Banking in Transition

*Studies in Economic Transition*

*General Editors*: **Jens Hölscher**, Commerzbank Professor for Money and Finance, University of Chemnitz, and Visiting Professor, Institute for German Studies, University of Birmingham; and **Horst Tomann**, Professor of Economics, Free University Berlin

This new series has been established in response to a growing demand for a greater understanding of the transformation of economic systems. It brings together theoretical and empirical studies on economic transition and economic development. The post-communist transition from planned to market economies is one of the main areas of applied theory because in this field the most dramatic examples of change and economic dynamics can be found. The series aims to contribute to the understanding of specific major economic changes as well as to advance the theory of economic development. The implications of economic policy will be a major point of focus.

*Titles include*:

Irwin Collier, Herwig Roggemann, Oliver Scholz and Horst Tomann (*editors*)
WELFARE STATES IN TRANSITION
East and West

Hubert Gabrisch and Rüdiger Pohl (*editors*)
EU ENLARGEMENT AND ITS MACROECONOMIC EFFECTS IN EASTERN EUROPE
Currencies, Prices, Investment and Competitiveness

Jens Hölscher and Anja Hochberg (*editors*)
EAST GERMANY'S ECONOMIC DEVELOPMENT SINCE UNIFICATION
Domestic and Global Aspects

Emil J. Kirchner (*editor*)
DECENTRALIZATION AND TRANSITION IN THE VISEGRAD
Poland, Hungary, the Czech Republic and Slovakia

Gregg S. Robins
BANKING IN TRANSITION
East Germany after Unification

Johannes Stephan
ECONOMIC TRANSITION IN HUNGARY AND EAST GERMANY
Gradualism and Shock Therapy in Catch-up Development

**Studies in Economic Transition**
**Series Standing Order** ISBN 978-0-333-73353-0
(*outside North America only*)

You can receive future titles in this series as they are published by placing a standing order. Please contact your bookseller or, in case of difficulty, write to us at the address below with your name and address, the title of the series and the ISBN quoted above.

Customer Services Department, Macmillan Distribution Ltd, Houndmills, Basingstoke, Hampshire RG21 6XS, England

# Banking in Transition

## East Germany after Unification

Gregg S. Robins
*Managing Director*
*International Personal Banking*
*Citibank*
*Switzerland*

Foreword by Jens Hölscher and Horst Tomann

palgrave
macmillan

Softcover reprint of the hardcover 1st edition 2000



Published by
PALGRAVE MACMILLAN
Houndmills, Basingstoke, Hampshire RG21 6XS and
175 Fifth Avenue, New York, N. Y. 10010
Companies and representatives throughout the world

PALGRAVE MACMILLAN is the global academic imprint of the Palgrave Macmillan division of St. Martin's Press, LLC and of Palgrave Macmillan Ltd. Macmillan® is a registered trademark in the United States, United Kingdom and other countries. Palgrave is a registered trademark in the European Union and other countries.

ISBN 978-1-349-41244-0 ISBN 978-0-230-28663-4 (eBook)
DOI 10.1007/978-0-230-28663-4

*Outside North America*

*Inside North America*
ISBN 978-0-312-22392-2

This book is printed on paper suitable for recycling and made from fully managed and sustained forest sources.

A catalogue record for this book is available from the British Library.

Library of Congress Catalog Card Number: 99–41754

Transferred to digital printing 2005

*To my daughters, **Gabriella**, **Casey** and **Raquel**, for always making me smile*

# Contents

# List of Figures, Plates and Tables

## Figures

## Plates



## Tables

# Foreword

This book looks at what the author calls a 'system transplant' rather than system transition. The East German example of overcoming the communist banking system was simply a takeover of the market by West German banks. This unique experience of transformation offers insights for the possible role of foreign banks in any transition economy on its way to a market economy. As we consider the financial sector being the core of the market economy, advanced knowledge in this area is of vital importance for policy-makers, the business world and academic economics. Robins draws the parallel between medical heart transplantation beginning in the early 1900s being perfect after numerous decades with institutional transplantation within systemic social change. This work contributes to a faster understanding of institutional change and behaviour.

*Chemnitz* JENS HÖLSCHER
*Berlin* HORST TOMANN

# Preface

In 1998 I attended a luncheon in Geneva where Paul Volcker was the keynote speaker. While he focused mainly on the hot issue of dormant accounts of Holocaust victims, he also included a broad-brush overview of some key trends in international financial markets. In his eloquent style, he remarked that the world financial system had become open to such a degree that national economies were particularly susceptible to capital flows and corresponding macro-pressures and potential imbalances. One clear consequence of this trend was the appearance of financial crises and the growing desire of countries to seek foreign financial institutions to 'rescue' failing banks through direct investments. Volcker cited Thailand, Mexico and Argentina as examples here, noting that the political will to keep banks in domestic hands had succumbed to the pressures of the market in a rather short period of time. This begged the question of whether this trend would continue and remain politically acceptable.

In this book we examine the trend outlined by Volcker from a different perspective and with a different group of countries. Rather than assess the political dimension, interesting and important as it is, we analyse the impact of foreign bank entry on the economy and indeed the banks themselves – domestic and foreign. In doing so, we ignore a key motivation for local regulators in transition economies to bring in foreign banks: the political and symbolic importance of foreign banks. In Hungary, for instance, the New Economic Mechanism (1968 onwards) saw foreign banks allowed in to position the country in the direction of the capitalist world. According to one senior Hungarian central banker who was involved in the debates, a most pressing policy dilemma was: 'Do you have a McDonald's and do you have a Citibank?'

I currently work for Citibank, arguably the most global bank in the world. Recently, Citibank placed an advertisement in the *Financial Times* to note the opening of its 100th country office: Ukraine. The message of the advertisement actually goes to the heart of this book:

> It's not just *that* we're there. It's *how* we're there. Completely local. Entirely at home. The way we are in 99 other countries. Understanding a country by its people, not just by its airports. Growing our

customers' business by understanding the kind of issues that are literally around the corner. Not just around the world.

The question is why being *local* is so important, why *knowing* the people and the environment is so important. It should become apparent to the reader in the chapters that follow why these attributes matter so much.

The book is based on my doctoral dissertation which I submitted in the Spring of 1996, one day before joining Citibank. My brief, albeit hectic, career in the bank has been tremendously rewarding, demanding and challenging, – clearly to blame for the book being published now rather than in 1996. My career has also made it impossible to carry out follow-up fieldwork in Germany, and rather than updating the data sections within the main text I have added a summary section in Chapter 7 to assess whether the trends I discuss persist to the present day. The lessons and insights remain valid for debates on the subject, and this point is made again in Chapter 7 when I revisit the current situation.

The book has been edited down somewhat from the dissertation, and the reader may consult the original work for a more comprehensive literature review, and a more detailed explanation of the research methodology. Further, while the text has been streamlined the notes at the end are comprehensive and – in many cases – rich with detail for the interested reader. The Bibliography remains complete. Another modification for the publication has been the removal of interviewees' names from the text. While it helps to know the person and context of the comments, a decision has been made that the confidentiality of all sources must be preserved. Where possible, I have indicated the person's organisation (and, where possible, position) so as to help the reader better understand the context.

I need to thank those that helped me so much to complete this work. Of course, my first thanks go to my supervisors at Oxford University, Peter Oppenheimer and Nick Woodward. Peter's careful and critical commentary was always much appreciated, particularly after the initial shock had set in, along with his concern and support. Nick's continued enthusiasm and open mind gave me inspiration to entertain new ideas and explore new areas which proved essential in making sense of the whole fieldwork experience.

Oliver Prill needs special thanks for countless insightful discussions on banking. Mihaela Kelemen helped me sort through the methodological minefield with encouragement along the way. Her other half, Csabi Sinka, contributed graphical assistance as well as good humour. Marina Moretti's critical and extensive commentary was greatly appreciated.

Carl Aaron has always been a good friend and fellow D. Phil patient. Frank Bönker always made helpful comments and accelerated my learning process by introducing me to the work of Karl Deutsch. Peter Sternhell's medical knowledge and ability to walk me through lymphocytes, homo-grafts, and so on, was much appreciated. Christoph Sahm engaged in helpful conversations on East Germany, and was always quick to challenge existing stereotypes. The people in the Templeton College Information Centre were always most kind in chasing up my frequent queries. Several other people made helpful suggestions in the course of the research: Ralf Dahrendorf, Deborah Pretty, Peter Richthofen and Jonathan Story.

Naturally, I owe a great debt to the many Germans who took time from their busy lives to address my questions. While they must forgive me for not mentioning all of them by name, a few need particular mention for their help and support: Hans Bauer, Wilfried Baum, Georg Gebhardt, Joachim Liese, and Hans-Jörn Weddige. Special thanks go to my dear friend Sascha Lenhart and his family for taking me into their home for the duration of the fieldwork. In this respect, thanks also go to Axel Sommer and Charlotta Adamczick for looking after me in Berlin.

The research would not have been possible without generous financial support from the Marshall Association, the Royal Bank of Canada, Templeton College, the University of Oxford and Citibank. David Gibson of Citibank needs special mention for taking an interest in my ideas and showing me the way to my new career. Within Citibank, I also need to thank my many colleagues across the world who have shared experiences with me as well as welcoming me into this complex and fascinating organisation – which thanks to the recent merger with Travelers (to form Citigroup) promises only to become more so.

I need to thank my many teachers without whom I would probably still be in the Bronx and hating school! A few need particular mention here: Dona Schwab of The Bronx High School of Science; Dennis Huston, Bill Martin, Mark Scheid and Rich Smith of Rice University; and Michael Kaser of Oxford University. Last, but not least, my family knows how much I love them and appreciate their patience and encouragement. My parents have always allowed me the freedom to grow and explore. *Mis suegros me han ayudado y amado mucho.* My grandfather in particular wanted so much to see my thesis completed, and I hope that he somehow is aware of it – somewhere. Thanks also to my brothers, brother-in-law, sister-in-law and brother by mutual consent. I have dedicated this book to my wonderful daughters, who have touched my life in ways I would never have imagined. Finally, my wife Jenny has stood by me throughout the difficult years of doctoral research, lack of finances and moving away from her home, family, and friends. The Citibank years have brought new challenges, and she has been the best mother in the world, and remained patient with my hectic schedule. Thanks, honey, for being you.

GREGG S. ROBINS

# Acknowledgements

The author and publishers acknowledge with thanks permission from the following to reproduce copyright material: Prentice-Hall, for Figure 2.1, from G. Peebles, *A Short History of Socialist Money* (1991); Gresham Books, Woodhead Publishing Ltd, for Figure 4.2, from M. Weber, 'Universal Banks', in N. Walter and R. von Rosen (eds), *German Financial Markets* (1995); *Deutsche Bundesbank*, for Figure 4.3, from 'The Monetary Union with the German Democratic Republic', *Deutsche Bundesbank Monthly Report* (July 1990); *Der Spiegel*, for Figure 4.4, 'Das Zinsenwunder in Osten' (October 1994); WZB, for Figure 5.4, from W. Carlin and P. Richthofen, 'Finance, Economic Development and the Transition: The East German Case', *Discussion Paper*, FSI 95 (1995) and for Figure 6.6, from S. Vitols, 'German Banks and the Modernization of the Small Firm Sector: Long-Term Finance in Comparative Perspective' (1994); John Wiley & Sons, for Figure 6.1, from J.F. Yates and E.R. Stone, 'The Risk Construct', in J.F. Yates (ed.), *Risk Taking Behaviour* (1992); Pan Books, for Figure 6.3, from T.A. Harris, *I'm OK–You're OK* (1967); *Sparkasse*, for Table 4.1, from *'Das Bankwesen in der Deutschen Demokratischen Republik'* (1990); IMF, for Table 4.2, from L. Lipschitz and D. McDonald (eds), 'German Unification: Economic Issues', *IMF Occasional Paper*, 75 (December 1990).

# List of Abbreviations and Acronyms

| | |
|---|---|
| *AG* | *Aktiengesellschaft* |
| *Altkredite* | Old loans (made before unification) |
| *Aufsichtsrat* | Supervisory Board |
| *Ausgleichsforderungen* | Equalisation claims |
| *Bankenverband mittel- und ostdeutscher Länder* | Bankers' Association for the Eastern *Länder* |
| *BDB* | *Bundesverband deutscher Banken* (German Bankers' Association) |
| *BDI* | *Bundesverband der deutschen Industrie* (German Association of Industry) |
| *Beirat* | Advisory Board |
| *BHF* | *Berliner Handels- und Frankfurter Bank* |
| *BHG* | *Banken für Handwerk und Gewerbe* |
| Big Banks | *Deutsche Bank, Dresdner Bank, Commerzbank* |
| *BKB* | *Buro Kommunikation System* |
| *BLN* | *Bank für Landwirtschaft und Nahrungsegüterwirtschaft* |
| *BMWi* | *Bundesministerium für Wirtschaft* |
| *BSB* | *Berliner Stadtbank AG* |
| *Bürgschaftsbanken* | Guarantee Banks |
| CDU | Christian Democratic Union |
| CIB | Central European International Bank |
| CIS | Union of Independent States |
| CMEA | Council for Mutual Economic Assistance (also known as COMECON) |
| CoCom | Coordinating Committee for Multilateral Export Controls |
| CPE | Centrally planned economy |
| CSFR | Czech and Slovak Federal Republic |
| *DABA* | *Deutsche Aussenhandelsbank AG* |
| *DG Bank* | *Deutsche Genossenschaftsbank* |
| *DHB* | *Deutsche Handelsbank AG* |
| *DIH* | *Deutsche Industrie Holding* |
| *DIW* | *Deutsches Institut für Wirtschaftsforschung* |
| *DKB* | *Deutsche Kreditbank* |
| DM | Deutschmark |

| | |
|---|---|
| *DtA* | *Deutsche Ausgleichsbank* |
| EBO | Employee buy-out |
| EBRD | European Bank for Reconstruction and Development |
| ECU | European Currency Unit |
| EDP | Electronic data processing |
| EIB | European Investment Bank |
| ERP | European Recovery Programme |
| EU | Expected utility |
| EVCA | European Venture Capital Association |
| FDI | Foreign direct investment |
| FIBOR | Frankfurt Interbank Bid–Offer Rate |
| FRG | Federal Republic of Germany |
| FSU | Former Soviet Union |
| GDR | German Democratic Republic |
| GEMSU | German Economic, Monetary and Social Union |
| *Genossenschaftsbanken* | Credit cooperatives |
| *Geschäftsbericht* | *Annual Report* |
| *Geshäftsführer* | Managing Director |
| *GMbH* | *Gesellschaften mit beschränkter Haftung* |
| GRMF | German Risk Management Framework |
| IBRD | International Bank for Reconstruction and Development (World Bank) |
| *IKB* | *Industrie Kreditbank* |
| *Industrie- und Handelskammer* | Chamber of Commerce |
| IPO | Initial public offering |
| *KfW* | *Kreditanstalt für Wideraufbau* |
| *Kombinat* | Large collection of enterprises (GDR) |
| *Kreditanwicklungsfund* | Debt processing fund |
| *Länder* | German regions/provinces |
| *Landesbanken* | Regional offices of the *Bundesbank* |
| M | Ostmark |
| MBO | Management buy-out |
| MBI | Management buy-in |
| *Mittelstand* | Small and medium-sized (usually family-owned) German enterprises |
| MNC | Multinational corporation |
| NBFI | Non-Bank Financial Institution |
| NBH | National Bank of Hungary |

| | |
|---|---|
| *NBL* | *Neue Bundesländer* |
| NBP | National Bank of Poland |
| NPL | Non-performing loan |
| OECD | Organisation for Economic Cooperation and Development |
| OMO | Open market operation |
| *OSGV* | *Ostdeutscher Sparkassen und-Giroverband* |
| PCPE | Previously centrally planned economy |
| R&D | Research and development |
| *RIKO* | *Rückstellungen für Richtungskoeffizienten* |
| SEU | Subjective expected utility |
| SMEs | Small and medium-sized enterprises |
| SOB | State-owned bank |
| SOE | State-owned enterprise |
| *Sparkassen* | Savings Banks |
| *THA* | *Treuhandanstalt* |
| USSR | Union of Soviet Socialist Republics |
| VM | Valuta Mark |
| *Vorstand* | Management Board |
| *West LB* | *Westdeutsche Landesbank* |
| *Wirtschaftswunder* | Economic miracle |

# 1
# Introduction

At the turn of the twentieth century, mankind began its quest to make organ transplantation a reality. The quest began in 1905 when two scientists at the University of Chicago removed the heart from a small dog and inserted it into a larger one. What followed were several decades of research devoted to perfecting the 'technique' of transplanting organs into the human body. According to Dr Simon Gelman, Professor of Anesthesiology at the University of Alabama:

> the origin and infancy of organ transplantation were extremely difficult, accompanied by failure, frustration, and disappointment rather than success and gratification.[1]

Nevertheless, the techniques involved in transplantation were virtually perfected by the 1940s–1950s. Despite this, some scientists still characterised cardiac transplantation as 'a fantastic speculation for the future'.[2] The reason for this assessment was that it had become apparent that technique, though essential and arduous to develop, was not the main obstacle to achieving success in a transplant.

Organ transplantation exposed the degree to which the human body is a *complex system*, with its own internal defence mechanisms. Thus the real obstacle to surgeons was that once the organ was put in place it was quickly rejected by the 'host' (body). In the words of one group of scientists working at Georgetown University:

> It is readily seen that the failure of the homotransplanted heart to survive is not due to the technique of transplantation but to some biologic factor which is probably identical to that which prevents survival of other homotransplanted tissues and organs.[3]

The biological factor to which they were referring stems from the body's immune system, whereby certain cells (*lymphocytes*) act as the body's police force. These cells monitor the body and distinguish between things which are 'self' and those which are 'not self', such as viruses or bacteria. In transplants, the problems that emerge *after the surgery* involve a rejection of the transplanted organ, whereby it is attacked and destroyed.

In response to this problem, scientists in the 1950s devised ways to prevent the transplanted organ from being attacked. This process of *immuno-suppression* entailed injecting chemicals into the host body which would disable its immune system and thus enable the new organ to survive. The problem, however, was that the chemicals would often produce side-effects worse than the initial condition had been before the transplant itself. In addition, experiences in kidney transplant showed that, 'if the anti-rejection treatment is to be successful the drugs must be administered in very large doses' and, moreover, on some occasions, 'in spite of sometimes full and poisonous doses of the anti-rejection treatment, the kidney is nevertheless rejected'.[4] At the same time, it became apparent that – even if successful – chemicals would have to be administered indefinitely, for when they are removed the organ is attacked in any case – i.e. *dependence* may occur.

What emerges from this discussion is that any form of transplant must be seen as a difficult *process*. Surgery – the actual transplant itself – is perhaps the main *event*, but it is only the beginning. In the words of R.Y. Calne, Professor of Surgery at the University of Cambridge,

> The success of an operation is blazoned across the headlines, sometimes before the surgery has been completed, whilst the subsequent fate of the patient occupies a small paragraph in the paper weeks or months later.[5]

* * * *

This book explores a different kind of transplant, though the lessons are strikingly similar. The patient is an economic system in transition from central planning to a market economy. The heart of the economic system is the banking system. The central case study in the book represents not only a heart transplant, in metaphorical terms, but also a transplant of the entire institutional structure surrounding it – the 'tissues' of the system. In examining this case, we focus on both the surgery as well as the after-effects on the patient and, indeed, on the newly transplanted organ itself. With this in mind, we turn to the situation in East Germany, the patient.

On 1 July 1990, some 16 million East Germans awoke to find a new set of laws, a new currency and a new banking system. These had been transplanted as a result of the overwhelming support East Germans had given in the election in March of that year to the 'Alliance for Germany' coalition which supported rapid economic and monetary union. The unification treaty was signed in May, making the five Eastern *Länder* and East Berlin part of the Federal Republic of Germany. The East German commercial banking system was purchased by the two largest West German banks, *Deutsche Bank* and *Dresdner Bank*, and in addition other West German banks rapidly established operations on its territory. The *Deutsche Bundesbank* became the central bank for the whole of Germany. All that now remains of the East German banking system are its local Savings Banks and Credit Cooperatives.

As a result of the transplant of 'good' banks as well as a 'good' institutional structure into the East, expectations were high that its economy would soon catch up with West Germany, especially since the West German banking system had been credited with playing a leading role in West Germany's successful reconstruction after the Second World War. Against these expectations, however, was the fact the transplanted institutions needed to function within the East German environment. On this view, German sociologist Klaus Offe raised 'the alarming prospect that the transplanted tissue from West German institutions may well encounter a socio-cultural incompatibility syndrome, and even rejection symptoms'.[6] In short, the operation needed to overcome possible negative reactions, and also create the underlying conditions necessary for the transplanted banks to develop their business. If it could not, it would be necessary to administer immuno-suppression for a shorter or longer period.

While providing a unique opportunity to examine a banking transplant, the East German case has not so far been extensively researched by comparison with the large literature on the financial experiences of other transition economies. This gap presents an opportunity to contribute to the broader debate on the role of banks in the transition process. To appreciate the special nature of the East German transplant, we need to say a few words about the broader context in which it takes place.

Beginning in 1989, the former communist countries in Eastern Europe and the Soviet Union, including East Germany, abandoned their planned economic systems and set out on the transition to a market economy. Most existing market economies had generally *evolved* rather than been created, with the path of evolution proceeding across decades and generally coinciding with industrialisation. The former communist countries had already achieved a certain level of industrialisation, and also hoped to speed up the transition process, not least in order to appease the expectations of their populations: transition to a market economy was generally accompanied by one to liberal democracy, and thus the *effectors* of the transition were dependent upon the votes of those *affected* by it.

Attention was focused on the potential for banks to play an active role in bringing about a market economy. This was partly because these economies had no other financial institutions, but it also reflected the important role the banking system has played in developing market economies. Writers such as Alexander Gerschenkron had long argued that banks could help a country overcome 'backwardness' by not only mobilising funds and directing them to those that would best use them, but also by getting involved in the investment process and promoting entrepreneurship.

As it turned out, indigenous banks in transition economies were for the most part not up to the task of playing the role they had been assigned. Recognition that it might be many years before these banks could be restructured – they were burdened with large non-performing loan portfolios – and also learn to operate in a market economy, led to suggestions that it might be better sooner rather than later to introduce 'good' banks into the economy from outside; in other words, foreign banks. Rostowski recommended that transition economies should consider 'importing' foreign banks on a large scale to hasten their respective transitions.[7]

While this was not politically or culturally feasible in most cases, East Germany was different, since the banking system of West Germany represented economically foreign yet linguistically and (after unification) politically native institutions. This study accordingly investigates the East German experience as a (relatively) pure or extreme model of banking-system transplant in the transition process. Despite – or rather, because of – its unique features, the German case allows some general insights to be gained into the possible role of foreign banks in any transition economy seeking to establish a market-oriented financial system.

The book is organised in six chapters (Figure 1.1). Chapter 2 begins by reviewing the literature on the role of the financial system in the planned economy and also the initial attempts made to reform it. It

*Figure* 1.1 Outline of the book

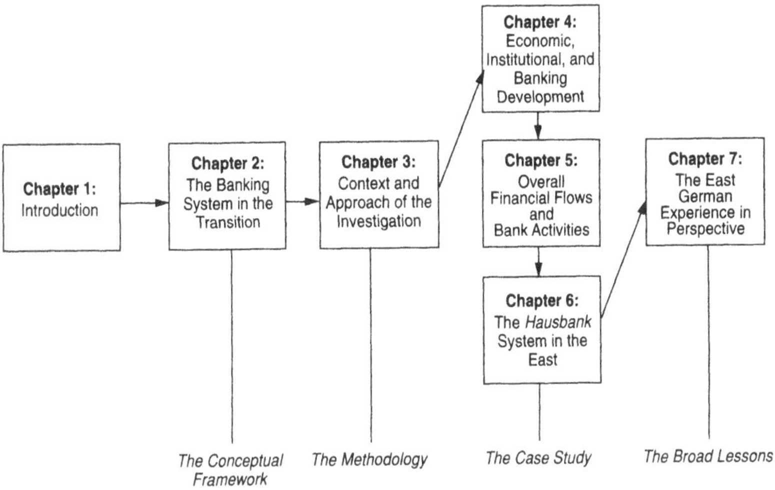


then discusses the role of institutional change in economic development and considers a range of proposals on how the financial system may be handled in the transition to market. These proposals focus on both the *structure* of the banking system and on questions of *ownership*.

Chapter 3 defines the central research question, including the selection of the East German case and the methodology that has been used in examining it. The chapter explains the fieldwork undertaken, and the advantages and limitations encountered.

The next three chapters provide the substantive analysis of the East German case. Chapter 4 begins with a review of the performance of the East German economy after unification, both to highlight the problems that emerged and to explain the general context in which the banking system had to function. It next outlines mechanisms that emerged to manage some of these problems, focusing especially on the banking system and on the various financial flows to non-financial sectors of the East German economy.

In Chapter 5, an empirical examination of overall financial flows highlights both the large role played by West German banks in handling the flows and, at the same time, the high level of risk borne by the state. This is followed by an examination of bank deposit- and lending activities (1990–4), with attention to the differences between West and East German bank groups. Next, case studies of two West German banks with different strategies provide insights into the opportunities and problems offered by the transition process. The chapter concludes with an analysis of survey results of borrowers in the East to see whether financing difficulties existed – and, if so, whether they applied to particular groups of borrowers.

Chapter 6 seeks to provide some analytical underpinning for the picture emerging from the data on banking and financial flows. Emphasis is placed on the importance of bank–borrower relationships in lending, and on the difficulties that emerged for West German banks in extending their business eastwards after unification. The discussion explores sociological and psychological perspectives on the unification process to place the banking activities into a broader perspective.

In the concluding Chapter 7, we review the main findings and examine some longer-term implications of the banking transplant to East Germany, including possible lessons for other transition economies.

# 2
# The Banking System in the Transition: A Conceptual Framework

While there are an array of financial structures found in different capitalist economies from which the newly emerging democracies can choose, it is not evident that any represent the 'optimal' financial structure ... In the case of some capitalist countries, the defects in the financial system are all too apparent. The newly emerging democracies have ahead of them a delicate balancing act: once they settle upon a financial structure, they will find that change is difficult and costly. (Joseph Stiglitz, 1992)

Social scientists, historians, and political observers in general agree on one point about the Eastern European revolutions of 1989: no one foresaw them. The collapse of communist power in Eastern Europe, the fall of the Berlin Wall and the reunification of Germany, the implosions in the Soviet Union – the end of the cold war, in short – all these developments unfolded in a remarkably short time and as a huge surprise to 'experts' and ordinary television viewers alike. But the lesson – that the utmost modesty is in order when it comes to pronouncements about the future of human societies – does not seem to have sunk in. As soon as the astonishing changes in the world's political and economic map took place, numerous voices were heard uttering self-assured opinions about the implications of those changes for this or that country or group of countries. It does not seem to have occurred to these people that if the events, which are the point of departure for their speculations, were so hard to predict, considerable caution is surely in order when it comes to appraising their impact. (Albert O. Hirschman, 1990)

This first chapter is partly a review of the literature and partly an attempt to construct a conceptual framework within which to understand the role of the banking system in the transition. While there is a large literature on banking in the transition, the conceptual framework presented brings in the concept of learning and allows us to differentiate proposals on banking reform in terms of their assumptions about the learning process. Before examining banking in the transition to a market economy, however, we need to outline why these countries embarked on complete transformations of their systems. To understand where they are going, we first have to explain where they have been; thus we begin our discussion with the centrally planned economy.

In the second section, we turn to the *financial system* within it, and explain why it played a passive yet important role. In the third section, we discuss the *transition to a market economy*, emphasising the magnitude of the task, particularly in terms of the behavioural changes required, while outlining the objectives concerning the banking system in the transition. We also review the *initial banking reforms* and the associated problems. The fourth section covers the *role of institutions* and the issues surrounding their creation and function. In the fifth and final section, we examine *financial system design* and the underlying issues of financial restructuring and learning.

## The centrally planned economy (CPE)

There is a considerable literature on the theory and practice of the CPE.[1] Our brief discussion begins with the question: what were the significant elements of the CPE? Fundamental was *Marxist–Leninist ideology*, which provided the justification and basis for its entire political, economic and social structure. According to it, socialism represented a more advanced form of society than capitalism and, therefore, would outperform the latter since it allowed people to reach their productive potential. At the same time, people were given certain promises from the state regarding their quality of life, including the right to work, as well as basic needs such as food, healthcare, education, vacations and cultural opportunities. These promises put the onus on the state to deliver: the right to work, for instance, meant that the state needed to ensure full employment on a macro level. In order to meet its promises, the socialist system was centrally planned so that the state could maintain complete control over the allocation of resources which, under its ideology, it claimed as superior to the laws of supply and demand in the market mechanism.

Flowing from the state's need to control the planning process, three features were essential to the CPE. First, there was a *plan* – indeed, a variety of plans – which determined the disbursement of the *budget* and thus the allocation of real and financial resources. In addition to the plan was *state ownership* of the means of production, including land, minerals, buildings, enterprises, machinery and so on, except for a very small amount of private property. The purpose of this ownership structure was twofold. On the one hand, private property in the capitalist system was seen as encouraging secretive and competitive behaviour to gain from it, whereas under socialism the ideal was that all economic gains – innovation, for example – would be for the good of all people. On the other hand, state ownership reinforced its control over the economy through *state-owned enterprises* (SOE). This stemmed from Lenin's idea that the SOEs should manage the 'commanding heights' of the economy, such as mining, manufacturing, transport, energy, and also banking. Alongside these features was a huge *administrative apparatus*, comprising both economic and political organs, which carried out the directives of the plan, monitored its performance and made recommendations for future plans. The central political organisation in the CPE was the *Communist Party*, it being a one-party system, but the *Ministries* and many other bodies existed as well.

These essential features formed the basis of the *formal institutional structure* of the CPE. In functional terms, the structure was marked by what Kornai termed 'bureaucratic coordination', as opposed to market coordination.[2] Bureaucratic coordination means that actors in the economic system are related in a vertical structure as opposed to the more horizontal structure of a market, where buyers and sellers interact. The establishment of bureaucratic coordination and the reliance on the plan led to the *passive nature of prices* for goods, capital and labour – these prices being administratively determined – and the corresponding absence of factor markets. This had to be the case, for if prices could influence the allocation of resources control would be removed from the planners who might then not be able to deliver on their promises – upon which the legitimacy of the system rested.

In addition to the passivity of prices, central planning also led to two other important effects. The first was what Kornai termed the 'soft-budget constraint', referring to the fact that SOEs could regularly overspend because they were assured of receiving routine external assistance – in the form of state subsidies, tax breaks, soft bank credits and favourable prices on inputs.[3] The expectation of this assistance meant that managers lacked incentives to use resources efficiently. Yet the soft-budget constraint was a necessary requirement for the system to function, enabling enterprises to meet (physical) plan targets and thus maintain employment levels. The soft-budget constraint was maintained within the state-owned sector, with households and actors in the underground economy facing hard constraints.

A second effect of central planning was that the CPE became a *shortage economy*.[4] Planners were plagued by severe informational asymmetries *vis-à-vis* enterprises and households as well, and were often forced to use data which was outdated in any case. As a result, they were unable to ensure that demand for products in the system was met, either for consumer goods or wholesale goods as inputs to enterprises. The result of this is that, 'those living in a socialist country ... experience the countless frustrations of thwarted purchasing intentions, queuing, forced substitution, searches for goods, and postponement of purchases in their daily lives as consumers and producers'.[5]

Underlying these effects, the allocation of resources – although formally planned – had much to do with personal relationships and hence political processes. The shortage economy was an important indication that in reality planners could not account for every last detail, particularly as an economy grows and becomes more complex. As Ericson described:

> The inefficiency of a Soviet-type economic system is aggravated by the growing complexity that accompanies, and indeed defines, successful economic development. Successful development means an increasing number of products, components, services, resources, factors, technologies, needs, and desires that must be incorporated into planning by the central authorities, and an increasing number of subordinates to implement those plans.[6]

As a result, within the CPE there developed an *informal institutional structure* and processes alongside the formal one. This structure was governed by the process of 'bargaining', whereby plan targets were negotiated from one plan to the next, occurring between enterprises and between planners and enterprises.[7] Bargaining was an important activity in enabling enterprises to preserve their soft-budget constraints, and in allowing all actors to cope with the shortage economy. Indeed, the informal institutional structure acted as a *lubricant* to the CPE, and allowed it to exist for as long as it did. As Olson observed,

> Paradoxically, they [the CPEs] performed as well as and survived as long as they did in part because of the many markets, legal and

> illegal, explicit and implicit, that they contained ... the mother wit of the peoples of the planned economies enabled them to obtain huge gains from trade from the networks of contracts, swaps, deals, arrangements, reciprocal relationships, and black markets they ingeniously (and usually informally) worked out.[8]

Taken together, informal elements combined with the formal to create a complex system, what Ericson described as 'a coherent whole – a true *system* – with its own inherent logic, necessary components, and natural interaction of these components'[9] (emphasis in original).

## The financial system within the CPE

Within the CPE, the financial system had to play a far different role than it does in a market economy.[10] Simply stated, the financial system needed to ensure that the plan was implemented, and thus was an integral, yet *passive* part of the economic system. Similarly, money also played a functional, yet limited role in the CPE, being largely unable to play the role it plays in a market economy. In Ericson's words, 'money as a generalized, universal command over goods and services cannot exist [in the CPE]'.[11]

### The role of money

In a market economy, money performs three functions. First, it acts as a *unit of account*, enabling uniform accounting to be undertaken, and to facilitate all transactions (present and future); prices, for instance, are represented in units of the currency. Second, it acts as a *means of payment*; this is its most important function. It can be used to settle all debts, and is universally accepted and guaranteed by the sovereign authority. Third, it is a *store of value*. As a store of value, money may be less desirable than other assets – such as investments in financial or real assets – which may appreciate in value. Although the nominal value of money is fixed, its real value may decline due to inflation.

In the CPE, money performed only the unit of account function completely, it being important in the planning mechanism for accounting purposes. The passive nature of prices, however, meant that they did not necessarily reflect the underlying value of the good or service. The other functions of money were highly restricted through the *segmentation* of financial flows which allowed planners maximum control over financial resources by removing outlets for actors in the system to make transactions not prescribed by the plan (Figure 2.1).[12]

*Figure* 2.1 Financial flows in the CPE

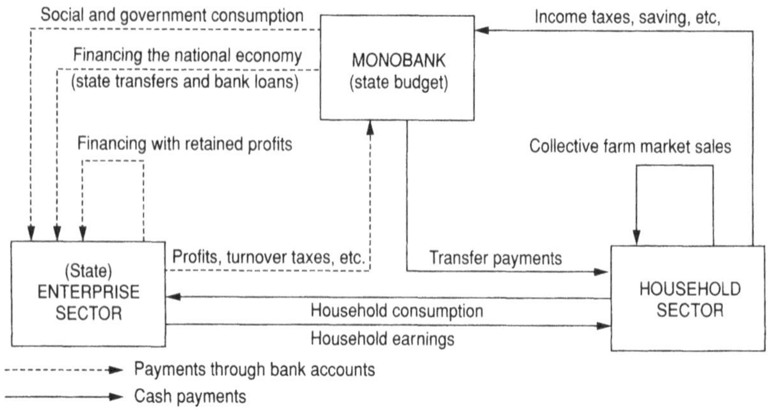


*Source*: Adapted from Peebles (1991, p.45).

The enterprise sector was entirely dependent on bank credits and its own retained earnings, which were closely monitored by the state, while the household sector used cash. Through this segmentation, therefore, savings and investment decisions were separated. Savings were placed in the Savings Bank which passed them directly to the budget where they were allocated according to the plan.

This segmentation meant that money could be used as a means of payment by enterprises only insofar as it corresponded to a direct allocation in the plan. Money was 'earmarked' in the plan. Money earmarked for wages could not be used to purchase materials, for instance, nor could money earmarked for materials be used to pay wages.[13] In addition to the restrictions on money as a means of payment, there were also severe restrictions on the legal exchange of money into foreign currency. That is to say, *external* and, more importantly, *internal inconvertibility* were imposed. For the plan to be enforced, all import and export transactions had to be planned as well, making the CPE a *closed economic system*. As a result, foreign currency was exchanged only according to planned orders.

By extension, money also played a limited role as a store of value since it did not guarantee – far from it – that it would be accepted as a means of payment. This primarily affected enterprises which were tied to plan targets. In the household sector, money was controlled and distributed as wages and could be used to purchase any goods which were available.[14] But in a shortage economy there was no certainty that there would be anything which one would want and be able to buy with money.

## The banking system within the CPE

The banking system in the CPE represented an institutional arrangement which functioned to implement the plan and ensure that the formal structure of central planning was maintained. In the absence of capital markets, the only financial institutions were banks. In fact, the CPEs were generally marked by a single, large bank which was broken into various 'arms' to deal with certain sectors, such as foreign trade and industrial development, and also a savings bank to service households. What Garvy termed the 'monobank,' stemmed from the vision Lenin had of 'a single giant State Bank, the biggest of the big, with branches in every rural district, in every factory'[15] and played an integral role in the CPE, being responsible for implementing the plan by allocating and monitoring credit.

The monobank fused central bank and commercial bank functions into a single institution. Although it was the central bank, it did not possess the functions of a central bank in a market economy. Monetary policy was managed along direct rather than indirect lines, with plan directives rather than interest rates (discount rates), open market operations (OMOs) and reserve requirements being the primary instruments.

Commercial banking functions in the monobank were also tailored to the needs of the CPE. The investment process in the CPE was carried out through plan directives with the issuance of credit being an important control function for the state. According to Garvy, 'all plans ... are tied together in an overall financial plan, usually prepared at the Ministry of Finance or by the central planning authority, which shows intersectoral financial flows, particularly the sources of investment funds and in some cases the use of credit in the economy'.[16] What this meant was that investment finance was channelled directly through the budget via subsidies. At the same time, the banking system generally supplied short-term working capital. Through its supply, banks were given an important control function to ensure that enterprises adhered to plan guidelines. Moreover, the dependence on bank credits was reinforced through the ban on credits between enterprises. In Russia, for example, Stalin issued a decree on 30 January 1930 to ban all inter-enterprise credit.[17] But plan targets to enterprises were given in physical output, which meant that bank loans were functional to the system in that they preserved the soft-budget constraints of enterprises to ensure that these plan guidelines were met. As a result, bank loans were not subjected to credit analysis as in a market economy. Apart from having no relation to credit risk, bank loans in the CPE were generally made at negative real interest rates, giving managers incentives to take bank credit to accumulate real assets and inventories.[18] Moreover, the credit process became subject to bargaining and patronage.

At the same time, the household sector was served by a single savings bank, which offered low levels of service, a minimal range of products, and low real deposit rates for savers. Owing to the shortage economy, however, households generally accumulated high levels savings despite the financial disincentive to do so. The passive role and corresponding low status of banking in the CPE meant that the monobank did not attract the best personnel. In Czechoslovakia, the banking sector was staffed by roughly 90 per cent women who took jobs in banks because they could not find other work.[19]

## The transition to a market economy

The inefficiency and waste inherent in the CPE worsened over time, as shortages became more acute and increasingly seen as a way of life. These problems raised questions about the system's viability, and certainly showed it to be falling behind its capitalist rivals. Moreover, efforts at reforming the CPE were not successful.[20] Imperfections in the CPE became more apparent in the 1980s, and strongly contributed to its demise.

Unlike the many reform efforts which preceded the transition process, the new goal of creating a market economy involved a complete move away from the CPE. Thus the formal institutional structure needed to be both broken down and replaced with private ownership, including the development of a private sector and trust in the market mechanism for resource allocation. Fundamental to the transition process was the need to harden the budget constraints of all state enterprises. Kornai referred to this process as the 'evolution of financial discipline', arguing that it was likely to be lengthy and painful.[21] The process rested on a few simple rules: (1) *Buyers*: Pay for the goods you buy; (2) *Debtors*: Abide by your loan contract; pay back your debt; (3) *Taxpayers*: Pay your taxes; (4) *Enterprises*: Cover your costs with your revenues.

The monumental task of destroying the CPE legacy and building a market economy represented a new endeavour in economic organisation. No ready-made 'blueprint' existed. Two broad concerns in the transition could be distinguished. On a macro level, there was the need for stabilisation, including creating and tightening fiscal and monetary policies, adjusting internal and external imbalances, including freeing prices on goods, capital and labour, and foreign trade liberalisation. On a micro level, there was the need for enterprise restructuring, institution building, and privatisation. On the latter point, the creation of a private sector involved privatising small and large SOEs, as well as enabling start-up enterprises to develop alongside the privatisation process. These macro- and micro-concerns were linked. For the fruits of stabilisation to be realised, the highly inefficient enterprise system and trade patterns had to be corrected. Otherwise, the supply response might be correspondingly lower than expected and could lead to extreme falls in output and rises in unemployment, with accompanying social and political tensions. In short, the transition needed to be comprehensive, a 'seamless web'.[22] There were, however, many divergent views on its ideal speed – a debate developed between proponents of 'Shock Therapy' and those of 'Gradualism'[23] – and on the issue of *sequencing*.[24] The sequence and pace of reform depended on many factors, including the political will of the country, the starting point of the economy,[25] and the extent to which capital was made available for the transition.[26]

## Banking system reform

Central to the transition was that money and the banking system would play an *active* role in the process and, taking over from the plan as the main allocative mechanism for financial resources, impose hard-budget constraints on enterprises and hence enforce financial discipline. Calvo and Kumar observed that 'it is widely acknowledged that the success of the stabilization policies and the structural reforms depends in an important way on the development of efficient financial intermediaries and of credit and capital markets more generally'.[27] The active role of the banking system centred on the broad macro- and micro-concerns of the transition process, and can be broken down into macro- (central bank) and micro- (commercial bank) objectives.

On a macro-level, there were two central objectives concerning the banking system. First, to establish a central bank with an effective and responsible *monetary policy* based upon indirect rather than direct instruments, including reserve requirements, OMOs, an efficient clearing system, along with money and interbank markets. Second, to establish a system of *prudential supervision and regulation* of the banking system.

On a microlevel, three primary objectives pertained to the commercial banking system. First, to establish *payment services*.[28] Second, to promote *financial intermediation*, involving the traditional functions of accumulation and allocation of capital to those that would use it most efficiently and, in doing so, to harden the budget constraints of enterprises by denying capital to those that were performing poorly. Third, to promote effective *corporate governance*, by monitoring enterprises in order to promote restructuring, and to ensure that the restructuring would not be reversed in the longer term. The need for banks to undertake corporate governance stems from the special nature of the transition whereby product, capital and labour markets are underdeveloped and hence do not exert strong competitive pressures on enterprise managers. Corporate governance is particularly important for large enterprises in which there is a separation of ownership and control. Of these objectives, our primary focus is on financial intermediation.

**The initial reforms**

The initial financial system reforms in virtually all the previously centrally planned economies (PCPEs) involved, to a greater or lesser extent, the creation of a two-tier, centrally banked system, partitioning the monobank by hiving off its commercial operations. Rostowski described the 'main sequence' of these reforms as consisting of: (1) splitting the monobank into a number of state-owned commercial banks (SOBs); (2) liberalising entry by private (mainly domestic) banks; (3) trying to privatise the SOBs.[29] Hence, the initial reforms were firmly rooted in the neo classical approach – i.e. *financial liberalisation*. The roots of the financial liberalisation approach appeared in the early 1970s with the work of McKinnon and Shaw (referred to as the 'financial repression paradigm') who argued that government intervention in the financial system, in the form of direct controls over interest rates or government-directed credits, led to distortions which inhibited growth. As a result, it was maintained that higher interest rates would lead to higher levels of saving and more efficient capital allocation.

In the early stages of the transition process, while macroeconomic stabilisation was achieved, microeconomic restructuring progressed at a much slower pace. As things turned out, credit markets in the PCPEs operated far from efficiently, and hence undermined the transition process as a whole.[30] Not only did the financial system fail to play an active role in the restructuring of enterprises, but it also became the source of several problems in its own right. The central assumption of the transition to a market economy was that the market would be more efficient than the plan in allocating real and financial resources. Initial financial system reforms, however, found the market worked less than optimally. In the analysis that follows, we divide the problems which developed into their *symptoms* and *causes*, though we acknowledge that these are inter-related to a certain extent.[31]

**Symptoms and causes of problems**

The first symptom was a *lack of finance for private enterprises*.[32] Even in a liberalised credit market, credit rationing may occur in equilibrium due to informational asymmetries.[33] To a large extent, finance for the private sector was crowded out by *lending to many insolvent SOEs*.[34] The persistence of lending to inefficient SOEs stemmed both from the skewed incentive structure and learning difficulties of commercial banks, issues which we examine shortly. In addition, *lending to the government* redirected resources from the private sector and contributed to the high real interest rates for loans. The large borrowing requirements of the government stemmed from high spending – large levels of social spending required in the transition – and shortfalls in revenue due to underdeveloped tax systems and also tax evasion.[35] In addition to being limited in quantities, the finance that was offered was predominantly of a short-term nature,[36] and also often expensive. Prill presents evidence that in Russia, albeit a worse case than many PCPEs due to its unstable macro-position, short-term lending (less than one year) as a percentage of total corporate lending was: 94.8 per cent in 1992; 96.5 per cent in 1993; 94.9 per cent in 1994; and 87.5 per cent by March 1995.[37]

SMEs experienced particular problems securing finance from banks. One study on Hungary noted the 'high costs and general unavailability of bank credit' for business start-ups.[38] It should be said, however, that SMEs have financing problems in many market economies. As Dedek observes,

> When pondering failures of commercial banks in the provision of financial services for SMEs, it is important to distinguish between transitional or non-systematic failures on the one hand and permanent or systemic features which one can encounter even in developed market economies.[39]

But permanent problems are aggravated by transitional problems in the credit markets in PCPEs. Dedek distinguishes several of the latter based on the experience of the Czech Republic, noting: the lack of providers of long-term finance (the slow development of credit guarantee schemes and lack of development banks); the heavy dependence of SMEs on an underdeveloped banking system; and the distinct lack of collateral by SMEs.[40] At the same time, the low availability of venture capital in PCPEs has aggravated the financing difficulties of SMEs and start-ups in particular.[41] For the Czech Republic, Dedek adds that, 'the absence of risk capital facilities may be considered as another gap in the present financial infrastructure'.[42] David Hexter of the EBRD cites the lack of venture capital as first among deficiencies in PCPEs which inhibit the flow of funds to local private enterprises.[43]

A second symptom was the *build-up of non-performing loans* by the newly-created banks and the recognition that the *banks were undercapitalised*.[44] While bank portfolio problems were partly the result of the non-performing stock of loans which they inherited, the rise in non-performing loans was primarily a *flow* problem – i.e. they were being generated in the period after the two-tier banking systems were created. Writing in 1993, Blommestein and Lange note that 'while the bad debt problem is frequently considered a financial legacy of the past, the biggest increase in bad debt has occurred over the past two years'.[45] The rise in non-performing loans was due in large part to the recessions in the PCPEs,[46] though it also reflected the high numbers of loans to inefficient SOEs, a point which underlines the inter-related nature of the symptoms.

A third symptom was the rapid build-up of *inter-enterprise debts*.[47] These debts grew in response to the lack of finance being provided by banks and also to the high price of finance which was available.[48] In other words, inter-enterprise debt functioned as an alternative source of working capital[49] and contributed to the maintenance of the soft-budget constraint. It also, however, stemmed from the problems faced by debtors in making payments, the incentives which existed to avoid bankruptcy proceedings and from the tight macroeconomic policies which squeezed credit issued to enterprises. Winiecki noted that it was ironic that tight monetary policies actually achieved the opposite result of that for which they were designed. Rather than hardening the budget constraints on inefficient enterprises they tended to penalise new private enterprises by lowering the overall amount of credit available.[50]

A fourth symptom was that *enterprise restructuring proceeded slowly* and often not at all.[51] The lack of restructuring went together with preservation of the soft-budget constraint and the 'rolling over' of loans to failing SOEs. There was little 'exit' from markets and entry was impeded for start-up enterprises. Moreover, the lack of financial discipline being imposed by banks on enterprises discouraged discipline *between* enterprises. Begg and Portes argue that 'there is a significant relationship between bank credit and interfirm credit. The greater the creditor passivity of banks, the more probable is creditor passivity in interfirm credit'.[52]

A fifth symptom was that developments in credit markets were *undermining macroeconomic stabilisation*.[53] Growth in the number of banks and corresponding levels of non-performing loans placed strains on supervisory organs to monitor these banks and also aggravated inflationary pressures since the loans put strains on the budget to absorb them. McKinnon cites Poland, the USSR and Vietnam, as examples where the mushrooming of commercial banks undermined monetary objectives and fuelled inflation.[54] He argues too that in the early stages of the Russian reforms, the rapid growth in small, 'wildcat' banks undermined the government's ability to control its monetary and fiscal policies by attracting away surplus funds from enterprises and, at the same time, softening the budget constraints of enterprises through soft loans.[55] At the same time, the growing commercial banking sector was attracting away many of the most qualified people from the supervisory organs themselves.

These symptoms arose due to a variety of causes. First, the *ownership patterns* of banks.[56] The privatisation of SOBs proved to be a slow process and hence the banks remained state-owned and slow to become profit-oriented. These SOBs were also pushed by the state to allocate credit for political objectives, such as maintaining employment levels. Moreover, many of the smaller, 'private' banks were in fact created by their owners, making them more like enterprise treasuries than true profit-oriented banks. This was common in the former USSR (FSU), as state organs formed large numbers of what came to be termed – 'pocket banks', since they were said to be in the pockets of the organisations that created them.[57] By owning these banks, enterprises could use them to attract low-cost funds provided by the central bank, and also exploit the banks' limited liability.

Second, the *lack of competition* in the banking system created little incentive for banks to improve and broaden their services, and little incentive to lower their lending and deposit margins and fees.[58] An oligopolistic structure emerged after the partition of the monobank with the SOBs being dominant in their particular areas, such as trade, savings, industrial, or regional finance. The concentration in the banking system created inefficiencies between the sources and uses of funds, with the savings banks continuing to hold the majority of household savings but with underdeveloped interbank markets which would have allowed these funds to be efficiently made available to banks prepared to lend them.

Third, the SOBs *inherited large volumes of non-performing loans* (NPLs) when the monobank was partitioned.[59] In addition, the *stock* of bad loans they inherited was concentrated which did not enable diversification in the early stages and hence increased banks' vulnerability.[60] Banks faced strong disincentives to foreclose on their customers, many of which were regarded as 'too big to fail.' Yet while these problems were significant, for many PCPEs the stock problem of bad debt was quickly overshadowed by the flow problem. In the words of Aghion and Carlin,

> In most of the Central and East European Countries, the distortions created by the inheritance of loans from the planned economy have been minimised. For example, in Poland the value of the debt was wiped out by hyper inflation and in the Czech and Slovak Federal Republic, a programme for transferring the debt from the banks to a new Consolidation Bank has been implemented.[61]

Fourth, the *slow development of the bankruptcy mechanism* in the PCPEs, stemming both from administrative and legal inadequacies in the system and from unclear property rights,[62] made bankruptcy not only difficult to enforce but extremely costly even if successful, often costing more than the underlying value of the assets.[63] In addition to the banks' incentives to continue lending to inefficient SOEs, however, there was also an 'option' value of waiting for the state to bail out both undercapitalised banks and their business customers. This reinforced the soft-budget constraint on banks and enterprises and also led to creditor passivity were creditors lacked strong incentives to collect on debts outstanding.[64]

Fifth, aside from the skewed incentives, the SOBs and the newly created private banks needed to *undergo a learning process* to operate in the new formal institutional structure of a market economy. As Dittus observed: 'Curtailed lending to enterprises may not only reflect prudent behaviour, but also the limited capacity of banks to evaluate risks and monitor borrowers in a market environment. Building up those skills will take time.'[65] The point has been well put by Johnson:

> The old skills that bankers developed under communism are entirely different from those necessary to function within a market

> economy. Such tasks as how best to manipulate the money supply, evaluate borrowers, and operate in securities markets takes years even for would-be bankers in the West to learn. In the chaotic economic situation in Russia today it would be ridiculous to expect Russian bankers to behave like capitalists all of a sudden, despite the growing incentives for them to do so.[66]

In the absence of learning, bankers in the new environment may rely on their former patterns of credit assessment, with *personal ties* continuing to play a central role.[67] This reliance further reinforces the previous lending patterns.

The foregoing symptoms and underlying causes demonstrated that in order to achieve financial discipline in the PCPE more had to be done than simply remove all controls. Writing in 1993, Thorne argued, 'while Eastern European Governments have made substantial progress in reforming their banking systems, in most countries the banking system still plays a passive role'.[68] Institutional arrangements, which had largely been overlooked in the initial push to liberalisation, now began to attract more attention,[69] particularly within the financial system. It was recognised that transition was a *process* rather than an *event*, a process in which institutions and organisations play an important role. Given this important role, we briefly turn our attention to some general features of institutional economics.

## The new institutional economics

Over the past two decades, increasing attention has been drawn to the inadequacy of traditional neo-classical economics in explaining economic change and development.[70] The New Institutional Economics holds that economies do not operate under the Walrasian assumptions of perfect information and competition, free entry and exit and costless transacting. Given imperfect information[71] and significant transaction costs,[72] the institutional approach holds that different institutional structures provide different levels of efficiency in terms of exchange.

According to North, 'institutions are the rules of the game in a society or, more formally, are the humanly devised constraints that shape human interaction', which 'reduce uncertainty by providing a structure to everyday life'.[73] Within North's definition, institutions are both *formal* – such as laws, constitutions and contracts – and *informal* – such as behavioural codes or unwritten rules i.e. culturally derived. Accordingly, institutional analysis considers a wide range of explanations on a variety of levels and across disciplines. According to Sjöstrand,

> One basic difference between institutionalists and mainstream economists is that the former do not sharply delimit their field of study from the other social sciences but function as more of an open, learning research system. In accordance with its broader perspective, the political and social frameworks for economic activities are not excluded, nor is the past or the future.[74]

Formal and informal institutions act jointly to provide a basis for exchange and, indeed, for virtually all interactive activity in people's lives. In the United States, for example, formal contracts play a central role in exchange which accounts for the huge number of lawyers. Japan, on the other hand, relies less on formal legal arrangements and more on trust and honour. Institutions not only regulate the behaviour of individuals, but also of groups of individuals – i.e. organisations. These organisations have their own internal institutional structures regulating interaction and exchange, and are also governed by the general institutional structure of the society, which in turn regulates, for example, interactions *between* organisations.

Institutional change is an important part of economic development, since institutions can bridge informational asymmetries, lower transaction costs and thus create incentives to encourage exchange and corresponding mechanisms to enable exchange to be efficient. Moreover, the process of institutional change must be understood on both formal and informal levels. 'Looking at formal rules themselves', according to North, 'gives us an inadequate and frequently misleading notion about the relationship between formal constraints and performance'.[75] The imposition of the US constitution on many countries in Latin America, for example, did not elicit the same effects as it did in the United States because – although the formal rules were the same – the enforcement mechanisms, behavioural norms and the subjective actions of individuals led to different outcomes. 'The way by which the mind processes information', writes North,

> not only is the basis for the existence of institutions, but is a key to understanding the way informal constraints play an important role in the makeup of the choice set both in the short run and the long run evolution of societies.[76]

In short, formal rules do not guarantee certain patterns of behaviour but can play an *enabling* role.

Formal institutions can facilitate exchange and reduce uncertainty only to the extent that the people are prepared to recognise them, abide by them, and expect others to do the same. North further argues that the process of institutional change is an *incremental* one primarily owing to the lag in changing informal constraints and patterns of behaviour: 'what is most striking (although seldom observed, particularly by advocates of revolution) is the persistence of so many aspects of a society in spite of a total change in the rules'.[77] It is not surprising, then, that in times of rapid and fundamental change, many people rely on their established patterns of transacting while they are adjusting to the new rules, or simply disregard the new rules entirely:

> Although a wholesale change in the formal rules may take place, at the same time there will be many informal constraints that have great survival tenacity because *they still resolve basic exchange problems among the participants, be they social, political, or economic*'[78] (emphasis added).

Institutional change in PCPEs, therefore, has not only to be effected on a formal level but also to elicit appropriate responses on an informal level. Neuber sums up the issues:

> The principal debate about the appropriate speed and sequencing of reform policies, often couched in the none-too-helpful dichotomy of gradualism versus 'big-bang', is based on different assumptions about the relative ease with which behavioural patterns and institutions in emerging market economies can, and ought to be changed as a result of policy.[79]

The unwillingness to accept new institutions can be understood as both a rational reaction to a new set of rules but also as a reliance upon established patterns of behaviour. According to Rose, for individuals it was 'rational' to continue to operate outside the formal institutional structure, with their participation in formal and informal economies representing a carryover from the past which enabled them to *cope with the changing institutional structure.*[80] Etzioni formulated the implementation problems in institutional change with the concept of 'friction', or resistance to the new institutional structure, arguing that individuals were likely to revert back to behaviour *to which they were accustomed.*[81]

'Far from having fixed self-interested preferences', argued Etzioni, 'individuals are penetrated by the institutions and cultures in which they spend their formative years and various parts of their childhood'.[82] In short, institutional change can be effective only if the new institutions are accepted and are able to function.

Tensions between formal changes being imposed and informal resistance to them help to explain the behaviour of banks in the transition. The concept of 'creditor passivity', referring to the build-up of NPLs and inter-enterprise debts, stems in part from the low skill levels of bankers operating in the new system and is compounded by informational asymmetries and a general lack of transparency which support the discretionary behaviour of enterprise managers.[83] There is also evidence that some banks found ways to conduct their business outside of the new rules which had been established. A survey of Ukrainian banks found that banks minimised their transaction and agency costs by using informal mechanisms for credit decisions, including personal contacts and private sources of information.[84] The Russian weekly *Commersant* found that banks in Russia tended to make a small percentage of loans based on credit analysis, a large portion being through a personal acquaintance (44 per cent), some form of official guarantee and, of course, through 'commissions' (i.e. bribes).[85]

Thus while policymakers were faced with the dilemma of creating institutions which would be accepted, the early stages of reform were often marked by an institutional vacuum in which the new actors in the nascent market economy were left without formal support. While informal support networks existed, and were used to a certain extent, these networks did not compensate entirely for a lack of formal institutions to provide finance, advice and other forms of support. The lack of finance being provided to private enterprises was rooted in part in the lack of an adequate institutional base:

> under communist regimes, the private sector, if at all permitted, was allowed to exist but not to expand. Besides legal limitations there was also a lack of financial institutions geared to the needs of small private firms, artisans, etc. Now, legal restrictions are gone but the network of institutions supporting the expansion of the small business sector does not yet exist.[86]

With these concerns in mind, attention was drawn to financial system design in order to reform its structure and enable it to play an active role in the transition.

## Design of the financial system

Financial liberalisation in itself being insufficient to impose financial discipline on actors in the economic system, there is a need to design an appropriate institutional arrangement of the financial system. Saunders and Walter argue that

> to the extent that Eastern European financial systems are likely to follow the stylized development (benchmarks) of Western financial systems in some accelerated fashion ... there arises a number of organisational issues regarding what might provide a *more* efficient transition than has historically occurred in some Western countries.[87]

The majority of proposals on financial system design underline the *important role of banks in the provision of finance*,[88] particularly for SMEs which are less able to borrow directly from capital markets and unable to rely on high levels of own funds.[89] While the development of capital markets is also significant as a complementary mechanism which can undertake intermediation and governance functions along with banks,[90] our focus is on the banking system.

The search for an ideal banking model for the transition centres primarily on the institutional freedom to be given to banks to engage in various activities. The greater the proposed scope for bank activities, the greater the assumption that banks would be able to operate effectively in the transition. We begin our discussion by examining *financial restructuring and privatisation* to improve incentives, and *learning* to enable banks to function within the new incentive structure.

### Financial restructuring and privatisation

The need to improve the incentive structure for banks reflects two sets of problems: bank portfolio problems and ownership patterns. A large literature has developed of proposals on *managing NPLs in bank portfolios*.[91] Initially, many proposals, Brainard's work being among the first, had recommended a 'fiscal solution', whereby the government would absorb the bad loans by bringing them onto the state balance sheet while crediting the balance sheets of banks through government bond issues. In this way, banks could start over with a clean slate and the government could spread the financial burden of the bad loans over time. Moreover, since most of the bad loans belong to SOBs, transferring them to the budget would actually represent a bookkeeping operation rather than a real change in the state's fiscal position. While this may have been true, political pressures, such as the strong pressure on governments to stay within strict budgetary guidelines, might have led governments to deal with the problem later rather than sooner.[92] But, further, the approach is strictly *static*. It addresses only the stock problem of NPLs, leaving aside any consideration of new flows. In so doing, it creates the problem of *moral hazard* – e.g. it signals the expectation to banks that future bail-outs will occur. A number of alternative methods have also been proposed to manage NPLs, such as debt-for-equity swaps.[93] Whatever the method of managing these loans, however, flow problems undermining financial discipline arise from additional factors. The removal of NPLs from banks' balance sheets, therefore, is a *necessary but not sufficient condition for restructuring banks*.[94]

Another condition seen as necessary for restructuring – which addresses the flow problem – is to correct the ownership structures of banks by *privatising* them. The rationale for privatising banks is that property relations would improve the incentive structure facing banks, make banks less subject to government attempts to use them to preserve failing enterprises, and accelerate the banks' learning process, thus allowing them to adapt more quickly to the formal institutional structure. Moreover, the proceeds of privatisation sales would provide short-term relief to the government's financing burden and hence lessen the degree of crowding-out of funds to private enterprises. Nuti sums up the issue as follows:

> The case for the privatisation of state financial institutions is partly the same as for other state enterprises, namely the expectation ... of higher efficiency through the subjection of state managers to bankruptcy rules and stock market discipline; the raising of budget revenue to contain or pay off government debt, or to allow a less severe deflationary stance than otherwise might be necessary; and the search for a model of property owning democracy.[95]

Privatisation in itself is no panacea, however, since a simple change in property relations might not *ab initio* overcome the learning process.[96] Moreover, in practical terms, bank privatisation in PCPEs has proceeded slowly.[97]

**Learning**

Even if the incentive structure facing banks is improved, there remains the need for banks (organisations) to learn to operate within the new incentives (institutions).[98] In proposals on financial system design, learning is seen as an eventual by-product, the primary distinction being placed on the length of time the learning might take rather than the underlying conditions and mechanisms which might help or indeed hinder it from occurring.[99] Rostowski addresses directly the need for learning in terms of the change from 'systematically bad credit into systematically good credit', pointing out that while some systematically bad credit may be recoverable, the difference between bad and good credit is in the mechanisms of selecting loans (i.e. screening).[100] His argument is that,

> banks which have never made such choices before suddenly have to decide which enterprises to continue financing, and which to cut off from credit. They are likely to make many mistakes.[101]

The rise in NPLs in PCPEs (i.e. the flow problem) suggests that bankers in these countries may be making mistakes which are part of their learning process.

The view that learning involves mistakes suggests that learning is a *process*, following Arrow's notion of 'learning by doing', and underlining the significance of *experience*.[102] Training is only the beginning. In a study of UK managers, accustomed to working within a market economy, Parker and Lewis found that

> Planning or training for promotion can do a lot to improve competence via technical abilities and general experience, but the real problems start for individuals when they actually sit in the new chair, and that unfortunately is when most training stops![103]

The learning process may not be linear and will certainly not be instantaneous and costless as held in neo-classical economics. This has long been recognised in the literature on development economics.[104]

We are more concerned with how learning occurs and hence what conditions may enable or constrain it from taking place.[105] As Arrow remarked:

> It has been assumed here that learning takes place only as a by-product of ordinary production. In fact, society has created institutions, education and research, whose purpose it is to enable learning to take place more readily. A fuller model would take account of these additional variables.[106]

How then can we understand what it means to enable learning? Moreover, how can we characterise conditions which might not be conducive to learning? Deutsch's examination of the political process introduces important concepts on the learning process.[107] First of all, Deutsch argues that the *learning capacity* of a system is

> related to the amount and kinds of its uncommitted resources. The larger the proportion of uncommitted resources within a system, the greater the set of new kinds of behaviour it can learn.[108]

Learning involves a mental process and the creation of new ideas and policies, but it also involves a physical process of implementation which demands that resources are committed. Uncommitted resources are not synonymous with idle resources, however, for the key point is whether an organisation can deploy resources, be they idle or in use for another task.[109]

Even in the presence of excess learning capacity, an organisation may experience what Deutsch terms *pathological learning*, whereby 'the organisation learned something that has reduced its subsequent capacity to learn'.[110]

> By pathological learning in the case of an individual or an organisation we may understand a learning process, and a corresponding change in inner structure, that will reduce rather than increase the future learning capacity of the person or organisation. Will and power may easily lead to such self-destructive learning, for they may imply the overvaluation of the past against the present and future, the overvaluation of the experiences acquired in a limited environment against the vastness of the universe around us; and the overvaluation of present expectations against all possibilities of surprise, discovery and change.[111]

Based on the above discussion, we may examine the inter-relationship between learning and incentives – and, indeed, why institutional change tends to be incremental, with institutions which are seemingly more efficient not adopted or adopted more slowly than would be expected.[112] In PCPEs there are strong incentives for banks to cling to their existing informal mechanisms in order to mitigate – or, indeed, avoid entirely – the slow and painful learning process, not least for fear of losing their market position to other banks which are more capable of working within the new institutional structure. Moreover, they have the power to do so given the limited degree of competition in their respective banking sectors. Deutsch observes that 'power' can give actors the ability to *avoid learning* – i.e. act as a learning pathology.[113]

For banks to initiate learning, therefore, they need to recognise the potential benefits of rearranging their resources to respond to the more market-oriented incentive structure. As banks recognise that other organisations are prepared to play by the new rules of the market – enterprises, for example, may make their accounts more transparent – they will have a greater incentive to do the same. But learning goes beyond will, for it involves capability and thus the need to build and allocate resources within the organisation effectively. Efforts to reform the banking systems in PCPEs need, therefore, to address the incentive structure as well as the issues surrounding the banks' learning process. These aspects underlie the debate on the banking structure PCPEs should adopt in the transition.

**Structural proposals on the banking system**

The debate on banking structure considers whether restrictions should be placed on bank activities such as the division between commercial and investment banking which exists in the United States, or whether banks should be free to engage in the entire range of financial activities, including equity participations (such as the universal banking which exists in Germany). The structures proposed address both intermediation and possible governance functions of banks, and differentiate between large enterprises (where there may be a separation of ownership and control) and SMEs. No matter which model is advocated, our discussion of institutional economics underlies the difficulty of universalising it, since the model may perform quite differently when placed in another system. Wagener adopts this view:

> A governance structure that seemingly led to reasonable efficiency and welfare in a 'western' country may have a quite different outcome when implemented in Central or Eastern Europe, or somewhere else. What we have called the oligarchic governance structure of Germany, for instance, depends in its functioning upon many different factors, political, cultural, historic, above all upon the intense international competition to which [West-] Germany traditionally exposed itself. Implanted in, say, the Czech republic one or several of these side conditions, of which economic analysis may not even be aware, could be lacking and hence performance would be different from the German experience. This is no argument

> against learning and imitation, but, as said, only a warning against too high expectations.[114]

Recognising, then, the possible limitations involved in applying any model to a PCPE, we turn to an analysis of the proposals that have been made.

At one end of the spectrum are proposals in which bank activities would be severely limited.[115] In many of these proposals, bank activities are constrained beyond a simple distinction between commercial and investment banking. Separation between payment and intermediation functions is envisaged, the latter being limited in addition. These proposals are based on the notion that banks are different from other enterprises in that they manage the population's deposits as well as the payment system, and that they are highly geared. On this view, the payment system and savings must be protected, even at the cost of less rapid progress in enterprise restructuring.[116] The high volatility in PCPEs would lead many 'good' banking decisions to go wrong owing to changes in their environment, and the learning process of banks would be long and marked by mistakes. In this process, given the impact on public deposits and the payment system, the government would likely be required to step in and bail out financial institutions in the event of distress – creating a moral hazard problem. Diaz-Alejandro recognised the long learning process of banks in the Southern Cone and advocated limits to banking activity in the development process:

> The new financial institutions in the Southern Cone attracted fresh entrepreneurs and stimulated the creation of new conglomerates and economic groups. While the new entrepreneurial blood has an attractive aura, experience indicates that such venturesome animal spirits are better channelled toward non-financial endeavors, where the disciplining threat of bankruptcy could be more credible.[117]

As a result, limiting the range of bank activities could also limit the degree of shocks to the system that might result from the bad loans that were made.[118] In short, these proposals make assumptions about the capability, or lack thereof, of banks to carry out their functions efficiently.

McKinnon proposes perhaps the most 'draconian' set of measures for banks in PCPEs.[119] His proposal entails two stages. In the first, there is an immediate distinction between state- and private enterprises, and within state enterprises, a further distinction between those that would be rescued and then allowed to fend for themselves (what he terms 'liberalised' enterprises) and those which the government would take over given their bad condition (the 'traditional' enterprises). During this stage, the state is responsible for maintaining the integrity of the payments system, and *no lending is allowed*, thus denying banks the opportunity to engage in financial intermediation. Private and liberalised enterprises are confined to own funds and capital market issues, while traditional enterprises continue to be financed by SOBs until further arrangements are made. In the second stage, banks are allowed to engage in some financial intermediation, such as highly collateralised lending (what McKinnon refers to as the 'real bills doctrine'). These measures are designed – first and foremost – to ensure macroeconomic stability, and only gradually to allow restructuring to take place.

The main problem with McKinnon's proposal is that the economy might collapse since many enterprises suffer from negative cash flow during restructuring. Another problem is that it assumes that the formal structure as proposed would be adhered to, and that organisations would not create informal arrangements in order to arbitrage the system. Moreover, the learning and skill development of local banks would be slowed. McKinnon concedes that the 'development of ordinary commercial banking may well have to be deferred for several years'.[120]

Rostowski also envisages a long learning process for banks, and argues that banks' ability to play an active role in the transition process depends on:

> the development of credit assessment, liability management and other banking skills in the banking systems of post-communist economies, and sophisticated bank supervision skills in the bank supervisory authority – in other words through the development of the skills necessary to provide the microeconomic underpinning of a banking system along lines current in the West.[121]

Yet Rostowski skirts the issue of when banks might be prepared to make 'systematically good credit':

> It is not easy to imagine a 'gradualist' solution to the problem of the switch from good to bad credit – after all, banks either are or are not responsible for the loans they make. Yet it is in this area that the costs of 'shock therapy' are likely to be particularly high given the duty to decide about the fate of a large part of the productive sector.[122]

Accordingly, Rostowski recommends a 100 per cent reserve banking system, where payment functions and intermediation functions are kept separate in order to protect the payment mechanism.[123] Over time, he argues, 'banks need to learn to allocate credit effectively by first learning to allocate short-term, self-liquidating credit for working capital'.[124] In short, bank freedoms should be increased only *gradually* as banks are able to learn and as the formal institutional framework is put into place.[125]

While the above proposals address a major cause of the problems – i.e. bank capabilities – others focus directly on a primary symptom – the lack of financing for private enterprises. One possibility is that the government introduces selective credit controls to limit funds to SOEs and hence ease the financing problems of private enterprises.[126] Selective controls would offer only a short-term administrative solution, however, a point taken up by Begg and Portes, who argue that,

> credit controls are a useful stop gap. They can be implemented quickly. But precisely because they deal with the symptom not the cause of the problem, they cannot represent an efficient long run solution.[127]

A second possibility is the creation of development banks. Lipton and Sachs argue that 'it is probably worthwhile for the government to encourage the formation of financial institutions catering to the needs of small businesses'.[128] A third possibility is to privatise a small group of banks which would then deal exclusively with the private sector, while the remaining state banks sort out the difficulties in the SOEs.[129] Pohl and Claessens support this approach for PCPEs based on the experience in Russia where a core of private, profit-oriented banks has emerged.[130] The critical issue, however, is that creating the core is only half of the battle, for once created these banks may not fulfil the lending expectations which are placed upon them. We return to this point in Chapter 7.

### The universal banking model

At the other end of the spectrum, the universal banking model – allowing banks to engage in a broad range of activities – also receives wide support in the literature.[131] First, it is seen as providing stronger *corporate governance* through more active participation by banks, as both shareholders and creditors (i.e. insiders). On this view, Corbett and Mayer argue that only universal banks could accomplish the huge task of enterprise restructuring by providing the necessary degree of corporate control.[132] Their analysis is based on existing patterns of corporate finance in market economies and the view that insider systems provide closer ties between banks and industry, as well as greater long-term industrial finance. Secondly, it is argued that universal banks would better perform their intermediation function, being more willing to take risks and provide longer-term industrial finance as a result of their increased levers of control and better information. *Relationships* between banks and industry would enhance the banks' ability both to achieve effective governance and to increase their scope for intermediation, an issue we discuss at length in Chapter 6. A further reason for recommending the universal banking model is that it would reduce costs in the banking system through economies of scale and scope.[133]

Unlike proposals which aim at constraining banks' scope for action in the transition on the basis that banks need to learn, proposals advocating a universal banking structure are based on the idea that banks can learn quickly and function effectively within the freedoms provided by the new institutional structure. Actually, the learning process is largely disregarded in these proposals. 'While progress in some areas may be frustratingly slow', write Corbett and Mayer, 'there is little doubt that the necessary reforms will *eventually* materialize'. (emphasis added).[134] The emphasis on the structural dimension (institutional) as opposed to the learning dimension (organisational) does not escape criticism in the literature. Phelps *et al.* note that:

> the idea that the existing offshoots of the communist banking systems in Eastern Europe could be rapidly transformed into the future analogues of *Deutsche Bank* seems to slide over the tremendous obstacles that lie in the way of reforming the existing banking institutions.[135]

Given the long learning process of domestic banks, perhaps they would simply not be able to perform their functions effectively in the transition, and so would either have to be constrained in their functions or the PCPE concerned would risk having its macro- and micro-concerns undermined or simply left unaddressed. Further, given the lack of competition in PCPE banking markets, it may be that if banks were able to engage in a wide range of activities they would maintain the status quo, thus making little progress in developing financial discipline among actors in the system.[136] That is to say, universal banking structures might increase the potential learning pathology inherent in banks' already dominant market positions.

## A possible role for foreign banks in the transition process

Up to this point, we have discussed reform proposals on the banking system using bank *structure* as the main variable. Another variable is bank *ownership*, however, and we next consider this dimension. We have drawn attention to the perceived benefits of *private* ownership of banks. Our focus now turns to the possible implications of *foreign* ownership of banks in PCPEs.

Given the many obstacles to achieving financial discipline in PCPEs, and the critical functions banks must perform, the question arises whether foreign banks could play a role in the process. In the words of Brainard,

> the rapid creation of a modern commercial banking system is feasible only if human skills and knowhow can be transferred quickly and on a significant scale. This seems unlikely unless countries are willing to grant interested foreign banks a significant domestic banking franchise without the legacy of past corporate debts.[137]

Nevertheless, while various alternatives – or, at least, complementary arrangements – to direct foreign ownership have been examined, including 'twinning' arrangements with foreign banks,[138] joint ventures,[139] and participations by international institutions,[140] foreign *ownership* of banks has remained a sensitive subject, given the critical functions entrusted to banks.

Terrell outlines some general arguments for restricting foreign banks from local markets:[141] (1) *reciprocity* – that domestic banks are unable to enter the banking market of the foreign bank in question; (2) *control is more difficult* – that domestic banks would be easier to control and, hence, ensure that they perform functions seen as critical to the economy; (3) *export local deposits* – that foreign banks might cause a 'net outflow' of funds from the country; (4) *the infant industry argument* – that domestic banks need protection in order to learn and improve their operations;[142] (5) *regulation is more difficult* – that foreign bank activities occur outside the border of the country and hence would be difficult to monitor; and (6) *possible 'overbanking'* – that the market would become too saturated through the foreign bank presence.

Saunders and Walter suggest that the costs arising out of foreign control over a large share of domestic banking assets include: (1) concerns over possible loss of 'moral suasion powers' by the central bank; (2) concerns over who would bear the costs in the event of failure of foreign institutions; and (3) concerns over the banking environment becoming more difficult for domestic financial institutions.[143] Stiglitz also points out that

> ... foreign banks, in allocating capital, will have different objectives than those of domestic banks, so that the disparity between social and private returns may be particularly large.[144]

Perhaps for some of these reasons, several proposals (for example, those of McKinnon) call for a low degree of foreign ownership of banks, suggesting that domestic banks should (and would have to) play the largest role in the transition (and beyond). Corbett and Mayer take a cautious approach to foreign ownership:

> Nor does foreign ownership of either enterprises or the financial system offer much solution. There is, of course, a great deal that Eastern Europe can learn from financial experience and management practice in the West. But that transfer of knowledge should not be achieved through ownership. Economic development requires the indigenous creation of enterprises and institutions that ensure that control at the highest level is retained domestically.[145]

This bold assertion notwithstanding, the issue of foreign bank entry in PCPEs has generally received little more than a passing mention in many proposals on financial system design.[146]

A potential immediate benefit to foreign bank entry is that by buying existing ailing banks foreign banks could both ease the government's revenue problems and, at the same time, also assist in restructuring the domestic banks that were purchased. Indeed, there is evidence that foreign investment in the non-financial sectors of PCPEs has led to effective restructuring.[147] This benefit has not been overlooked by PCPEs. Poland has attempted to force foreign banks to enter the Polish market through acquisition (of an ailing Polish bank), but the process has proved a slow and difficult one.[148]

This 'instrumental' use of foreign banks aside, in the literature we find several proposals which recommend open entry to foreign banks, a large foreign-bank presence, and full competition between foreign and domestic banks.[149] Schmieding and Buch argue that the entry of foreign banks would be beneficial to PCPEs since foreign banks would help to mobilise savings and allocate them more efficiently. This view is somewhat narrow in holding that foreign banks (organisations) would simply be more efficient than domestic banks (organisations) in performing the function of financial intermediation.

A more dynamic perspective on foreign bank entry in PCPEs is provided by Saunders and Walter, who argue that:

> emerging Eastern European financial systems should be fully open to the potential and actual entry of banks and other financial firms from the West. This will help assure the kinds of technological infusions, training, management, and capital adequacy needed to capture the relevant static and dynamic gains. Foreign-based institutions should be able de novo to establish branches, agencies, or subsidiaries, purchase existing banking assets, take equity stakes in emerging local financial institutions, form strategic alliances with such institutions, and generally benefit from national treatment vis-à-vis their local competitors. By forcing local financial institutions to live under a credible competitive threat from internationally active players, the transition to Western levels of performance in financial intermediation and control will be promoted. The cost of having a significant segment of the domestic financial services industry under the control of foreign-based institutions may be small in comparison to the gains.[150]

Three assumptions are incorporated in the above passage. First, that foreign banks can operate effectively in PCPEs. That is to say, that these banks would be able to engage in financial intermediation and other activities in the transition environment without having to undergo a learning process. Second, that foreign banks can exert the necessary competitive pressures on domestic banks to accelerate the learning process of domestic banks. This assertion evidently also assumes a certain response from domestic banks, which would clearly depend on the extent that they are able, willing, and forced to learn – recalling Deutsch's enabling and disabling conditions. Third, that by virtue of these benefits, the foreign banking contribution would outweigh its costs (such as those outlined earlier).

On the basis that foreign banks possess many advantages (outlined in Chapter 3) over domestic banks, Rostowski presents the most radical proposal: that foreign banks should be allowed – and, indeed, encouraged – to take over the banking system in a given PCPE since they will be better able to achieve the primary objectives of the banking system in the transition. Given the long and difficult learning process for domestic banks envisaged by Rostowski, he proposes a highly restrictive regulatory stance towards them and, in addition, home regulation of foreign banks. In this way, he argues, it should be possible for foreign banks to take over the entire banking system by virtue of their advantages and favourable regulatory position. Moreover, he argues that this option should be seriously considered:

> given the argument that a secure banking system is vital for macroeconomic stability, and that macroeconomic stability is vital for a successful transition to a market economy, then some post-communist economies may find it most efficient to import foreign banks to create their banking systems, just as they have to import foreign machinery for their productive investment. The law of comparative advantage does not only apply to goods.[151]

The proposal also has an added benefit of placing less pressure on domestic supervisory organs which are overburdened with supervising domestic banks and, moreover, short on resources – particularly human resources, given the exodus of many of the best personnel to new commercial banks.

Using Rostowski's proposal as a point of departure, we find overall that proposals on financial system design contain implicit views on the expected pace of learning and financial restructuring and privatisation. The typology of proposals is summarised in Table 2.1.

Our focus concerns the lower two boxes, where high foreign bank participation is recommended. These proposals are based on a particular view that foreign banks will be able to function effectively in

*Table* 2.1 Proposals on financial system design in PCPEs

| | | *Domestic bank role (degree of operating freedom allowed)* | |
|---|---|---|---|
| | | *Small (long learning)* | *Large (short learning)* |
| *Foreign bank role* (degree of ownership allowed) | *Small* | McKinnon | Corbett and Mayer |
| | *Large* | Rostowski | Saunders and Walter |

PCPEs, that they will act as catalysts to the development of domestic banks and that they will impact positively on the non-financial sectors of the economy. On these issues, the existing general literature on foreign banks is largely silent,[152] being focused primarily on motives and strategies of foreign banks in entering markets.[153] In Chapter 7 we revisit these issues in light of our investigation.

## Summary

We began this chapter with a discussion of the CPE, emphasising its formal and informal institutional structure and underlining the difficulty inherent in reforming – or, indeed, transforming – it. We also noted the passive role that the financial system played in the CPE, pointing out that for a successful transition to a market economy the financial system needed to play an *active* role. Despite financial liberalisation, the financial system has hitherto continued to play a largely passive role in PCPEs, thereby slowing the transition to a market economy. This transition rests upon the imposition of financial discipline, and has been hampered by problems which have emerged in the banking system. Our discussion of these problems provided the basis on which to focus on the institutional aspects of the transition, viewing the transition as a process whereby *both* formal *and* informal institutions need to be changed for the transition to be successful.

We then considered the issue of financial system design in the transition and highlighted the need for learning and financial restructuring and privatisation. Our discussion of these aspects underlay the subsequent analysis of the existing proposals on financial system design. We concluded the chapter by creating a typology, categorising the proposals in terms of their recommendations on bank structure and ownership, and signalling our focus on the latter – particularly the issue of foreign bank ownership.

# 3
# Context and Approach of the Investigation

> If a common ground exists between the artists and the scientists, that ground is explanation. Neither art's appreciation of the uniqueness of occurrences nor science's grasp of occurrences as mere instances of more general propositions is limited to explanation. But central to both enterprises is an attempt to understand and explain why events occurred. The artist may appear (to the scientist) overly fascinated with nuance and randomness that would be better treated as extraneous fluff around common, recurring elements. The scientist may seem (to the artist) to ride roughshod over relevant, particular details in the quest for generality. (Graham Allison, 1971)

> Facts and theories are different things, not rungs in a hierarchy of increasing certainty. Facts are the world's data. Theories are structures of ideas that explain and interpret facts. Facts do not go away while scientists debate rival theories for explaining them. Einstein's theory of gravitation replaced Newton's, but apples did not suspend themselves in mid-air pending the outcome. (Stephen Jay Gould, 1983)

This chapter applies the conceptual framework to the specific case which is examined in the book. Underlying the discussion which follows are the difficult choices and problems confronting PCPEs, for without an explanation of these the 'special' nature of the East German case cannot be fully appreciated. The discussion also covers in brief the approach taken, along with the methods that were employed.

*Table* 3.1 Respective advantages of foreign and domestic banks[a]

| *Foreign banks* | *Domestic banks* |
|---|---|
| Quality of service | Branch network |
| Marketing | Local knowledge and contacts |
| Technology | Local deposit base |
| Organisational structure | |
| Lower cost base (streamlined) | |
| Reputation | |

*Note*:
[a] One point omitted from Table 3.1 concerns balance sheet size. The reason is that balance sheet size may be an advantage for a large domestic bank but also for a foreign bank. The position of the latter depends on the organisational status of the foreign bank: branches are able to access a larger capital base, (i.e. the capital of the parent bank) than subsidiaries which are bound by domestic regulatory restrictions based on local balance sheet size. Even in the case of branches, internal controls on capital may restrict the foreign bank's access to funds.

## The research question

A central question which emerged in our conceptual framework was whether foreign institutions and organisations could be *transplanted onto a PCPE*, following from Rostowski's proposal which recommended a foreign bank 'import.'[1] The basis for the import is that foreign banks possess many advantages *vis-à-vis* domestic banks (Table 3.1).

### The 'limiting case' of East Germany after unification (GEMSU)

The decision was made to limit the primary focus of the research to East Germany after unification (GEMSU), on the basis that this represented the most developed and extensive case of foreign bank entry. One may, however, question whether West German banks were actually 'foreign,' these banks having been local German banks in the East prior to the Second World War and possessing a rich historical legacy there. The point requires a more detailed exposition.

#### *The legacy of the West German banks in the East*

The legacy of the banks stems from their important contribution in the building of the German nation in the eighteenth and particularly nineteenth centuries.[2] 'The dominant position of the universal banks in Germany,' writes Weber, 'must be seen against the emergence and development of the industrial society in Germany.'[3] In the latter part of the nineteenth century, as Germany underwent rapid industrialisation, there was a high demand for capital. At the same time, there was also a clear deficit in developed capital markets as well as wealthy individuals who could channel funds through these markets to satisfy the long-term financing needs of industry. Coinciding with the unification of Germany by Otto von Bismark in 1871,

> The existing capital gap ... was closed by an 'institutional innovation': the creation of joint-stock banks. Between 1870 and 1872, over 100 joint-stock banks ... were founded with the active assistance of private bankers.[4]

Among the joint-venture banks established were the present 'Big Three' – *Deutsche Bank* and *Commerzbank* in 1870, and *Dresdner Bank* in 1872.[5] In line with their growing importance, these banks also grew rapidly in size. In less than forty years after unification, *Deutsche Bank* grew its deposit base to more than 162 times its original size.[6] By 1910, *Deutsche Bank* and *Dresdner Bank* were among six banks in Germany to possess more than 100 mn marks in capital, having 200 mn and 180 mn, respectively; *Commerzbank* had 85 mn.[7] As the banking sector became more concentrated, a process began of 'converting the network of banks in scattered locations into a hierarchical structure with its apex at Berlin.'[8]

More than 100 years after Bismark, as the German nation was unified once again in 1990, West German banks were anxious to promote their past involvement in the East prior to the Second World War, implying that in many respects they were simply picking up where they left off. In its 1989 *Annual Report, Dresdner Bank* announced,

> *Dresdner Bank* has now returned 'ad fontes', to its origins ... It is no coincidence that *Dresdner Bank* was the first West German bank, indeed the first West German firm, to open an office in its home city of Dresden, followed by other cities in the GDR ... Just as the Bank's history extends far deeper into the past by the takeover of the private Dresden banking house of Michael Kaskel, established in the $18^{th}$ century, than the founding date of 1. 12. 1872, so are its house colours of green and white associated with the old electorate of Saxony colours.[9]

*Deutsche Bank* was heavily involved in the East: before the Second World War, it had more than 70 branches there and its headquarters located in what later became East Berlin.[10] *Commerzbank* also stressed its prior engagement in the East: 'Throughout what was then Germany [before the Second World War], including parts that were in 1945 ceded to Poland, *Commerzbank* had 300 branches.'[11]

*The treatment of the West German banks as foreign*

The preceding discussion notwithstanding, the selection of the limiting case was based upon a working assumption that West German banks in the East should be treated as foreign. As it turned out, the assumption was validated by the findings of the fieldwork. As will be outlined (Chapter 6), the West German banks encountered significant problems adjusting to the operating environment in the East.[12] Indeed, many of the problems they experienced were similar to those experienced by foreign banks in other PCPEs (Chapter 7). It is still necessary, however, to explain the basis upon which the initial assumption rested since it was important in the design of the research question.

The treatment of the West German banks as foreign banks was based on two considerations. First, that the West German banks were established, successful financial institutions in an advanced market economy and, therefore, possessed significant advantages in terms of experience and knowhow *vis-à-vis* the East German banks. This consideration follows from the discussion in Chapter 2 which characterised foreign banks as 'good' banks in terms of their human skill levels and knowhow. That is to say, it was assumed that the West German banks had already undergone a long learning process and thus could operate more effectively from the outset. In addition, the West German banks could operate without the burden of old debts on their balance sheets and hence commitments to existing customers (Chapter 4). In short, the West German banks possessed the operating advantages outlined in Table 3.1. as well as the further advantages shown in Table 3.2 (p.44).

In addition to these functional characterisations, the second consideration in treating West German banks as foreign was that they would probably have found a significant lack of familiarity with the East in 1990 following the passing of more than a generation since the Second World War when it was transformed into a socialist state. In this transformation a monobank structure was created to replace the strong (commercial) banking tradition. As West German banks were forced to retreat from the East, Berlin ceased to be Germany's financial centre, which shifted to Frankfurt.[13] As a result, few people in the East after 1990 would have remembered well the West German banks and the banking tradition that existed prior to the Second World War. Moreover, most of the younger generation would have been influenced by propaganda labelling West German banks as evil products of the capitalist system.

There was an important difference, however, between the West German banks in the East and foreign banks in other PCPEs. After unification in 1990 the East became technically part of the Federal Republic of Germany, thereby placing the West German banks within their home country legislative environment.[14] This difference had two important implications. First, unlike foreign banks in other PCPEs, West German banks did not have to manage the sovereign risk of operating within another state: in many countries this may be a significant disincentive for foreign banks to enter and expand in the domestic market. Second, West German banks were treated as local banks in terms of the pressure they faced to support the transition in the East, both from the German government as well as the media. This pressure had a significant impact on their behaviour in the East (see Chapter 6, p.135). While foreign banks do face pressure in the markets where they operate, it does not compare with that felt by the West German banks as they developed their business in the East.

*Additional favourable conditions in the East*

In addition to the virtual takeover by West German banks (i.e. 'good' banks), the East possessed many other favourable, or 'limiting' conditions, which seemed to eliminate the primary causes of banking problems in most PCPEs (outlined in Chapter 2). Here we list the limiting conditions; we examine them in detail in the chapters that follow.

(1) the *ownership problem* was addressed through a complete privatisation of the former East German commercial banks[15]
(2) The *lack of competition* was addressed through open entry and the corresponding presence of many banks
(3) The *inheritance of non-performing loans(NPLs)* was addressed by transferring all former debts of East German enterprises to a separate institution (*Treuhandanstalt*) – i.e. no financial restructuring was necessary[16]
(4) The *incentives problem* was addressed by the complete West German institutional transfer to the East[17]
(5) The *learning problem* was (seemingly) addressed through the transfer of experienced West German banks.[18]

Phelps *et al.* had argued that domestic banks 'would not turn into Deutsche Bank overnight,' and hence should not be expected to

*Table* 3.2 Foreign bank advantages and disadvantages in East Germany and other PCPEs

| | *West German banks in East Germany after GEMSU* | *Foreign banks in PCPEs* |
|---|---|---|
| 1. Common language | Yes | No |
| 2. Information on local economy | Some | Little |
| 3. Used to banking structure | Yes | Variable |
| 4. Used to existing institutional structure | Yes | No |
| 5. Existing relationships with bank customers | Many (West German firms) | Few (only MNCs) |
| 6. Common history and culture | To some extent[a] | No |
| 7. Political and economic stability[b] | Yes | Variable |
| 8. Risk-sharing by the state | Extensive | No |
| 9. Branch network (in the local market) | Yes | No |
| 10. Restrictions on activities[c] | None | Some |

*Notes*:
[a] Hancock and Welsh (1994, p.7) outline the point in detail.
[b] The institutional transfer under GEMSU meant that the East would have a stable and credible political structure, hence avoiding the PCPE problem of 'time-consistency'.
[c] In some PCPEs, restrictions were placed on the activities of foreign banks, such as on the extent to which they could establish additional branch offices outside of the main branch (these are outlined in Chapter 7). In the East, no restrictions were placed on the West German banks which entered.

perform as effectively as universal banks. In the East after GEMSU, the largest branch network formed by a West German bank was established *by Deutsche Bank*. In addition to these various advantages, thanks to significant external transfers from West Germany the East German state did not crowd out the private sector by borrowing in domestic markets.

There were, moreover, further favourable conditions for West German banks which entered the East after GEMSU (Table 3.2).[19]

In addition to the West German Banks which entered the East, the remaining (domestic) East German banks – the publicly owned Savings Banks (*Sparkassen*) and also the Credit Cooperatives (*Genossenschaftsbanken*) – were relieved of their former debts and supported through financial and technical assistance from West Germany.

Furthermore, these limiting conditions were transferred to the East *overnight*, making it the most extreme case of shock therapy amongst the PCPEs. As a result, it represented an ideal case with which to test the success of a complete institutional transplant. In the words of Offe,

> researchers have had the good fortune to see a 'natural experiment' of such dimensions as could not even approximately be reproduced under 'laboratory conditions' ... place us in the unique position of being able to study the impact of the characteristic West German variety of democratic-capitalist institutions on a society which has not been democratic for nearly 60 years, and for 40 years has certainly not been capitalist.[20]

**The focus of the study**

This study considers the limiting case of the East as a possible model for banking reform in the other PCPEs. In the words of Carlin and Richthofen:

> The incorporation of a former planned economy into an advanced industrialised country with an efficient banking system would have permitted the solution of several of the major transitional problems with relative ease – irrespective of whether it was a German or Anglo-American type of financial system.[21]

Schulmann also claims that, 'the example of the GDR also shows that a complete takeover by Western financial institutions can be a very efficient way of providing instantaneous banking reform.'[22] Dornbusch and Wolf share a similar degree of optimism:

> With a banking system that has secured access to the world capital market in place, the East should not find it difficult to finance further investments in new small and medium-size firms.[23]

We examine the effects of the limiting conditions on West German bank activity in the East – including balance sheet development, profitability, and operating problems experienced. Given the lending difficulties facing banks in PCPEs, we set out to discover whether these difficulties would also be present in the East. As Rostowski stated,

> The former GDR is the sole example of massive entry of western banks onto the domestic market of a PCE, and a study of the quality of new lending there should be most instructive.[24]

In addition, we seek to measure effects on the non-financial sectors of the economy, and on the East German domestic banks. In other words, given that the causes of banking problems in PCPEs had been addressed, *were the symptoms eliminated as well*, or did some persist? Moreover, if some did persist, *what were the underlying reasons*?

## The research approach

The broad scope of the research question was deliberate, stemming from the special nature of the East German case. That is, the case was indeed a limiting one, and hence had no parallel case to use as a reference point to guide the research. In their study of East German management, Edwards and Lawrence similarly observed,

> there are no precedents, no literature, no accumulated wisdom ... There can be no definitive study, since no-one knows in what terms it could be defined.[25]

The case study approach was chosen, therefore, since it allowed for flexibility and an in-depth analysis of the bank transplant in the East.

### The limited literature on banking in the East after GEMSU

Although the literature on the general unification process has steadily grown, literature specific to banking developments was virtually non-existent when the research was undertaken – including English as well as German sources. Moreover, of the three key papers which have addressed the subject, only one was available to the author at the time the fieldwork was commenced.[26] Early literature on the topic tended to be descriptive and generally focused on the development of the banking system without examining the activities of the (West or East German) banks or the effects on the non-financial sectors or on the East German banks. In these narrow terms, it found that the banking transplant was a success, with the banking system having been largely transformed and hence functioning as it had in West Germany.[27] While this conclusion was essentially correct, it failed to address the broader questions surrounding the system's performance.

Subsequent literature has been more critical of the transplant, as bank activities have become more apparent, addressing to a certain extent the broader questions we have raised.[28] A few general comments may be made on this literature. First, there is consensus that the banking transplant in the East has *not provided an ample flow of finance or equity* to East German borrowers, despite the favourable initial conditions. Second, the literature underscores the *significant role of the state* in the allocation of credit, as both a direct provider and an indirect facilitator (through guarantees or refinancing mechanisms) of credit to the non-financial sectors in the East, particularly SMEs.[29] This highlights an additional limiting condition of GEMSU: namely, the well established and proven state-support structure, consisting of guarantee schemes and development banks (see Chapter 4). Third, within the literature there are different, though not necessarily conflicting, *explanations for the performance of the transplant.* One explanation is that bank behaviour in East Germany has increasingly mirrored that in West Germany, a process termed 'normalisation.'[30] Another explanation is that the West German banks entering the East were unable to cope with the severe valuation problems there, stemming from the intangible nature of most assets.[31] This book builds on these explanations in trying to explain the problems which developed in the transplant.

## The timing of the study

A potential objection to the selection of the East German case is that it is too soon to make an informed judgement about the lessons that have emerged. Carlin and Richthofen argue that, 'Of course, it is still too early for an empirical evaluation of the effectiveness of the banking system in East Germany.'[32] As economists, they base their assertion upon a particular notion of what evidence is required for an empirical evaluation.

Apart, however, from the implications of what constitutes 'evidence' and whether it is available, there arises the broader issue of perspective – that is, is it too soon to draw any meaningful lessons whatsoever from the banking transplant in East Germany after unification?

Historian Simon Schama quotes the well known Chinese comment on the significance of the French Revolution (two hundred years after it occurred) attributed to Zhou En-lai: 'It's too soon to tell.'[33] Schama argues, however, that while historians have maintained that 'distance' (in 'time') confers objectivity, perhaps there is a case for 'proximity.' In this research, 'proximity' is seen as an advantage, allowing those who are currently operating in East Germany to be interviewed. According to Edwards and Lawrence,

> If one wants to know what it was like at and after reunification, the message is to get in quickly, or memories will have faded and events will have passed.[34]

By waiting, valuable opportunities to collect data could be lost.[35] These considerations are not intended to deny, however, that there are also downsides of the decision. One problem, for example, emerged in the comparative cases studies of *Deutsche Bank* and *Commerzbank*, where it was shown that the 'results' of their different strategic approaches were still difficult to discern and compare (see Chapter 5).

### The sample

At the organisational level, the primary objective was to understand how and in what context the transplant of West German banks operated. Of the West German banks to move into the East, the three 'Big Banks' were the most active initially, heavily involved in both own lending as well as handling of various flows through the state-support network (see Chapter 4). Of the Big Banks, the decision was made to prepare case studies on *Deutsche Bank* and *Commerzbank*. These banks adopted different strategies, with *Deutsche Bank* taking a joint-venture approach, which included existing East German bank buildings and staff, and *Commerzbank* setting up greenfield sites. The contrast between the two was designed to examine whether there were problems common to the West German banks, or certain ones particular to the approach. Apart from the West German banks, the East German Savings Banks and Credit Cooperatives offered a good representative sample of domestic banks, and their performance was examined *vis-à-vis* the West German banks.[36] In addition, the views of several other institutions were regarded as important, including the *Bundesbank* and its regional centres (*Landeszentralbanken*), the privatisation agency for the East (the *Treuhandanstalt*), and the Specialised Development Banks (the *Kreditanstalt für Wiederaufbau, Deutsche Ausgleichsbank*, and the *Bürgschaftsbanken*).

On an individual level, the approach taken was what has been termed 'opportunistic sampling' or 'chain sampling,' whereby interviews are arranged on short notice, often through contacts of those already interviewed. An important reason for this approach was that it was difficult to identify the right people in advance in view of the high staff turnover between East and West Germany. Moreover, despite the initial planning, some sampling decisions were altered on the basis of information that became available in the field. Chain sampling was particularly effective within *Deutsche Bank* and *Commerzbank*, with internal calls allowing further interviews to be arranged. Within other large organisations, such as the *Bundesbank* and the Treuhandanstalt, a similar pattern emerged. A total of sixty-nine interviews were conducted. The final sample contained a good distribution of organisations, with a concentration on the West German banks and other significant organisations (Figure 3.1).

The sample also spanned a wide geographic distribution (Figure 3.2). There were, however, more West Germans interviewed than East Germans overall. The larger number of West Germans was partly a function of the chain sampling employed and also due to the fact that West Germans (apparently) tended to work in managerial positions, the level at which access was usually granted. The main interviews were conducted between June and August 1994 (Figure 3.3), although

*Figure* 3.1 Distribution of the sample[37]

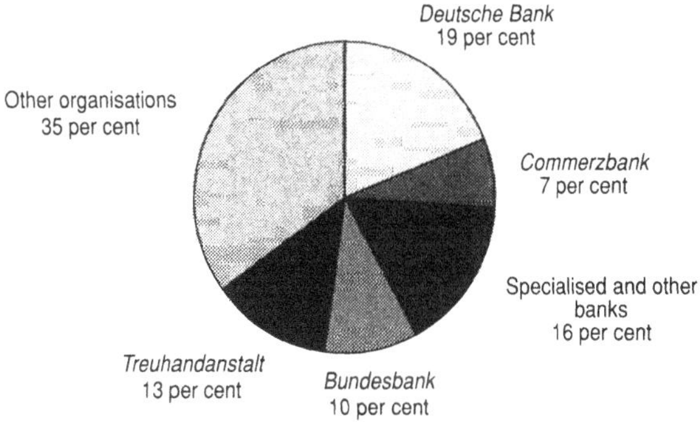

*Figure* 3.2 Map of fieldwork locations

*Note*: The area comprising the five Eastern *Länder* is shaded.

*Figure* 3.3 Chronology of the interviews

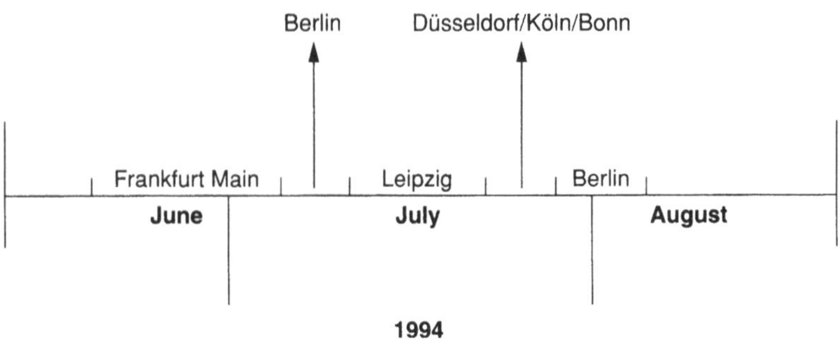

these were supplemented with follow-up questions and requests for further information.

### The statistical sources

In terms of the statistics on bank activities in the East, there is first of all a simple lack of data. Since the West German banks established branch networks in the East, the data on their operations in the East is consolidated in the balance sheets of their parent banks in West Germany, including profit and loss figures. Nevertheless, some figures are periodically released at the banks' discretion in press releases and summary statistics compiled by the *Bundesverband mittel- und ostdeutscher Länder* from Landeszentralbanken data. Internal (anonymous) *Bundesbank* sources have suggested, however, that West German banks have manipulated their accounts to shift loans to their East German accounts to demonstrate their commitment to the East.[38] These summary statistics, moreover, take time to produce, and for this reason much of the data analysis in this book covers the period 1990–4, with some, more recent data being added where they are available. An update through to 1997 is found in Chapter 7. The German Bank Association (*Bundesverband deutscher Banken*) also prepares annual reports of West German private bank activities in the East,[39] but these are also subject to bias owing to the sensitive nature of the topic, with political pressure on banks leading them to justify their activities in the East.[40] The *Bundesverband deutscher Banken* exists to promote the banks and to defend their interests; according to Manfred Weber, himself former Managing Director of the *Bundesverband deutscher Banken*, 'the task of the [bank] associations is representing the particular interests of each group of banks in the political arena, *vis-à-vis* the authorities, the rest of the economy and the general public.'[41]

## Summary

In this chapter, we have made a link between the conceptual framework and the selection of the limiting case of East Germany after unification. We also discussed the research strategy that was employed, including the methods that were used. Having outlined the context and approach of the investigation, we turn now to the substantive chapters of the book, beginning with an overview of banking and institutional development in the East after unification.

# 4
# Economic, Institutional and Banking Development after GEMSU

> As communist countries went – Westerners never learned more about communism than they did from its disintegration – the GDR was long regarded as the soundest until the opening of the Wall revealed its glaring weaknesses for all to see. (Peter H. Merkl, 1993)

> The universal banking system in Germany has proved itself over the years. Its benefits have been demonstrated particularly in difficult phases of Germany's economic development under the special German conditions: in the early stages of industrialization, during the Great Depression, when banks converted many bad loans into shareholdings, after World War II, when they went beyond their customary role of lender to carry a share of the business risks, and in the recent past, through the swift construction of an efficient, market-oriented banking system, which did not exist in the former socialist GDR. (Manfred Weber, 1995)

Having established the special nature of the East German transition, we turn to an examination of what happened following GEMSU. The chapter is structured in three sections. In the first, we describe the *economic collapse* that occurred after GEMSU, and outline its causes. In addition, we outline the approach that was adopted to restructure and privatise East German industry and the problems surrounding ownership rights which hindered this process. In the second, we outline the *institutional framework* that developed after GEMSU, primarily by examining the West German system upon which it was based. The framework in the East, what we term the 'German Risk Management Framework' (GRMF), involves a range of financial flows and risk-sharing arrangements between the public and private sectors. In the third, we examine the *banking system in the East* specifically by first looking at the structure of the West German banking system (what it came to reflect) and then examining how the East German banking system was rapidly transformed to West German standards.

## The economic collapse

Despite the favourable (limiting) conditions which existed after GEMSU, the overnight shock therapy applied to the East led to 'one of the worst and sharpest depressions in European history.'[1] It has been argued that the collapse was worse than that experienced in the US Great Depression,[2] and perhaps also worse than in other PCPEs.[3] GDP declined 13.3 per cent in 1990, and 20 per cent by the last quarter of 1991.[4] This fall represented double the decline in Poland which until then had experienced the highest fall amongst the other PCPEs.[5] Although the collapse occurred across all sectors, industrial output registered the most dramatic fall, dropping 40 per cent between June and August 1990.[6] Industrial output continued to fall to 49 per cent of its pre-GEMSU level by the end of 1990, reaching a low of 33 per cent in 1991.[7]

As output declined, unemployment rose rapidly. By official measurements, the unemployment rate jumped from 1.6 per cent in June 1990 to 3.1 per cent in July, and then to 7.3 per cent by the end of the year.[8] The 'effective' unemployment rate, however, showed a far steeper rise: from zero at the time of GEMSU to 7.2 per cent after one month, 25 per cent by the spring of 1991, and 30 per cent by this year-end.[9] The 'effective' rate includes workers who were taking part in job creation schemes and retraining programmes, with 'short-time' workers being counted in full-time equivalents. By the end of 1992, overall employment had fallen by more than 3 million, of which 2.25 million was in manufacturing. In the service sectors, employment was more stable, and even increased in some areas (such as the professions).[10]

### Causes of the collapse

The collapse was the result of both *supply-* and *demand-side* factors. Supply-side factors centred on the inefficiency of the industrial structure, stemming from the high cost base which most enterprises faced after GEMSU, and the low productivity which could not offset these costs. These factors were combined with demand-side factors, including the loss of both domestic and export markets for goods produced in the East.

The *currency conversion* played an important role in the collapse by raising enterprise costs as well as forcing enterprises to sell their goods for DM at world prices. In accordance with GEMSU, East German Marks (M) were exchanged for West German Deutschmarks (DM) at a rate of M 2: DM 1 for most accounts. The *Bundesbank* was concerned that a total conversion at parity 'would have implied massive gains in purchasing power for GDR savers, gains which might have led to an inflationary spate of buying.'[11] Some savings accounts were exchanged at more favourable rates to compensate savers,[12] leaving the average rate for the (overall) conversion at M 1.8: DM 1.[13] The rates chosen for the conversion reflected the outcome of a fierce debate.[14] In the end, the conversion – at favourable rates for East Germans[15] – was driven primarily by two important political factors: fears of mass migration – the feeling amongst East Germans that 'if the DM does not come to us, we will go to the DM' – and also the election on 18 March 1990. Chancellor Helmut Kohl publicly announced the terms of the conversion just five days before his party's (the CDU's) overwhelming election victory.[16]

There were two significant implications of the conversion rates which were selected. First, there was the stock implication whereby the chosen rates determined the *distribution of wealth* in the East after GEMSU. The main items affected were the wealth of savers – East Germans held the bulk of their asset portfolio in financial assets as opposed to real assets[17] – on the one hand, and the level of old debts issued in East German enterprises, on the other. The enterprise perspective was another important part of the *Bundesbank*'s argument against a M 1: DM 1 conversion, in that it would leave East German enterprises with a debt burden of DM 260 bn which would not be serviceable at market rates of interest.[18] Some individuals also had loans outstanding, primarily consisting of housing credits.

Second, there was the flow implication of the conversion whereby the chosen rates affected the post-GEMSU starting levels of wages and prices. At the time of GEMSU, the *industrial structure* in the East was highly concentrated, autarkic[19] and inefficient, as in all PCPEs, and needed to undergo massive restructuring in order to become competitive *vis-à-vis* West German and international firms.[20] Before GEMSU, almost all productive activity in the East took place within one of the 126 *Kombinaten*, which were collections of enterprises.[21] As in all PCPEs, the service sector was greatly underdeveloped, the emphasis having been on heavy industry.[22] The capital stock was 'technologically outdated, physically run down, and economically and ecologically obsolete.'[23] This industrial structure was in desperate need of restructuring.

The task of restructuring enterprises and making them competitive was made more difficult as a result of the rate chosen for the currency conversion, since it made the East German cost base after GEMSU very high. Under the terms of the currency conversion, wages were converted at M 1: DM 1, reflecting the political pressure to discourage mass migration:[24] converted at parity, wages could not remotely have been supported by productivity levels.[25] Their initially high levels notwithstanding, wage levels actually rose rapidly after GEMSU, even in the face of growing unemployment. Only four months after GEMSU (October 1990), Eastern wages had risen from 30 to 38 per cent of West German levels, reaching almost 50 per cent by the first quarter of 1991 and 65 per cent by the end of 1992.[26] The rise was largely the result of union pressure in both East and West Germany,[27] but was also due to other reasons.[28]

Though by far the most important, high wages were not the only significant costs. *Ecological costs* were also important.[29] The OECD reported that,

> 'high energy consumption and a complete disregard for the pollution consequences of production have also created substantial environmental damage and contingent liabilities for enterprises.'[30] Although these costs were more significant in the longer term, they nevertheless increased further the shorter-term cost base of enterprises in the East.

Against these high costs, *productivity* lagged badly behind West Germany levels, though estimates varied with respect to the differential.[31] A *Deutsche Bank* study suggested that East German productivity was generally below 50 per cent of the West German level.[32] The OECD estimated that aggregate labour productivity was about 33 per cent of the West German level,[33] drawing the conclusion that 'one in three eastern German enterprises could be profitable at wages and prices prevailing in the second half of 1990.'[34] A still more pessimistic account estimated that labour productivity in manufacturing was only 28 per cent of the level in West Germany before GEMSU.[35] These differences notwithstanding, the competitiveness of East German enterprises was clearly insufficient after GEMSU. Dornbusch and Wolf summed up the resultant dilemma facing East German enterprises:

> The eastern German productivity level resembles Mexico's or Korea's, while the wage level matches that of the United States and is already ten times that of the neighboring Czech and Slovak Federal Republic. Such a discrepancy is obviously not a recipe for economic success.[36]

At the same time, East German enterprises were forced to compete overnight with West German and international firms, both in their export markets and at home in the East.[37] Prior to GEMSU, most East German enterprises had a small export base, primarily to other PCPEs. Roughly 60 per cent of all exports went to CMEA members, of which about half were for the USSR.[38] GEMSU introduced a lack of exchange rate flexibility and also an immediate imperative to trade in hard currencies with other PCPEs. East Germany's CMEA trading partners were unable to keep importing East German goods since these goods were now more expensive and could be paid for only in hard currency.[39] The collapse in trade with the PCPEs, particularly the USSR, was postponed through export guarantees, but these expired in 1991.[40] It was estimated that between 900 000 and a million industrial jobs in the East were directly dependent on sales to CMEA countries, with more than half of this number corresponding to the former Soviet Union.[41]

Alongside this decrease, the recession in West Germany – and Western economies more generally – led to a drop in East German exports to Western countries.[42] Moreover, the initial consumption surge in East Germany after GEMSU was primarily marked by a switch to West German goods by East Germans *who could afford them* as a result of the currency exchange and their inflated wages.[43]

These factors underscored the importance of significant enterprise restructuring in the East if its enterprises were to become competitive. According to one account:

> At the time of currency union it was widely rumoured that one-third of East German firms would go out of business. The microeconomic data that have been presented in this paper offer a far more pessimistic view of the likely viability of the East German economy. In the absence of massive productivity improvements or substantial subsidisation, most Eastern industry will have to close down.[44]

## Enterprise privatisation and restructuring

The task of enterprise restructuring and privatisation was given to the privatisation agency in the East, the *Treuhandanstalt* (*THA*).[45] The *THA* took over the entire enterprise portfolio in the East, comprised of more than 8000 enterprises which had formerly been in the *Kombinaten*. The *THA*'s initial (clearly competing) functions included: *reorganising* the *Kombinate*; *restructuring* enterprises to make them more competitive; *selling* as many enterprises as possible to private investors; *maintaining* a maximum number of jobs; and *creating* new jobs for those who had lost their old ones.[46] The *THA*, therefore, became the most important actor in the governance and restructuring of enterprises in the East, and hence lessened the extent to which banks would be expected and able to play the governance role. The *THA* was responsible for creating supervisory boards (*Aufsichtsräte*) for all of its enterprises which had more than 500 employees.[47] To carry out its various functions, the *THA* had to assess the viability of its enterprise portfolio, which it did by dividing enterprises into six categories ranging from profitable to non-salvageable.[48] On this basis, 70 per cent of *THA* enterprises were classified as 'potentially viable.'[49]

Throughout its existence, the *THA* was forced to strike a delicate balance between restructuring and privatising its enterprises. In the first year after GEMSU, its approach adhered to that prescribed in the law on its establishment: 'to reduce, by means of privatisation, the entrepreneurial activity of the state as fast and as far as possible.'[50] This approach contributed to the economic collapse and deindustrialisation in the East,[51] and resulted in widespread protests and public demonstrations, possibly even including the assassination on 1 April 1991 of the then *THA* president, Detlev Karsten Rohwedder.[52] Unemployment came as a shock to East Germans who, as in all PCPEs, had been accorded the 'right to work' under their constitution (Article 24). The importance attached in political terms to promoting employment led banks consistently to point out the 'employment effect' of their investments in the East (discussed later in the chapter).

Criticism of *THA* policies led to a reassessment of its objectives and the adoption of a more 'employment-friendly' approach, with a greater emphasis on restructuring:

> The THA got under increasing public pressure to undertake 'regional structural policies' in Spring 1991, when the East German economy began to collapse, and the overwhelming part of the formerly state-owned firms was still under the control of the *THA*. Indeed, in March 1991, in a crisis consultation between the Federal Government, the heads of the new east German states, and the *THA*, the *THA* acknowledged its responsibility to cooperate in such policies.[53]

Under the new approach, the *THA* continued to privatise in a rapid fashion, but placed more emphasis on the employment guarantees made by purchasers as defined in the purchasing contracts. These contracts became increasingly focused on purchaser promises of investment and employment. Moreover, the 'price' of the enterprises was also pushed down because of the rising cost of capital (i.e. relative attractiveness of investment in financial assets).

By the end of 1994, most *THA* enterprises had been sold, and the *THA* formally ended its existence in January 1995.[54] This is not the place to assess the *THA*'s performance. Indeed, any assessment would be difficult given that the majority of *THA* contracts remain to be fulfilled in terms of investment and employment guarantees.[55] The mere fact that as of May 1994, the *THA* had privatised 14 160 enterprises, whose purchase agreements contained promises for investments of DM 198.1 bn and jobs totalling 1 461 560,[56] does not in itself warrant the extravagant praise by *The Economist*,[57] among others. One striking result was clear at the end of the period. When the *THA* was established, it was projected that it would raise roughly DM 600 bn in revenue.[58] In the end, it actually wound up roughly DM 205 bn in debt.[59]

### Ownership uncertainties

Apart from the factors we have outlined, a further major obstacle to privatising and attracting investment was the *uncertain ownership situation* after GEMSU. Under the unification treaty, the full restitution of property was granted to its original owners.[60] In the GDR, all property had been 'the people's property' (*Volkseigentum*).[61] After GEMSU, this property needed to be placed into private hands within the framework of West German law. Full restitution meant that all property that was seized or property whose owners had fled would be returned to its original owners,[62] with the notable (and controversial) exception of property seized by the Soviet Union in the period 1945–9.[63]

While an uncertain ownership situation existed in many PCPEs, the situation in East Germany was fundamentally different, a point well articulated by Siebert:

> The distinction between ill-defined property rights and ownership uncertainty is crucial for the comparison of the German, Eastern European and the USSR cases. In the German case, property rights are clearly established, but there is uncertainty with respect to ownership. In the USSR and to some extent in Eastern Europe, property rights themselves are uncertain.[64]

Full restitution may have been desirable from a moral, financial and political point of view, but it was disastrous for investment.[65] The restitution process was both uncertain and decidedly slow.[66] Once a claim was placed on a property, competing claims were often made. Moreover, the case would need to be settled before any sale of the property could be considered.[67] In some cases, claims would arise after the property had been sold. The inability of the East German administration to apply a new, complex, and rapidly changing legal framework (see Chapter 6) led to vast delays in property restitution. By the end of 1993, only 694 563 claims had been processed in the East out of a total of 2 171 000 (i.e. 32 per cent).[68]

In this environment, the first 'breakthrough' was the Obstacle Removal Law of March 1991, under which certain priorities were given to interested investors over former owners.[69] This law also contained problems,[70] however, and what followed was a *gradual* process of legal and administrative modification of the restitution process so that investment could be facilitated.[71] One attorney specialising in restitution issues observed that the revised laws represented merely 'exceptions to the exceptions.'[72] The (complexity of the) subject of restitution was such as to support at least two journals specifically devoted to it.[73]

## The institutional framework

To mitigate the effects of the obstacles to investment that existed in East Germany after GEMSU, given the need for enterprise restructuring, an institutional framework was developed to enable finance to flow to the East by sharing and allocating risk between the public and private sectors. It has been argued that risk management is widely practised at an organisational level,[74] but less understood on a national level.[75] In the East Asian economies,

> it may very well be that a major point of departure in economic management ... is not the intervention in credit allocation, but how these governments absorb risks of the private sector, or co-insure such risks with the private sector during the development process. In other words, there may have been risk management strategies that have encouraged private sector growth, without the usual negative effects of direct government intervention.[76]

The institutional framework that developed in the East reflected the extent to which GEMSU represented (in Schrettl's words) an 'insurance plan' offered by West to East Germany.[77] Under the plan, much of the risk in the transition was shifted to West Germany which – for its part

– exacted a 'price' from the East (to be discussed in Chapter 4 below). The result of the shift in risk was that:

> regardless of the details of the policies adopted, German unification meant from the outset that the pains of political and economic transformation in the East were to become mere regional problems of a much larger unit whose overall stability would be only marginally affected by whatever difficulties the switch to a market economy in the East would entail.[78]

The parallel to an insurance plan represents an abstraction of the chaotic events and agreements surrounding GEMSU. 'Although there was no talk of an insurance contract, at least an implicit understanding of the risk transfer involved in the deal seems to have prevailed.'[79] The stylised presentation of the institutional arrangement after GEMSU (Figure 4.1, p.64) similarly represents an abstraction, and is not meant to imply, therefore, that German policymakers had constructed a 'framework' for the transition in the East. To a large extent, the arrangement was (a West German) one designed to manage the risk of providing finance to the East based on the principles of the West German 'social market economy' (*Soziale Marktwirtschaft*):

> it has always been part of the political philosophy of 'social market economy' that the economic development and its modernisation should be supported and aided by a system of public credits and guarantees, tax relief, programmes for the improvement in weak regions, harmonised between the Federation and the Länder.[80]

The basic principle of the social market economy is that the division between public and private participation in the economy is blurred, with the synergy between them allowing the proper risk balance to develop. In West Germany, public support for industry is widespread. According to Randlesome,

> backing from the federal government includes 18 per cent of the start-up costs of any manufacturing company establishing itself in a depressed region, grants for specific sectors, training handouts, and tax breaks.[81]

It was, of course, unsurprising that faced with the task of reconstruction in the East, West Germans would rely upon a system which had enabled reconstruction in the postwar period in West Germany and continued to function effectively. In the words of the *Bundesbank*,

> When mapping out the promotional policy for eastern Germany, the public sector did not have to break new ground at all. On the contrary, it could largely fall back on the conceptual and institutional framework of the subsidy policy practised in western Germany for a long time, with a wide range of promotional instruments which had been developed over several decades.[82]

In East Germany, the public role in reconstruction has been large. According to the *Bundesbank*,

> Since the introduction of monetary, economic and social union on July 1, 1990, united Germany has seen an expansion of government support for the economy, the nature and extent of which are unprecedented both historically and by international standards.[83]

The strategy of the public support was threefold. First, to provide *access to financing* to borrowers that might otherwise be unable to invest. The *Bundesbank* notes: 'while the various forms of interest subsidies reduce the cost of financing, it is often public guarantees that give access to the credit market in the first place.'[84] Second, to *lower the cost* of investment finance to enterprises selectively below market levels.[85] Third, to provide such low-cost finance on a *long-term basis*. These aspects are particularly important for small- and medium-sized enterprises which otherwise would be at a distinct disadvantage *vis-à-vis* large enterprises that generally have better access to low-cost funds. Vitols argues, for example, that

> one of the major advantages that German small firms have relative to US and UK small firms is access to long-term fixed-rate financing at interest rates comparable to that available to large firms.[86]

Owing to the high level of public support, the non-financial sectors in the East were 'virtually insulated from interest rate effects.'[87] This insulation was especially important because the period after GEMSU was marked by *high real interest rates*, reflecting the West German decision to finance unification by borrowing rather than by raising taxes.[88] The *Bundesbank*'s discount rate rose from 6 per cent in 1990 to $8\frac{1}{4}$ per cent by November 1992.[89] The OECD observed that the interest rate levels in Germany in Summer 1992 had been reached only twice in the previous twenty years, in 1973–4 and 1980–1 (i.e. following the oil shocks).[90] Put another way, the risk (premium) for financing the non-financial sectors in the East was shifted to the West German government either directly or indirectly – i.e. via other institutions (a point examined further in Chapters 5 and 6).

A particular priority in the East was the development of a *Mittelstand* (small and medium-sized business sector), following the important role these firms had played – and continue to play – in West Germany in the postwar period. Indeed,

> According to Ludwig Erhard, this term (Mittelstand) does not stand for a collection of small and medium-sized firms, but for an 'attitude in the socio–economic and political process' and he referred primarily to the fact that the firms in the Mittelstand are owner-managed, with the most desirable feature that the owner is fully responsible and accountable for his own decisions.[91]

The West German *Mittelstand* have been termed the 'Hidden Champions' of the West German economy.[92] Although less well known than many of the large corporations, such as Siemens or Daimler Benz, the

> *Mittelstand* produce two-thirds of Germany's gross national product, train 9 out of every 10 apprentices, and employ 4 out of every 5 workers.[93]

For these reasons, the development of a *Mittelstand* was seen as crucial to the overall development of the East German economy. One West German Senator in West Berlin maintained that if the West German ratio of small and medium-sized businesses to large ones could have been replicated in the East, as many as 4 million new jobs could have been created, jobs which could have offset the anticipated 2–3 million unemployed.[94] To this end, the *THA* developed a specific programme entitled, '*Treuhand-Initiative Mittelstand*.'[95]

The institutional structure of the West German economy may be said to *operationalise* the principle of the social market economy. Thus the West German Banks play a critical role not only in supplying their own finance to industry, but also in administering public funds and guarantees. In performing what has been described as a 'filter function' (*Filterfunktion*),[96] the banks contribute their branch networks and credit-analysis skills and hence alleviate the need to create government structures to allocate public funds.[97] Moreover, the subsidised loans and the guarantees are designed to make up only a percentage of the borrowers' liability portfolio, to be accompanied by (own-risk) bank lending. The object of the arrangement is a 'multiplier effect,' whereby public support generates additional private investment. The bank which handles the flow of public funds to a borrower is generally referred to as the borrower's '*Hausbank*.' This is the functional definition, simply meaning 'handling bank.' The broader definition of '*Hausbank*' is addressed at length in Chapter 6.

## The German risk management framework (GRMF)

Having discussed the basis for the institutional structure of the social market economy, we now outline the particular institutional arrangement of the GRMF (Figure 4.1). The GRMF consisted of a web of financial flows reflecting various risk-sharing arrangements with the (East and West German) banks playing the central role. Three types of financial flows were supplied to the non-financial sectors of the East German economy: loans, non-repayable transfers and venture capital.

## Loans in the GRMF

The first type of financial flow consisted of *loans* to the East. The simplest type of loan is made to the borrower at the bank's *own risk*. In their role as creditors, banks provide loans which are returned with an agreed interest charge. The risk to the borrower is that these payments must be made or the creditor may seize the enterprise's assets. Some loans are *refinanced*. This means that the originating bank, acting as *Hausbank*, screens and monitors the loan on behalf of the lender, but then actually shifts ('refinances') it to one of the Specialised Banks (rather than using its own balance sheet). The refinancing aspect (and general function) of two Specialised Banks is significant in the GRMF and warrants further exposition.

### *Refinancing through the Specialised Banks in the GRMF*

The Specialised Banks which refinance loans are the *Kreditanstalt für Wiederaufbau* (*KfW*) and the *Deutsche Ausgleichsbank* (*DtA*). The *KfW* is a public institution which was formed after the Second World War (1948) to administer Marshall Aid funds made available under the European Recovery Programme (ERP). Over time, the *KfW* became increasingly oriented to assist the *Mittelstand*. The *KfW* defined its main task in East Germany after GEMSU as the granting of loans with the following characteristics: (1) favourable interest rates; (2) long

*Figure* 4.1 Stylised model of financial flows in the GRMF

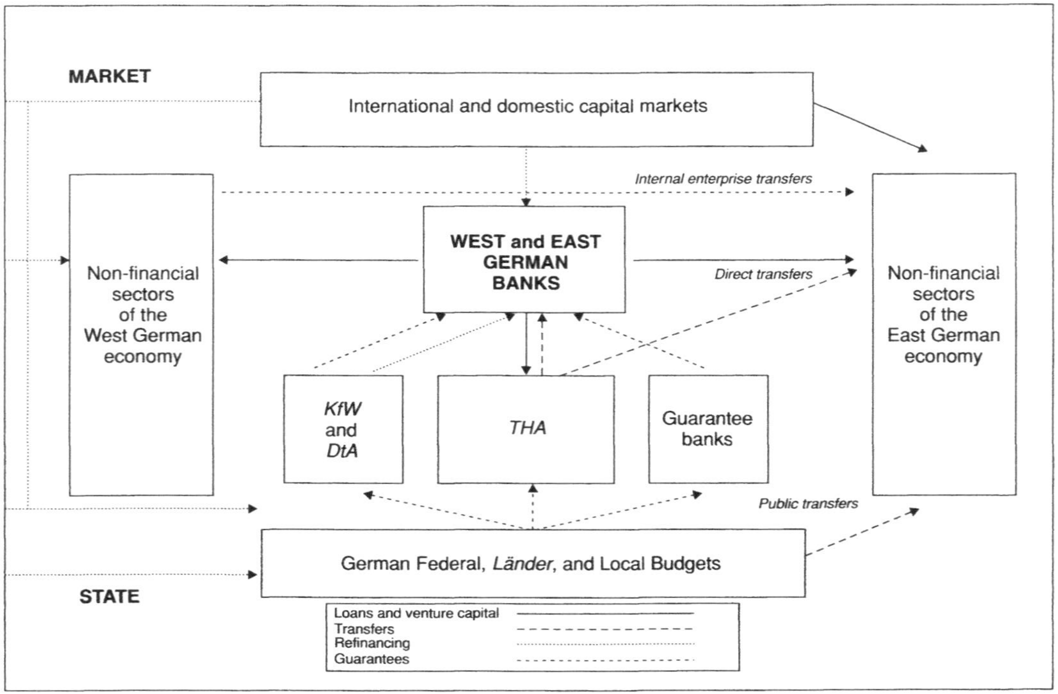


*Note*: See text for definition of *KfW* and *DtA*.

maturities and grace periods; and (3) simple application procedures and fast handling.[98] To perform this task, the *KfW* raises funds (cheaply) on capital markets and lends them to enterprises at low (sub-market) interest rates.

The process by which *KfW* lending takes place is as follows. A borrower applies to its *Hausbank* for a loan. The *Hausbank* evaluates the loan application and decides that it is unable to approve it but recommends that the borrower apply for *KfW* funds. Alternatively, the borrower may itself approach the bank with the request to borrow from the *KfW*. The *Hausbank* applies on the borrower's behalf to the *KfW*, performing the standard credit analysis required for the application. If the *KfW* approves the loan application, which it does in the vast majority of cases,[99] the funds are distributed to the borrower at a guaranteed long-term rate while the *Hausbank* receives a (pre-agreed) margin on the loan.[100] In other words, the *Hausbank* does not bear the interest rate risk for the loan, nor does it use its balance sheet.

The *Hausbank* does, however, bear the credit risk for the loan in most cases, which gives the *Hausbank* an incentive to screen it properly – another reason for the *KfW*'s high approval rate. According to the *KfW*, 'As the handling banks generally take full liability for the loans, the standing of the applicants has to be checked to banking criteria'.[101] This arrangement suits the *KfW*, which does not have a branch network, and also utilises the *Hausbank's* experience and resources in screening loan applications. The credit risk can, in certain instances, also be shared between the *KfW* and the *Hausbank*. In East Germany, there are provisions which allow the *Hausbank* to be released from up to 75 per cent of its liability for the loan.[102] For the loan to be approved, the 'multiplier principle' applies: *KfW* loans cannot make up the entire financing needs of the borrower, so the *Hausbank*, needs to provide additional loans at its own risk, using its own balance sheet.[103]

The other Specialised Bank which refinances loans is the *Deutsche Ausgleichsbank* (DtA). Founded in 1950 for the purpose of providing finance to refugees and expelled people from the former German territories, the *DtA* – like the *KfW* – changed its role over time to financing start-ups, and also employed ERP funds for this purpose. The *DtA* lending process is identical to that of the *KfW*, apart from two things. First, while the *KfW* tends to support existing, medium-sized enterprises, the *DtA* tends to finance *start-ups*. Second, the *DtA* more often shares the default risk with the *Hausbank*.[104] In addition to loan refinancing, the *KfW* and *DtA* both provide *advice* and *assistance* to enterprises to help them with the application process and with their financial planning more generally.

*Guarantee mechanisms in the GRMF*

While refinanced loans relieve the *Hausbank* of the interest rate risk, and in some (limited) instances a portion of the credit risk, loan *guarantees* (by a third party) relieve the *Hausbank* of a portion of (or, in some cases, the entire) credit risk. Unlike the refinanced loans, guaranteed loans do require the bank to use its own balance sheet. In the East after GEMSU, the importance of guarantees was underscored by the Bundesbank:

> In view of the mostly very low profitability, the fairly uncertain sales prospects in many places and the frequently unclear property conditions, the importance of the guarantee instrument for fund raising, especially in the new Länder, can hardly be overestimated.[105]

Within the GRMF, there are several guarantee mechanisms. First, the *THA* issued umbrella guarantees for (short-term) loans to all enterprises in its portfolio to help them to overcome liquidity constraints and problems in attracting outside finance in the first two years after GEMSU (1990–2), when uncertainty was high. These liquidity loans were intended to be a stop-gap measure, as the Bundesbank observes:

> Loan guarantees by the Trust Institution (THA) and the government for liquidity loans to GDR enterprises can therefore only be justified as a start-up and interim measure for the private sector. They must not become a permanent feature.[106]

Over time, the global guarantees were reduced, being replaced by firm-specific (individual) guarantees which were issued on a case-by-case basis, often to facilitate the sale of an enterprise.

Guarantees were also provided by the Specialised Banks (*KfW* and *DtA*) to a limited extent – and more generally by the approximately 30 guarantee banks (*Bürgschaftsbanken*). These banks were founded in the 1950s to overcome credit rationing primarily for start-ups which lacked the necessary collateral to obtain commercial loans. They offer guarantees for up to 80 per cent of the loan volume, with 20 per cent of the risk being retained by the *Hausbank*. The loan values they guarantee tend to be quite small, and the application process much the same as for the *KfW* and *DtA*. It is possible – and quite common – for a single borrower to receive a funding package from the *KfW* and *DtA*, or with one of the guarantee banks as well, containing both guarantees and refinancing.

*West German firms in the GRMF*

The majority of privatised enterprises in East Germany were purchased by West German firms and investors, making East Germany unique amongst the PCPEs in the large degree of 'foreign ownership' it had in the non-financial sectors of its economy (a breakdown is presented in Chapter 5). Thus West German enterprises may have provided guarantees for loans to their East German subsidiaries; in some cases, they may have (alternatively) offered *informal* guarantees of liability. In the author's interviews, several bankers mentioned one large West German enterprise that would offer only a 'letter of comfort' for loans to its subsidiaries in East Germany. Even if no guarantee was provided, formal or informal, West German subsidiaries often carried an *implicit guarantee* since the West German parent enterprise, even if not legally bound, might stand to damage its reputation if the subsidiary were to default on its loan commitments. Even without guarantees, West German-owned enterprises are more creditworthy for banks, particularly West German banks, for reasons which we shall explore in detail in Chapter 6.

**Transfers in the GRMF**

Transfers to the East were provided at no specific risk to the recipient, these funds not needing to be repaid. Three types of transfers may be distinguished. First, *government transfers* from West to East Germany were intended to sustain (temporarily) aggregate demand in the East after GEMSU.[107] Transfers went to the social security system, pension schemes, unemployment insurance and directly to East German *Land* and local authorities.[108] The majority of these transfers have been used for consumption rather than investment purposes.[109] Second, *THA direct transfers* to East German enterprises were used for restructuring and also for paying off old debts from before GEMSU.[110] Although the *THA* is guaranteed by the federal government, which helps it to access funds at favourable rates, it is treated as an enterprise in the measurement of financial flows in Germany and, therefore, not counted in the public transfers. We isolate the *THA* as a separate source of flows not only because of this somewhat arbitrary – and perhaps misleading – distinction, but also because of the important direct role it played in the provision of finance to borrowers in the East, in addition to the loan guarantees which it provided on a wide scale.

Third, West German enterprises supply *internal enterprise transfers* to West German-owned enterprises in the East. While we noted that West

German subsidiaries in the East were less risky for banks to finance, these firms may also be financed by their East German operations *directly* through intra-company transfers. These intra-firm transfers may not have been 'gifts' at all but rather conducted on a market basis at agreed rates within the organisation. For the purposes of risk management on a national scale, however, risk is internalised within the West German parent enterprise and is not shared with the government or banks. This is not to say, however, that the West German enterprise may not have risk-sharing arrangements in West Germany which thus impact on the East German subsidiary, albeit indirectly.

### Venture Capital in the GRMF

Venture capital represents the third type of flow. Here risk is held by the provider of the funds. As against loans, venture capital, as equity, is provided at a higher risk but offers the prospect of a higher return which is not limited to interest payments and principal but also includes a share of the profits. Apart from venture capital, which is predominantly channelled through financial institutions, borrowers may also be able to access capital markets directly via equity issuance.

In addition to lending and handling other flows, expectations were placed on banks – particularly West German banks – to take equity stakes in enterprises in the East. This expectation was based both on the perception that banks hold equity stakes in enterprises in West Germany, and on economic logic which suggests that equity positions can accomplish valued ends. First, through venture capital, banks can capture risk-related returns. Second, through equity stakes, banks can become *insiders* to industry and improve their information flow as well as lessen any governance problems that may exist.

## Banking system development

Just as the GRMF as a whole was rooted in the West German social market economy, so the banking system within it was also based on the West German system. In the period after GEMSU, the Eastern banking system was quickly transformed to mirror the West German one in terms of its structure and mode of operation. The need for this 'normalisation' was underscored by the *Bundesbank*:

> To enable the Bundesbank to discharge the mandate laid down in the State Treaty effectively in the territory of the GDR as well – i.e. to enable it to exercise monetary policy control over the money and

> credit creation process – specific regulatory prerequisites also have to be met in that part of the extended currency area, so as to ensure that the Bundesbank's traditional interest rate and liquidity policy measures will work there, too. These include, in particular, the establishment in the GDR of an independent commercial banking system organised in line with free-market principles.[111]

Indeed, the transplant of the West German banking system to the East was an important limiting condition in its transition process (as outlined in Chapter 3), and was crucial in the effective administration of the GRMF. Before examining in detail how this transformation occurred, we present an overview of the structure of the West German system it came to reflect.

**Structure of the West German banking system**

The West German banking system is dominated by Universal Banks (as defined in Chapter 2), both in terms of the number of banks and the total business volume they possess (Figure 4.2).[112] Collectively, these Universal Banks accounted for roughly 80 per cent of the overall business volume of all banks in 1950, and 77 per cent even in 1993.[113] It is the Universal Banks which perform the *Hausbank* role within the social market economy. Universal Banks are divided into three sectors – Commercial, Savings and Cooperative – covering both private and public ownership.

The privately owned Commercial Bank sector saw its share of business volume decline from 36.7 per cent in 1950 to 24.5 per cent in 1993. This group includes the three Big Banks – *Deutsche Bank, Dresdner Bank* and *Commerzbank* – which have the highest profile among German banks with their large branch networks. However, the Big Banks account for a smaller share of the overall business volume of the banking system than is generally thought, it having shrunk from 19.5 to 9.4 per cent between 1950 and 1993. The decrease in the Big Bank share highlights the *high level of competition* in the banking system.[114] While the Big Banks may account for a relatively small share of the overall business volume, their importance is underscored by their off-balance sheet activities, international operations, and their governance role *vis-à-vis* (large) German enterprises.[115]

The Savings Bank sector is publicly owned and accounts for the largest share of overall banking business, having grown from 32 to 37.7 per cent of the banking system total business volume between 1950 and 1993.[116] The Savings Bank sector is divided into three tiers:

*Figure* 4.2 The structure of the German banking system, 1993

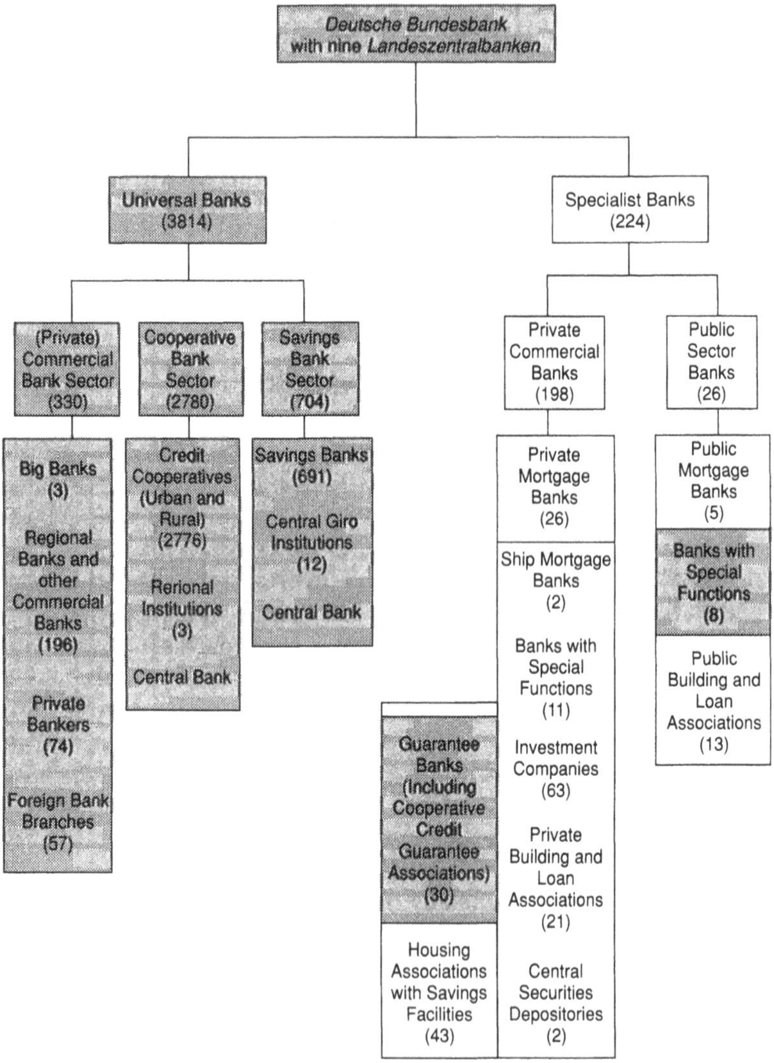


*Note*: The numbers of banks in each group includes East and West Germany. The shaded areas represent the primary focus in the book (though other groups are mentioned in passing).

*Source*: Weber (1995, p.37)

Savings Banks (*Sparkassen*), which are responsible for local business; Central Giro Institutions (*Landesbanken*), which are the regional offices for the Savings Banks; and the main office (*Deutsche Girozentrale/Deutsche Kommunalbank*).

The Credit Cooperative sector is collectively owned by its members. It accounts for the smallest share of the banking business, having grown from 10.4 to 14.9 per cent between 1950 and 1993.[117] As with the Savings Banks, the group is divided into three tiers: Local cooperative banks (*Kreditgenossenschaften*), which consist of urban credit cooperatives (*Volksbanken*) and agricultural credit cooperatives (*Raiffeisenbanken*); three regional institutions; and a main central bank (*Deutsche Genossenschaftsbank*).

Both sectors benefit greatly from their refinancing mechanisms.[118] These banks have access to cheap funding through deposits, but if they lend these funds out long-term they may face interest rate and liquidity risks. Intra-organisational refinancing mechanisms overcome these risks by raising funds long-term on bond markets – at the regional and national levels – and using these to refinance local banks. In addition, local banks deposit their surplus funds in the regional and national associations to create a nation-wide internal money market for refinancing local banks.

### *Corporate governance by German banks*

An important feature of the West German banking system is the significant governance role it plays *vis-à-vis* non-financial enterprises. To understand this role, we need briefly to delineate the legal forms of business that exist in Germany.[119] The largest businesses are publicly listed enterprises (*Aktiengesellschaften* or AGs). The share of total business turnover accounted for by *AG*s rose from 16.5 to 21.1 per cent between 1950 and 1986.[120] The rest of the businesses are unlisted, with the largest segment consisting of limited liability companies (*Gesellschaften mit beschränkter Haftung* or *GMbH*s), whose share of overall turnover rose from 15.4 to 25.5 per cent between 1950 and 1986.[121] It is unnecessary to examine the other legal forms in detail, but they are generally smaller than *AG*s and *GMbH*s and account for the remaining share of business turnover, which fell from 68.1 to 53.4 per cent between 1950 and 1986.[122] These smaller businesses along with the bulk of the *GMbH*s are what make up the German *Mittelstand*.[123]

In examining the governance role played by banks, it is important to bear in mind that it applies primarily (but not solely) to AGs – i.e. a minor share of the non-financial business sector.[124] The governance role functions through three main institutional levers: share holdings, share proxy holdings, and supervisory board participation.[125] *Share holdings* represent the banks' ownership stakes in enterprises (i.e. the insider role). *Proxy holdings* represent the second lever of bank governance, reflecting the non-bearer nature of German shares and the corresponding need to safe-deposit them.[126] Under the proxy voting system (*Depositstimmrechtssystem*), shares are deposited in banks. These banks, acting as trustees, are able to exercise the voting rights of the shares on behalf of the shareholder in the shareholders' general meeting (*Haupversammlung*). To understand *supervisory board participation*, we must note that large German enterprises have two governing boards: the supervisory board (*Aufsichtsrat*) and the management board (*Vorstand*).[127] The main lever for bank governance here is through board nominees' participation on the supervisory board.

### Financing of large enterprises

The extent to which banks actually exercise a governance role is the subject of considerable controversy.[128] The *traditional literature* on the German banking system highlights the extent to which the banks – particularly the Big Banks – have played a central role in financing and governing industry in Germany.[129] To a large extent, it was this traditional view of German banking that conditioned the high expectations which were placed on the *transplant of this system to the East*. The view holds that Universal Banks with close ties to industry are able to provide low-cost finance in large amounts, and are also able and willing to assist enterprises which are undergoing difficulties. Gerschenkron argued that the banks historically played an entrepreneurial role as well as being providers of finance, and that this role was significant in overcoming 'backwardness'.[130]

> the German investment banks – a powerful invention, comparable in economic effect to that of the steam engine – were in their capital-supplying functions a substitute for the inefficiency of the previously created wealth willingly placed at the disposal of the entrepreneurs. But they were also a substitute for entrepreneurial deficiencies. From their central vantage points of control, the banks participated actively in shaping the major – and sometimes even not so major – decisions of enterprises. It was they who very often mapped out a firm's paths of growth, conceived far-sighted plans, decided on major technological and locational innovations, and arranged for mergers and capital increases.

The high degree of bank control over industry is an important element in the traditional view, exemplified by Schonfeld's (1995) 'organised capitalism' model that banks circumvent the market through their tight control over industry and thus coordinate economic activity in the country.

A more recent literature (which we refer to as the contemporary literature) on the German banking system highlights the extent to which the Big Banks have increasingly ceased to play the leading role in governing industry, and highlights the importance of the Savings Bank and Cooperative Bank Sectors in the financing of non-financial businesses.[131] A study by Edwards and Fischer questions whether the postwar German industrial system has benefited from any special banking role.[132] Large enterprises have at all events become increasingly reliant on self-finance during the postwar period, and the Big Banks thereby lost many of their main loan customers.[133] In parallel with the drop in their lending to AGs, the Big Banks began selling equity holdings in these firms.

*Financing of small businesses*

The contemporary literature also maintains that the Big Banks have grown increasingly conservative, which has enabled (or forced) the German state to play a larger role in the provision of finance to small businesses.[134] At the same time, as regards the Savings Banks and Credit Cooperatives,

> In the mid-1970s the savings banks group surpassed the entire private commercial banking sector as the largest source of business loans. When only loans to manufacturing industry are considered, this shift between the three banking groups is even stronger. Contrary to what the organized capitalism model would lead us to believe, the savings and cooperative groups together provided roughly one half of all loans to manufacturers in the early 1980s – the big three commercial banks provided less than one-fifth.[135]

In West Germany, the significance of Savings Banks and Credit Cooperatives in financing industry is particularly evident with respect to small borrowers, to which Savings Banks and Credit Cooperatives have traditionally been the main suppliers of finance.[136] The Savings Banks tend to handle urban areas, with the Credit Cooperatives focusing more on rural areas. There are historical antecedents to the relationships that have formed between small banks and small businesses, since in the immediate postwar period the Big Banks were primarily occupied with financing and servicing large enterprises. Partly in response to their drop in business with large customers, the Big Banks have made progress in extending their lending business to the *Mittelstand* in West Germany.[137] Big Bank loans to *Mittelstand* enterprises rose as a per centage of their overall corporate loans in the late 1970s and early 1980s.[138]

## Banking development in the East before GEMSU

Before GEMSU, the banking system in the East looked nothing like the West German system we have outlined, under either the traditional or the contemporary view. The East German system was set up by the Soviet occupation authorities, and was modelled after the monobank system (outlined in Chapter 2). Its central bank was originally called the *Deutsche Notenbank*, and became the *Staatsbank der DDR* in 1967.[139]

While the system functioned along the lines of a typical monobank system – with a single institution responsible for central and commercial banking and a functional separation between lending and retail savings – there was one significant difference:

> in contrast to other countries of Eastern Europe, savings banks [operated] in East Germany under primarily local authority, rather than as a single nationwide network.[140]

Although an unusual feature for a CPE, the importance of these smaller banks reflected the West German system during the same period. And these banks played an important role:

> For the citizens of the GDR who seek advice on money matters and require banking services, the savings banks are the most important money and credit institutions.[141]

At the end of 1989, there were 196 Savings Banks, with 2400 branches, and around 20 000 employees.[142] With their large branch network providing access to the population, Savings Banks received the bulk of deposits in East Germany (Table 4.1).

East Germany also had a network of about 230 smaller cooperative banks for artisans, *Banken für Handwerk und Gewerbe* (*BHG*), and a large (3150) network of farm credit cooperatives (*Bauerliche Handelsgenossenschaften*).[143]

*Table* 4.1 GDR, deposits held in the Savings Banks, 1950–88

| *Year* | *Savings bank deposits (M mn)* | *Total deposits (M mn)* | *Savings bank share (per cent)* |
|---|---|---|---|
| 1950 | 1 062 | 1 275 | 83 |
| 1960 | 13 120 | 17 498 | 75 |
| 1970 | 39 737 | 52 149 | 76 |
| 1975 | 58 890 | 75 315 | 78 |
| 1980 | 79 337 | 99 730 | 80 |
| 1981 | 82 089 | 102 960 | 80 |
| 1982 | 86 034 | 107 573 | 80 |
| 1983 | 90 864 | 113 193 | 80 |
| 1984 | 95 339 | 118 655 | 80 |
| 1985 | 100 161 | 124 577 | 80 |
| 1986 | 106 533 | 132 315 | 81 |
| 1987 | 114 496 | 141 851 | 81 |
| 1988 | 122 619 | 151 590 | 81 |

*Source*: Ashauer (1990, 13–14); own calculations (percentages).

While the small banks 'survived' the imposition of the monobank system, the system otherwise manifested the general institutional arrangement of the monobank system. There were three main state-owned banks:[144] the *Deutsche Aussenhandelsbank AG* (*DABA*) and the *Deutsche Handelsbank AG* (*DHB*), responsible between them for all international trade and financial transactions in the GDR;[145] and the *Bank für Landwirtschaft und Nahrungsgüterwirtschaft* (*BLN*), responsible for the agricultural sector, including the farm credit cooperatives.

*The initial banking reforms*

In preparation for GEMSU, East Germany introduced reforms in its banking system (Figure 4.3). While these reforms proved to be short-lived, they were significant in the development of the institutional structure of the system after GEMSU. On 6 March 1990, the East German Parliament passed a law creating a two-tier banking system.[146] The Staatsbank remained the central bank (until GEMSU), while its commercial operations were split off to form the new commercial banks: *Berliner Stadtbank AG* (BSB) for Berlin, and the *Deutsche Kreditbank* (*DKB*) for the rest of East Germany.[147] Initially, the East German state held 100 per cent ownership of these banks. This was transferred to the *THA* in April 1990 for the *DKB* and in June for the

*Figure* 4.3 The East German banking system at the time of GEMSU[a]

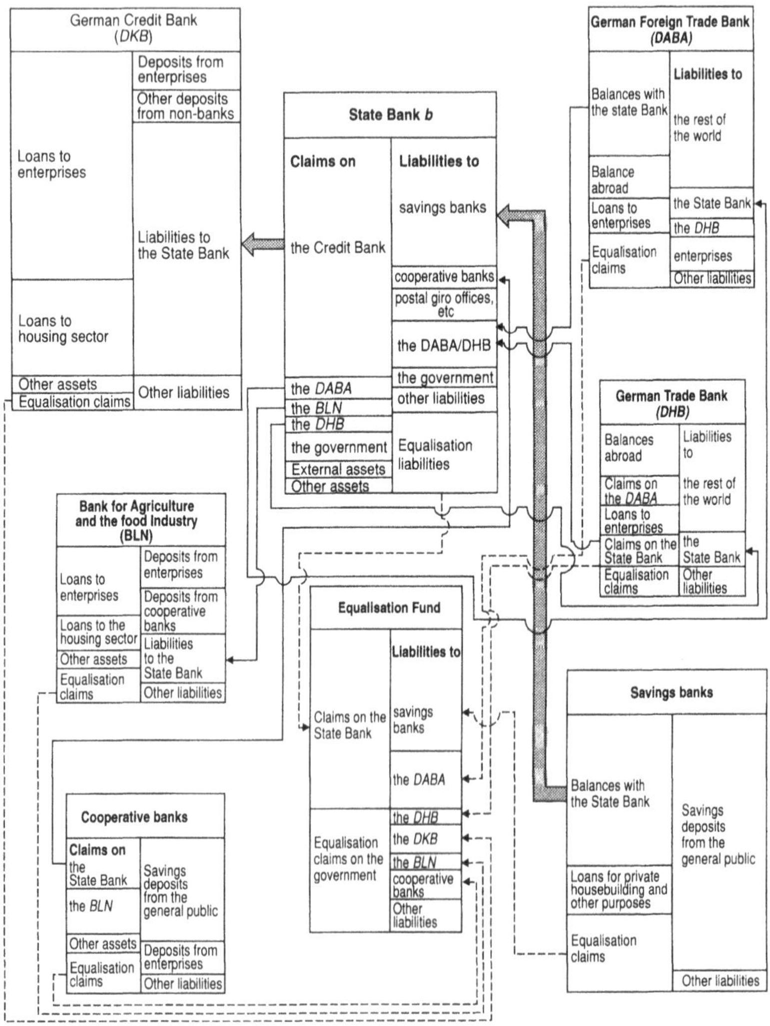


*Notes*:

*a* The joint venture banks established since the currency conversion and the restructuring of the GDR banking system effected since then are not included.

*Source*: *Deutsche Bundesbank* (1990*b*, p.17).

BSB. The main office of the *BLN* became the *Genossenschaftsbank der DDR*, while its branches were hived off and merged with those of the *BHG* to create rural cooperative banks.[148] The Savings Banks remained intact and, along with the *Genossenschaftsbank der DDR*, were organised as public companies. The local credit cooperatives kept their cooperative status.

The newly created 'commercial' banks were deficient in many respects. The *DKB* lacked any operational banking experience and expertise, as well as key infrastructure and technology. Moreover, it had to support a large branch network of around 13 000 employees who, as in other PCPEs, lacked the necessary skills to function in a market economy. One East German who joined Deutsche Bank after GEMSU, observed that in East Germany before GEMSU he would not have considered entering a banking sector which would have 'disabled me', being staffed by more than 99 per cent women.[149] This apparently sexist comment is an indication of the status and skills involved in banking operations: the employees were mainly clerical/administrative front- and back-office workers, with little or no decisionmaking or discretion. Bankers were the worst paid workers in East Germany with gross monthly wages of M 750,[150] the equivalent of roughly £35 in 1989.[151]

## Institutional change after GEMSU

The transitional reforms of March 1990 were quickly overridden at GEMSU, and significant institutional change occurred.[152] The only banks not to be acquired by West German banks after GEMSU were the Savings Banks and Credit Cooperatives. In institutional terms, these banks needed to integrate into the wider Savings Bank- and Credit Cooperative Sectors in West Germany to take advantage of the important support structure they provided, particularly with regard to refinancing. The integration process was simpler for the Credit Cooperatives than for the Savings Banks, since the former benefited from the acquisition of the Credit Cooperative central bank (*Genossenschaftsbank Berlin*) by its West German counterpart (*Deutsche Genossenschaftsbank*). For the Savings Banks, the process was more cumbersome primarily because of internal, political dissension within the West German sector itself. Initially, the Eastern Savings Banks were placed into a single Eastern Savings Bank Association (*OSGV*), but the association began to fragment, beginning with the departure of Thüringen (an East German *Land*) for the Hessen (a West German *Land*) Savings Bank Association.[153]

### *Financial problems for East German banks after GEMSU*

In addition to the institutional changes that were required, East German banks suffered severe financial problems at the time of GEMSU as a result of two factors: the terms of the currency exchange, and the existence of old loans made under the East German regime which remained on the banks' books. The currency exchange not only effectively redistributed wealth within the former state sector – the state, the banks and the enterprises – but also affected banks differently on account of different rates which were used for converting assets and liabilities (Figure 4.3).

Total assets were converted at an average rate of M 2.03 = DM 1, while liabilities where converted at M 1.81 = DM 1. In other words, since liabilities were converted to a higher value than assets, the banking sector experienced a *net conversion loss* of DM 26.4 bn (Table 4.2). Within this total, the biggest loss fell upon the Savings Banks and Credit Cooperatives, because the bulk of their liabilities consisted of deposits from the population which were converted at the higher rates.

Besides these conversion losses, the East German banks inherited the old loans (*Altkredite*) issued under the former regime. Many were non-performing under the market conditions that existed after GEMSU. The combination of conversion losses and old loans meant, according to Meinecke of the *Bundesbank*, that 'by western standards, most of the banks were virtually bankrupt on the day of the currency conversion, 1 July 1990'.[154]

To handle the situation, an Equalisation Fund was set up – as in 1948 at the time of the (West) German currency reform – to top up the assets of the banking system. Banking claims resulting from GEMSU were assigned to a Debt Processing Fund (*Kreditabwicklungsfund*), and corresponding equalisation claims (*Ausgleichsforderungen*) were provided to banks. First, the conversion loss represented a stock loss which needed a one-off correction to all banks. Equalisation claims were distributed in accordance with each individual bank's status after the conversion (Figure 4.3) Once transferred to the banks' balance sheets, equalisation claims carried market interest rates (three-month FIBOR).[155] While all banks and some enterprises were eligible to receive these claims, the Savings Banks and Credit Cooperatives were the primary users. The Savings Banks experienced the worst conversion loss and, therefore, received the highest share of equalisation claims. The Staatsbank was allocated a liability to the equalisation fund because it had gained in the currency conversion with the elimination of the *RIKO* fund – a significant liability – from its books.[156]

*Table* 4.2 Consolidated balance sheet of the East German credit system before and after currency conversion
Based on figures for 31 May 1990

| *Assets* | *M (bn)* | *Conversion Rate* | *DM (bn)* | *Liabilities* | *M (bn)* | *Conversion Rate* | *DM (bn)* |
|---|---|---|---|---|---|---|---|
| Domestic credit | 397.4 | | 180.7 | Domestic deposits | 249.0 | M 1.6 = DM 1 [a] | 156.6 |
| Enterprises | 231.7 | M 2 = DM 1 | 115.8 | Enterprises | 57.0[b] | M 2.05 = DM 1[a] | 27.8 |
| Housing | 102.6 | M 2 = DM 1 | 51.3 | Households | 182.1 | M 1.48 = DM 1[a] | 123.4[c] |
| Consumers | 2.5 | M 2 = DM 1 | 1.3 | Government | 10.8 | M 2 = DM 1 | 5.4 |
| Government | 60.6[d] | M 2 = DM 1 | 12.3 | | | | |
| Foreign assets | 45.0 | | 36.3 | Foreign liabilities | 56.1 | | 55.6 |
| State-trading countries | 17.4 | M 2 = DM 1 | 8.7 | State-trading countries | 1.1 | M 2 = DM 1 | 0.6 |
| Other | 27.6 | M 1 = DM 1 | 27.6 | Other | 55.0 | M 1 = DM 1 | 55.0 |
| Participations | 1.1 | M 1 = DM 1 | 1.1 | Currency in circulation | 13.6 | M 2 = DM 1 | 6.8 |
| Other assets | 3.1 | M 2 = DM 1 | 1.5 | Other liabilities | 127.0 | | 27.0 |
| | | | | Equity | 23.4 | M 1 = DM 1 | 23.4 |
| Sub-total | 446.6 | M 2.03 = DM 1[a] | 219.6 | RIKOs | 96.4 | – | – |
| | | | | Other | 7.2 | M 2 = DM 1 | 3.6 |
| Equalisation claims | – | – | 26.4 | | | | |
| **Total** | 446.6 | M 1.81 = DM 1[a] | 246.0 | Total | 446.0 | M 1.81 = DM 1[a] | 246.0 |

*Notes*:
[a] Average conversion rate.
[b] A small part was deposited after 31 December 1989 by non-residents and was therefore converted at M 3 = DM 1.
[c] M 2000 for each of 3.2 mn residents under age 14, *plus* M 4000 for each of 10.1 mn residents between ages 14 and 58, *plus* M 6000 for each of 3 mn residents over age 58, were all converted at M 1 = DM 1; the remaining deposits were converted at M 2 = DM 1.
[d] Of this, M 31.2 billion constituted credits to the government for the revaluation of *Richtungskoeffizienten* – (*RIKOs*) (see later) and M 4.9 bn was a credit to the government for the minting of coins and currency during the conversion of 1948. Thus, only M 24.5 bn was actually converted.
*Source*: IMF (taken from Shinasi, Lipschitz, and McDonald 1990, p.146).

Secondly, in addition to the stock conversion loss, the banks were also undercapitalised as a result of the old loans on their balance sheet. These loans had been approved under the old regime and were not based on credit analysis. A large percentage of them were non-performing. To address this problem, the banks were permitted to make claims on the Equalisation Fund to increase their capital adequacy to 4 per cent of their total balance sheet and 7.7 per cent of the risk weighted assets that were held.[157]

Although the uses of the equalisation claims were in principle clear, their valuation and disbursement proved to be complicated because they were tied to the balance sheets of enterprises, and these balance sheets took time to produce and, moreover, were frequently amended.[158] The total value of the equalisation claims to cover the asymmetric conversion (DM 26.4 bn) and also recapitalise the East German banks was estimated by the *Bundesbank* to be DM 57 bn, of which roughly DM 30 bn would be covered by the Staatsbank – given its liability to the Equalisation Fund – and the remainder by the Federal government.[159] Despite the careful projections, the *Bundesbank* later (in 1991) stated:

> Because of the delays in drawing-up and auditing the Deutsche Mark opening balance sheets, the processing of only eight equalisation claims of Savings Banks and Credit Cooperatives totalling DM 102 million ... had been completed by the Federal Banking Supervisory Office by mid-March 1992. Until the end of 1994 the allocations are provisional only, so that any changes to the Deutsche Mark opening balance sheet ... will affect the level of equalisation claims.[160]

Despite the delays in their disbursement, the equalisation claims comprised a significant, albeit decreasing, percentage of the business volume of the East German Savings Banks and Credit Cooperatives. In June 1992, these claims represented 23.7 per cent of the Savings Bank business volume and 21 per cent for Credit Cooperatives,[161] but by the end of 1992, these per centages had declined to 12.4 and 11.1 respectively.[162] The overall amount of equalisation claims allocated by the end of 1992 was already roughly DM 65 bn, with subsequent adjustment still being made.[163] By the end of 1994, the figure had risen to roughly DM 75 bn.[164]

### *Refinancing problems for East German banks after GEMSU*

Although the East German banks were compensated for the asymmetric currency conversion and the inherited NPLs, they faced an additional problem after GEMSU. They could not access ordinary *Bundesbank* refinancing because they had no assets acceptable to the *Bundesbank*. The main instruments for bank refinancing in West Germany are discount credits (rediscounting trade bills) and Lombard credits (loans against collateral), both of them subject to limitation by the *Bundesbank* both quantitatively and qualitatively.[165] Of these, Lombard credits are generally used in more exceptional circumstances and carry a higher rate. After GEMSU, East German banks had neither trade bills at the standard demanded by the *Bundesbank*,[166] nor collateral.[167] The *Bundesbank* Act had to be amended, according East German banks special treatment for refinancing. East German banks were allowed to use their own promissory notes as collateral, these bearing no further signature apart from the bank's.[168] Apart from what were effectively bank 'IOUs', equalisation claims could also be used as collateral for refinancing with the *Bundesbank*. Given the delays in the disbursement of equalisation claims in the first two years after GEMSU, East German banks were effectively accessing *Bundesbank* refinancing during this period purely with their own IOUs.[169]

To accompany the special concessions on refinancing, special refinancing quotas were also introduced for East German banks. Intended as a temporary measure until the banks could accumulate an alternative asset base, the quotas were initially set quite high: at GEMSU, quotas were first set at an aggregate level of DM 25 bn – compared to DM 60 bn for *all* West German banks which had business volumes of roughly 37 times the size of East German banks.[170] Unlike in West Germany, where quotas are allocated on a bank-by-bank basis, depending on the particular bank's own funds and asset and liability maturity structure, the quotas in the East were offered across-the-board on the sole basis of the size of the bank's balance sheet. This arrangement was regarded by the *Bundesbank* as 'provisional'.[171] The quotas were gradually reduced to DM 10 bn on 2 January 1992,[172] returning to normal levels (DM 2.3 bn) (i.e. allocated under the same criteria as West German banks) by November 1992.[173] In essence, for the first two years of the transition, a *parallel refinancing mechanism* based on different forms of collateral and different quota levels was established to meet the specific needs of East German banks. The joint-venture banks established after GEMSU (see below) were prevented from accessing this mechanism. For joint-venture banks with more than 25 per cent owned by a West German parent, quotas on their East German operations were to be deducted from the West German parent bank's overall standard rediscount quota.[174] The same provisions applied to Lombard loans.

*Acquisitions by West German banks*

Apart from the Savings Banks and Credit Cooperatives, the former East German banks were clearly marked for future extinction. During the short transition period leading up to GEMSU, West German banks set up representative offices and were well represented at local fairs and market-oriented promotions which facilitated information gathering.[175] After GEMSU, the new, East German commercial banks were quickly privatised via West German banking acquisitions (Figure 4.4).

The *BSB* and the *DKB* became joint ventures. *Deutsche Bank* and *Dresdner Bank* took over the branch networks and employees of the *DKB* but none of the old loans outstanding. The *BSB* was bought by the

*Figure* 4.4 West German banking acquisitions in the East, November 1991

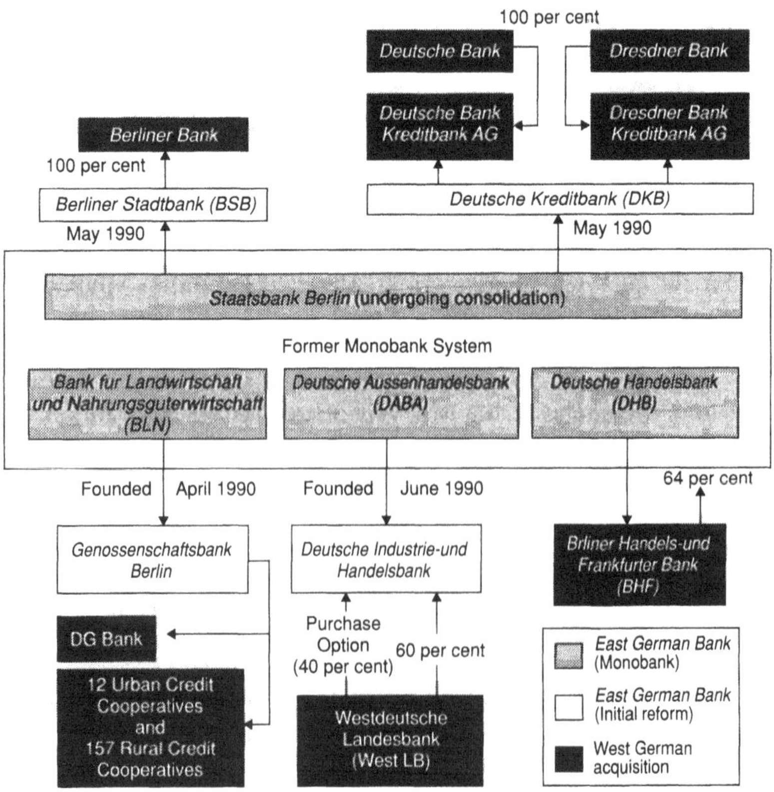


*Source*: Adapted from '*Das Zinsenwunder im Osten*', *Der Spiegel* (October 1994, p.57).

*Berliner Bank*, which took the existing old debt onto its balance sheet but avoided responsibility for it.[176] The speed of the banks' privatisation was caused by two factors: on the one hand, recognition that the *BSB* and *DKB* lacked the necessary expertise to carry out the currency reform[177] and to implement an efficient market-oriented credit allocation system; and on the other hand the immediate removal of the old debt from their balance sheets.[178] The other state-owned banks were rapidly acquired as well. *DABA* was acquired by *Westdeutsche Landesbank* (*West LB*), which took over more than 200 branches and 1200 employees. West LB originally took a 60 per cent stake in the joint-venture,[179] called *Deutsche Industrie- und Handelsbank*, and eventually raised its share to 100 per cent in 1995.[180] The *DHB* sold a 64 per cent share to the *Berliner Handels- und Frankfurter Bank* (*BHF*). The *Genossenschaftsbank Berlin* – the successor in the March reforms to the *BLN* – was acquired by the *Deutsche Genossenschaftsbank* (*DG Bank*), the central bank of the cooperative bank sector, which took over the main office (at GEMSU). The individual credit cooperatives were newly founded under new contractual agreements.[181]

*The Staatsbank role and the management of old loans after GEMSU*

The *Staatsbank* turned over its central banking functions to the *Bundesbank* but remained as the '*Staatsbank Berlin*', acting as a money-market bank to ensure the refinancing of the former East German commercial banks – namely, *DKB* and *BSB*, which lacked a deposit base[182] (Figure 4.5). In the early stages after GEMSU, the *Staatsbank Berlin* also managed the resources of the East German Savings Banks and Credit Cooperatives. Although these banks developed their lending to non-financial enterprises at a slow pace, they increasingly placed their funds into money markets.[183] In turn, the *Staatsbank Berlin* borrowed directly from capital markets – which, because the bank was 100 per cent-owned by the Federal government and borrowed with a full government guarantee, was not difficult to manage. Already by 6 September 1990 – barely more than two months after GEMSU – *Staatsbank Berlin* had raised DM 24 bn,[184] a figure which almost quadrupled in the following twelve months.[185] The size of the *Staatsbank Berlin* balance sheet declined steadily after GEMSU, owing to the decrease in the level of old loans in the *BSB* and *DKB*. At GEMSU, its asset base was DM 154 bn, but by 31 December 1993 it had declined to virtually half that at DM 84.5 bn.[186] On 1 October 1994, the *Staatsbank Berlin* ended its existence through a merger with the *KfW*.[187]

*Figure* 4.5 Simplified model of the new arrangements for old industrial loans

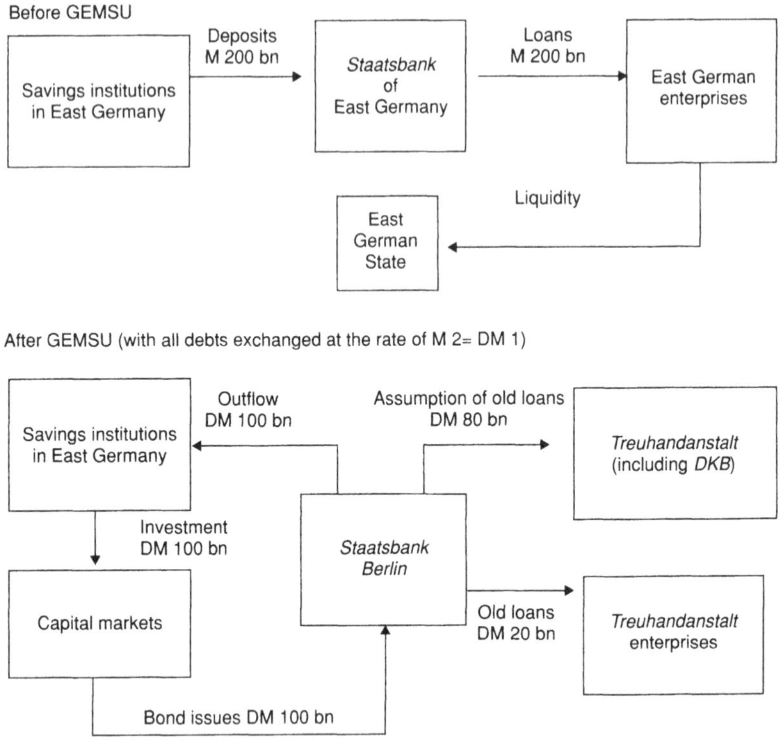


*Note*: The model presents a highly stylised description of the flows. For the sake of simplicity, housing loans (approximately DM 40 bn) are left out.

The process of managing and allocating the old loans from the former regime was messy. The most important point for the banking sector was that *all banks were relieved of the burdens of these loans*. For East German Savings Banks and Credit Cooperatives, all NPLs were compensated to their full value with equalisation claims. Overall, total old loans (of all banks) at GEMSU came to DM 176.5 bn.[188] Of this total, roughly DM 100 bn were industrial loans and DM 40 bn housing loans.[189] The industrial loans were placed in a 'shell' institution called the *Deutsche Kreditbank* (*DKB*), which was owned by the *THA*.[190]

Rather than arrange a global write-off of the old loans, the *THA* chose to handle them on a case-by-case basis while servicing the interest due:

> The Union Treaty stipulates that the companies do not have to service these debts for two years starting from 1 July 1990 or until they are privatised.[191]

In many cases, responsibility for the existing bad loans was factored into the sale price of an enterprise, becoming a bargaining point between the *THA* and prospective purchaser, similar to investment and employment commitments.[192] Some loans were maintained after the enterprise had been privatised. Others were simply removed and settled by the *THA*. In the final analysis, the *THA* absorbed responsibility for the bulk of the old loans.[193]

*DKB* contracted *Deutsche Bank* and *Dresdner Bank* to manage the debt-collection process, a service which the banks provided for a fee.[194] In addition, *DKB* was able write off some debts and finance others through the Equalisation Fund. Like the *Staatsbank Berlin*, the *DKB* was designed to end its existence upon completing its task, and witnessed a similarly sharp decrease in its balance sheet size, from roughly DM 124 bn in 1990 to DM 57.7 bn at the end of 1993.[195] In January 1995, the *DKB* was acquired by *Bayerische Landesbank*.[196]

*The banking environment after GEMSU*

The *Bundesbank* officially became the central bank for the whole of Germany on 1 July 1990. It set up a provisional office in East Berlin along with 15 branches across the Eastern *Länder*. Less than two years later, in October 1992, the *Bundesbank* wound up its administrative office in the East, calling it the 'end to the integration of the new states into West Germany's currency and central banking system'.[197] This rapid consolidation involved a reorganisation of the *Bundesbank*.[198]

With GEMSU, the *Bundesbank* assumed all regulatory functions in East Germany in conjunction with the Federal Supervisory Office.[199] While the regulation of the new commercial banks posed few problems because they were mostly joint-ventures, the Savings Banks and Credit Cooperatives did present difficulties. The regulatory treatment of East German banks was by necessity somewhat relaxed so that these banks could undergo a *gradual* transition to the West German framework:

> Laws regulating financial markets in the FRG were adopted by the GDR although, in certain circumstances, they could be applied more flexibly than in the FRG.[200]

With respect to financial reporting, the domestic banks were allowed to supply rudimentary monetary statistics until they were able to offer more detailed information.[201]

The range and quality of banking services in the East was rapidly improved to West German standards. Prior to GEMSU, the *Staatsbank* system in East Germany provided a minimal level of services. East German savers were offered a choice of two types of savings accounts: the savings giro account and the savings book, both which paid 3.25 per cent interest. After GEMSU, East Germans were offered a variety of new products, including: time deposits, various types of securities, and insurance services. According to the *Deutsches Institut für Wirtschaftsforschung* (Berlin) and *the Institut für Wirtschaftsforschung* (Kiel), in 1991 'the spectrum of financial services on offer in terms of variety and conditions is now virtually as extensive as in West Germany'.[202] These improvements were largely the result of the high level of West German acquisitions in the banking sector. East Germany was used by the West German banks as a testing ground for new ideas and products. For example, a subsidiary of the *Hypo-Bank*, the *Hypo-Service Bank*, offered only nine retail products compared with the roughly sixty on offer at a normal retail branch in West Germany. The reduced number of products was designed to cut costs and speed up service, with the prospect of being used in West Germany after a trial period.[203] As services improved, many banks rapidly established themselves in the East, and Leipzig became one of the leading financial centres in all of Germany with 96 banks registered by the end of 1993.[204]

The payments system in the East was also rapidly improved from its previous rudimentary state. According to the *Bundesbank*, 'the GDR [paper-based] payments system (which basically was very cost effective) was not suitable for credit institutions after the transition to a market economy'.[205] After GEMSU, there were problems in implementing a system of paper-less payments, and many East German banks continued to operate under the old clearing system.[206] Following a transition period in which the West and East German systems were employed, the switchover process was completed as scheduled on 31 December 1991.[207] At that time, the *Bundesbank* reported that the process was carried out effectively, and that a state of 'normalisation' had been achieved.[208]

The poor transport and telecommunication infrastructure which also presented problems to the banks, including the *Bundesbank*, was also quickly sorted out. One banker from Commerzbank commented that 'there was nothing there' and that the telecommunications were 'antique', but that they improved rapidly.[209] According to Marsh:

> The *Bundesbank* launched its own eastern modernisation drive by bringing in up-to-date computers for the new east German network. Requiring sophisticated frequency regulating apparatus to improve supplies of electricity to the new offices, the *Bundesbank* fell foul of western technology transfer rules. It had to apply for a special dispensation from controls operated by the shadowy CoCom watchdog body. Telephone lines were a particular problem. But once the *Bundesbank* gained entry to the old Berlin Reichsbank extension building on the Werdersche Wiese, officials realised they could make use of high-performance secret police lines to connect up provincial branch offices.[210]

In essence, bankers needed to be flexible and creative to handle the infrastructural deficiencies in the short term. The same *Commerzbank*er commented that 'they [bankers] had to be flexible even in technical terms which bankers are usually not'.[211] Sometimes this meant navigating around some of the institutional obstacles to bringing in high technology, – such as CoCom. *Deutsche Bank* experienced such severe problems with the phone system that it initially set up an internal system for its own use.[212]

The improvements in the banking system in the East were the result of a massive undertaking by West German banks that had set up ventures and also by local East German banks who benefited from the assistance of West German Savings Bank and Credit Cooperative Associations.[213] The West German Private Banks invested DM 4.3 bn in their Eastern branch network by the end of 1993,[214] roughly DM 8 bn by the end of 1994[215] and some DM 10 bn by 1995.[216] Through this investment, these banks expanded their Eastern branch network from 750 at the end of 1991 to 1117 at the end of 1993[217] and to roughly 1500 by the end of 1994.[218] East German Savings Banks also spent heavily on their branch network. By the end of 1993, they had invested DM 5.6 bn, of which DM 3.4 bn was for real estate and building improvement, and the other DM 2.2 bn for modern equipment in the branches.[219] The Savings Banks had some help from their West German counterparts, but 'had to rely primarily on their own funds to finance their technical modernization'.[220]

*Staffing issues for banks after GEMSU*

Training was essential to enable East German staff to handle the new banking environment, to understand the new products and services on offer and to be socialised into the culture of the respective banking institutions. While the joint-venture banks could send over some West German staff to assist at a management level, the majority of the staff would have to be East German. This was even more the case for the Savings Banks and Credit Cooperatives who did not have a West German partner to rely on for managers. A large number of training schemes were arranged by the *Bundesbank*, the Banking Associations and the West German banks, the latter often seconding staff directly to East German branches. Here we find the sort of apprentice scheme which is so important in German management, whereby training is 'on the job' with the trainers coming to the trainees.

The German Bankers' Association outlined the further training offered to West German bank staff in East Germany. Between GEMSU and the end of 1993, 95,000 staff received training at some point, or 22 per cent of the total staff trained in East and West Germany in the Private Banks.[221] In terms of actual days of training, East German staff received 515 000 – i.e. 31 per cent of the total in East and West Germany. The Association also proposed a measure of training intensity (*Ausbildungsintensität*) which showed that in proportion three times as many East German staff were trained as West Germans.[222]

East German Savings Bank staff received training as well, primarily through assistance from the West German Savings Banks who seconded West German managers and also provided technical assistance, much of it through partner bank relationships.[223] Of the total 42 000 staff, roughly 5600 were (currently) trainees,[224] a similar proportion to that of the West German commercial banks in the East.[225] According to the German Savings Bank Association, this represents around 50 per cent more than the average of all German banks, and a third more (in relative terms) than in the West German Savings Banks.[226]

Overall, despite some transitional problems and adjustments, the transformation of the East German banking system was widely regarded as successful. Writing in 1993, Wagner asserted:

> The goal of quickly constructing an efficient banking system that corresponds to Western standards in East Germany has largely been reached. The necessary adjustments in the financial sector have gone comparatively smoothly and are largely finished.[227]

In their analysis, Carlin and Richthofen called Wagner's statement 'uncontroversial'.[228] Deeg pointed out that 'the banking industry itself is arguably the most successful case of a restructured sector in East Germany'.[229] The *BDB* remarked that with a similar transfer of knowhow (*Transfer von Köpfen*) in other industries, the 'development of East Germany' (*Aufbau Ost*) could have been more successful.[230] This view was also expressed by bankers in the East in interviews with the author.[231]

## SUMMARY

In this chapter, we found that the East German economy was not saved from severe economic difficulties despite the many favourable preconditions it had. After outlining the difficulties that emerged, and the negative effect they would have on investment flows, we turned to the institutional framework that developed to enable finance to flow to the East. At the heart of the system were the Universal Banks which could play a critical role in the transition by providing and facilitating funds through the GRMF. In the chapter that follows we look at the financial flows which developed and the overall performance of the banking system.

# 5
# Overall Financial Flows and Bank Activities

> Never learn to do anything: if you don't learn, you'll always find someone else to do it for you. (Mark Twain)

After GEMSU, the banking system in the East was quickly transformed or 'normalised' to resemble closely the West German banking system in terms of its structure and infrastructural development. The present chapter begins with an empirical examination of the broader *financial flows to the East* after GEMSU, underlining the banks' role handling these as well as the state's role in absorbing the requisite risks. In the second section, it analyses *activities in the banking sector as a whole*, distinguishing between East German (Savings Banks and Credit Cooperatives) and West German (Commercial) banks.[1] The third section examines the *experiences of two West German Commercial Banks* which employed different strategies. The fourth section explores the *availability and allocation of financing* to the various non-financial sectors of the economy from the borrowers' perspective.

## Financial flows and guarantees to the East

We begin by measuring the distribution of financial flows and guarantees to the East within the GRMF (see Chapter 4, Figure 4.1), p.000 for the period 1990–3. The objective is to put into perspective the role played by East and West German banks and to examine the distribution of risk associated with the flows. The flows shown represent those 'approved' rather than 'paid out', though the difference is not significiant.[2] Guarantees facilitate flows rather than contributing them.

For the financial flows which entered the East through the GRMF in the period 1990–3, the risk involved was distributed among the

*Table* 5.1 Overall (approved) financial flows[a] and guarantees through the GRMF to the East; 1990–3

| *Source of Funds/Guarantees* | *Total* | |
|---|---|---|
| | *DM bn* | *Per cent* |
| *Loans* | 331 | 67 |
| Bank loans[b] | *218* | *44* |
| *of which:* | | |
| East German Banks | 63 | 13 |
| West German Banks | 155 | 31 |
| Specialised Banks[c] | 113 | 23 |
| *of total loans:* | | |
| Loans to West German Firms[d] | 199 | 40 |
| *Transfers*[e] | | |
| *THA* (Total debt) | 168 | 34 |
| West German subsidiaries | – | – |
| *Venture capital* | 0.498 | 0.1 |
| Total (approved) flows | 499 | 100 |
| *of which:* | | |
| Total (approved) guarantees[f] | | |
| *of which:* | 92 | 18 |
| *THA* | 88 | 18 |
| Specialised Banks | 4 | 1 |
| *Memorandum items:* | | |
| *Public Transfers*[g] | | |
| Gross | 461 | (93) |
| Net | 352 | (71) |

*Notes*:

[a] The flows are not actual flows to the East but those that were approved. While the magnitudes may thus be slightly overstated, the relative size of the flows is accurate.

[b] See Table 5.6 (p.106).

[c] See Table 5.2 (p.92).

[d] Based on the assumption that West German firms borrow in proportion with their ownership and investment (see below for a full discussion). Of the remaining 40 per cent, a certain portion represents loans to foreigners, making the East German share less than 40 per cent.

[e] See Table 5.5 (p.100). Based on the assumption that all *THA* funds go to East German enterprises. Transfers from West German enterprises to their subsidiaries in the East are not included since no data are available.

[f] See Table 5.3 (p.94).

[g] For the period 1991–3 only.

*Source*: *Landeszentralbanken data*: *Bankenverband mittel- und ostdeutscher Länder, KfW, DtA*, EIB; and *Verband der Bürgschaftsbanken*; *THA* internal data; *Bundesverband Kapitalbeteiligungsgesellschaften*; OECD (1994).

German state, West German enterprises, and banks (Table 5.1). The state guarantees the *THA* and *Bürgschaftsbanken*, supplies public transfers and guarantees the refinancing of all *KfW/DtA* loans. As noted earlier, some enterprises may have received *both* guarantees and *KfW/DtA* funds – an instance of overlap between categories.

What emerges from Table 5.1 is that high levels of financial flows entered the East but the corresponding risk (premium) for these flows was borne largely by the German state. A high percentage of the total flows consisted of loans. Of these, however, a significant share were guaranteed loans and loans refinanced by the Specialised Banks. Public transfers to the East were huge – almost as much as the overall financial flows combined. At the same time, venture capital played almost no

*Table* 5.2 Loans through the Specialised Banks to the East, 1990–3[a]

| *DM mn* | *1990* | *1991* | *1992* | *1993* | *Total* |
|---|---|---|---|---|---|
| *Kreditanstalt für Wiederaufbau (KfW)* | | | | | |
| *Total loans*[b] | 4 177 | 24 149 | 22 938 | 16 397 | 67 661 |
| of which: | | | | | |
| Loans to SMEs[c] | – | 10 538 | 8 404 | 6 388 | 25 330 |
| *Deutsche Ausgleichsbank (DtA)*[d] | | | | | |
| *Total assistance* | 4 044 | 12 020 | 10 993 | 10 517 | 37 574 |
| Start-up Programmes | 3 061 | 8 569 | 8 792 | 8 051 | 28 473 |
| *of which:* | | | | | |
| ERP Start-Up Programme | 2 518 | 5 044 | 4 884 | 4 506 | 16 952 |
| Capital Assistance Programme | 514 | 3 170 | 3 539 | 2 954 | 10 177 |
| *Bürgschaftsbanken* | | | | | |
| Total loans | – | 536 | 1 321 | 1 284 | 3 141 |
| *European Investment Bank (EIB)*[e] | | | | | |
| *Total (loans)* | – | 640 | 1 343 | 2 263 | 4 246 |
| Total loans | 8 221 | 37 345 | 36 595 | 30 461 | 112 622 |

*Notes:*
[a] Not including East Berlin. Figures represent the value of loans approved by year-end.
[b] Also including export finance loans.
[c] Including foreign branches and the technology programme.
[d] Including East Berlin.
[e] Loans are denominated in ECU and converted at the rate of 1 ECU = 1.833 DM (9 May 1995). The EIB is a European rather than a German Specialised Bank, but is included in the analysis because it provided loans on a large scale to the East which were handled by East and West German Banks.

*Source*: 1990, 1991, 1992 and 1993, *KfW* and *Deutsche Ausgleichsbank, Annual Reports*; EIB 1993, *Annual Report; Verband der Bürgschaftsbanken*, 1992. 1993–4; *Institut für Wirtschaftsforschung, Institut für Wirtschaftsforschung Halle*; own calculations.

role in the overall flows. In all, the GRMF with its risk-allocation mechanisms allowed for funds to flow to the East while minimising the level of East German (interest rate and credit) risk borne by banks. As we break down these flows into their component parts, we underscore the large handling role played by West German banks in the GRMF.

### Specialised bank loans

The activity of the Specialised Banks was valuable in generating a multiplier impact on financial flows to the East. Specialised Bank loans are thought to have generated investment of DM 132 bn.[3] Moreover, the handling banks did in fact bear the majority of the (credit) risk for the loans of the Specialised Banks. As of December 1994, of the *KfW's* total loans to enterprises in the East (DM 77 bn), only 1.4 per cent (DM 1.1 bn) were made without the handling banks assuming the full (credit) risk.[4]

There was a decline in all of the programmes between 1992 and 1993 for two reasons (Table 5.2).[5] First, some lending programmes expired, having been introduced as stop-gap measures after GEMSU. Second, with particular reference to *KfW* loans, some borrowers delayed their long-term financing because of the general recession in Germany and in the hope that interest rates would fall further. The decline in Specialised Bank loans is consistent with the Specialised Banks' role in providing 'seed money' designed to help enterprises build their own funds and develop long-term with banks (see Chapter 4).

### Guarantees

The guarantee mechanisms in the GRMF played a significant role in the provision of finance of East German enterprises under the *THA* and, to a far lesser extent, through the guarantee banks (Table 5.3).

The decrease in *THA* guarantees reflects the privatisation of more and more *THA* enterprises. In some (limited) cases, guarantees were maintained even after privatisation, often being used as part of the sales package.

### Banks' role in handling financial flows

In the immediate aftermath of GEMSU, West–East financial flows were handled predominantly by West German Commercial Banks (Table 5.4). These banks handled the vast majority of *THA* liquidity loans.

The distribution of *Bürgschaftsbanken* guarantees similarly highlights the large role played by West German Commercial Banks in the

*Table* 5.3 Loan guarantees to borrowers in the East, 1990–3

| *Item* | *1990*[b] | *1991* | *1992* | *1993* |
|---|---|---|---|---|
| *THA (Total approved – DM bn)*[a] | *28.6* | 30.5 | 28.8 | 20.2 |
| Global guarantees | 28.6 | 26.2 | 15.2 | 0.1 |
| Individual guarantees | – | 2.3 | 8.8 | 13.9 |
| Other warrantees[c] | – | 2.0 | 4.8 | 6.2 |
| *Bürgschaftsbanken (Total – DM mn)* | – | 423 | 1030 | 1009 |
| *Memorandum item* | | | | |
| THA Guarantees repaid[d] | – | 3.4 | 8.5 | 13.0 |

*Notes*:
[a] The *THA* figures represent guarantees approved, which are higher than those actually taken up by enterprises.
[b] From 1 July to 31 December 1990.
[c] Including export guarantees, credit sale insurance, leasing guarantees and interim financing for foreign trade organisations.
[d] This level is perhaps the amount of liquidity loans which went into default. The actual amount of liquidity loans which the *THA* paid would seem to be higher. Perhaps the loans which were serviced before the privatisation were not included.
*Source*: *Deutsche Bundesbank* (1994*d*); *THA* data (Hornef, 1994a); own calculations.

1990–3 period. By 1994, however, East German Credit Cooperatives had greatly increased their participation (47 per cent) as West German Commercial Bank participation declined (45 per cent), particularly by the three Big Banks (24 per cent). Thus the development ('normalisation') of East German banks' lending activities was accompanied by a similar process in handling guarantees.[6]

Loans through the *DtA* show an even distribution amongst bank groups, but this masks the large role played by West German Commercial Banks in the 1990–3 period. These banks handled a far higher share of these loans in the East than in West Germany, where *DtA*-receiving enterprises (mostly start-ups) tend to be traditional customers of Savings Banks and Credit Cooperatives in particular.[7] For *DtA's* Start-Up and Capital Assistance programmes, in 1991 West German Commercial Banks handled twice the volume (in relative terms) *vis-à-vis* Savings Banks and Credit Cooperatives as they did in West Germany. Of total *DtA* flows to the East in 1992, West German Commercial Banks handled 41 per cent, compared to 25 per cent in West Germany. Additional programme breakdowns only reinforce this trend.[8]

*KfW* loans likewise show an even distribution, though it is possible that the figures are somewhat misleading being for the whole of Germany.[9] In 1990 and 1991, in particular, when East German Savings

*Table 5.4* Breakdown of the handling of Specialised Bank loans and guarantees in the East, by bank group, 1990–3

| *Handling bank* | *THA (approved) guarantees*[b] *(per cent)* | *KfW loans and guarantees*[c] *(per cent)* | *DtA programmes*[d] *(per cent)* | *Bürgschaftsbank loans and* guarantees[c] *(per cent)* |
|---|---|---|---|---|
| *West German Commercial Banks* | | | | |
| *(Total)*[a] | | | | |
| 1990 | 90 | 48 | 39.6 | – |
| 1991 | 90 | 60 | 41.1 | 52 |
| 1992 | 90 | 57 | 35.7 | 68 |
| 1993 | – | 54 | 35.3 | 60 |
| *Of which:* | | | | |
| Big Banks[f] | | | | |
| 1990 | 77 | 25 | – | – |
| 1991 | 80 | 30 | – | – |
| 1992 | 83 | 26 | – | 53 |
| 1993 | 59 | 20 | – | 35 |
| *East German Banks* | | | | |
| Savings Banks | | | | |
| 1990 | 0.04 | 29 | 30.3 | – |
| 1991 | 0.10 | 26 | 31.6 | 28 |
| 1992 | 0.17 | 28 | 37.2 | 15 |
| 1993 | 0 23 | 31 | 39.7 | 15 |

*Table 5.4* *continued*

| *Handling bank* | *THA (approved) guarantees*[b] *(per cent)* | *KfW loans and guarantees*[c] *(per cent)* | *DtA programmes*[d] *(per cent)* | *Bürgschaftsbank loans and* guarantees[c] *(per cent)* |
|---|---|---|---|---|
| Credit Cooperatives | | | | |
| 1990 | 7.6 | 23 | 29.0 | – |
| 1991 | 7.0 | 14 | 27.3 | 18 |
| 1992 | 6.4 | 15 | 27.2 | 19 |
| 1993 | 0.3 | 15 | 25.1 | 25 |

*Notes*:
[a] May not total to 100 per cent owing to rounding errors. The volumes of the flows handled are presented in Tables 5.2 and 5.3.
[b] *THA* data for 1993 contains a large amount (18 per cent) of loans without a specified handling bank.
[c] Based on figure for Germany overall (figures for the East not available)
[d] Based on an average of the two largest programmes–in terms of outflows: the ERP Start-Up Programme and the Capital Assistance Programme.
[e] The data for 1991 is for Mecklenburg-Vorpommern only, whereas for 1992 and 1993 it is an average of Mecklenburg-Vorpommern and Berlin-Brandenburg. The figures for the Big Banks are for Berlin-Brandenburg only.
[f] The levels represent the percentage of the *total* loans handled by the Big Banks.
– = not available

*Source*: *THA* internal data; *KfW* 1993, *Annual Report*; *DtA* internal data; *Bürgschaftsbank Berlin–Brandenburg* internal data; *Bürgschaftsbank Mecklenburg-Vorpommern* 1993, *Geschäftsbericht*; own calculations.

Banks and Credit Cooperatives were in an early stage of their development and reorganisation, it is likely that they handled a lower proportion of these in the East. According to the *KfW*, Savings Bank levels in the early years after GEMSU reflect their large role in handling (high levels of) housing loans (rather than enterprise investment funds).[10]

**Lending to West German-owned companies**

While the levels of financial flows to the East were substantial, a significant portion of them were *targeted for West German-owned enterprises*. It is difficult, however, to determine their precise amount. Carlin and Richthofen point out that lending figures for East Germany refer only to banks or bank branches that are *located* there, and do not include loans which are made by banks *located* in West Germany to East German enterprises or individuals.[11] While it is difficult to quantify lending flows, we can begin an examination by looking at ownership and investment patterns in the East.

*Ownership patterns in the East*

The *THA's* approach to selling enterprises did not allow many East Germans to enter the process and become owners, resulting in a large sector of East German industry being owned by West German companies (see Chapter 6). Carlin summarises the position as follows:

> Privatisation in East Germany has produced an ownership structure quite different from elsewhere in transitional economies. The basic type of privatisation in East Germany shares key characteristics with some kinds of foreign direct investment elsewhere–namely, the new owner with a majority ownership stake is a Western enterprise. The most common form of ownership of larger privatised East Germany companies (with at least 100 employees) sold by the Treuhand is one in which there is a dominant owner (with a stake of at least 50 per cent) which is a West German company. In other words, privatisation has created subsidiaries of West German companies.[12]

In 1994, roughly 60 per cent of enterprise employees in former *THA* enterprises were working for a new West German owner; for 30 per cent, the owner was East German (or resident in East Germany); and for the remaining 10 per cent foreign.[13] These figures may overstate the total ownership of West Germans because they ignore start-up firms, where East German owners are more prevalent.[14] Of *THA* enterprises which had become 'private *Mittelstand*', 45 per cent were owned by

West Germans, 44 per cent by East Germans, and the remaining 11 per cent were under mixed ownership of the two.[15] The primary vehicle for East Germans to become owners was the Management buy-out (MBO). Most MBOs were for enterprises with less than 200 employees.[16]

*West German investment in the East*

As one would have expected, German investment in the East increased between 1990 and 1993 both absolutely and as a share of total enterprise investment in Germany:

> Almost one Deutsche Mark in every four that were spent by [East and West] German producing enterprises on gross capital formation in 1993 was accounted for by the new Länder; a year before it had been one in six and in 1991 only one in seven Deutsche Mark.[17]

Investment by West German-owned enterprises in the East represented 63 per cent of total enterprise investment in the East in 1992, 65 per cent in 1993 and 56 per cent in 1994.[18] These figures roughly correspond to the new ownership structure in the East.

Data measuring investment flows of West German enterprises in the East do not, however, disclose the *financing* of the investment. That is, we do not know the extent to which the investment is financed by, say, own funds as opposed to bank loans and, in the case of loans, whether the loans are recorded as being made in East or in West Germany. Bundesbank sources report that West German banks adjusted their loan books to show loans to West German parent companies (i.e. loans which will function as intra-enterprise transfers) as loans to the East.[19] Carlin and Richthofen argue that 'the true flow of loans from banks in West Germany to either East Germans or West Germans investing in East Germany is extremely hard to quantify'.[20]

Assuming that the pattern of enterprise ownership and investment is mirrored in the pattern of borrowing by West German-owned companies in the East,[21] we can estimate that West German-owned enterprises account for 60 per cent of lending to the East. Deeg reports evidence to support this view:

> The Deutsche Bank, which is clearly the dominant lender among commercial banks in the East, has indicated that 60–70 per cent of its by small- and medium-sized firms in the East is actually going to West German firms.[22]

Some West German banks have stated as a matter of policy their preference for lending to firms with West German owners. *IKB Deutsche Industriebank*, which primarily finances long-term investment for *Mittelstand* enterprises,[23] stated in 1992 that 90 per cent of the investment projects it had funded in the East flowed to 'IKB customers in West Germany'.[24] This figure was reduced to 75 per cent in 1993, but the bank still claimed, 'our long-standing western German customers remain the most important target market for our lending operations in the new *Länder*'[25]

West German-owned enterprises are eligible in addition to receive loans through the Specialised Banks. There is evidence that West German-owned firms received a significant share of such loans as well.[26]

## Transfers

The high levels of public transfers to the East have been the most widely publicised feature of the East German transition to date. Annual transfers to the East over the period 1991 to 1993 equalled 58, 49 and 42 per cent of East German GDP, respectively.[27] West German transfers to the East in 1991 were equal to three times the GNP of the Czech and Slovak Federal Republic (CSFR), which has roughly the same populaton.[28] It is important to note that the transfers led to a significant rise in German public debt: from 42 per cent of GDP in 1989 up to 60.5 per cent in 1996,[29] and that (West) German banks absorbed just under half of this total.[30]

The *THA* played a large role in funding enterprises through direct transfers (Table 5.5). To finance these, the *THA* borrowed heavily from banks in the first two years after GEMSU, but thereafter increasingly borrowed from capital markets because it was able to get better terms than from banks.[31] The *THA's* average cost of borrowing was about 9.33 per cent at the end of 1991, which was reduced to just under 7 per cent by the end of 1993.[32] Although the *THA* was treated as an enterprise, and therefore not included in the public budget directly, there is a fine line between *THA* transfers to enterprises, which were refinanced through market sources (with, of course, the guarantee of the German state), and public transfers.[33]

While the steep rise in *THA* transfers may have reflected its increasingly favourable access to funds, and thus a changeover from guaranteeing funds to transferring them directly, another possible explanation is that it was in response to the inability of banks to meet the financing needs of enterprises under *THA* stewardship, particularly as guarantees were removed.

*Table* 5.5 THA transfers to enterprises in the East, 1990–3[a]

| *Item (DM bn)* | *1990*[b] | *1991* | *1992* | *1993* |
|---|---|---|---|---|
| *Debt level (total)* | 14.1 | 39.4 | 106.8 | 168.3 |
| Credit market debt[c] | 4.3 | 24.2 | 54.7 | 134.5 |
| Assumption of old debt | 9.7 | 15.2 | 38.0 | 19.7 |
| Liabilities arising from enterprises' equalisation claims[d] | – | – | 14.1 | 14.2 |

*Notes*:
[a] *THA* liabilities are taken as a proxy for transfers.
[b] For the second half of the year (i.e. after GEMSU).
[c] Including export guarantees, credit sale insurance, leasing guarantees and interim financing for foreign trade organisations.
[d] This level is perhaps the amount of liquidity loans which went into default. The actual amount of liquidity loans which the *THA* paid would seem to be higher. Perhaps the loans which were serviced before the privatisation were not included.
– = not available.
Source: *Deutsche Bundesbank* (1994*e*); *THA* data (Hornef, 1994*a*); own calculations.

## The provision of venture capital

Banks have been reluctant to take equity stakes in the East on any significant scale. By the end of 1993, the total amount invested in the East was DM 498.49 mn, spread across 253 enterprises.[34] The bulk of the acquisitions occurred in 1991, when the total value rose from DM 77.21 mn to DM 455.65 mn (a 378 per cent increase).[35] West German Commercial Bank investments represent a large share of the total, larger than those of East German banks for the same period. The combined holdings of East German Savings Banks and *Landesbanken* was DM 150 mn at the end of 1993.[36]

Big Banks naturally accounted for a significant portion of the above totals. Commerzbank elected not to form a venture-capital subsidiary, but *Deutsche Bank* invested equity in East German enterprises through majority and minority stakes. By the end of 1993, it had invested DM 121 mn in minority stakes through its subsidiary, *Deutsche Beteiligungsgesellschaft mbH*.[37] As of October 1994, it had provided more than DM 250 mn to 25 enterprises (purchased from the *THA*) through *Deutsche Industrie Holding*, which took majority stakes.[38]

The level of venture capital from abroad was also low. The largest foreign venture capital holding was by The East German Investment Trust plc. which, by the end of March 1994, had a portfolio of 18 enterprises and had invested DM 135 mn, a figure which rose to DM 157 mn by the end of March 1995.[39]

## Banking activities in the East after GEMSU

Banking deposit and lending activities in the East after GEMSU reveal a path of *normalisation* in which (East and West German) bank groups achieve market shares in line with those in West Germany.[40] According to a *Deutsche Bundesbank* (1994) report, 'their [East German Savings Banks and Credit Cooperatives] relevant benchmarks and their balance sheet structures are drawing progressively closer to West German conditions.'[41]

Nevertheless, while growing closer in broad terms to West German benchmarks, the banking sector in the East displayed certain differences, especially in the period immediately following GEMSU. On the lending side, the West German Commercial Banks initial large role proved to be a temporary phenomenon; East German banks gradually caught up. On the deposit side, East German banks maintained their strong market position – at higher levels than their counterparts in West Germany – despite some loss of market share following GEMSU. It is the latter activities with which we begin our analysis.

### Deposit activities

Savings increased in the East after GEMSU, following an initial temporary surge in consumption by East Germans. Before GEMSU, the savings rate increased–largely in anticipation of the currency exchange–in the first two quarters of 1990 from 18.4 to 22.4 per cent. It then fell sharply after GEMSU to -1.8 per cent in the third quarter, before climbing back to 13.4 per cent in the fourth quarter.[42] Consumption still continued to increase in absolute terms, with a striking displacement of East German goods by West German imports.[43]

Bank deposit levels mirrored the movement of savings, experiencing an initial drop and then rising rapidly (Figure 5.1). Immediately following GEMSU there was a fall in bank deposits as East Germans either withdrew deposits in order to consume[44] or simply left the country.[45] Thereafter, the increase in bank deposits primarily took the form of time and savings deposits, showing a heightened desire for interest-bearing and higher-yielding instruments and marking a shift from an initially strong liquidity preference. Nevertheless, liquidity preference remained higher in East than in West Germany: as of December 1994, East Germans still held 34 per cent of their deposits as demand deposits, whereas in West Germany the overall level of demand deposits was only 18 per cent of the total.[46] Stronger liquidity preference in the East may reflect a lower yield consciousness among East

*Figure* 5.1 Total deposits of non-banks in the East,[a] 1990–4

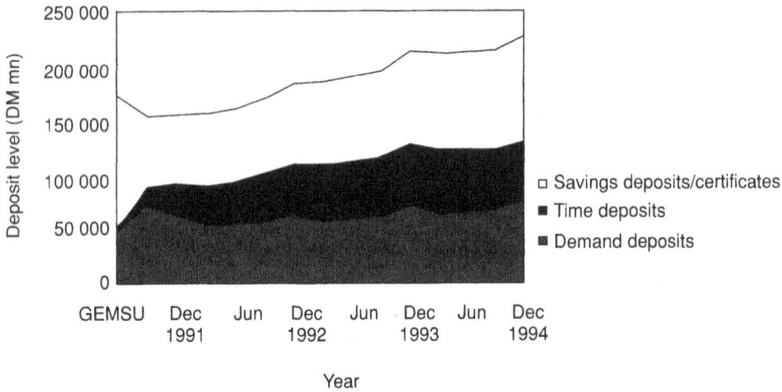


*Note*: [a]Not including East Berlin.

*Source*: *Deutsche Bundesbank, Regionalergebnisse der monatlichen Bilanzstatistik für Kreditinstitute in Ostdeutschland; Landeszentralbanken* data (see Appendix 3, Table A3.1, p.198).

Germans. On the other hand, it may reflect the greater wealth possessed by West Germans and the corresponding lower need for liquidity as a percentage of the overall asset portfolio. In any event, East Germans' savings levels and investment behaviour were becoming increasingly similar to those in West Germany.[47]

We do not find significant normalisation in deposit levels across bank groups. According to the *Bundesbank*, the East German Savings Banks' traditional role as 'reservoirs of capital' had not been 'severely shaken by increasing competition from West German credit institutions with branch networks'.[48] At the time of GEMSU, West Germans banks did experience significant success in attracting deposits away from East German banks. Thus the initial displacement of East German *products* by those from the West was accompanied by a similar displacement in banking *services*. However, this tendency did not continue for long (Figure 5.2).[49] As a result, the East German Savings Banks' market share of total deposits declined from the 80 per cent it had been in the GDR, but continued at a high level: at the time of GEMSU, these banks held 59 per cent of total deposits, and as of December 1994 still had 60 per cent.[50] Savings Bank deposit levels in the East have remained significantly higher than those of Savings Banks in West Germany,

*Figure* 5.2 Breakdown of total deposits in the East,[a] by bank group, 1990–4

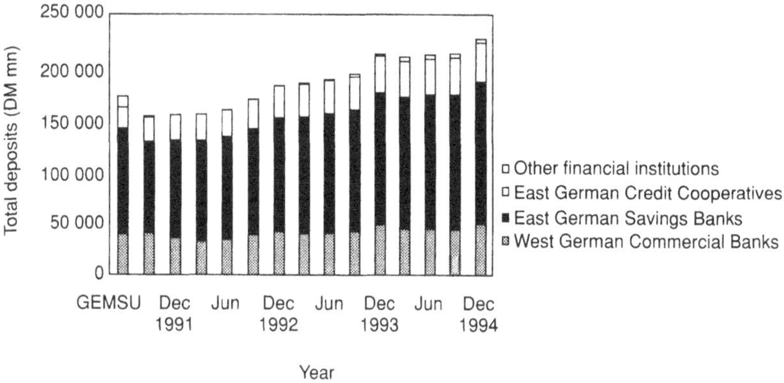


*Note*: [a]Not including East Berlin.

*Source: Deutsche Bundesbank, Regionalergebnisse der monatlichen Bilanzstatistik für Kreditinstitute in Ostdeutschland; Landeszentralbanken* data (see Appendix 3, Table A3.2, p.199).

whose market share of total deposits was 34 per cent as of December 1993, and 32 per cent as of December 1994.[51]

The dominance of the Savings Banks stemmed from their high market share in retail deposits: between 1991 and 1993, the Savings Banks held an average of 71 per cent of all such deposits, with West German Commercial Banks holding 13 per cent and East German Credit Cooperatives 16 per cent.[52] An important explanation is that the East German Savings Banks still had a much larger branch network than the West German Commercial Banks, proximity being perhaps the most important buying factor for retail customers.[53] In mid-1991, the Savings Banks had 2248 branches while *Deutsche Bank, Dresdner Bank* and *Commerzbank* combined had 380.[54] The figures also reflect a certain degree of inertia on the part of East Germans who were content to leave their money at lower yields rather than go to the trouble of changing their accounts to one of the West German Commercial Banks. In the GDR, people had managed all of their financial transactions through the Savings Banks, and after GEMSU simply didn't want to undertake the time-consuming process of changing over all of their paperwork to another bank.[55] Further, there may also have been a certain familiarity with and trust in the East German Savings Banks.[56] Such a general preference of individuals to bank with East German banks mirrors the underlying trend of East German consumers who quickly switched back from West German to East German goods.[57] An additional factor which needs mentioning is that the mass migration that occurred leading up to and following GEMSU saw many potential customers of the West German banks move to West Germany, where they would probably have shifted their accounts to a West German bank in any event.[58] Perhaps for these reasons, West German Commercial Banks were unsuccessful in attracting away East German depositors, despite offering higher deposit rates as well as concessions on fees: *Dresdner Bank* and *Commerzbank* offered one year of free banking services for East Germans, and *Deutsche Bank* offered its services at reduced rates.[59] These higher rates appear to have exerted some competitive pressure on the Savings Banks, however, as they gradually responded by raising theirs.[60]

West German Commercial Banks maintained a dominant share of enterprise deposits. Between 1991 and 1993, they held an average of 55 per cent of all enterprise deposits, with Savings Banks holding 27 per cent and Credit Cooperatives 16 per cent.[61] This segmentation was not surprising given that the vast majority of *THA* enterprises became customers of the West German Commercial Banks by virtue of banks supplying them with *THA* liquidity loans (examined in more detail below); in return, enterprises would likely have been obliged to give them their deposit business (i.e. cash management). It is surprising, however, given the shock of GEMSU on the enterprise sector, and the huge drop in output (Chapter 4), that enterprise deposits were so high in the first year. One commercial banker attributed the initial high levels of enterprise deposits to artificially high levels of *THA* liquidity loans. Another possible explanation is that many enterprises continued to receive export guarantees – particularly for exports to Russia – which cushioned the shock of losing their traditional CMEA markets until 1991, when these support measures were removed.[62]

The East German Savings Banks' dominant position did not hold for all types of deposits. While maintaining high levels of demand deposits and savings deposits, they gathered a proportionately lower share of time deposits (Figure 5.3).

Time deposits were an easier target for West German Commercial Banks for several reasons. First, for these deposits yield was a more important factor for customers – as opposed to the quality of banking services or proximity, for instance – which allowed pricing to become a more significant competitive lever. Second, it may have been that the West German Commercial Banks had a higher share of high net-worth

*Figure* 5.3 Breakdown of time deposits in the East,[a] by bank group, 1990–4

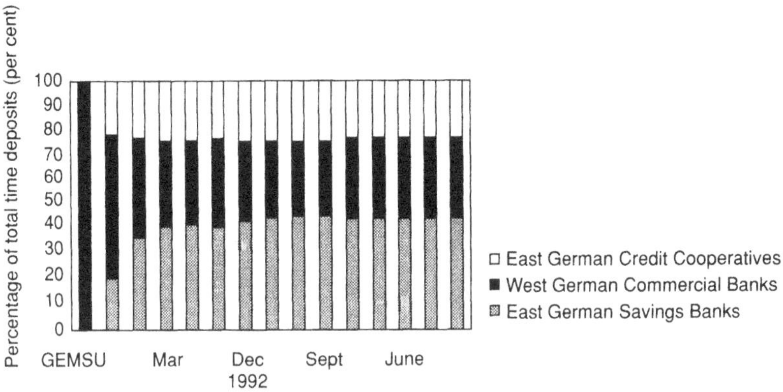


*Note*: [a]Not including East Berlin.

*Source*: *Deutsche Bundesbank, Regionalergebnisse der monatlichen Bilanzstatistik für Kreditinstitute in Ostdeutschland; Landeszentralbanken* data (see Appendix 3, Table A3.3, p.200).

individuals, who would hold higher time deposit balances.[63] Third, time deposits represented a new product that was not offered in the GDR – that is, West German banks found it easier to compete for deposit products which the Savings Banks were less suited to offer. An additional explanation for the West German Commercial Banks' initial hold over time deposits is that enterprises developed their yield consciousness more rapidly than private persons and were thus over-represented in the aggregate levels. In 1993, enterprises held 38 per cent of their total deposits as time deposits, whereas private persons held only 20 per cent.[64]

## Lending activities

Overall bank lending increased in the 1990–4 period. We can estimate the total amount of bank loans to the East at approximately DM 218 bn at the end of 1993, and DM 279 bn at the end of 1994 (Table 5.6).

This does not include loans which banks handled through the Specialised Banks, even though these were also made – to a large extent – at the banks' own (credit) risk. Mortgage Banks were responsible for more than half of the total lending by West German Commercial Banks to the East, not including East Berlin. Presumably the high level of housing incentives offered by the government and the construction boom led to a

*Table* 5.6 Total bank lending in the East, 1990–4

| *Bank group* | *Total loans* | | | |
|---|---|---|---|---|
| | *1993* | | *1994* | |
| | *DM bn* | *% of total* | *DM bn* | *% of total* |
| *West German Commercial Banks (total)* | 93 | 43 | 122 | 44 |
| Universal Banks | 43 | 20 | 52 | 19 |
| Mortgage Banks | 50 | 23 | 70 | 25 |
| West German Landesbanken[a] | 62 | 28 | 80 | 27 |
| *East German Banks (Total)* | 63 | 29 | 77 | 28 |
| Savings Bank | 47 | 22 | 58 | 21 |
| Credit Cooperatives | 16 | 7 | 19 | 7 |
| Total | 218 | 100 | 279 | 100 |
| *Memorandum item: East Berlin* | | | | |
| West German Commercial Banks[b] | – | – | 20 | – |
| East German Banks | – | – | – | – |

*Notes*:
[a] The West German *Landesbanken* made loans totalling DM 53 bn up to mid-1993. The figures cited are estimates made by averaging post-GEMSU loans over six-month periods and adding additional periods as required (*Deutsche Sparkassen- und Giroverband e.V.*, 1994). Data not available for 1994.
[b] Estimate by the *Bankenverband mittel- und ostdeutscher Länder* (Friedmann, 1995) representing roughly one-third of the total loans by West German Commercial banks in Berlin (DM 66 bn).
– = not available.
*Source*: *Landeszentralbanken* data; *Deutsche Sparkassen- und Giroverband e.V*; own calculations.

surge in mortgage loans.[65] The result was that West German Commercial Banks lent a decreasing proportion of their portfolio to enterprises and an increasing proportion to private persons (Table 5.7).

The German Bankers' Association points out that West German Commercial Banks have taken on an increasing share of own-risk lending, (i.e. non-guaranteed).[66] Figure 5.4 displays graphically the figures shown in Table 5.7. Loans to *THA* enterprises – virtually all guaranteed – declined significantly between 1990 and 1993. At the same time, non-*THA* loans – virtually all non-guaranteed – increased substantially over the same period.

Similarly, the increase in lending activities of the East and West German Banks was primarily in personal loans and loans to self-employed persons (Figure 5.5). Even excluding Mortgage Bank lending, West German Commercial Banks increased their market share of total

*Table* 5.7 Lending profile for West German commercial banks in the East, 1990–3[a]

| | *End 1990* | | *End 1991* | | *End 1992* | | *End 1993* | |
|---|---|---|---|---|---|---|---|---|
| | *Amount (DM mn)* | *% of total* | *Amount (DM mn)* | *% of total* | *Amount (DM mn)* | *% of total* | *Amount (DM mn)* | *% of total* |
| **Total loans**[c] | **22 964** | **100** | **49 415** | **100** | **73 496** | **100** | **96 900** | **100** |
| *Personal loans*[b] (approved) | 1 778 | 8 | 7 243 | 15 | 15 322 | 21 | 23 800 | 25 |
| housing loans | 240 | 1 | 1 741 | 4 | 4 178 | 6 | 11 500 | 8 |
| housing loans paid out | 204 | 1 447 | 3 239 | – | – | | | |
| *Commercial loans* (approved) | 21 186 | 92 | 42 172 | 85 | 58 174 | 79 | 73 100 | 75 |
| loans paid out | 18 306 | 80 | 34 952 | 71 | 47 934 | 65 | 56 900 | 58 |
| *of which:* | | | | | | | | |
| *THA enterprises* | 13 557 | 59 | 20 618 | 42 | 18 683 | 25 | 8 000 | 8 |
| guaranteed | 12 771 | [94] | 18 993 | [92] | 16 372 | [88] | 7 040 | [88] |
| non-guaranteed | 786 | [6] | 1 625 | [8] | 2 311 | [12] | 960 | [12] |
| *Non-THA enterprises* | 4 749 | 21 | 14 334 | 29 | 29 251 | 40 | 48 900 | 50 |
| guaranteed | 691 | [15] | 2117 | [15] | 1990 | [7] | 4890 | [10] |
| non-guaranteed | 4 058 | [85] | 12 217 | [85] | 27 261 | [93] | 44 010 | [90] |
| *Mittelstand*[d] | 4 598 | 20 | 8 786 | 18 | 12 502 | 17 | 17 700 | 18 |

*Notes:*

[a] *Bundesverband deutscher Banken* data not available for 1994. The data is based on nine reporting banks: *Baverische Hypotheken- und Wechsel-Bank AG; Baverische Vereinsbank AG* (without *Vereins- und Westbank AG*); *Berliner Bank AG; Berliner Handels- und Frankfurter Bank; Commerzbank AG; Deutsche Bank AG; Dresdner Bank AG; SchmidtBank KGaA*; and *Vereins- und Westbank AG* (i.e. it includes Mortgage bank loans).

[b] *KfW* and *DtA* loans not included.

[c] Personal Loans are all together (irrespective of amount).

[d] *Mittelstand* loans are defined as greater than DM 5 bn (irrespective of borrower).

Source: Compiled from *Bundesverband deutscher Banken*, 1992, 1993 Reports.

*Figure* 5.4 Breakdown of West German commercial bank lending to enterprises in the East, 1990–3

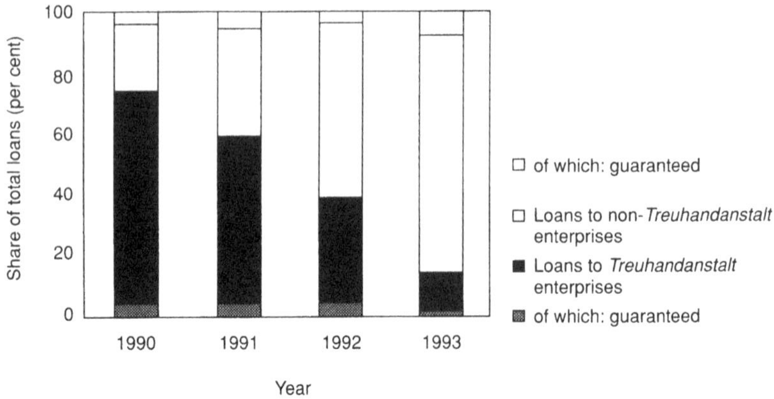


*Note*: Data on guaranteed loans not publicly available for 1994, though the percentages in all likelihood continued to fall.

*Source*: *Bundesverbank der deutschen Banken*, 1992, 1993 Reports (see Table 5.7). Figure as presented by Carlin and Richthofen (1995, p.19).

*Figure* 5.5 Total bank lending in the East, 1991–4[a]

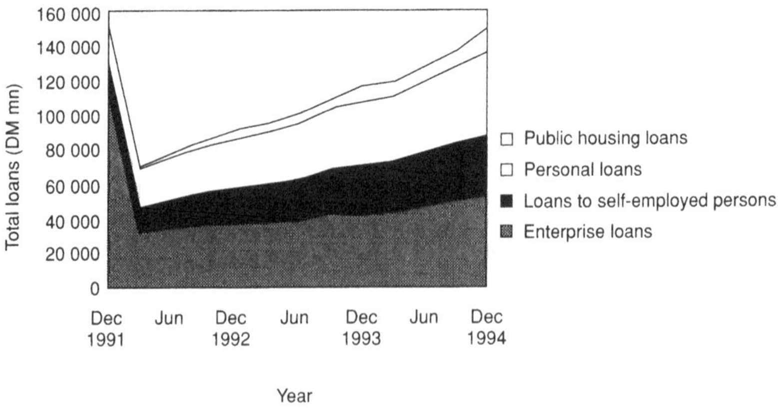


*Note*: [a]After March 1992, the lending statistics do not include *Staatsbank Berlin* and *DKB* accounts. Does not include *KfW/DtA* loans. The figure corresponds to Table 5.6, apart from Mortgage Bank loans which are excluded, as are West German *Landesbank* loans and loans in East Berlin.

*Source*: *Landeszentralbanken* data (see Appendix 3, Table A3.4, p.200).

*Figure* 5.6 Term structure of bank lending in the East, 1991–3[a]

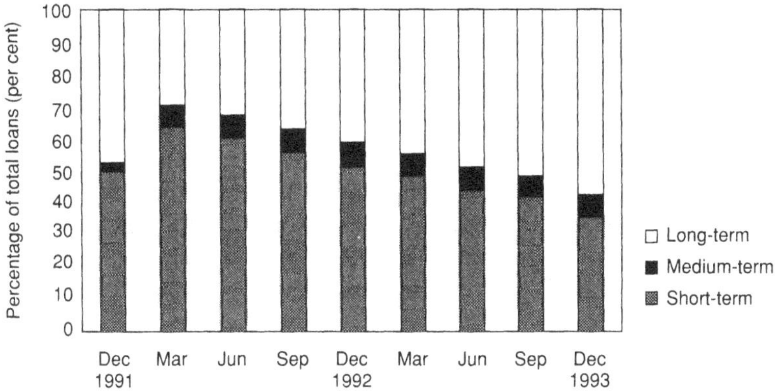


*Note*: [a]After March 1992, the data does not include *Staatsbank* and *DKB* accounts. Term structure data not available for 1994. 'Short-term' is up to and including 1 year; 'medium-term' is more than 1 year but less than 4; 'long-term' is for 4 years or more.

*Source*: *Landeszentralbanken* data (East German Banks and West German Commercial Banks, excluding Mortgage Banks) (see Appendix 3, Table A3.5, p.201).

personal loans from 15 per cent in 1991 to 27 per cent in 1993.[67] This increase came mostly at the expense of the Savings Banks which saw their share decrease from 63 per cent in 1991 to 53 per cent in 1993.

Enterprise lending showed no significant increase between 1991 and 1994. An important reason was that THA (guaranteed) liquidity loans were dramatically reduced. This is reflected in the term structure of lending (Figure 5.6). As the main suppliers of THA loans, West German Commercial Banks saw their loans outstanding to enterprises decline from DM 25 477 mn in December 1992 to DM 23 839 mn in December 1994. Their share of overall enterprise loans decreased from 67 to 45 per cent. The Big Banks handled the bulk of the THA liquidity loans; their overall lending volume fall from DM 25 470 mn in 1992 to DM 22 618 mn in 1993, a decrease of 11.2 per cent.[68]

### *The development of East German Bank lending activities*

The low level of lending by East German Banks directly after GEMSU was primarily due to three factors. First, following the currency conversion, they (Savings Banks especially) were overwhelmed with the logistics of converting their high volume of deposit accounts from M to DM. While this was the responsibility of the banks' accounting rather than credit departments, the magnitude of the task placed strains on the overall capacity of the bank to develop new business.[69] Second, East German management needed to learn to evaluate creditworthiness.[70] The banks became cautious after the unfortunate experience of Savings Banks in Halle, where local managers squandered more than DM 400 mn in loans to West Germans who had prepared fraudulent documentation.[71] Third, West German banks played an abnormally large role immediately after GEMSU in lending to enterprises and in handling additional financial flows into the East, particularly *THA* liquidity credits (Table 5.4), and it took time for the East German banks to build their customer base.

In the first two years after GEMSU, East German Savings Banks placed most of their deposits in the money market, with non-bank lending remaining at low levels. A large percentage of these funds went to the (West German) *Landesbanken* which subsequently lent them out, primarily to enterprises (Table 5.6). Thus, as of June 1992 East German Savings Banks held 23.7 per cent of their assets in non-bank loans, versus 64.6 per cent for West German Savings Banks; East German Credit Cooperatives 36.4 per cent in loans, versus 60.9 per cent for West German Credit Cooperatives.[72] Even by 1994, East German Savings Banks – and to a lesser extent the Credit Cooperatives – had a small proportion of their deposit base lent to non-banks (Figure 5.7).

The gradual expansion of lending activities by East German banks was encouraged by several factors, both positive and negative. First, the banks received assistance from West German Savings Bank and Credit Cooperative Associations in the form of training, technical assistance, and some limited financial assistance for modernising East German branch networks. The banks also receive equalisation claims to offset the negative effects they experienced on their balance sheets as a result of the currency conversion (see Chapter 4).

Second, East German banks maintained a large, low-cost deposit base owing to the low yield consciousness of East German depositors. The banks' liability structure mirrored that of total bank deposits we outlined earlier, giving them comparatively much cheaper funding than their West German counterparts.[73] By placing this large deposit base in the money market, which had attractive rates in 1991–2 owing to the high interest rates, East German banks were able to build their network infrastructure, provision against potential and existing NPLs, and invest in training for employees.[74]

Over time, as money market rates fell and their cost of funds rose,[75] East German Banks were forced to lend more funds to non-banks

*Figure* 5.7 Ratio of lending/deposits in the East, by bank group, 1994

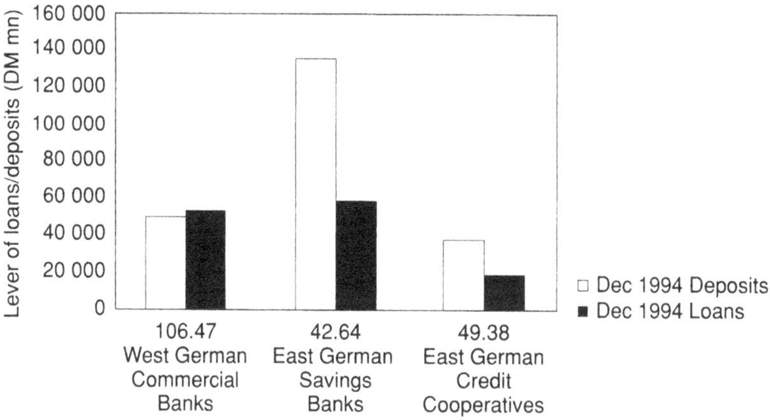


*Source*: *Landeszentralbanken* data.

(i.e. accept more risk) in order to maintain their margins.[76] East German Savings Banks overtook West German Commercial banks (in *absolute* terms) in total loans extended by the end of 1993, becoming the largest lender in the East (Figure 5.8).[77]

*Figure* 5.8 Bank lending in the East, by bank group, 1991–4[a]

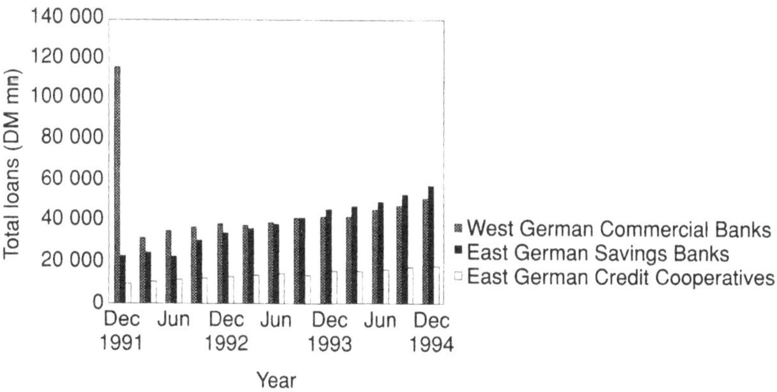


*Note*: [a]After March 1992, the data does not include *Staatsbank* and *DKB* accounts.

*Source*: *Landeszentralbanken* data (see Appendix 3, Table A3.6, p.202).

West German Commercial Banks, by contrast, had higher lending than deposit levels in 1994. In other words, they accounted for a *net inflow* of funds to the East. This may explain why they began decreasing their lending, despite the fact that money market funds became cheaper, thus underlining the significance of their lack of success in taking more deposits away from East German banks.

All in all, the development of the East German banks' loan portfolio and preservation of their deposit base took West German bankers by surprise. According to Peter Krakow, Chairman of the Board of the Leipzig Savings Banks,

> The big western banks thought they'd have it easy when they came here ... , of course we have lost customers and market share – but not on the scale that other banks were expecting.[78]

Kurt Kasch of Deutsche Bank shared this view: 'We underestimated the speed with which they [East German Savings Banks] would change.'[79]

## The experiences of *Deutsche Bank* and *Commerzbank*

Not all West German Commercial Banks followed identical strategies in developing their business in the East. In this section, we compare the experiences in the East of two of the largest West German Commercial Banks: *Deutsche Bank* and *Commerzbank*. The case studies are designed to highlight different organisational approaches to banking in the transition process and, in so doing, identify the common and particular difficulties experienced by West German Commercial Banks. Because of data problems, the analysis depends relatively heavily on interviews.[80] The analysis is in three sections, covering strategy, performance and lessons to be learned.

### *Deutsche Bank's* strategy: the joint-venture approach

*Deutsche Bank's* entry to the East involved the purchase of a significant stake in the former East German *Staatsbank*: the *Deutsche Kreditbank* (*DKB*). In the process, *Deutsche Bank* reoccupied many of its old branches which it owned before their expropriation in 1945. *Deutsche Bank* entered into early negotiations (March 1990) with the *THA* to discuss the extent of the role it would play in the East. According to Axel Osenberg, member of the board of the joint-venture, 'preference was given to Deutsche Bank because we were prepared, from the very beginning, to contribute not only all our know-how, but also our international connections, our operational organisation, including EDP [Electronic Data Processing], our design and our logo.[81]

*Deutsche Bank* decided to share the acquisition with *Dresdner Bank*, which formed a separate joint-venture with *DKB* – a decision motivated primarily by political constraints. In the words of *Deutsche Bank's* Chairman, Hilmar Kopper,

we couldn't take the whole lot because we wouldn't have had the political support to do it. We pondered it, but it created an outrage in the media when Allianz took 100 per cent of the East German insurance industry.[82]

Indeed, when the initial letter of intent was signed between *Deutsche Bank* and *DKB* on 17 April 1990, public attention at once focused on implications for competition in the banking industry in the East.[83]

In the end, *Deutsche Bank* took over 122 of the 170 branches of *DKB* and approximately 8500 *Kreditbank* employees – the others going to *Dresdner* – in addition to opening 18 more branches of its own (Figure 5.9).[84] Altogether it invested DM 300 mn, which gave it a 49 per cent stake in the venture.[85] '*Deutsche Bank* only reluctantly undertakes shareholdings with such a low share'; but 'given the Joint Venture Law in force in the GDR at that time, we had no choice'.[86] *Deutsche Bank* aimed, however, to increase its share and ultimately gain 100 per cent ownership,[87] which it achieved in 1991.[88] In the period when the venture remained jointly owned, its board (*Vorstand*) consisted of three representatives from each organisation. It is not clear to what extent the *DKB* representatives had input, but suggestions have been made that their assistance was valuable in explaining how the former (GDR) banking system operated, and in understanding the East more generally.[89]

For *Deutsche Bank*, the joint-venture approach assumed that people would not respond well to too much change too quickly. According to one report,

Their [Deutsche and Dresdner] argument is that east Germans like to walk into old east German branches and talk to east German counter staff. New, western-style branches and western staff are intimidating.[90]

*Figure* 5.9 Organisation development of *Deutsche Bank* in the East, 1945–90

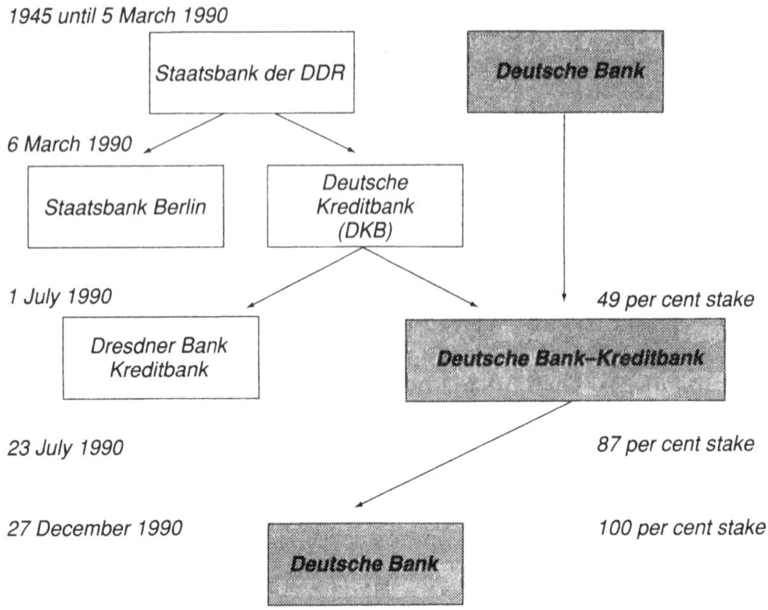


Nevertheless, there were signs the approach was being abandoned. *Deutsche Bank* kept its links with the past through its employees, but when it took over 100 per cent of the venture it dropped the 'Kreditbank' name. One *Deutsche Bank* manager suggested that this was because the name acted as a disincentive to prospective customers (i.e. it signalled the former system).[91]

### *Advantages and disadvantages of the* Deutsche Bank *strategy*

*Deutsche Bank's* joint-venture strategy contained both advantages and disadvantages. The main advantages were office space and staff. Given the problems in the East concerning property restitution, it was a benefit to take over existing *DKB* branches, even though they needed significant levels of investment to improve them to a suitable standard in technical and aesthetic terms (see Plates 1 and 2).[92] With respect to the staff, it was beneficial to begin with an established workforce. *Deutsche Bank* Chairman Hilmar Kopper said that, 'it was important to recruit their staff, because we knew we wouldn't be able to collect enough people here to send over there'.[93] On the other side, the staff needed training and appeared over-large. In the first six months after

Plate 1 *Deutsche Bank* (Leipzig), 1994

the venture was established, *Deutsche Bank* staff took part in over 6000 seminars. More than 1000 people attended training courses in the West.[94] Two years after the acquisition, *Deutsche Bank* still claimed that it was 'overstaffed'.[95]

Although staff from the East were lacking in banking expertise, lending especially, particularly within the [West German] social market economy, they had contacts and information across industries in the East. The information was the less important of the two since all data in the East were dubious and being frequently updated.[96] The contacts proved valuable since they facilitated *Deutsche Bank's* large share of the

Plate 2 *Deutsche Bank* (Kamenz), 1994
(Regional Head Office)

profitable *THA* liquidity loans, and its large enterprise portfolio immediately after GEMSU.

Further, as a result of the decision that old loans (*Altkredite*) on the *DKB* balance sheet would be split off and placed in another institution (see Chapter 4), *Deutsche Bank* (and *Dresdner*) managed to acquire the fixed assets and human capital of *DKB* without taking on its balance sheet obligations.

Deutsche Bank's *operating strategy*

The *Deutsche Bank* strategy centred on capturing market share, particularly in the *retail market*, which had previously been serviced in only a rudimentary fashion. 'I am interested in the 17 million people as customers', said Hilmar Kopper, *Deutsche Bank* Chairman, 'I want more market share. I don't want more corporate business.'[97] This strategy was based on two assumptions. First, that there would be little opportunity initially to take deposits from and lend to East German enterprises. Second, that the retail market, deposits in particular, would be easy to penetrate given the poor state of the local East German Savings Banks and Credit Cooperatives. Both assumptions turned out to be false (see below).

### *Commerzbank's* entry strategy: the greenfield approach

Underlying the *Commerzbank* strategy was the desire to distance the bank from the past in East Germany, and also from *Deutsche* and

*Dresdner* who were seen to be in favour of some continuity with the past. In the words of a *Commerzbank* press release:

> Unlike its two major competitors, it [Commerzbank] deliberately chose not to cooperate with existing East German banks, in order to be able to present a *genuine alternative in no way associated with East Germany's past*[98] (emphasis added).

'*Commerzbank* attempted to use its disassociation with the past as a competitive advantage *vis-à-vis Deutsche Bank*. *The Economist* commented:

> *Commerzbank* ostentatiously asks all new East German staff to sign a declaration that they have not been members of the Stasi, the former East German secret police force. This enables some *Commerzbankers* to drop none-too-subtle hints about the number of ex-Stasi folk who may or may not be on Deutsche's and Dresdner's payrolls – and who would want to do business with people like that?[99]

*Commerzbank's* decision not to participate in the joint-venture with *DKB* may have been by design or simply by default. In other words, the bank adopted its strategy only after being excluded from the *DKB* venture. Interviews revealed a widely held view that *Commerzbank* had reacted slowly and lost out on potential opportunities to take part in the splitting up of the former Staatsbank.[100]

Whether the greenfield approach was its preferred choice or not, *Commerzbank* adopted the strategy and promoted its positive aspects.[101] First, it avoided the large investment required to transform the existing branch network. Second, it avoided taking on the large and unskilled workforce. Third, it avoided responsibility for old loans on the East German banks' balance sheets, it being unclear initially how responsibility for these would be allocated.

These advantages, however, were accompanied by corresponding disadvantages in the early years of *Commerzbank's* operations. First, it had no buildings. It had severe problems purchasing new branches for operation, managing to secure only twelve existing sites.[102] As a result, the bank started with mobile branches in the form of buses (see Plate 3), and also built transportable banking containers – which *Commerzbankers* prefer to call 'pavilions' (see Plate 4).

The illustrations show the differences between the banking infrastructure with which the West German banks began their operations in

Plate 3 *Commerzbank* Minibus (Leipzig), 1994

Plate 4 *Commerzbank* Container (Leipzig), 1994
(white structure in the foreground)

the East.[103] The *Deutsche Bank* branches are those the bank had owned before the Second World War.

Secondly, *Commerzbank* suffered from staff shortages. *Commerzbank* established an organisational structure based on partner cities, East and West. Between these, managers would be exchanged and promote both locations. Immediately after GEMSU, the vast majority of *Commerzbank* employees in the East came from West Germany. This put extreme strains on the bank, both in East and West Germany, particularly at the management level. Third, *Commerzbank* had no contacts initially with the old system and as a result lost out on much of the lucrative business of providing *THA* liquidity loans (and hence developed its loan portfolio more slowly).

**Bank performance**

It has been surprisingly difficult to evaluate these two different approaches in comparative perspective. Interviews proved inconclusive, partly owing to the banks' different points of comparison. In competitive terms, *Commerzbank* frequently evaluated its position with respect to *Deutsche Bank*. Several *Commerzbank* employees referred to *Deutsche Bank* branches in a sarcastic manner as 'our friendly competitors'. This approach was not adopted by *Deutsche Bank*, which perhaps did not see *Commerzbank* as a significant competitor. Rather, the *Deutsche Bank* benchmark was its market share in East as compared to West Germany. These considerations notwithstanding, some observations can be made.

By July 1991, after only one year of operations, *Deutsche Bank* had collected DM 14.4 bn in deposits and made DM 10.6 bn in loans, whereas *Commerzbank* had taken DM 3 bn in deposits and made DM 2 bn in loans.[104] At the same time, *Deutsche Bank* had around 600 000 customers while *Commerzbank* had around 150 000.[105] As noted, *Deutsche Bank's* intended strategic focus was not initially on corporate business, but this changed when the *THA* introduced its policy of providing enterprises with liquidity loans. These loans represented an opportunity for banks to make (credit) risk-free loans at high margins. *Deutsche Bank's* significant early advantage of contacts with *THA* enterprises led to its high levels of liquidity loans. In addition, by managing the old loans (*Altkredite*), *Deutsche Bank* kept well informed about financing patterns of these enterprises. *Commerzbank* employees claimed that *Deutsche Bank* enjoyed an unfair competitive advantage by virtue of its close relationship with the *THA* and with *THA* enterprises.[106]

*The handling of THA liquidity loans*

In the first year of operations, *Deutsche* and *Dresdner Bank's* dominant position with liquidity loans prompted other banks – led by *Commerzbank* – to write a letter to the *THA* to try to spread loans more broadly.[107] Whether the *THA* responded to this request is not clear, but other banks did gain a greater share of liquidity loans over time. *Commerzbank* even developed a task force with the objective of increasing its share of liquidity loans. Unfortunately, however, not only the

*Table* 5.8 'Approved'[a] liquidity loan levels of the Big Banks, 1990–3

| | *Deutsche Bank* | | *Commerzbank* | | *Dresdner Bank* | | |
|---|---|---|---|---|---|---|---|
| | *Credits (DM mn)* | *% of total* | *Credits (DM mn)* | *% of total* | *Credits (DM mn)* | *% of total* | *Total (DM mn)* |
| 1 August 1990[a] | 5 050 255 | *49* | 193 397 | 2 | 2 911 889 | 28 | 10 249 767 |
| 31 December 1990[a] | 13 466 000 | 46 | 1 276 000 | 4 | 7 685 000 | 26 | 29 329 500 |
| 31 December 1991[b] | 11 000 000 | – | 1 500 000 | – | 6 500 000 | – | 25 000 000 (estimate) |
| 31 December 1992 | 8 774 600 | 46 | 1 627 500 | 9 | 5 293 100 | 28 | 18 888 100 |
| *31 December 1993* | 3 330 200 | *30* | 1·114 400 | *10* | 2 093 900 | *19* | 11 026 200 |
| Average %[c] | | 44 | | 6 | | 26 | |

*Notes*:

[a] All above figures are for approved liquidity credits, and do not represent those which were actually disbursed (*Inanspruchname*). The data represent (flow) values of approved liquidity loans in the year ending on the date specified.

Based on consolidated figures for: *Deutsche Bank* (*Deutsche Bank/Kreditbank AG* and *Deutsche Bank Berlin AG*); *Dresdner Bank* (*Dresdner Bank AG, Dresdner Bank/Kreditbank AG* and *Dresdner Bank Berlin AG*); and *Commerzbank* (*Commerzbank AG* and *Berliner Commerzbank*). The reason for the separate organisations is that the banks had not yet consolidated their Berlin subsidiaries which were created in the postwar period to comply with regulations that the Big Banks could not extend branch networks into Berlin (Edwards and Fischer, 1994, p. 102, note 4).

[b] Data unavailable for 1991. The estimate of total liquidity loans for the year comes from a *THA* presentation (Hornef, 1994*a*) and the division between banks based on the four-year average.

[c] A weighted average based on the years for which data exists.

*Source*: *THA* internal data; own calculations.

levels of liquidity loans declined, but also the margins on them. The bulk of the profits initially available in this area went to *Deutsche Bank* and *Dresdner Bank* (Table 5.8).[108]

According to the *THA*, bank margins on liquidity loans were quite high (approximately 3 per cent) in the first one and a half years after GEMSU, but then declined in 1992 and 1993 (to approximately 1.5 per cent). At these rates, the loans were a large source of risk-free revenues, and with little work. Based on actual figures for loans paid out and based on estimates, we find that *Deutsche Bank's* total interest income from liquidity loans for 1990–3 was approximately DM 540 000 mn.[109]

The actual amount of credits taken up ('paid out') rose gradually over time as a percentage of those approved (Table 5.9), more because of *a fall in the level of approvals* rather than *an (absolute) rise in credits paid out*. A possible reason for this was that the *THA* learned how to adjust more appropriate levels and, in addition, changed from its somewhat indiscriminate policy of giving blanket guarantees to all enterprises (*Globalbürgschaften*) to more tailored guarantees on a company-by-company basis (*Einzelbürgschaften*) (see Table 5.3).

*Deutsche Bank's* head start in the competitive race in the East did not translate into permanent gains. Between 1991 and 1993, *Commerzbank* improved its position. In terms of credit volume, *Commerzbank* made only 19 per cent of *Deutsche Bank's* volume in the first year after GEMSU, but raised this to 37 per cent of *Deutsche Bank's* by 1994.[110] At the same time, *Commerzbank* judged itself more profitable than *Deutsche Bank*, largely owing to its lower cost base, particularly in terms of human resources.[111] *Commerzbank* had only one-ninth of *Deutsche Bank's* 9000 or more employees in its network in the East in the first year after GEMSU,[112] and still had only one-fifth in 1994 (Table 5.10). In addition, by 1994 it had invested less than one-tenth as much in its network. Given that its lending volume was roughly a third of *Deutsche Bank's*, it is likely that its cost per unit of business was lower.

Given the nature and obscurity of the data available, however, measuring profitability is a tremendous task. Various sources have published conflicting reports. Some claimed that *Deutsche Bank* was profitable in its first year of operations.[113] But in April 1994, *Deutsche Bank* board member Georg Krupp stated that (despite its high levels of investment in the East) *Deutsche Bank* had yet to realise any profits.[114]

Perhaps more important than short-term profitability, *Deutsche Bank's* reliance on liquidity lending represented a *lost opportunity to learn to lend in the East*. While banks were meant to screen all loan

*Table* 5.9 'Paid-out' liquidity loans handled by the Big Banks, 1990–3[a]

| | *Deutsche Bank* | | *Commerzbank* | | *Dresdner Bank* | |
|---|---|---|---|---|---|---|
| | *% of loans paid out* | *Total paid out (DM mn)* | *% of loans paid out* | *Total paid out (DM mn)* | *% of loans paid out* | *Total paid out (DM mn)* |
| 31 December 1990[b] | 46 | 6 347 000 | 65 | 831 000 | 68 | 5 200 000 |
| 31 December 1991 (est.)[c] | 61 | 6 710 000 | 78 | 1 170 000 | 73 | 4 745 000 |
| 31 December 1992. | 77 | 6 735 800 | 91 | 1 486 900 | 79 | 4 186 200 |
| 31 December 1993 (est.)[c] | 93 | 3 097 086 | 100 | 1 114 400 | 84 | 1 758 876 |

*Notes*:

[a] Data for 1991 and 1993 are not available. The data represents (flow) values of liquidity loans paid out (*Inanspruchname*) in the year ending on the date specified.

[b] Based on weighted averages for the banks: *Deutsche Bank* (*Deutsche Bank/Kreditbank AG* and *Deutsche Bank Berlin AG*); *Dresdner Bank* (*Dresdner Bank AG, Dresdner Bank/Kreditbank AG* and *Dresdner Bank Berlin AG*); and *Commerzbank* (*Commerzbank AG* and *Berliner Commerzbank*).

[c] No data exist for these years. Estimates assuming that the banks increased their percentage of 'paid-out' loans in proportion to the existing figures of 1990 and 1992. For 1991, since there are no figures for 'approved' liquidity loans, the estimate is based on the average for the bank over the 1990–3 period as a percentage of the DM 25 000 mn estimate for the year.

*Source*: *THA* internal data, own calculations.

*Table* 5.10 Profile of *Deutsche Bank* and *Commerzbank* activities in the East, 1990–4

| | *Deutsche Bank*[a] | *Commerzbank*[b] |
|---|---|---|
| *Credit volume* (DM mn) | 21 724 | 8 000 |
| *Deposits* (DM mn) | 27 400 | – |
| *Customers* | 1 536 000 | 300 000 |
| of which | | |
| Corporate | 44 000 | – |
| Self-Employed | 117 000 | – |
| *Risk level* (per cent) | 88.7[e] | 80 |
| *Employees* | 8 563 | 1 800 |
| *Branches*[d] | 303 | 120 |
| *Level of investment* (DM mn) | 4 000[f] (approx.) | 300 |

*Notes*:
[a] The *Deutsche Bank* network in the East is run through two regional head offices (*Hauptfiliale*) in Berlin and Leipzig. The aggregate figures presented represent the Berlin (as of 24 September 1994) and Leipzig (as of April–May 1994) regions. It is not clear whether the figures include East Berlin, but likely that they do because they correspond to the proportions of branches (between the regions). The breakdown is as follows: Credit volume– Berlin (13 424), Leipzig (8300); Deposits–Berlin (18 000), Leipzig (9400); Customers–Berlin (935 000), Leipzig (601 000); Corporate customers–Berlin (26 000), Leipzig (18 000); Self-employed customers–Berlin (71 000), Leipzig (46 000); Employees–Berlin (4900), Leipzig (3663); and Branches–Berlin (152), Leipzig (151).
[b] The *Commerzbank* network is also run in a regional structure (Berlin and Leipzig), but no disaggregated data are available. All figures are as of 6 September 1994 unless otherwise noted and are taken primarily from the press conference given by the bank's Chairman, Martin Kohlhaussen, in Leipzig (6 September 1994).
[c] Berlin region only.
[d] Not including branches in West Berlin.
[e] Berlin region only. The risk level is the percentage of total loans which the bank has outstanding at its own risk.
[f] Krupp (1994*a*, p. 2).
[g] As of end-1993.
– = not available.
*Source*: *Deutsche Bank* internal data; *Commerzbank* 1993, *Annual Report*; various press conferences and speeches; other reports; own calculations.

applications, the usual liquidity credit application contained little more than the phrase: 'has the *THA* guarantee'.[115] Some screening and monitoring was done to evaluate the enterprises' creditworthiness and prepare for the time when the guarantees would no longer be available.

Through this analysis, *Deutsche Bank* estimated that between 8–10 per cent of the *THA* enterprise portfolio was potentially viable.[116] While it is unclear to what extent *THA*-guaranteed enterprises were screened and monitored, it is likely that they were not screened and monitored as carefully as they would have been without the guarantees.[117] Further, a significant share of *Deutsche Bank's* portfolio was made up of these loans, evidenced in a comparison of overall lending (Table 5.10) and 'paid-out' liquidity credits (Table 5.9).

The lost opportunity of learning in credit assessment in the East gradually took on greater importance as the banking market became more competitive. In the Berlin region, the risk level for *Deutsche Bank* was 66 per cent in 1992, 76 per cent in 1993 and 88.7 per cent in 1994.[118] The increase in own-risk lending was due partly to an increase in non-guaranteed credits, but was also the result of shrinkage in the loan portfolio due to a decrease in *THA* enterprises. That is to say, the *relative* increase in own-risk lending is partly the result of an *absolute* decrease in the portfolio. In the Leipzig region, for instance, the number of *Deutsche Bank* enterprise customers which had increased to 11 000 in the last six months of 1990, 16 000 in 1991 and 17 500 in 1992, grew only to 18 000 in 1993 and in the first quarter of 1994 fell back to 17 750.[119] As *Deutsche Bank* tried to find new customers, the risk level began to increase and NPLs became more apparent. In 1993, *Deutsche Bank's* bad-debt provision ratio of 7 per cent was more than twice that in West Germany (3.4 per cent).[120]

As *Deutsche Bank* saw its portfolio decrease and the banking market for enterprise customers become more competitive, it increased its involvement with small, primarily East German Management buy-outs (MBOs). This was a fruitful way of developing relationships with East German *Mittelstand* alongside its large *THA* portfolio. By January 1991, the bank had lent DM 400 mn to customers starting new businesses in addition to DM 7–8 bn in *THA*-guaranteed liquidity loans.[121] Of the approximately 2000 MBOs in the East in May 1993, one-quarter were said to be *Deutsche Bank* customers.[122] By November 1993, the bank claimed to have loaned approximately DM 700 mn to them.[123] Unlike *Commerzbank*, *Deutsche Bank* was also active in providing venture capital in the East via *Deutsche Beteiligungsgesellschaft* and *Deutsche Industrie Holding*.[124]

By this time, however, *Deutsche Bank's* ability to expand its lending to the *Mittelstand* appears to have reached its limit. According to *Deutsche Bank* Director Herbert Zapp, more generous lending would not be fair to shareholders or depositors and would not, moreover, be appropriate towards 'inexperienced' borrowers.[125] By 1995, the loan credit risk in the East was said to be several times higher than in West Germany, so that 'the scope for lending is exhausted. Any more would be irresponsible'.[126] In short, *Deutsche Bank* tried to diversify its portfolio by taking on risky MBOs only to find that the risks involved quickly became excessive.

*Commerzbank* – along with most other West German banks – had to build a portfolio of predominantly private enterprises from the start, and seems thereby to have acquired an underlying advantage over *Deutsche Bank*. That is to say, it acquired customers which would remain creditworthy without guarantees and, at the same time, learned to screen and monitor loans in the East, where conditions were very different from West Germany. In short, *Commerzbank's* strategy was more appropriate for the longer term. In the words of a *Commerzbank* board member responsible for East Germany, Axel von Ruedorffer, 'We are targeting our corporate activities at those firms which promise a long-term relationship'.[127] Even so, it encountered difficulties as it tried to expand its loan portfolio. Klaus von der Hyde of *Commerzbank* complained that 'our bad loans are three times higher than in the west. We have made a lot of mistakes, lending money to people we shouldn't have'.[128]

### Lessons from the case studies

Contrasting strategies by individual banks did not, in short, lead to markedly different performance. Several problem areas seem to have been common to West German banks.[129] First, even though *Deutsche Bank's* early entry through acquisition enabled it to avoid the severe staffing problems experienced by *Commerzbank*,[130] both banks faced a lack of qualified staff in the East, loan officers especially (see Chapter 6). Second, both banks faced constraints on their local deposit base, owing to the continued hold by the Saving Banks over local deposits. Third, while the foregoing problems were more acute for *Commerzbank*, the problem for *Deutsche Bank* was that its early reliance on *THA* liquidity loans made it more difficult for the bank to build its portfolio as these were withdrawn by the *THA*. The liquidity loans represented – in Deutsche's words – a 'learning pathology'.

## The borrowers' perspective

Investment levels in the East rose rapidly after GEMSU, largely a result of West German enterprises shifting their investment there. Gross capital investment *per capita* in the East as a percentage of West German levels rose from 65.8 per cent in 1991, to 88.8 per cent in 1992, and 113.9 per cent in 1993.[131] This might suggest that the high levels of financial flows in the GRMF were adequate for reconstruction. Without even considering bank loans, the *Bundesbank* asserts that

> if one considers the entire range of economic assistance provided by the central, regional and local authorities (including the special funds, the public promotional banks, and the Treuhand agency), then one cannot but infer that it was not the financing which presented a bottleneck to the reconstruction of the East German economy.[132]

Carlin and Mayer similarly argue that

> it would be wrong to conclude that the *availability* of finance is the constraint on the development of East German enterprises[133] (emphasis in original).

**Financing problems**

Surveys on borrowers in the East, however, suggest that many have experienced financing problems. The importance attached to the development of the *Mittelstand* in the East has provided the basis for many studies and surveys that have been conducted to identify obstacles faced by enterprises in the East, *Mittelstand* especially. Two specially noteworthy studies are a survey by the Association of German Industry (*Bundesverband der deutschen Industrie (BDI)*) and an internal study for the Federal Ministry of Economics (*Bundesministerium für Wirtschaft (BMWi)*) undertaken by the *ífo Institut für Wirtschaftsforschung* (Munich) and *Institut für Wirtschaftsforschung Halle*. The *BDI* survey was conducted in December 1993/January 1994 among *Mittelstand* in the East, and there were over 1000 responses.[134] Approximately three-quarters of these claimed that banks were more cautious (*zurückhaltend*) in East than in West Germany. The study for the *BMWi* was carried out by two teams of academics from the institutes involved through a series of mail and phone surveys and an analysis of the existing data.[135]

The lack of financing appears to be a particular problem which affects only some borrowers. In other words, the non-financial sector structure is segmented, with lending being *spread unequally across industries and enterprises*. The result is that aggregate measures of financial flows may mask existing inequalities in allocation. In the following sub-sections we survey this issue in more detail, making use of the existing studies on

East German borrowers. We argue that borrower segmentation occurs by industry, borrower size and ownership origin, with manufacturing enterprises, especially those that are small and East German-owned, experiencing the most difficulties in securing financing.

*Segmentation by industry*

East Germany's economy after GEMSU suffered deindustrialisation[136] (see Chapter 4). For manufacturing enterprises, poor performance led to difficulties in obtaining finance. A *Bundesbank* study of 1464 enterprise balance sheets in the East in 1992 found that manufacturing enterprises (568 in the sample) were experiencing the greatest operating difficulties and correspondingly 'comparatively difficult access to bank loans'.[137] This conclusion is consistent with the findings of a similar study of East German enterprise balance sheets conducted by the Bundesbank a year earlier, where the sample was slightly smaller (863).[138]

The data on bank lending tell the same story.[139] Total lending to manufacturing enterprises declined significantly between 1991 and 1993, in *absolute* as well as *relative* terms. As a percentage of overall loans to enterprises and self-employed persons, manufacturing loans declined from 42 per cent in March 1992 to 23 per cent in December 1993. In absolute terms, the decline was from DM 19 719 mn to 16 275 mn.[140] Among manufacturing enterprises, financing dropped particularly sharply from 1992 to 1993 for the chemical industry (24 per cent); the electronics, mechanics and optics industry (28 per cent); and the leather, textile and clothing industry (56 per cent).[141] These drops do not necessarily mean that enterprises were being denied finance. They may indicate that large drops in output led to downsizing in industry and hence a lower borrowing requirement.

Survey evidences suggests, however, that finance was not being provided to match demand in these enterprises. In the *BDI* survey, the allocation of bank credit *by industry* was emphasised, with about one-quarter of the responding enterprises claiming that they were part of a 'not eligible sphere' (*nicht förderungswürdiger Bereich*), including machine building, chemicals, timber, metals, electronics and textiles. According to the person who supervised the *BDI* survey, 'Banks put people into small boxes and characterise them'.[142] A survey of 5400 industrial enterprises conducted by the *Deutsches Institut für Wirtschaftsforschung* found that more than 50 per cent of the enterprises surveyed noted a 'lack of medium-term investment finance as a problem', although the number declined from 1992 (at 63 per cent) to 1993–4 (at 53 per cent).[143]

*Segmentation by borrower size*

Not surprisingly, large enterprises in the East have had fewer financing problems than small- and medium-sized ones.[144] A major finding of the *BMWi* study was:

> Despite the extensive range of assistance available, small- and medium-sized enterprises complain about financing problems.[145]

Of manufacturing enterprises surveyed in the study, those with less than 50 employees represented the highest percentage with financing difficulties, and were the only group which experienced an increase in the number of enterprises with financing problems in the 1991–4 period.[146] A 1992 survey found that while 63 per cent of all responding enterprises had significant financing problems, for enterprises with more than 500 employees the figure was only 37 per cent.[147] In June 1994, the *ifo Institut für Wirtschaftsforschung* telephone survey was most revealing in terms of equating enterprise size with financing problems.[148]

*Mittelstand* enterprises indicated growing problems due to a low level of own funds (see below), a shortage of liquidity, and a lack of collateral. By contrast, large enterprises indicated substantially less problems (less than half as many enterprises complained) and, moreover, demonstrated a steady downward trend in the problems indicated.[149] In May 1994, an enterprise survey revealed that these problems increase as enterprise size decreases – in terms of the number of employees (Figure 5.10).

Against these problems, while West German Commercial Bank loans to *Mittelstand* borrowers increased in the 1990–3 period in absolute terms, they hardly changed as a percentage of the overall amount of loans (Table 5.7, p.000). Furthermore, these figures may actually overstate the loans which reached *Mittelstand* borrowers since they are categorised by the size of the loan, rather than the borrower.[150]

With *KfW* funds, East German *Mittelstand* received far more on average than *Mittelstand* in West Germany. Between 1990 and 1993, *industrielle Mittelstand* in the East received 51 per cent of all investment funds refinanced by the *KfW*.[151] Seidel's analysis of industrial *Mittelstand* supported by *KfW* funds show that more *KfW* resources were directed to *Mittelstand* in East Germany than in West Germany: in the period 1990–3, in the East, 8200 of these enterprises received an average of DM 4 mn per enterprise and DM 38 100 per worker, whereas in West Germany, 7400 enterprises received an average of DM 2.7 mn per enterprise and DM 28 100 per worker.[152] Moreover, East German

*Figure* 5.10 Financing obstacles for Manufacturing enterprises in the East, May 1994

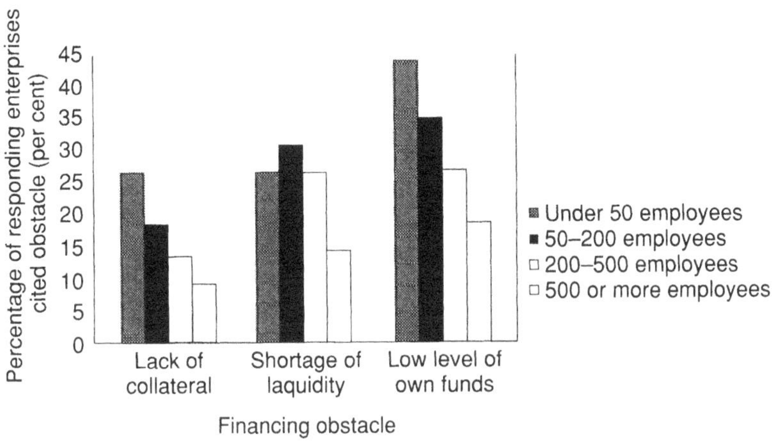


*Source*: Hummel, Ludwig *et al.* (1994, p.31).

enterprises seem to have received a high proportion of these loans.[153] This level is perhaps not surprising given that East German ownership levels of *Mittelstand* enterprises were higher than their overall ownership levels. In absolute terms, however, *KfW* loans continued to decline (Table 5.2, p. 92).

One possible result of financing patterns is a distinct deficit of *industrielle Mittelstand* in the East.[154] By the end of 1993, the East had 440 000 enterprises (compared to roughly 2 000 000 in West Germany), of which only 11 000 were *industrielle Mittelstand.*[155] These 11 000 enterprises employed 550 000 people (of a total from all *Mittelstand* enterprises of 3 000 000). This may well be the result of a lack of financing for start-ups in industry, which have received only a small fraction of the start-up development funds. (Table 5.11)

The apparent preference by banks for financing large enterprises only fuelled the political pressure on them to allocate more funds to smaller enterprises. The president of the Small- and Medium-sized Business Association, Klaus Bregger, claimed that banks were 'criminally neglecting their supervision duties and are foolishly giving undeserved preferential treatment to major customers'.[156] We may recall that one of the central aims of the GRMF was to enable the development of *Mittelstand* enterprises in the East.

*Table* 5.11 Breakdown of DtA flows to the East, by borrower type, 1990–3

| *Programme*<br>*Borrower type* | *1990* | | *1991* | | *1992* | | *1993* | | *Total* | |
|---|---|---|---|---|---|---|---|---|---|---|
| | DM mn | % of total | DM mn | % of total | DM mn | % of total | DM mn | % of total | DM mn | % of total |
| *Equity capital assistance programme* | | | | | | | | | | |
| • Crafts | 131 | 28 | 955 | 27 | 1436 | 39 | 1179 | 41 | 3701 | 33 |
| • Professions | 212 | 34 | 1095 | 37 | 568 | 19 | 383 | 17 | 2258 | 28 |
| • Industry | 10 | 1 | 97 | 1 | 217 | 3 | 323 | 5 | 647 | 3 |
| *ERP business start-up programme* | | | | | | | | | | |
| • Crafts | 797 | 33 | 1816 | 30 | 2389 | 47 | 2079 | 46 | 7081 | 37 |
| • Professions | 807 | 24 | 1474 | 36 | 124 | 5 | 104 | 4 | 2509 | 21 |
| • Industry | 61 | 1 | 188 | 1 | 332 | 3 | 440 | 5 | 1022 | 2 |

*Source*: *Bundesministerium für Wirtschaft* (published in Wieczorek, 1994). Percentages do not add up to 100 per cent because some types have been omitted (e.g. trade). The types listed are for comparative purposes.

*Segmentation by borrower ownership*

There is a link between size and ownership, since virtually all large enterprises in the East have West German owners. One member of the *Bundesbank* remarked, 'For them [subsidiaries of West German enterprises] there is no financial problem',[157] a comment which is supported by survey evidence. The *BDI* survey revealed that larger enterprises had fewer financing problems – by virtue of West German ownership or a *THA* guarantee: 'The *larger* an enterprise, the *less complicated* its application is arranged'[158] (emphasis in original). In addition, the general impression among enterprises in the *BDI* survey was that collateral demands were reduced for enterprises with 'West Germany parent enterprises'. The *BMWi* study distinguished between new (i.e. East German) investors and those that have an enterprise in the background (West German or foreign), noting that while the former face a myriad of problems, including a general lack of finance, the latter have access to short- and long-term finance and must focus primarily on the actual financing and operation of the project at hand.[159] A different survey found that enterprises owned by West Germans or foreigners experienced a lower degree of financing problems (34 per cent versus the 63 per cent average).[160]

*Investment in intangibles*

A problem in the East which has been attributed to the financial system is that East German enterprises invest proportionately less in research and development (R&D) activities than their counterparts in West Germany – based on a study of *KfW*-sponsored enterprises.[161] East German enterprises' lower investment in intangibles may signal a lack of willingness on the part of banks to invest in assets which are not recoverable if the enterprise should default on its loan commitments. Carlin and Richthofen note that

> in spite of the scale on which development bank finance is flowing to East Germany and the clear incentive characteristics of the system of screening loan applicants through commercial bank branches and local banks, there is a major concern with ability of the system to solve the funding problems of East German entrepreneurs wishing to invest in intangibles.[162]

But this behaviour may be the result of the borrower's choice rather than the bank's. First, many enterprises in the East are in the early stages of development and may out of choice be acting as suppliers to West German enterprises.[163] Second, many East German enterprises are owned by West German or foreign enterprises and the R&D investment may take place at the parent enterprise.

### Credibility of the evidence

There are certain possible biases in the surveys which should be noted. First, they may contain an over-representation of certain industries.[164] Second, borrowers who were dissatisfied with banks were more likely to have responded. Third, it is difficult for East German borrowers to make comparisons with conditions in West Germany where they have no experience. Fourth, it is not clear whether responses would have been different in West Germany, or in other countries for that matter, since borrowers can always find fault with their banks in some respect.[165] While these points suggest that we should treat the survey evidence with a degree of scepticism, the variety and sample size of the surveys suggests that there probably have been financing problems for some borrowers.

The important question, then, is why these problems exist for *Mittelstand* enterprises in the East, when it has had transplanted into it a banking system which has been widely considered as devoted to providing significant levels of financing to the *Mittelstand*.[166]

### Lack of own funds (*Eigenkapital*)

Perhaps the financing problems expressed by borrowers result from their lack of own funds. After all, West German *Mittelstand* enterprises finance a larger part of their investments through bank loans than do larger enterprises, but they still finance roughly three-quarters of their investment with internally generated funds.[167] The significance for *Mittelstand* enterprises in the East is twofold: first, a lack of own funds does not enable them – as their counterparts in West Germany – to invest with their own resources; second, a lack of own funds may be a significant obstacle to these enterprises in obtaining bank loans.[168]

Despite the perception that *Mittelstand* enterprises in the East suffer from a lack of internal funds,[169] own-fund ratios in the East have been shown to be surprisingly high. Three studies here deserve mention.[170] First, Elsser examined 1991–2 balance sheets of 909 enterprises (manufacturing, construction and services) which received *KfW* funds and found that the average level of own funds (29.7 per cent) was higher than in West Germany (17.5 per cent).[171] Second, the *Bundesbank* examined 1991–2 balance sheets of 1464 enterprises (manufacturing, construction and services) and found a lower own-fund ratio (19.3 per cent) than in the Elsser study, but nevertheless a higher level than in West Germany.[172] A further *Bundesbank* study of 1993 balance sheets of 2380 enterprises found that although own fund levels had fallen somewhat during 1991–3, 'it does not appear to be justified to talk generally ... of a sustained erosion of the capital base or of an increasing weakness of the East German enterprises' capital base'.[173]

There are several reasons why it is difficult to judge the level of own funds in a comparative context. First, West German enterprises have high levels of 'hidden reserves' – such as private pension funds.[174] Second, many enterprises in the sample are West German-owned. Third, East German enterprises may have deceptively high own-fund levels because they were cleansed of their old debts after GEMSU, bringing down their debt burden and making their low levels of own funds seem high *in relative terms*. On this view, their *absolute* own-fund levels may be insufficient to accommodate their desired investment level. These explanations must be taken seriously in light of the strong perception by the thousands of enterprises surveyed that there is an 'own-funds' problems.[175]

Another possible explanation for the high relative own-funds ratio is that it may reflect a low availability of external finance, returning us to the question of *Mittelstand* financing. In West Germany, while *Mittelstand* borrowers generally enjoy good access to finance, there may be problems for start-ups and relatively young enterprises. A 1993 *ifo Institut für Wirtschaftsforschung* (Munich) survey of 702 West German borrowers revealed that 81 per cent found that West German banks provided too little risk capital for innovation in new enterprises, and applied unduly strict conditions to new enterprises (75 per cent).[176] An important explanation for this is the high insolvency ratio among these borrowers.[177] On this view, while young borrowers represent a relatively small percentage of *Mittelstand* borrowers in West Germany,[178] they represent the vast majority of those in the East. With this in mind, we turn in Chapter 6 to an examination of why problems arose in the East for borrowers and banks alike.

## Summary

In examining financial flows to the East in the aftermath of GEMSU, it was argued that these were large, but that only a small degree of East German borrower risk was borne entirely by banks. At the same time, it emerged that lending activities followed a path of 'normalisation', with

East German banks showing significant increases in their lending levels. The experiences of two West German banks revealed that both faced difficulties in the East, albeit for somewhat different reasons. Deposit activities, however, remained dominated by East German banks, particularly the Savings Banks. Concluding the chapter from the borrowers' perspective, extensive survey evidence suggested that some borrowers appear to have experienced significant obstacles to obtaining finance, with borrower size, sector and ownership being the critical differentiating factors.

# 6
# The *Hausbank* System in the East after GEMSU

What good is a banker who cannot see at first sight from the face of his client whether or not he has got money in his pocket? (Alexander Dumas)

As a general proposition, the community believes in the banker who believes in the community. (Elbert Hubbard)

In the preceding chapters, we found that after GEMSU the banking sector in the East quickly transformed itself to resemble the one in West Germany in terms of institutional structure and infrastructure (Chapter 4). Yet alongside the rapid development – 'normalisation' – of the banking sector and bank lending activities, as well as significant levels of financial flows (Chapter 5) and other advantages present in the transition in the East (Chapter 3), many East German borrowers complained of financing difficulties (Chapter 5), and accused the banks (particularly the West German banks) of not supporting *Mittelstand* enterprises in the East. At the same time, four years after GEMSU West German banks were decreasing their loans to manufacturing enterprises – as *THA* guarantees were removed – and publicly declaring that they had to decrease their overall lending exposure to the East. While the declarations were to a certain extent politically motivated – to demonstrate that banks *intended* to develop their lending activities but were unable to do so – they signalled the difficulties banks' faced in credit assessment.

Behind these developments is the fact that the banking sector in the East developed *too well* and *too quickly*. In the first two years after GEMSU, lending activities were dominated by West German banks. As *THA* guarantees were removed, these banks expected to lend according to West German risk assessment criteria. In the words of one senior manager at *Deutsche Bank*, 'by traditional Western standards you couldn't lend any money to anybody, based on the West German banking tradition'.[1] In short, the normalisation process that was taking place in the banking sector was not paralleled by simultaneous change in the non-financial sectors of the economy. The transformed banking sector in the East needed to function within a region which, for all the West German institutions transplanted to it, was still dominated by East German managers, workers and administrators. There were discussions within *Deutsche Bank* about whether to lower credit standards in the East so as to make it easier to finance East German enterprises. The decision was made to stick to West German standards but to extend them to the 'furthest possible point' (*meistmögliche Punkt*).[2]

The purpose of this chapter is to explain why East and West German banks changed their roles over time in financing East German borrowers, and why many of these borrowers experienced financing difficulties. We argue that West German banks were unable to *measure, manage* and *price* risk for East German borrowers because of a variety of problems with the *Hausbank* system in the East. East German Savings Banks and Credit Cooperatives – traditional lenders to the Mittelstand – were, in the meantime, only gradually building their loan portfolios.

The chapter is in four sections. In the first section, we examine the concept of *risk*, and note the presence of ambiguity in its measurement. The second section discusses *risk management* and associated bank–borrower relationships. In the third section, we assess the *Hausbank* system in the East within the context of the GEMSU process, and examine why West German banks found it difficult to cope with risk in the East. The concluding section contrasts the *development of East German banks* with that of West German banks and tries to explain why the former appear to have apparently had more success in taking on East German risk.

## Risk

There is no universally agreed definition of risk. In their study on the 'risk construct', Yates and Stone observe that 'if we were to read 10 different articles or books about risk, we should not be surprised to see risk described in 10 different ways'.[3] Risk is often defined as simply 'the possibility of loss'. Steil, however, emphasises that risk must be defined more quantitatively as a 'measure of the likelihood and magnitude of *unanticipated changes*'[4] (emphasis in original). In our argument, risk involves *measurement*, both of the probability of unanticipated changes and of the loss that will occur as a result of them.

In his seminal study, Knight formalised the distinction between risk and uncertainty:

> To preserve the distinction ... between the measurable uncertainty and an unmeasurable one we may use the term 'risk' to designate the former and the term 'uncertainty' for the latter.[5]

When we talk of 'attitudes to risk', then, we are referring to those founded upon some basis for measurement. Luce and Raiffa refer to completely measurable risk as 'objectivity', and to unmeasurable risk as 'ignorance'.[6] A simple example of objectivity is tossing a fair die which has a one-in-six chance of turning to the number four. An example of ignorance is trying to guess the colour of an object which cannot be seen. Between the two extremes of completely measurable risk (objectivity) and completely unmeasurable risk (ignorance), there is a range of situations in which risk can be measured to a certain extent (Figure 6.1). This range has been designated by Ellsberg as *ambiguity*.[7]

The distinction between ignorance and objectivity has not featured prominently in the literature on decision theory. *Expected-utility theory* (EU) assumes that probabilities of outcomes are known, while *subjective expected utility* (SEU) assumes that probabilities are not necessarily objectively known, but that actors operate *as if* they were.[8] We are less interested, however, in whether actors act as if they know the probability of an outcome, than in whether they behave differently when they are better able to measure the probability. In other words, we are interested in what Ellsberg termed 'ambiguity avoidance', or whether actors avoid decisions which are harder to objectify.

*Figure* 6.1 Levels of uncertainty

*Source*: Yates and Stone (1992, p.15).

## Ambiguity avoidance

There is evidence that behavioural patterns are affected by an actor's ability to measure a situation. March and Shapira cite survey and interview data to support the view that 'managers see risk in ways that are both less precise and different from risk as it appears in decision theory'.[9] Empirical studies on managers, particularly in the insurance sector, reveal clear preferences by actors to take on risks which are measurable to some degree as opposed to those which are not.[10] A series of studies on insurers found a preference for avoiding risks that are most uncertain – i.e. ambiguity avoidance.[11] Shapira found that managers 'make a sharp distinction between *gambling* (where it is impossible to learn anything to reduce uncertainty) and *risk taking* (where skill or information can reduce uncertainty)'.[12] It has also been argued that managers hope to do better than a 'fair bet' (i.e. objectivity) by applying their specialist knowledge to a situation: 'Executives' remarks about the reducibility of uncertainty suggest that levels of uncertainty beyond objectivity should be acknowledged'.[13] These levels have been called 'prescience' (Figure 6.1). There also appears to be a normative element involved, where 'good' managers are seen as taking risks but not gambling, suggesting that it is more respectable in society to take informed risks than to be seen as gambling.[14]

## Risk in banking

In banking, although some risks can be measured with more precision than others, all risks must be *objectified* for the purpose of carrying out credit analysis and pricing loans. Objectification of risk allows consistency across lending officers and locations and also enables the bank to control the credit process in these locations through guidelines from the head office. There may also be an element of ambiguity avoidance involved, whereby bankers feel more comfortable taking on lending risks that seem measured. Bankers generally objectify risks through a rating system that ranks prospective borrowers in terms of risk categories. There are various types of risks, including credit risk, interest rate risk, liquidity risk and foreign exchange risk. In this book we are most concerned with *credit risk*, or default risk, which Wood defines as:

> the degree to which a lender's entitlement ... may be impaired by the non-performance of the counterparty. Measurement of default risk is therefore important to a lender because it affects loan profitability of particular loans[15]

Credit risk can be further decomposed into *specific risk factors,* which affect the particular borrower in question, and *systemic risk factors,* which affect all borrowers in the economy. Risk ratings – measures of risk – cover a broad spectrum of potential credit risks, ranging from insignificant to enormous. In some cases, at least in theory, lending may involve zero or near-zero (credit) risk – e.g. government securities. Banks charge a *risk premium* in the price of the loan to offset the risk of the loan not being repaid, as well as an *intermediation margin* which covers the costs associated with processing the loan, such as information gathering, and return on capital. Taken together, these contribute to the overall price of the loan. (Figure 6.2) By the 'price of the loan' we mean the interest rate, although the price may also include some fees or other expenses which are incorporated into the loan contract.

While our framework is highly simplified, it is meant to show that banks' lending depends both on the costs to the bank and the (measured) risk of the loan in question.[16]

In order to set the price of the loan and determine its conditions, a bank must perform two crucial functions: screening and monitoring. *Screening* is the process of evaluating the borrower – and thus objectifying the risks of lending to it – before actually giving the loan. *Monitoring* is the process of ensuring that the borrower uses the funds according to the terms of the loan contract, and that it repays the loan as agreed. To screen and monitor loans effectively, banks must have adequate *information,* as well as *enforcement* mechanisms to recover loans in the event that the borrower is unwilling or unable to pay.

*Figure* 6.2 Simplified model of the components of the price of a loan

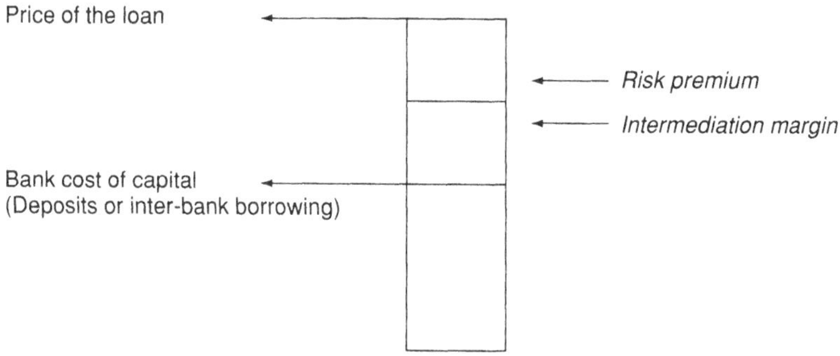

## Informational asymmetries and enforcement mechanisms

In order to assess the risk premium for any borrower the bank needs sufficient information concerning the borrower.[17] Information is imperfect, costly, and subject to asymmetries – i.e. the borrower has more information on its situation than the bank. The bank, therefore, needs to make a trade-off between gathering additional information, which is costly but reduces ambiguity, and minimising information costs but operating under a higher level of ambiguity. In general, *quantitative* information is less costly to obtain, measured in terms of the bank's time commitment, than is *qualitative* information. An example of the latter might be an evaluation of the quality of the management of the borrower in question, or even a feeling based on the borrower's demeanour.[18]

As a result of informational asymmetries, and the costs associated with overcoming them, banks often require assets which are used as *collateral* or *security* for a loan to reduce their losses in the event the borrower does not pay back the loan. In a system where enforcement is perfect – i.e. where banks can seize and market the assets they have accepted as collateral in all cases and without transaction costs, such as legal fees – credit risk can be reduced to zero by requiring collateral to the full value of each loan. But many borrowers cannot provide collateral to the full value of their borrowing requirements. Hence a policy of full collateralisation may limit the bank's potential to expand its loan portfolio. In addition, transaction costs make even fully collateralised loans which do not perform costly to the bank.

From the above description, we can see the importance of efficient institutions (enforcement mechanisms) for banks' lending activities. An important function of institutions is that they allow banks not only to *seize* assets in the case of default, but also to *value* assets at the time of the screening process. This function underlines the importance of a system of clearly defined property rights. In the event that information is imperfect and institutions are inefficient, the risk of a given situation may be difficult to measure – i.e. high ambiguity.

With loans that are not fully collateralised, the bank stands to lose (the loan amount or some of it) in the event of default. The possible loss is the bank's *exposure*, which Donaldson defines as:

> The maximum credit loss on a transaction, or group of transactions, on the worst possible assumptions. For a loan, this is the face amount of the loan. The concept involves no view that the worst will happen.[19]

With such loans, informational asymmetries impede a bank's ability to distinguish good credit risks from bad. As the interest rate rises, two types of problems may appear: *adverse selection*, where the pool of loan applicants may contain a higher proportion of bad credit risks since good credit risks will be discouraged to borrow; and *moral hazard*, where having received a loan, the borrower may be induced to use it for a morc risky purpose than agreed. For these reasons, as the interest rate rises, the bank's returns will not rise proportionately, and at a certain rate will begin to decline. As a result, the bank will lend up to the interest rate at which its returns are maximised and then refuse to lend at a higher rate despite the existing demand for loans. On an aggregate scale, *credit rationing* by banks means that some borrowers may be unable to secure a loan no matter the premium they are prepared to pay.[20]

## Risk management

From the above discussion, it would seem that banks can try only to measure risk, and then either accept to operate under a given level of ambiguity or refuse to. Risk (and ambiguity) is not only accepted, however, but *managed* and *reduced*. Yates and Stone describe risk handling as when

> rather than merely selecting among the options that that just happen to present themselves, the individual more aggressively tries to formulate options that reduce risks without sacrificing advantages.[21]

In other words, the individual tries to avoid 'gambling'. Champernowne offers three possible methods for reducing ambiguity: acquiring more information; influencing the probabilities of the situation; and providing insurance against the possible loss.[22] On the latter point, risk can be shifted, from banks on to the government, for example, or on to any institution which is prepared to guarantee a loan. That is, the guarantor uses its assets as security so as to allow the loan not only to be offered, but made on better terms and at a lower interest rate than it otherwise would have been.

We have been referring to individual loans, but banks can also manage risks on an aggregate level through their loan *portfolios*.[23] Not only can they avoid exposure to too many large risks, but they may also be able to choose risks which offset each other (hedging), thus making the risk of the overall portfolio less than the sum of the individual risks. The process of *diversification* is analysed in the literature on portfolio theory.[24] In theory, a bank's portfolio can be diversified sufficiently to remove specific risk entirely – by combining risks which have off-setting co-variances – and leave the portfolio risk equal to the systematic risk of the overall economy. Portfolio diversification does not, however, reduce ambiguity in the lending environment; it is a tool which allows banks to reduce individual risks *once quantified*.

**Bank–borrower relationships**

We now turn to the first two ambiguity-reducing methods mentioned above: gathering more information, and influencing the probability of the situation. These approaches come together in the screening and monitoring process of banks, and can be particularly effective when banks develop long-term relationships with borrowers.

Banks perform their screening and monitoring functions to improve the quantity and quality of information that they have on any given borrower, thereby facilitating the management of specific risk. The importance of bank–borrower relationships, however, stems not only from the provision of financial information, but also from the development of trust between bank and borrower. This may reduce ambiguity in the bank's lending decision and, therefore, allow the bank not only to price the loan more accurately, but to be more inclined to offer it. Moreover, through the relationship the bank may be able to influence the performance of the borrower (via corporate governance) so as to reduce the probability that the borrower will default on the loan. Schumpeter captures the essence of the bank–borrower relationship:

> the banker must not only know what the transaction is which he is asked to finance and how it is likely to turn out but he must also know the customer, his business and even his private habits, and get, by frequently 'talking things over with him', a clear picture of the situation.[25]

Being close to the customer is essential since loan officers may have a fair amount of discretion over 'objective' risk ratings. In many (west) European banks, 'the internal ratings often said more about the likes and dislikes of individual account officers and their superiors than about the underlying credit risks'.[26] Since Schumpeter, the bank--borrower relationship has received extensive treatment in the literature, and the specific benefits have become more formalised.

*Conceptual work on bank–borrower relationships*

Diamond focuses on the concept of banks as 'delegated monitors', whereby banks gather information on borrowers over time.[27] The process involves what Diamond calls 'delegation costs'. The result, according to Diamond, is that 'there is a "life-cycle" effect in the use of borrowing through intermediaries'.[28] That is to say, a credit record is established over time which at first serves to facilitate bank lending and which ultimately makes it more possible for the firm to borrow directly from capital markets. In a similar vein, Fama argues that over the course of the bank–borrower relationship 'inside information' is generated which – in our terminology – reduces the level of ambiguity in the lending decision.[29]

Within the bank–borrower relationship, 'implicit contracts' are drawn between bank and borrower. The bank knows that it has a creditworthy customer and the borrower that it can generate more favourable conditions over time as a result.[30] Von Thadden suggests on an *a priori* basis that

> if banks engage actively in monitoring, their clients will be less liquidity constrained in times of financial distress, as long as their substance justifies continued bank assistance.[31]

An additional incentive for the bank is that the initial screening costs are an investment into the lending relationship, a 'relationship-specific' investment which is lost if the borrower moves to another bank.[32] According to Binks, Ennew and Reed:

> The collection of information over and above simple descriptive statistics causes a discrete and disproportionately large rise in costs to the financial institution concerned because the assessment of more qualitative aspects such as management skills is more time consuming to perform and requires a much higher level of investment in the training of those undertaking the evaluation.[33]

Overall, then, theoretical arguments hold that banks and borrowers benefit from long-term relationships between them. Banks gain a creditworthy customer, continue to benefit through reduced screening and monitoring costs, and moreover *learn* over the course of the relationship so that lending conditions can be optimally set over time. Borrowers gain increased availability of finance – and are less liquidity-constrained as a result – and also lower borrowing costs, in addition to building their reputations (and corresponding creditworthiness).[34] In addition, they are less constrained in their borrowing by the collateral they are able to offer. Potentially, both banks and borrowers can gain through consultation whereby the bank advises the borrower on specific or more general business decisions. Moreover, it enables the bank to *influence* the borrower's performance. An additional benefit to banks which should not be overlooked is that relationships allow banks to cross-sell their products, so that they can earn profits from the borrowers' cash management and other fee-related services – i.e. the German concept of *Allfinanz*.[35]

*Empirical work on bank–borrower relationships*

These theoretical arguments have received empirical support. Berger and Udell examined a sample of 3400 small businesses in the United States and found that 'borrowers with longer banking relationships pay lower interest rates and are less likely to pledge collateral'.[36] Peterson and Rajan examined the same firm sample and found that

> the availability of finance from institutions increases as the firm spends more time in a relationship, as it increases ties to a lender by expanding the number of financial services it buys from it, and as it concentrates its borrowing with the lender.[37]

In Japan, several studies suggest similar findings. According to Corbett, close bank–borrower relations allow the parties to communicate and adjust the terms of the loan contract in a manner beneficial to both.[38] Fukada and Hirota find that Japanese firms with so-called 'main bank' relationships have greater financing available.[39] Hoshi, Kashyap and Scharfstein conclude that Japanese firms with strong ties to a main bank, and those that are members of industrial groups, perform better – invest and sell more – after the onset of financial distress than those which lack these relationships.[40]

## The German *Hausbank* system

The German *Hausbank* system is widely regarded as the leading example of close bank–borrower relationships.[41] Nevertheless, the author's interviews with bankers revealed a lack of consensus on what exactly it means. Is it based on the *institutional levers of control* which banks have over public companies, as Edwards and Fischer define it? Does it more narrowly refer to the '*filter function*' performed by banks in administering state support?[42] Does it depend on the *length of time* of the bank–borrower relationship? Does it imply that the relationship is *exclusive*? In interviews, many bankers noted that it is rare for an enterprise to work with a single bank. The more common arrangement is a *Hausbank*, perhaps two, which works with other banks (*Nebenbanken*) that handle less of the borrower's financing needs.[43]

The definition of the term is not straightforward, and it certainly contains different meanings depending on whether we refer to *Mittelstand* or to large enterprises. For the *Mittelstand*, Quack and Hildebrandt describe the system in the following manner:

> In the German 'Hausbank' relation, SMEs give priority to one bank which runs the core of their banking business, banks give priority to their 'Hausbank' customers, the relationship is long-term, stable and regarded as a partnership.[44]

In Germany, most attention has focused on long-standing relationships between Big Banks and big enterprises (*Aktiengesellschaften* AGs), empirical studies suggesting that such relationships have benefited both parties.[45] Relationships between banks and smaller-sized borrowers have been less investigated. Mullineux found empirical support for the importance of relationships between banks and *Mittelstand* enterprises in West Germany.[46] His interviews with German bankers were summarised as follows:

> The importance of relationship banking was repeatedly emphasised by the German participants. It benefited the banks by improving their loan screening and monitoring capabilities and generated numerous additional opportunities to provide service and earn fees as enterprises matured and grew. It also allowed them to build data bases which could be used, for example, to identify business areas and even potential clients that they should target in order to raise profitability and to guide bad debt provisioning.[47]

One could argue that relationships are more critical for banks when financing small and medium-sized enterprises because some of the traditional institutional control levers which banks use to exert control over large firms do not exist, and there is little – if any – public information available.

Given that banks do not possess the same degree of control through formal institutional levers *vis-à-vis Mittelstand* enterprises as with *Aktiengesellschaften*, the trust in the relationship takes on added importance. Gröschel suggests that a key component in building relationships and maintaining them is in the provision of 'trust capital' (*Vertrauenskapital*).[48] Similarly, Mullineux:

> By managing accounts of family members from childhood, trust was built up leading to a willingness on the part of banks to look at proposals, offer advice and structure finance appropriately to take account of the whole financial situation of the borrower.[49]

And *Deutsche Bank* Chairman Hilmar Kopper

> For us, the trust built up over the years between bank and customer is the basis for doing business. It establishes links which, as a rule, last even in hard times for customers.[50]

State-support mechanisms in the West German social market economy act as a catalyst to help bank–borrower relationships develop. They do so by providing refinancing mechanisms (which remove interest rate risk from loans), and guarantees (which remove credit risk from loans) to enable enterprises without collateral to initiate relationships with banks. We have referred to this state function as providing 'seed money' for *Mittelstand* enterprises, since Specialised Bank loans must be accompanied by (own-) bank loans to meet the financing needs of the enterprise. Over time, relationships are developed which allow bank and borrower to be less dependent on state assistance – financial or otherwise.[51]

## The *Hausbank* system in the East

Despite the apparent benefits, the *Hausbank* system failed to develop in the East in the early years after GEMSU. This was for several reasons.

### Difficulties in risk measurement in the East

Some bankers estimated lending risk in the East at four to five times greater than in West Germany.[52] A study by one of the Big Banks reportedly put the difference as high as seven times.[53] Not surprisingly, many bankers commented that it was difficult to say precisely how much riskier it is to lend in the East.[54]

While the problem affected East and West German banks alike, the latter were the main lenders after GEMSU and thus felt the difficulties most. Much of their gradual reluctance to lend stemmed from the inability to assess lending risk. In other words, West German banks exhibited 'ambiguity avoidance'. Moreover, these banks were unable to gain specialised knowledge and manage risks in the East, leaving the perception that the best they could do was gamble with loan decisions. The (West German) banks' perception was summarised by the *Bankenverband mittel- und ostdeutscher Länder*:

> The willingness of the private banks to take on risk in the new Länder is without exception higher than in West Germany. They go up to the bounds of what is justifiable. But one must consider that realistic risk assessment is inordinately difficult. The estimation of the existing risks and difficulties is more problematical than at first believed.[55]

Günther Schmidt-Weyland of *DG Bank* asserted, 'there's no way of assessing creditworthiness'.[56] Klaus von der Heyde of *Commerzbank* noted, 'People came to us with no collateral. We could only look into their blue eyes and ask ourselves: Will he make it or not?'[57]

Apart from the general uncertainty inherent in the transition process, the high level of ambiguity in the lending environment of the East stemmed from poor information. It took many months before even primitive balance sheets were available, and these in turn were frequently revised.[58] Under the *D-Markbilanzgesetz*, East German enterprises were given a grace period to produce balance sheets and then were allowed several years to 'update' them as their valuation methods improved.[59] As a result, enterprise data could not be compared from year-to-year. In West Germany most banks require a minimum of three years of balance sheets from a business in order to begin making loans to it.[60] In the East, without a business 'history', many bankers felt they were, or would be, lending 'blindly'.[61]

Griffin examined the information problems facing West German banks after GEMSU, arguing that the privatisation process 'favoured institutions that could provide certain information difficult for the big banks to obtain'.[62] His main conclusion was that East German enterprises were not established enterprises as such, but rather collections of assets which needed to be valued in strategic terms.[63] As a result, the *THA* relied on a

> complex network of East and West German managers, consultants, investment banks, accounting firms, buyers, and politicians that made an accelerated pace of information sharing and deal making possible.[64]

The information-gathering process, then, placed West German banks at a distance from enterprises, lending in the first two years after GEMSU typically through *THA* guarantees. This *distancing* process was reinforced by the banks' heavy reliance on third parties – primarily consulting firms – for financial information.[65]

*The problem of asset valuation*

Asset valuation was particularly important for West German banks. Like many other banks they prefer to base lending on asset valuations rather than on cash-flow projections.[66] According to both *BDI* and *BMWi* surveys, a major problem facing East German enterprises was the provision of collateral to obtain loans, with complaints that banks were requiring multiple forms of collateral (*Mehrfachbesicherung*).[67] The most frequently mentioned factor in the author's interviews with bankers was the lack of 'security' (*Sicherheit*), and its impact on lending. Perhaps for this reason banks were especially reluctant to finance investments in intangible assets by East Germans, as we noted in Chapter 5.

Banks focused on property as collateral, but the problems of restitution claims (see Chapter 4), together with the difficulty of valuing property in the absence of an established real estate market,[68] meant that banks were unable to measure (quantify) risks to their satisfaction. One important reason for the slow development of the housing market was the need to reschedule housing loans made under the GDR regime and outstanding after GEMSU – a striking incidence of the 'interconnectedness' of the implementation process in the East and its impact on banking behaviour. Another factor was the problem of assigning property rights. Griffin argues that restitution problems were particularly troublesome for banks since land was the one asset they had confidence in valuing consistently.[69] The German Bankers' Association, monitoring the banking environment in the East through a series of bank surveys in the period 1992–4, found *unsettled ownership issues* to be the most significant obstacle in the East both to general economic activity and to banking activity in particular. Two-thirds of participating banks described this obstacle as 'very serious' in each year from 1992 to 1994.[70]

*The role of institutions in screening and monitoring*

Institutions in the social market economy play a larger role in the screening and monitoring process than simply establishing and valuing property rights. The German government plays an important enabling role in the provision of finance to the *Mittelstand*. According to Mullineux:

> Government support for *Mittelstand* financing is primarily through the funding of loan guarantees and the provision of implicitly subsidised medium- to long-term loans. However, the government also provides: generous investment and depreciation allowances; export guarantees; and, *financial assistance for establishing data bases and providing information, training and consultancy to SMEs*[71] (emphasis added).

This information and assistance is provided through the institutions of the social market economy. These function as a complete system which enables lending to occur through mechanisms which help both borrowers and banks in (overcoming ambiguity in) the lending process, thus reducing the corresponding costs.[72] For loans that receive guarantees from the *Bürgschaftsbanken*, Harm observes:

> Although monitoring the loan during its life is the responsibility of the (handling) bank, it is often mentioned that the detailed advisory efforts prior to the business inception ultimately lead to the relatively low failure rate of 2 per cent in the credit guarantee institutions' (*Bürgschaftsbanken*) loan portfolios. To the extent that banks rely on chambers [of commerce] and guilds to provide consulting services to the entrepreneur, the bank actually exploits an externality.[73]

In West Germany, all start-ups must obtain an official letter from either the local Chamber of Commerce and Industry (or Chamber of Artisans) stating that the venture is viable and that the qualifications of the owner are satisfactory.[74] Of course, the importance of a 'network' of institutional support for financing SMEs is not unique to Germany.[75]

While institutions can assist in the screening and monitoring process, in East Germany after GEMSU, the (overnight) transplant of West German institutions proved difficult to manage, leading to long delays in their main functions.[76] In the sections that follow, we examine the underlying reasons for the implementation problems as well as their implications.

*GEMSU as a process rather than an event*

GEMSU involved the wholesale integration of the East into the West German legal, administrative, economic and social system. The decision was made to transfer the West German constitution to East Germany through Article 23 rather than the more complex Article 146. The latter would have involved writing a new constitution for East Germany which would have been put to a popular vote, whereas the former allowed West German law to be transferred directly, with some modifications, by the East German states joining the West German Federation.[77]

The abruptness of the transplant of West German institutions imposed a *lack of flexibility* which may have actually slowed down the development of the East. Portes asserts that

> economic recovery in East Germany might have been faster if the new institutional structure had initially been simpler, less sophisticated and less demanding than that of the West.[78]

Moreover, the East needed to comply not only with West German laws and regulations, but also with those of the EC, making the transition even less flexible.[79] Severe strains were placed on eastern resources to implement the new institutional structure.

We argued in Chapter 2 that institutional change is a *gradual process*. Even though formal rules and regulations may be imposed overnight, a system needs to adjust and adapt. On this view, GEMSU should be seen as a *process* which involves learning and adjustment rather than a single *event*.[80] The latter view was expressed by Dornbusch and Wolf, for example, who declared that:

> Monetary, social, and economic union was accomplished almost by the stroke of a pen. The radical transition sent a clear signal that the break with the past was both complete and irreversible, thus setting the basis for rapid restructuring.[81]

This view only focuses on the formal institutional transplant and ignores the long adjustment process, whereby *implementation* occurs.

The impact of more than forty years of socialism on the people of East Germany is difficult to measure.[82] Comparisons are often drawn between the task of transforming East Germany and that of reconstructing West Germany after 1948; indeed, the basis for the GRMF was that the social market economy had worked so well in postwar West German reconstruction (see Chapter 4). Offe suggests that the current task is the more difficult.[83] The postwar period involved the replacement only of what he terms 'institutional hardware', – i.e. the destruction caused by the war created the need to rebuild the infrastructure and much of the physical basis of industry. Though some hardware problems exist, the reconstruction of East Germany primarily involves the development of 'institutional software', – i.e. the creation of new institutions and attitudes and – at the same time – the destruction of old patterns of behaviour. In the immediate postwar years, he argues, 'Capital just happened to be partially destroyed as a *physical* entity, not capital*ism* as an institutional reality'.[84] (emphasis in original). In short, there is a contrast between the reconstruction tasks, one involving the *continuity* of a system and its rebuilding, the other the *discontinuity* of a system and its dismantling. Offe also emphasises the distinction between formal institutional change and informal adjustment:

> The intangible or 'software' resources – mentalities, routines, habits, modes of coping, familiarity with institutional patterns – seem to be missing that turn out to be of a surprising strategic significance as determinants of a sustained and successful process of reconstruction.[85]

In addition, while West Germans after the Second World War were sober following their defeat yet determined to rebuild their country, East Germans after GEMSU were resentful and demanding, having felt cheated by the GDR system. Thus West and East Germans had quite different expectations upon entering their respective transitions. For the latter, all improvements were measured in *relative* terms *vis-à-vis* West Germany rather than in *absolute* terms.[86] For all these reasons, difficulties arose in the implementation of GEMSU, and affected the banking sector no less severely than other parts of the economy.

Implementation problems arose due to staff shortages as well as the inability of the existing staff to work within the new institutions. Many staff involved in the old regime were excluded from the new regime for political reasons.[87] Those that were not excluded suffered from

> 'functional' disqualification, as the rules and routines, standards and legal norms according to which they are now supposed to operate are entirely new and unknown to them. As a consequence, the judicial, managerial, administrative, political and academic personnel to operate the new institutions must also to a large extent be transplanted from West Germany.[88]

Lehmbruch terms GEMSU an 'exogenous' transformation by contrast with the 'endogenous' transformation within the CIS.[89] In the latter case, local elites play the leading role in the process; in the former case senior positions go largely to outsiders.

But West German human resources were limited too, as was illustrated in the case study of Commerzbank in the East (Chapter 5). Even in West German Banks, which brought over a relatively large number of West German employees compared to other sectors, West German employees made up only 21 per cent of the total East German workforce by the end of 1993.[90] Recognition of the shortage of qualified staff by the *THA* led it to concentrate its West German human resources in-house rather than spreading them throughout management teams of the enterprises being privatised.[91] In the legal system, it was difficult to attract a large number of qualified West Germans, because salaries were much lower than in West Germany (roughly one-third the level), and living conditions were unsatisfactory by West German standards. Many of the West Germans that did go for work assignments did not stay for long. In 1991, Saxony's Minister of Justice, Steffen Heitmann, stated 'we need over 1500 jurists and at present we have about 600, of whom we'll lose a third'.[92] Merkl presented a similar account:

> Unfortunately in 1990, the entire GDR had only about 700 'independent' attorneys – West Berlin alone had 2000 – and almost no trained assessors of property or land registry personnel to straighten out all the legal complications.[93]

A major consequence was very slow progress with property restitution claims despite administrative and legal efforts to speed it up the process.[94]

Many of those interviewed commented that East Germany simply couldn't handle the legal structure that had been imposed on it, leading to long delays in virtually all administrative functions.[95] One example is the registration of new enterprises, a process which takes on average two weeks in West Germany.[96] In East Germany, the process took between six months and a year in the early years after GEMSU.[97] Implementation problems meant that banks and other institutions:

> went to great efforts to collect local data on site, introducing themselves to local business chambers, economic development associations, and other bodies; the costs of doing so were [so] high, however, that structural information deficits often remained.[98]

Carlin and Richthofen similarly observe:

> The institutional infrastructure of local chambers of commerce, industry associations and firm–firm relationships which allow a flow of information to the banks relevant to the assessment of the viability of projects is not yet effective in East Germany.[99]

West German banks even provided assistance to the East German Chambers of Commerce, suggesting the importance banks attached to the chambers' role in the *Hausbank* system,[100] but problems developed nevertheless. A central difficulty was that the chambers were staffed by East Germans who were advising other East German entrepreneurs on projects to be presented primarily to West German banks. This problem became apparent in an interview with the head of the liaison department between banks and enterprises in the chamber of commerce in Leipzig – the financial centre of the East. When asked about his background, he explained that he had worked for more than 25 years in one of the *Kombinate* (electronics) and that he 'knew' many bankers; he demonstrated the latter point by revealing a pocket electronic rolodex with a long list of phone numbers. He clearly meant 'to know' in a different sense than suggested by West German bankers; the latter used the word 'know' (*kennen*) to suggest a relationship built over time, not simply knowing a name or a telephone number.[101] In short, the (informal) institutional framework that existed in the GDR, where contacts were most important in arranging transactions cut no ice with West German banks, and the quality of advice was also low. Many aspiring entrepreneurs who were told by the chamber that their projects merited financing, found themselves rejected – often abruptly – when they visited the bank.[102]

*Problems within management in the East*

Lack of financial and other quantitative information paralleled with the lack of institutional support meant the role of East German management in liaising with banks was critical (i.e. qualitative information). Kasch, Lowenthal and Cassuto, note that 'credit analysis [in the East] is replaced by talking to management to assess the likelihood of success'.[103] Another banker recalled the situation in the East: 'You sit down and talk to the management and get a gut feeling about the company'.[104]

By most accounts, however, management was unprepared. East German managers require a prolonged learning period to adapt to the new economic system.[105] In 1991, the OECD conducted a poll of West

German enterprises operating in the East: 75 per cent of the respondents found Eastern management to be inadequate, and possessing a 'lack of dynamism, qualifications and performance'.[106] A study by Mülder and Partner management consultants assessed 250 East German managers for their suitability as management board members in West German companies.[107] The study found that only seven would qualify, the others failing for their 'lack of market knowledge, lack of confidence, lack of creativity, lack of initiative, and lack of mental flexibility'. In the *BMWi* study, surveys of banks showed that they regarded the overall qualifications of East German entrepreneurs to be a major obstacle to lending.[108] According to Wolf-Dietrich von Bothmer of *Deutsche Bank*, 'In the eastern states, because of several decades of central planning, you do not have the memory, the habit, or the continuity of an entrepreneurial/enterprise culture'.[109] Bankers noted in interviews with the author that East German managers were excellent in technical fields such as engineering, but poor on financial control and marketing. The lack of confidence by the banks was felt by East German entrepreneurs, as illustrated in the *BDI* survey: 'The trust in the lending process placed in the management and marketing qualifications of East German entrepreneurs is not very pronounced'.[110]

Correspondingly, West German ownership brought additional advantages to Eastern subsidiaries apart from financial support (i.e. internal transfers). Experienced management was the most important. It could not have been transferred on the same scale through an arrangement other than direct ownership. This advantage was unique amongst PCPEs, the others having experienced much lower levels of FDI and needing, therefore, to develop local management and technology or contract it out. Experienced and qualified management from the West could be evaluated by West German bankers, which helps to explain why these banks directed a considerable share of their lending to West German enterprises.

Even West German subsidiaries were not immune, however, to management problems within their organisations. The West Germans that came over were often not the most qualified available.[111] It was suggested that in some cases West Germans had come over to get away from something in West Germany, either of a personal or a business nature.[112] Even where the management was capable, some West German subsidiaries still experienced problems, as illustrated by Antal and Merkens:[113]

> The philosophy behind the transition is to have this subsidiary manage and be managed the same way as every West German

> subsidiary. Standardization of the corporate identity is given a high priority. In order to achieve this, the structures, processes, and criteria have been introduced that were developed in the West German corporation, with the expectation that they will automatically lead to the same mentality. Clearly, this approach cannot function as simply as expected because the East German company is not a *tabula rasa*, an empty slate upon which one can write up whatever management system one chooses. Rather, it is a living entity made up of individuals with shared past and common experiences that shape their interpretations of events and their behaviour in their organization. In requiring the employees to function in the system gradually developed, by and for other people, and under very different circumstances, the parent organization is essentially expecting its new employees to separate themselves from their own biographies and take on new identities.[114]

Banks overcame many of these problems and – perhaps more successfully than any other sector – socialised their East German employees into their organisations. The problem, however, is that the staff fluctuation involved in doing so was detrimental to relationship building with borrowers, the topic to which we next turn.

**Bank–borrower relationships in the East**

Given the informational deficiencies in the East, it would seem that *Hausbank* relationships with *Mittelstand* enterprises could have been critical in overcoming banks' reluctance to lend. According to one Commerzbank manager, the *Hausbank* system is 'more important in the East than in the West'.[115] In the words of Deeg,

> The East affords a prime opportunity to revive and further adapt the Hausbank tradition which has long been weakening in the West (even with western Mittelstand firms). Quite possibly, an even more intense form of bank–firm cooperation might develop in the East.[116]

Yet even four years after GEMSU bankers acknowledged that the *Hausbank* system is not so established in the East.[117]

We have observed that banks relied on other organisations to help bridge information shortcomings in the East. At the same time, East German borrowers turned to organisations other than banks for guidance with their business strategies.[118] Brandkamp conducted a survey of small business start-ups and found that banks were viewed as less important sources of advice than professional consultants, friends from West Germany and local chambers of commerce, with more than one-quarter of all respondents receiving no external advice at all.[119] In 1990, the *KfW* established its Berlin office[120] as an information centre for prospective borrowers, but also to assist these borrowers in understanding the loan process and the funding possibilities on offer. For the above reasons, it is thus not surprising that in the *BDI* survey East German borrowers complained of a lack of a 'customer closeness' (*Kundennähe*) shown by banks in the lending process.[121]

In the following sections, we examine three important elements in developing bank–borrower relationships (lacking in the East): time, corporate governance, and people.

*The (lack of) time in relationships*

Time is a basic and necessary component of building relationships. It is needed to gather information on the borrower, and indeed for the borrower to build its own 'history'.[122] The point was made in many interviews that three or four years (after GEMSU) was insufficient to develop bank–borrower relationships. Bankers noted that in West Germany bank–borrower relationships have developed over more than forty years, and some over as many as eighty.

*The (lack of) corporate governance in relationships*

The institutional control levers which German banks possess *vis-à-vis* large enterprises in West Germany (Chapter 4) did not aid in relationship-building in the East because the economy consisted primarily of *Mittelstand* enterprises.[123] Banks were unable to hold proxies in East German enterprises since there were virtually no East German public companies. By 1994, there had been only two 'Initial Public Offerings' (IPOs) from the East, and one of these ended in a scandal in which the enterprise (*Sachsenmilch*) – with *Deutsche Bank* as the chief underwriter – went bankrupt shortly after going public.[124]

*The (lack of) insider status through equity holdings*

Despite the fact that they have not provided *equity* on a significant scale in West Germany, West German banks had hoped to become more active in the East immediately following GEMSU; but they quickly realised that 'very few opportunities in the East could meet the demands of Western investors'.[125] In addition, banks were unable to engage in Debt-for-Equity Swaps – which account for much of the bank-owned equity in West Germany[126] – because the DKB took over the responsibility for the old loans. Banks also had a further disincentive to take equity stakes in the East. According to the German law on limited liability companies (*GMbHs*) – which represented the majority of enterprises in the East – bank loans to an enterprise in which the bank holds an equity stake are treated as equity in the event of a bankruptcy.[127] In other words, banks' equity investments in East German enterprises would downgrade the banks' lending claims – which are much higher in value – in the pecking order of potential claimants on enterprise assets.

At the same time, the low amount of venture capital[128] – in contrast to loans and transfers – was possibly a reflection of the *THA*'s privatisation design:

> Concerning the point you raised that there seems to be a significant lack of venture capital in Eastern Germany as a result of a shortcoming of the German banking system, we can not fully support this argument. From the more than 1100 privatisations Roland Berger & Partner have successfully concluded on behalf of the German Treuhandanstalt, we know that the Treuhandanstalt is reluctant to sell companies to venture funds, and rather prefers to sell its companies to strategic investors exclusively.[129]

The *THA*'s approach was intended to bring committed owners to the East and – equally important – to transfer technology and knowhow (i.e. management) to the East in the most efficient manner. The decision was made that this would be best achieved through direct ownership by outsiders. Manfred Balz, General Counsel for the *THA*, justifies the approach in the following terms:

> All other things being equal one might say that there is a general policy to favour internal buyers over external ones. In practice, however, the 'other things' – especially the financial standing, the entrepreneurial concept and the capacity to offer sufficient future investment and job guarantees as well as, of course, the price offered are rarely equal. Usually – unless venture capital institutions help internal buyers – MBO/EBO transactions are a last resort device in cases where no strong outside investor is interested in the firm.[130]

Thus the *THA* promoted MBOs as a last resort only where it became clear that West German business investors were not interested.[131] Before that point was reached, top management in the East was denied opportunities to become owners, and in any case the most promising businesses went to West Germans.[132] The *THA* has not avoided criticism for this approach.[133]

Another explanation is that the low level of venture capital reflects its underdeveloped state in West Germany.[134] There are several reasons pertaining to Germany more generally which explain the low levels of venture capital provided. First, banks are not investors, though roughly half of the (low overall level of) venture capital in Germany is administered by banks.[135] There was a strong view amongst bankers interviewed that banks are – and *should be* – providers of loans and services, not equity capital.[136] Banking skills are focused on valuing loans rather than attempting to place value on the longer-term strategic value of a firm's assets. Second, in West Germany, for new ventures bank loans are often provided as a substitute for equity. Third, despite the traditional view that West German banks have actively invested in equity stakes and used these strategically, the contemporary literature on the German banking system points out that West German banks' equity stakes in industry are less significant than has been thought in the traditional view, and shows that levels of bank equity holdings have decreased in the postwar period (Chapter 4). Fourth, while banks are averse to providing venture capital,[137] other institutions are restricted in their provision of it.[138] Fifth, evidence suggests that there is a lack of demand for equity among German private investors who seem to *prefer fixed-income* securities, such as bonds or money market funds: West German households decreased their share holdings as a percentage of overall assets from 25 to 2.9 per cent between 1950 and 1990 and, at the same time, increased their share of bond holdings from 1.4 to 16.8 per cent.[139]

These arguments suggest that supply-side factors discourage the provision of venture capital in Germany. It may be, however, that demand-side factors have also been significant. *Mittelstand* enterprises are reportedly reluctant to accept equity participations, fearing a loss of control.[140] A report by the *Deutsche Beteiligungsgesellschaft* asserts that German entrepreneurs have a 'patriarchal' or 'master-of-the-house' mentality which dislikes accountability to an outside shareholder.[141] The reluctance to dilute ownership stakes stems in large part from the fact that the majority of West German *Mittelstand* are family-owned.[142]

### *The (lack of) supervisory and advisory board participation*

Banks were also largely unable to strengthen relationships with East German borrowers through supervisory board participations. A supervisory board (*Aufsichtsrat*) is required by law only for *AG*s and for *GMbH*s with more than 500 employees. Enterprises with less than 500 employees may have a voluntary advisory board (*Beirat*). In Saxony, the *Land* in the East in which lending levels are the highest,[143] an estimated 94 per cent of all enterprises had fewer than 500 employees in February 1994.[144] Carlin and Mayer suggested that banks did play a large role through supervisory board participation for large enterprises which were under *THA* stewardship:[145]

> Banks are heavily represented on the supervisory boards of *THA* enterprises, providing a quarter of the board members and a fifth of the chairmen. Bank representation in East Germany is commonplace even where no lending or equity investments occur. When asked to join a board, bank employees typically examine the restructuring plan of the firm as a way of evaluating the management. They are reluctant to chair the supervisory board of an enterprise with poor prospects for fear of tainting their reputations if failure occurs. Supervisory board positions, particularly those of the chairman, impose considerable demands on bank employees' time; in return they only receive modest direct remuneration (less than DM 8000 a year compared with DM 15 000–80 000 in West Germany). Banks' reasons for dispatching their personnel to sit on supervisory boards are a sense of social obligation and as an investment in creating customer bases in the East.

Some comments on these remarks are in order. First, in interviews with bankers and with the *THA*, the author found no confirmation of supervisory-board participation on the scale described. Second, even if the description is accurate, the experience of West German banks suggests that the information gathering process for *THA* enterprises was conducted by loan officers who spent minimal time on applications which were virtually all for guaranteed liquidity loans (Chapter 5). No suggestions were made in the interviews that additional information was obtained through supervisory-board participations.[146] Further, virtually all large *THA* enterprises were sold to West German firms, the vast majority of which have existing *Hausbank* relationships in West Germany. In the words of Mayhew and Seabright,

> larger enterprises seem to be inheriting the corporate control mechanisms of Western Germany, not by replication of those mechanisms in the East but by subsidiary incorporation of Eastern enterprises into their Western counterparts.[147]

For these enterprises there were no significant governance or financing problems.

In any event, the existence of supervisory boards on (large) *THA* enterprises has little to do with the bank–borrower relationships of *Mittelstand* enterprises, who form the vast majority of firms in the East.[148] Harm argues that in West Germany advisory boards (*Beiräte*) are used by *Mittelstand* enterprises (primarily) to provide consulting services as well as to provide the bank with information and – in certain cases – an institutional lever of control. He cites several studies which demonstrate broad advisory-board participation by banks in West Germany.[149] In the author's interviews, however, there was little mention of advisory-board participation in the East, and only one banker confirmed his representation on an advisory board.[150]

### *The (lack of) people to build relationships*

In the first years after GEMSU, the frequent fluctuation of bank staff obstructed the building of relationships which depend on stability.[151] Staff fluctuation occurred because East Germans were sent to the West for training, back to the East and once again to the West for further skill development. While the early years after GEMSU were exceptional in that mass training was needed for East Germans to be able to operate within West German banks, the problem was not confined to East Germans.

West German bankers tended to spend short assignments in the East, with the result that East German business managers were frequently corresponding with different loan officers. These short assignments were a further disincentive to build long-term relationships with East German borrowers. For young West Germans, working in East Germany was a quick way to make a name for oneself.[152] From the standpoint of relationship-building, however, West German bankers made little effort to integrate into East German society and hence to understand East Germans better. They were poorly positioned, therefore, to develop relationships in the manner suggested by Schumpeter, whereby the banker comes to know the habits of the borrower. West Germans who worked in the East left virtually every weekend, and every other chance they had, for West Germany. Even in 1992, there were still reports that flights to East Germany on Monday mornings and to the West on Friday afternoons were booked months in advance.[153] One West German banker in Dresden commented: 'We are outsiders. ... We will have to decide to become normal citizens, to participate more fully in the life of this city'.[154]

At least one West German bank did become aware of the detrimental effects this had on relationship-building, and tried to make adjustments, but only after two or three years had passed. *Commerzbank* introduced 'account managers' to handle a single customer – who earlier had corresponded with several different product divisions – and addressed the problem of staff fluctuation by introducing mandatory three-year contracts for employees in the East.[155]

Staff fluctuation was accompanied by a severe shortage of skilled banking personnel in East Germany in the first two years after GEMSU, particularly qualified loan officers. This occurred despite high levels of training (see Chapter 4), underscoring the importance of *experience* in credit assessment.[156] In interviews with West German bankers, referring to lending in West Germany, Edwards and Fischer note:

> It was commonly pointed out that accounting data are historic whereas the bank was interested in the future performance of the loan applicant, and that to evaluate likely future performance *there was no real substitute for the loan officer's personal experience and judgement*[157] (Emphasis added).

The poor state of accounting data in the East makes (the absence of) these qualities even more significant. In Kamenz, just north of Dresden, the manager of corporate lending for *Deutsche Bank* noted that when he first came to work in the branch in 1991 the most acute deficiency in the branch was in credit analysis, which he considered the most difficult task in East Germany for both East and West Germans.[158] The shortage of loan officers was especially felt in the East given the time and resources that are devoted to credit analysis in West German banks:

> In Germany, a good relationship manager for SMEs has not only to be a qualified sales person, he or she must also have passed some years in the credit department and have experience in the assessment of business information. As a standard, there are at least 'four eyes' involved in the credit decision. The business information is assessed independently of the relationship manager by a second employee in the credit department.[159]

The Big Banks were showing up to three-week delays in seeing prospective borrowers.[160] Griffin noted that West German bankers frequently complained in interviews of the 'huge mass of unviable business propositions'.[161] The low staff numbers may have been a further disincentive for loan officers to recommend and process loans through Specialised Banks, which require far more paperwork[162] and bring lower margins.[163] Indeed, given the sheer number of programmes[164] and the constraints faced by West German banks, it is not surprising that, 'nobody had a real overview of the programmes that could be used by the customers'.[165]

Nonetheless, West German banks were generally willing to handle Specialised Bank loans as was outlined in Chapter 5. Such loans, being refinanced, were free of interest rate risk. They also enabled West German banks which were at their maximum lending capacity (based on their local deposit base) to increase their lending. In addition, many *KfW* loans were handled for existing West German customers and, in any event, recipients of *KfW* funds are generally the most creditworthy borrowers.[166]

## A psychological perspective on GEMSU

Alongside the extensive implementation problems we have referred to (primarily of a sociological nature), GEMSU also ran into psychological barriers between East and West Germans, which had a negative impact on banking activities, including the development of bank–borrower relationships. In the words of Jarausch,

> Toughest of all was psychological reconciliation. Easterners struggled with a loss of identity, 'living in two worlds, but not feeling at home in either one'. Trying to adapt, they vacillated between self-pity and nostalgic defiance. With so many new demands placed upon them, they were disoriented and 'simply stressed out'. They resented even helpful advisers as arrogant. ... Westerners failed to understand why Ossis were not more grateful. Prosperous FRG citizens resented paying the costs or showed patronizing sympathy. Even after the psychological barriers were gone, the wall in people's heads continued to loom large.[167]

The East–West psychological divide has been well documented in surveys.[168] In October 1990, 75 per cent of East Germans regarded themselves as second-class citizens. In March 1991 the figure had risen to 91 per cent.[169] These perceptions stem partly from the manner in which GEMSU was carried out.

GEMSU created what has been perceived as a form of colonialism.[170] In 1994, Former German Chancellor Helmut Schmidt remarked that the East experienced a 'feeling of alienation and colonization'.[171] A poll conducted in Rostok revealed that 60 per cent of East Germans considered the East a 'colony'.[172] Schrettl argues that despite the common view that the East only benefited from the unilateral transfer of institutions and funds from West Germany, it actually paid a 'fee' for the insurance which these transfers provided:

> The fee comprises nothing less than the bulk of East Germany's endowment, i.e. capital stock as well as land. Some of the assets are to be returned, free of charge, to the previous owners, most of them West Germans.[173]

The colonial nature of GEMSU was evident in the *THA*'s privatisation policies whereby a large percentage of East German industry was purchased by West Germans. West Germans were also the prime beneficiaries of restitution.[174] During this process, 'the PDS daily newspaper, *Neues Deutschland*, trumpeted headlines about the "great raid" of the rich West Germans on East German real estate'.[175] Concerning West Germans working in the East, parallels with colonial regimes are not hard to find:

> In the typical colony the agents of imperial authority were a small group of expatriates who were appointed to fill posts there and who therefore regarded the colony as merely a place of work (and often an uncomfortable one which they looked forward to leaving) and eventually retired to hide in their European home country.[176]

The exogenous transplant we have outlined and corresponding functional disqualification created the possibility that,

> For a long time to come, new institutions will be perceived as alien, in particular since their executive positions are largely staffed with people from the West.[177]

There were criticisms that West Germans sought to wipe out the entire East German legacy, including its intellectual achievements.[178]

Overall, there existed the perception that GEMSU was in fact a West German 'takeover' of the East.[179] This perception of GEMSU did not go unnoticed in the (European) financial press (Plate 5). It helps to explain the reported reluctance of East German bureaucrats and others to facilitate the entry of West German enterprises and proprietors. A senior *Deutsche Industrie Holding* manager drew attention to the fact that

Plate 5 Depiction of GEMSU in the financial press, 1990

*Source*: 'Bridging the East–West Divide', *Euromoney* (March 1990, p.76).

privatisation in Potsdam was virtually stalled in the early years because the person responsible for giving licences decided not to issue any.[180]

*Transactional analysis as a way of understanding bank–borrower relationships*

The psychological barriers between East and West Germans clearly affect the relationships between them. In trying to capture the impact on bank–borrower relationships, we turn to an area of psychological analysis called 'Transactional Analysis'. The framework of transactional analysis which we employ is based on the work of Thomas Harris.[181] While Harris' work may be referred to as 'pop psychology', it provides a useful illustrative framework through which to understand the perceptions, concerns and problems between East and West Germans which emerged in the author's interviews as well as in the other surveys and accounts.[182]

Transactional analysis holds that psychological states co-exist within each person, but in different proportions, with one of the states being dominant on any given transaction. The states include those of *Parent*, *Child* and *Adult*. The *Parent* is the state based on *external events*, and adheres to a reality which is imposed or taught at an early stage in life. The *Child* is the state based on *internal events* expressed through feelings and reactions to what a person sees or hears. The *Adult* is the state based

*Figure* 6.3 The framework of transactional analysis

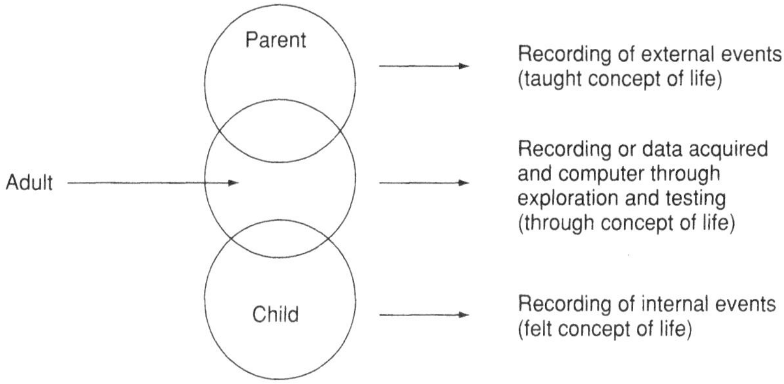


*Source*: Harris (1967, p.29).

on reason and assessment of information based on a *thought process*, as opposed to the first two states which are based on programmed reactions.

All three states are always present in each person. The overlap of the three states is not a static phenomenon, and must be understood within a dynamic process, whereby the person develops the Adult and, perhaps, breaks away from the Parent and the Child (Figure 6.3). Harris argues that the Parent and the Child are formed within the first five years of development, whereas the Adult, while beginning its development at around ten months, continues throughout the person's life. Harris designates four stages of development which correspond to the development of the states in any relationship, such as between an infant and its mother and father.[183] The first stage is generally identified by 'I'm not OK – You're OK', whereby the infant feels inadequate and helpless in comparison with its seemingly perfect mother and father. This first stage can then progress to a second stage of 'I'm not OK – You're not OK' or a third stage of 'I'm OK – You're not OK'. The fourth stage, 'I'm OK – You're OK', occurs when transactions are marked by two Adults who transact through reason and understanding rather than through emotions or accepted ideals. As we resume our analysis of bank–borrower relationships in the East, we examine the dominating Parent in West Germans in contrast to the dominating Child in East Germans.

The West German dominating Parent stems from the West German conviction that GEMSU was simply a repeat of postwar German reconstruction with little recognition of the peculiarities of the GEMSU process. This conception underscored the transplant of the

GRMF, and also the West German banks' refusal to disregard established risk-assessment criteria used in West Germany. Harris' description of the Parent highlights the acceptance of what the Parent has been taught at an early age:

> The significant point is that whether these rules are good or bad in the light of a reasonable ethic, they are recorded as *truth* from the source of all security[184] (emphasis in original).

The dominating Parent in West Germans became recognised in a punning colloquialism:

> From the word *Besserwisser*, which means a know-it-all, we now have the unfortunate pun *Besser-Wessie*, a person from the West who feels superior.[185]

At the same time, East Germans were often characterised by West Germans as if they were children in the united Germany. One *Deutsche Bank* manager said of East Germans, 'When they are responsible for themselves they have problems'.[186] According to East German psychiatrist Hans-Joachim Maaz, the former East German regime in many ways made adults into children. In the former GDR system, which Maaz calls 'Socialism As It Really Exists'.

> there emerges a picture of a system of extensive and continuous coercion, manipulation, constriction, control, and punishment; a system that inspired fear and humiliation. Societal structures exploited and perpetuated behaviour that had been instilled in childhood.[187]

After GEMSU, East Germans to a large extent became children in the united Germany, and had to begin a long learning process. In the course of this process, we may understand conflicts that may have developed between these Children and their West German Parents.

Take the concept of *time*. Conditioned by the long duration of bank–borrower relationships in West Germany, West German bankers expressed a cautious view that the lending process needed to be viewed in stages, and that these stages could allow for a *gradual* increase in lending over time if the borrower proved creditworthy. A *Deutsche Bank* manager suggested that enterprises needed to pass through a learning process which was *by necessity* gradual in nature.[188] Here for

West German bankers 'time' takes on a normative aspect which suggests that a long time period *has to be* part of a sound relationship. We noted earlier that time was necessary in logistical terms to build a history, but here we find the sense that bank–borrower relationships *ought not to develop over a short time period* – because they have not done so in West Germany.

In stark contrast to the West German Parent, the East German Child's conception of time is impulsive. As Harris observes, 'The Child wants immediate results'.[189] In interviews and in the responses in the *BDI* survey, a frequent complaint by East German borrowers was that loans were both processed and paid out too slowly,[190] obliging borrowers to take on bridging loans (*Zwischenfinanzierungen*) at much higher interest rates.[191] There were also complaints that lending amounts were begun at too low a level.[192]

In addition to these perceived delays, East German borrowers often felt misunderstood by banks. In the *BDI* survey, borrowers claimed that banks lacked empathy (*Einfühlungsvermögen*) for their difficult situation.[193] This underscores the difference between the postwar years in West Germany and the GEMSU process. In the postwar period, banks and borrowers both had to rebuild their business and achieve reconstruction; hence they identified with each other's interests. Under GEMSU, West German banks were already established international financial institutions, and hence viewed lending commitments to the East not solely as business decisions, but as fulfilment of patriotic and political duties, and perhaps as a form of charity.[194]

East German borrowers complained not only that banks failed to understand and empathise with them, but also that they were humiliated in some measure by the lending process. In the *BDI* survey, borrowers complained of feeling like 'beggars' (*Bittsteller*) rather than partners in the bank–borrower relationship.[195] Both in the author's interviews and in the *BDI* survey, borrowers pointed to the expensive bridging credits given by the *Hausbanken* in the early years after GEMSU, consistently citing 12 per cent as what was perceived as an exorbitant rate. On closer inspection, we find that under the GDR Staatsbank system, where interest rates were low, 12 per cent happened to be the penal rate (*Sanktionszinsen*) used for enterprises that needed emergency bank credits which were outside planned investment credits.[196] East German borrowers, moreover, were afraid to negotiate with West German banks (Parents) after GEMSU, and this left them paying high margins on liquidity credits.[197] *THA* board member Wolfram Krause argued: 'Our enterprises simply must learn to walk out the door if they are not offered better conditions [by banks]'.[198]

*Figure* 6.4 An example of a crossed exchange

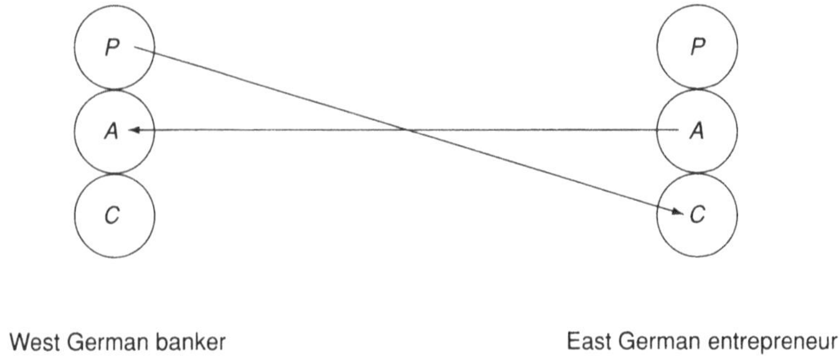


While these Parent–Child interactions clearly contained possible obstacles to building bank–borrower relationships in the East, the question arises whether transactions between banks and borrowers can improve – i.e. move onto an 'I'm OK – You're OK' basis, in Harris' terms. This is a difficult question to answer, but there is no guarantee that the transition will prove straightforward. As one party or the other begins to escape from the dominating Child or Parent role, there is the potential for a breakdown in communication, or what Harris terms a 'crossed transaction'.[199]

One East German entrepreneur recalled an episode when West German bankers had entered his factory to discuss possible financing. During the meeting, they commented that his office furniture was not very impressive (Parent remark to a Child since the furniture did not look like that in West Germany).[200] His reply was that he was selling his product and not his furniture (Adult response to another Adult question) (Figure 6.6). The result was an end to the communication. While there were no other such transactions described in interviews with the author, it is possible that others occurred.

## Difficulties in pricing risk: the political dimension

While West German banks were unable to measure and manage risks to their satisfaction, they were also *unable to price them* as a result of the political dimension of GEMSU. In general terms, political expediency underlay the decision to adopt GEMSU so quickly, the specific terms of it most notably the setting of the exchange rates between the M and the DM and the need to equalise income levels between East and West Germany for fear of migration.[201] In addition, the political discourse surrounding GEMSU raised expectations to unrealistic levels. Chancellor

Helmut Kohl promised that nobody would suffer from GEMSU and many would benefit, and also promised that no new taxes would be needed to finance unification.[202] In short, the feeling was fostered that GEMSU would quickly lead to another *Wirtschaftswunder*, with Chancellor Helmut Kohl talking of 'blooming landscapes' (*blühende Landschaften*).[203]

*Politicisation* of the GEMSU process placed the banks' actions under close public scrutiny. This in turn influenced the manner in which the banks' released information on their activities in the East and also on the content of the information (see Chapter 3).[204] In addition, close scrutiny of the banks' lending policies, in particular, created what one West German banker termed a 'transparency' in interest rate levels East and West.[205] The equalising of interest rates between East and West had serious implications for the banks' lending behaviour. The East had a much higher systematic lending risk than in West Germany – because of transitional problems (see Chapter 4) and the high number of start-ups in the East[206] – but banks were unable to charge an appropriate risk premium because the transparency in interest rates imposed an *informal interest – rate ceiling* on the East. This point has been largely overlooked in the literature, but captures the view expressed by bankers in interviews with the author.

The ceiling limited not only what banks could charge as a risk premium, but also (in some cases at any rate) the intermediation fee that could be levied (Figure 6.5). Thus not only were banks unable to charge for risks, but they were often unable to recover the high costs of developing bank–borrower relationships. It is logical to conclude that West German banks therefore deliberately restricted their lending in the East and endeavoured instead to develop other (off-balance sheet) activities, though there is no direct evidence of this.

*Figure* 6.5 Effect of the informal interest-rate ceiling in loan pricing

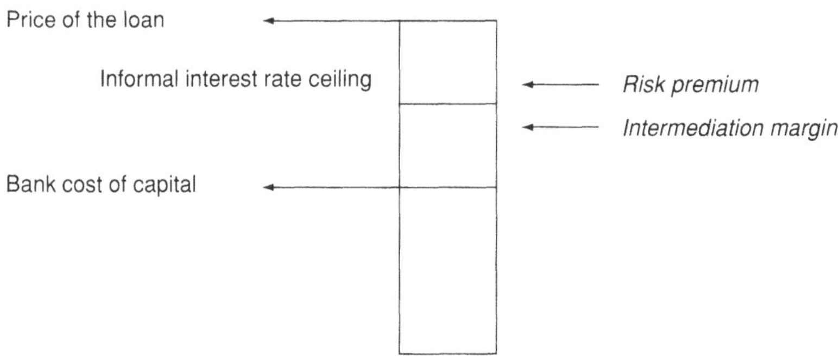

At the same time, the close scrutiny of the banks in the press and media exposed the ongoing battle between the State and the banks to shift the lending risk for the East.[207] Schrettl's metaphor of GEMSU as an insurance contract underscores the basis of the struggle:

> Although there was not talk of an insurance contract, at least an implicit understanding of the risk transfer involved [to West Germany] in the deal seems to have prevailed.[208]

Thus the West German government accepted the risk of the East's transition, and automatically expected the banks to be able to play a large role in managing this risk, as they had done in the early postwar period. The underlying tension in the East, therefore, centred on the division of risk between the public and private spheres, the essence of which is expressed in the following report:

> The idea of a sectoral superfund has come under fire from some banks and Kopper ruled out any preferred interest rates for troubled companies. That would not only derail the market mechanism, but would conflict with interests of depositors and banks' owners. The government could resolve the legal dilemma by offering some sort of guarantee for the funds made available by the banks. That, of course, would again make the German taxpayer the guarantor of the last resort.[209]

*The Bankenmilliarde*

The most visible result of the dilemma of finding ways to shift risk to the private sector and to expand the banks' (risk-related) activities in the East was the creation of the so-called '*Bankenmilliarde*', whereby in 1992 West and East German banks made available 1 billion DM to be used to purchase and restructure enterprises still under *THA* ownership.[210] The *Bankenmilliarde* created a sensation in the press, with numerous articles appearing daily. The proposal was motivated by politics rather than economics, but became unfortunately touted as a venture capital fund – which, of course, it was not.[211] The slow development of the proposal, and lack of corresponding purchases by the banks, gave the appearance of a fiasco, and criticisms against the banks were both fierce and plentiful.[212]

We may understand the *Bankenmilliarde* episode within our analysis as a result of the banks' inability to measure, manage and price risk in the East. As we have argued (Chapter 5), there does not exist a separate venture capital industry in Germany; rather, banks are largely responsible for its provision. The manager who oversaw the *Bankenmilliarde* in the *THA* observed in negotiations with the banks that they always returned to the basic problem that they could not acceptably measure risk in the East.[213] In the banks' defence it must be said that there were doubts about the legality of the scheme. The German Banking Act prohibits banks, because of their responsibilities to depositors, from lending to companies which are unable to service their debts. For private banks, there is the added responsibility to their shareholders, a point West German private banks have repeatedly made with regard to their activities in the East. Regarding the *Bankenmilliarde*, it remained unclear whether the investment of equity capital in enterprises which are not thought to have a future would actually be illegal.[214]

## West and East German banks within GEMSU

We have outlined the sort of obstacles which existed to the functioning of the *Hausbank* system in the East. The problems affected primarily West German banks in the early years after GEMSU; based on our analysis of the West German banks, we may ask how East German banks succeeded in building loan portfolios and whether they were in fact better able to measure, manage and price risk in the East. Given that East German banks faced the same implementation problems in the state-support structure as West German banks, and their borrowers the same general difficulties,[215] their growth in lending may have been due to greater success in building bank–borrower relationships. Perhaps this underlies Deeg's suggestion that in the East the 'cooperative and savings banks appear to have a higher risk tolerance than private commercial banks'.[216] In the following sections, we try to understand why they may have been more successful in building these relationships.

East German banks were more dependent on well developed bank–borrower relationships with East German borrowers. They managed only a small portion of the guaranteed lending, particularly through the *THA*, and did not have the option of lending to established West German enterprises. Thus they had to screen and monitor their borrowers from the beginning of the relationship. Further, East German bank loan portfolios consisted primarily of *Mittelstand* borrowers: the Bundesbank observes that the lending growth of East German Savings Banks and Credit Cooperatives was 'fuelled to a large extent by lending to medium-sized enterprises, private craft enterprises and small traders'.[217] For *Mittelstand* borrowers bank–borrower relationships are more critical than for larger borrowers, as we have argued.

In addition, East German banks were locally based, and had to build *local* portfolios of borrowers.[218] This is the view which was given by Horst Köhler, President of the East German Savings Bank Association, and which accords with the importance of bank–borrower relationships as described by Schumpeter:

> Our savings banks are generally managed by people who have spent much of their lives in the local area, people who have been dealing with their customers on a day-to-day basis for a number of years. As a result, the managers know their customers' businesses inside-out, and they know what services and assistance the customers need to operate profitably. From this expertise, the managers also know how to appraise projects and evaluate the risks involved – essential in the banking business.[219]

Having local East Germans in positions of responsibility regarding lending activities also probably allowed these banks to avoid the psychological barriers which obstructed relationship-building by West German banks.

Moreover, based on the experience of the West German system, there may also be organisational reasons why small banks have been better placed to finance and build relationships with smaller enterprises (Figure 6.6).[220] While Big Banks have a single vertical structure, small banks are local units – with a locally comprised portfolio and local focus. As a result, small banks operate with – rather than *under* as in a vertical structure – their respective associations on a regional and a national level. Pooled databases among member banks allow sharing of information.[221]

*Figure* 6.6 Organisational structure of large and small banks in Germany

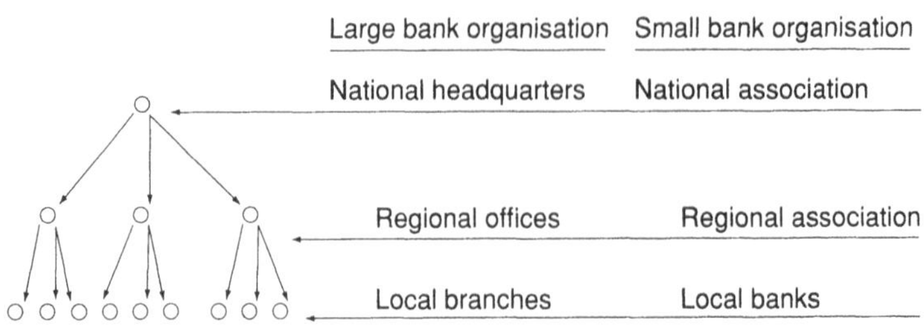


*Source*: Adapted from Vitols (1995).

Against this, Vitols asserts that Big Bank problems in lending to small businesses stem from (1) internal cut-off rates for loan size, (2) internal confusion over the extent of decentralisation of lending decisions to the local branches and (3) the fact that small accounts are often used as training for lending officers before they move on to 'bigger' customers, the result being that Big Banks offer the services of less experienced personnel to small businesses.[222] Moreover, attempts by the Big Banks to imitate the organisational structure of the small banks have not proven successful.[223]

As a result of their *local emphasis*, East German banks may suffer from a higher total risk in their portfolio than West German banks,[224] since the latter can more easily diversify across German industries as well as across regions and, moreover, can diversify abroad as well.[225] East German banks may therefore have needed to invest more in their screening and monitoring in order to minimise the ambiguity in the lending process and, hence, manage the specific risk factors for each individual borrower. Harm observes that small banks in West Germany:

> [face] significantly larger bank specific risk stemming just from the fate of being small. This disadvantage compared to the larger banks can obviously lead to a larger demand for information to assess the individual risk, as it is covered to a lesser extent through portfolio diversification.[226]

Costs were high in gathering information in the East, particularly qualitative information. It may be that the East German banks were more willing initially to incur these costs for the above reasons. Moreover, their initial (relationship-specific) investments may have in fact reduced these costs over time as trust and information were developed.

Thus East German banks had the need to build bank–borrower relationships, but also the advantage that they could *learn and develop their capabilities over time*, thanks to the West German banks' large role after GEMSU, which allowed East German banks *gradually* to build their asset portfolio. In terms of Deutsch's concept of learning capacity (see Chapter 2), the East German banks' spare *learning capacity* enabled them to focus their lending activities on local relationship building and allow loan officers to develop their skills and build their customer base over time. This was in stark contrast to West German banks whose loan officers were occupied with liquidity loans as well as serving (often existing) West German customers.[227] Moreover, West German banks were at their lending limits – given their deposit base in the East – and hence were not able to reallocate their asset portfolio whereas East German banks were able to divert more resources to local borrowers (see Chapter 5, particularly Figure 5.7 p.000). East German banks also avoided to a large extent the staff fluctuations experienced by the West German banks.

An alternative explanation for the growth in East German bank lending, however, is that East German Savings Banks are state-owned, and hence may have been less (profit-) constrained in allocating resources to screen and monitor loan applications, to invest time in bank–borrower relationships and to take on higher risk while forgoing the required risk premium.[228] Edwards and Fischer note that Savings Banks in West Germany,

> were originally conceived not as commercial profit-making concerns but rather as state institutions with obligations to provide banking services to less well-off members of the community, to furnish credit on favourable terms to public authorities and to finance local investment of benefit to the region in which the savings bank was located. Although the savings banks still have these obligations, they have developed into universal banks which compete with the commercial banks for most forms of banking business.[229]

Thus a further possibility is that East German banks may have been under pressure to lend by the municipalities, particularly as *THA* guarantees were reduced. Savings Banks, in particular, are required by their charters to take account of the general social and economic needs of their local area.[230] Some of their loans may be non-performing.

The evidence, however, suggests that East German banks have not in fact sacrificed profitability to the growth of their lending portfolio. The *International Herald Tribune* reports that:

> Because of this closeness, and because a number of communities and industrial monocultures have been struggling with the problems of reconstruction, it would not be surprising to find a number of struggling savings banks. In point of fact, these have become a rare species over the past few years. Savings banks show nearly across-the-board increases in individual capital-adequacy ratios and reserves – both already very high – and very low levels of loan write-offs.[231]

This optimistic-sounding account – published in a special advertising section for the Savings Banks – finds support in profitability figures released by the Bundesbank.[232] Even though this suggests that these banks performed well, it should be interpreted with some caution as there does not as yet exist any evaluation of the quality of the loans, most of which are long-term and not due.

For West German banks, in the meantime, besides the lack of learning capacity, there may have been other factors which inhibited their learning process in the East. The high dependence on *THA* liquidity loans and West German customers may have functioned as what Deutsch termed a 'learning pathology', hindering banks' ability to learn to properly screen and monitor East German borrowers. This pathology would only have been strengthened by the heavy reliance on collateral in lending decisions. Given the staff shortages facing West German banks, along with their inability to charge for high screening and monitoring costs, it is possible that they adopted a more standardised credit evaluation procedure for the East designed to minimise costs and give as little discretion as possible to inexperienced loan officers.[233] While there is no supporting evidence for this view, it is at least consistent with the fact that virtually all those interviewed in West Germany claimed that the banking environment in the East was little different from that in West Germany, yet those in the East insisted that their colleagues in West Germany were far removed from the situation, and that things were quite different there.[234] In addition, certainly in the first two years after GEMSU, the banking sector in the East was not very competitive in all but the largest cities. Thus the West German banks – Deutsche and Dresdner especially – had the *power to avoid learning*. In the absence of competition, bank–borrower relationships may not have been valued – or particularly needed.

It is possible that West German banks may have known that there would be many NPLs in the East, and hence decided not to become highly exposed to East German risk.[235] This would also explain their heavy reliance on guaranteed loans and loans to West German-owned enterprises. Griffin rejects this argument, however, for two reasons. First, if banks had reliable information on the state of industry in the East, why did they rely so heavily on third parties – such as consultants – for evaluations of enterprise assets? Second, if banks had superior information, why didn't they invest more venture capital into *THA* enterprises which were potentially profitable? But whether West German banks knew better, which our analysis also suggests was not the case, or were unable adequately to measure, manage and price risks, as we have argued, the question remains why they increased their lending to East German enterprises initially only to experience high levels of NPLs later, leading to a subsequent decision to decrease lending to East German enterprises.

There are many possible reasons for the early lending, and we may identify six. First, there was *increasing competition* in the West German banking market and the banks saw an opportunity to establish market share in the East at an early stage (i.e. less competition).[236] Second, there was a recognition that early support of East German enterprises was critical for the *future business* of the banks in the East. Third, there was *strong political pressure* on the banks to lend to improve their image. Fourth, there existed *sincere patriotism* on the part of the banks to help rebuild the East.[237] Fifth, loans were initially made for *internal reasons* within the banks, particularly owing to agency problems and the performance-minded agendas of many loan officers.[238] Lastly, West German banks may have simply *underestimated* the difficulties of lending in the East. In several interviews, bankers explained that due to the transitional nature of the economy in the East, many 'good' loans had simply gone bad.

## Summary

We began this chapter with a discussion of risk. The presence of *ambiguity* means that risk measurement is imperfect, with a corresponding enhanced need for risk management. With respect to banking, we argued that banks seek to objectify risks, and that the screening and monitoring process is critical to their ability to both *measure* and *manage* risk. We argued further that bank–borrower relationships can be beneficial not only to banks, in their efforts to measure and monitor risk, but to borrowers as well. After establishing the importance of these relationships in West Germany, particularly for financing *Mittelstand* enterprises, we switched to a discussion of GEMSU.

We defined the *Hausbank* system in the East, and distinguished its key components for financing *Mittelstand* enterprises: state support structures and bank–borrower relationships. Our discussion of GEMSU emphasised that it was a *process rather than an event in time*. As a process of implementation, GEMSU created obstacles to banks' ability to measure and manage risk in the East. We then set out to explain why banks faced obstacles in establishing bank–borrower relationships, particularly since these might have helped them to overcome difficulties in risk assessment and other problems which stemmed from the institutional structure.

The analysis highlighted the linkages between the GEMSU – on an institutional and psychological level – and the West German banks' behaviour, and was enhanced by the discussion of the political dimension of GEMSU. The central problem in the East was that West German banks were unable adequately to measure, manage, or charge for risk, while at the same time the East German banks were only gradually building their portfolios. *Mittelstand* enterprises, therefore, found a lack of banks willing and able to finance them. In the broader context, the German institutional framework for financial flows to the East represents a risk-management framework incorporating a delicate risk balance between the public and private spheres. An important point is that the framework contains *distancing* conditions which have allowed West German banks to avoid developing close bank–borrower relationships with East German enterprises and, moreover, called into question the prospects for risk devolution from the public to the private sphere.

# 7
# The East German Experience in Perspective

Returning to our opening analogy, we have examined the banking transplant in East Germany, focusing both on the 'technique' of the operation itself and also on the side effects which developed both for the patient as well as the organs (banks) that were transplanted. In this concluding chapter, we put the East German experience in perspective and seek to understand its implications.

## Summary of the main findings

Many factors favoured the transition process in East Germany. The West German institutional structure was transplanted to the East, with certain additions. The 'German Risk Management Framework' (GRMF) contained a combination of institutions and refinancing, guarantee, transfer, and lending mechanisms which enabled financial flows to go to the East. Within the GRMF, the (West) German state played a large role in absorbing lending risks, both directly and indirectly. Apart from the institutions of the social market economy, including the *KfW*, *DtA* and *Bürgschaftsbanken*, the *Treuhandanstalt* occupied a key position in the GRMF, providing significant levels of guarantees and transfers. Another significant feature was the high level of West German ownership in the East which enabled funds to flow to West German subsidiaries both through intra-company transfers and through guarantees for bank loans. In spite of all this, the new *Länder* experienced an economic collapse of unprecedented proportions.

At the heart of the GRMF was the banking system, which after GEMSU underwent a 'normalisation' process whereby it quickly came to resemble the West German one in terms of structure and infrastructural development. Though costly and arduous, this *technical* part of the transplant occurred fairly rapidly, within four years, thanks to a combination of West German bank acquisitions and various forms of assistance to the (remaining) East German Savings banks and Credit Cooperatives.

Bank activities in the East adapted correspondingly. On the deposit side, East German banks – particularly Savings Banks – maintained their hold over a dominant share of overall deposits. On the lending side, West German banks played an exceptionally large role after GEMSU both in handling flows through the GRMF and also in own lending. The latter, however, contained a high percentage of *Treuhandanstalt*- guaranteed loans and also loans to West German subsidiaries. At the same time, East German Savings Banks and Credit Cooperatives built their non-bank lending gradually but steadily. By 1993, the Savings Banks had become the biggest lending group in the East.

Despite the GRMF and the success of the bank transplant, survey evidence has suggested that many East German *Mittelstand* borrowers have experienced financing difficulties. We argue that these problems arose because East German banks were unable in the early stages to lend to such borrowers on any significant scale and, at the same time, West German bank lending in the East was in decline – in *absolute* terms – as NPLs grew. Further, case studies of *Deutsche Bank* and *Commerzbank* noted that these West German banks experienced (qualified) staff shortages and staff fluctuations, and also suffered as loan guarantees were reduced by the *Treuhandanstalt*.

The decline in West German bank lending was attributed to the fact that the banks were unable satisfactorily to measure, manage and price risk in the East. Informational deficiencies and other factors meant that banks were more dependent on subjective factors in making lending decisions. The associated ambiguity provided a disincentive to lend. Bank–borrower relationships were seen as significant in the management of risk, and thus as a key component of the German *Hausbank* system. In the East, owing largely to the short span of time since GEMSU and other factors, these relationships may not have developed sufficiently. Moreover, the political scrutiny placed on banks in the East may have imposed an informal interest rate ceiling, thus preventing banks from charging the appropriate risk premium for certain loans. The local banks – Savings Banks in particular – may have been more successful in building bank–borrower relationships and thereby expanding their loan portfolio, though the quality of their lending remains unclear.

## The banking sector in East Germany: An Update

While it has not been possible to engage in comprehensive research of a follow-up nature, several observations can be made based on a recent report by the *Bankenverband mittel- und ostdeutscher Länder.*[1] Thanks to continuing support from West Germany, the East German economy has shown steady improvement, with productivity increases relative to West Germany as well as more than 500 000 new small businesses having been created, employing more than 3.5 million workers. Nevertheless, it is clear that the transformation process continues for many enterprises, with continued reliance on assistance, and the need to improve capitalisation levels and increase productivity.

The trends outlined among the banking groups in the East remain largely in place. First, West German banks have (again) regained the leading lending position, but only marginally, over the East German Savings Banks, with some DM 90 bn (36 per cent share), as against DM 81 bn (32 per cent) for the Savings Banks and DM 25 bn (10 per cent) for the Credit Cooperatives. Secondly, West German banks also continue to lead in the handling of specialised loans: through the *Deutsche Ausgleichsbank* they handled more than 50 per cent of the total (the Savings Banks and Credit Cooperatives 30 per cent and 19 per cent, respectively); through the *Kreditanstalt für Wiederaufbau* they handled 40 per cent versus 25 per cent and 15 per cent for the Savings Banks and Credit Cooperatives, respectively. Thirdly, the Savings Banks still hold more than 60 per cent of the deposits in the East, with little relative change in this regard over the past few years.

The three bank groups have been steadily increasing their lending allocation from their asset base to non-bank enterprises, including to self-employed and other individuals (Table 7.1). While this evolution is expected, the East German banks are still well behind more normal allocation levels, suggesting that their learning process continues, with remaining caution. The West German banks' lack of success in increasing

*Table* 7.1 Ratio of lending/deposits in the East by bank group, 1994 and 1997

| *Year* | *West German Banks* (%) | *East German Savings banks* (%) | *East German Credit Cooperatives* (%) |
|---|---|---|---|
| 1994 | 107 | 43 | 49 |
| 1997 | 167 | 51 | 56 |

*Source: Bankenverband mittel- und ostdeutscher Länder* (1994, 1997/8).

their share of the deposit market has left them increasingly as 'importers' of capital to the East (which is in fact politically desirable for them).

It is helpful to view the current situation, but we should not assume too much from the numbers, for they could be scrutinised further to understand, for example, the degree to which the increase in West German bank loans has been to fund West German enterprises in the East as they expand. Furthermore, we understand little of the quality of the loan portfolios of the respective bank groups. Although there is a clear opportunity for further fieldwork here, it is important to underscore that the trends in the early 1990s largely continue, at least in statistical terms.

## Implications for the transition in East Germany

A crucial policy issue concerning the East is the timetable for dismantling the high level of state subsidies and transfers. We recall that as *Treuhandanstalt* liquidity loan levels were reduced, NPLs became more apparent, leading to a decline in lending. That is to say, as initial immuno-suppression was removed reactions quickly occurred. A *Bundesbank* study was widely quoted for its suggestion that the East had to avoid the spread of a subsidy mentality.[2] Central to becoming a self-sustaining economy is the development of a thriving sector of *Mittelstand* enterprises; hence the concern over the fact that these appear to be experiencing financing difficulties. Given that it may take some time before these enterprises can largely finance their growth through retained earnings, as does the West German *Mittelstand*, external financing is likely to play a crucial role. It is curious to note that in the German elections in September 1998, almost 10 years after GEMSU, continued aid to the East remained an important part of Kohl's CDU platform.

In assessing these prospects, we need to distinguish between implementation problems and possible fundamental or structural problems with the *Hausbank* system in the East. According to Pickel,

> Unintended consequences obviously are unavoidable in any attempt to bring about fundamental changes in socio-economic order. The crucial question ... is whether there are unintended consequences of a lasting nature – consequences that cannot be corrected and which ultimately subvert the basic goals of the transformation.[3]

Though implementation problems have proved detrimental within the context of the GRMF, many will eventually be overcome as East

German capacity to handle its new system is developed. Psychological barriers, however, may be harder to overcome.[4]

There is the possibility that the German *Hausbank* system is not well suited to an environment where high levels of risk capital are required.[5] That is to say, banks are unlikely to lend significant levels to new borrowers until the latter have established a credit record and possibly a relationship with the bank. The critical question in the East is thus how long it will take to realise a devolution of risk from the state to the banks in financing East German enterprises.

Our analysis suggests that local Savings Banks and Credit Cooperatives may be best positioned to build the appropriate relationships. Some evidence from West Germany suggests that this might be considered another form of 'normalisation'. In 1989, a survey of West German companies revealed that almost half (44 per cent) considered a Savings Bank its 'main bank', and roughly another third a Credit Cooperative, while only 13 per cent mentioned a similar relationship with one of the Big Banks.[6]

## Implications for banking in PCPEs

In order to assess the implications of the East German case for banking in (other) PCPEs it may be useful to recall the basis for examining this limiting case in the first place. We argued that a number of banking-related problems developed in PCPEs, and divided these into symptoms and causes. Among the latter were ownership patterns of banks, lack of competition, inheritance of NPLs, slow development of the bankruptcy mechanism and the need to undergo a learning process. In the East German limiting case, these causes were seemingly addressed through the transplant of 'good' private commercial banks, in addition to a number of other favourable limiting conditions in East Germany, including a 'good' institutional structure, a common language, and so on (see Table 3.1, p.000).

To use Offe's analogy, PCPEs experienced severe banking-related problems owing to deficiencies in the 'hardware' and 'software' of their systems. In East Germany, however, the hardware of the banking system was rapidly put into place after GEMSU. The question was whether the software would enable the hardware to function in the manner expected. If it were to do so, we would not expect to find the symptoms experienced by PCPEs: lack of financing for private enterprises; a build-up of NPLs by banks; accumulation of inter-enterprise debts; the slow pace of enterprise restructuring; and the undermining of macro-stabilisation.

As it turned out, most of these symptoms *were* absent in East Germany. *Macroeconomic stabilisation* was not undermined by the banking system, and was indeed secured through the transplant of the *Deutschmark*, the *Bundesbank* and access to significant levels of external funding. The accumulation of *inter-enterprise debts* was also not a problem in the East. On the topic of *enterprise restructuring*, significant progress has been made, however, it has been carried out primarily by the *Treuhandanstalt* – and also West German owners – rather than the banks. On the issue of *NPLs*, we do find evidence of these in bank portfolios, particularly those of West German banks. As in PCPEs, many of them stem from the difficult environment facing the non-financial sectors of the economy. A major difference in East Germany, however, is that loans are not extended to support inefficient SOEs via the banks, except in the case of *Treuhandanstalt* liquidity loans which are transparent. That is to say, loans are simply non-performing, rather than state subsidies in disguise. Against these numerous points, the one symptom noticeable in the East was an apparent *lack of financing* for (some) borrowers in the private sector, mostly SMEs.

While institutional hardware was thus quickly put into place, the associated software did show significant compatibility problems. As a result, what were 'good' banks and institutions with West German software were found to be less effective when transplanted into East Germany, with East German administrators, managers and workers. Several implications for banking in PCPEs are suggested.

First, the East German experience suggests that proposals which call for banks to refrain from lending will not enable these banks to learn. These banks need to begin their learning process as early as possible, and it may involve mistakes. In the absence of learning, the state only postpones the process of devolution of allocative responsibility to the banking system. In addition, it is likely that administrative attempts to segment the credit market will meet resistance by the actors in the system who may find ways to circumvent them.

A second point is that the East German experience calls into question the notion that 'good' private commercial banks will in themselves solve the financing problems of private enterprises. Pohl and Claessens, for example, praise the Russian banking reform for having created a sector of good banks:

> The dismantling of the old state banks and the emergence of new commercial banks not burdened by old loans and old management practices in Russia is much more likely to lead to a financial sector

> which plays an active role in enterprise restructuring and channels resources into the private sector than under the East European, gradual approach to banking reform.[7]

But these expectations fail to take account of the *environment* in which the banks have to operate. Prill's analysis of the Russian system finds that private, profit-oriented banks are reluctant to lend – to large enterprises, primarily because of their own lack of corporate governance (i.e. monitoring) capacity, and to small enterprises because of informational asymmetries and inaccessibility.[8] As a result, profit-oriented private banks invest primarily in government securities, with the government then channelling funds to inefficient enterprises through a second, non-profit-oriented banking system. When this pattern will change depends not on the banks, but rather on factors external to them, including governance mechanisms and borrower creditworthiness more generally. We may recall that in West Germany half of the large public debt which resulted from transfers to the East was financed by (West) German banks. While this mechanism is more transparent (i.e. direct subsidies rather than subsidies in disguise of bank loans) it is also a case of 'good' banks lending while the state absorbs the underlying risks; this in addition to the many other risk-sharing mechanisms in the GRMF.

There is also evidence in other PCPEs that private, profit-oriented banks have become more rather than less reluctant to lend to borrowers in the private sector, SMEs especially.[9] The important point, then, is that attention should focus not merely on 'banks', but on the institutional structure in which they operate and the condition of borrowers in the economy. *Deutsche Bank* Chairman Hilmar Kopper articulates the point particularly well:

> In Central and Eastern Europe ... new markets are opening up on the doorstep of many West European banks. However, I would warn against any euphoria. Banking business needs a foundation in terms of infrastructure, efficient administration, properly functioning supervision and an established market order. Bank lending is not suited to building up from scratch economies which are still in a phase of political self-discovery. What's needed here is, above all, cooperation between governments and international organisations. Banks can be called in wherever there are specific projects with calculable risks.[10]

In East Germany, *Treuhandanstalt* liquidity credits enabled borrowers to obtain loans in the early period after GEMSU where rapid restructuring occurred. Without these, banks would in all probability have refused to lend on any significant scale and, where they did, would likely have accumulated higher levels of NPLs.

Nevertheless, the East German case raises the possibility that (local) Savings Banks may help to provide finance to SMEs through their local knowledge, commitment and relationships, alongside their support network which provides refinancing and information sharing. In the summer of 1994, the European Savings Banks Group met and agreed on certain common principles, including 'close local and regional links', and the 'supply of products and services for private and business customers geared more especially to small and medium-sized enterprises'.[11] This point has been widely remarked in the literature. Gibb notes that 'the most significant successes in small firm "appropriate" banking seem to be via development of local savings and credit cooperative type institutions'.[12] In Russia, it was reported that the German Savings Banks' 'individual approach to each client' made a 'tremendous impression' on managers from the Moscow Savings Bank (*Sberbank*).[13] Yet for all the high-flown declarations, the East German Savings Banks had significant support in building their business, including refinancing privileges on rates and quotas and West German technical assistance. Moreover, apart from the capabilities of the particular banks, the East German case underscores the point that it is problematic to assume the universal application of any system developed in a specific context.

Given the learning process of banks and the deficiencies in their lending environment, it is likely that in the early stages of the transition process the government will have to play a role in absorbing the risks of financing certain segments of the non-financial side of the economy. It may do this directly through subsidies or indirectly by pressuring banks to make loans. The latter, less transparent option is likely to lead to a build-up of NPLs and, therefore, forestall the process whereby banks are in a position to play a more active role in lending to the most viable opportunities.

In the case of the government channelling funds to certain groups of borrowers, the East German case demonstrates that development banks and other institutions can play a role in facilitating the flow of these funds. In the GRMF, risk-sharing between the state and the banks employs the screening and monitoring capabilities of the latter and the funds of the former. This system helps banks to overcome informational asymmetries by both evaluating and advising borrowers, and also moral hazard by allocating some of the risk and hence monitoring burden on the banks. The problem for most PCPEs is that they are lacking two essential components needed to establish a state support system similar to the one used in East Germany: funding and banks capable of administering it.

## Implications for the role of foreign banks in PCPEs

We noted in Chapter 2 that experience with foreign banks in PCPEs showed that these banks did not fulfil expectations that they would purchase local banks, thereby providing budgetary funds as well as assisting the process of bank restructuring. The East German case suggests that foreign banks cannot solve all the financing problems of the local economy, even with a large foreign bank presence and significant favourable conditions. Even in East Germany, where West German banks bought out the entire commercial banking system, within four years the local banks were leading by far in overall deposits and also to a lesser extent in lending. Thus even in the East German case, where a foreign bank 'takeover' in the manner described by Rostowski takes place, it is in the end the local banks that play the largest role in financial intermediation. This supports the conclusion of Corbett and Mayer, and also McKinnon, that domestic banks will have to play a large role in the transition process.

As it happens, the experience with foreign banks in PCPEs is that nothing close to a takeover has taken place.[14] From the regulatory point of view, not only were foreign banks subjected to no formal restrictions[15] – except in Russia[16] – but they were actually provided with incentives to enter both the Polish and Hungarian markets. Nevertheless, their levels of involvement in these PCPEs have remained relatively low (Table 7.2).

In terms of the number of banks, it might appear that foreign banks do have a significant presence in these countries (apart from Russia). But the number of banks is a poor measure of penetration because it measures banks registered and does not consider that many foreign banks do little as yet in terms of operations. To be sure, there are also many small, undercapitalised domestic banks that have little impact on the banking market, Russia being the most extreme example. A better measure then is the level of bank assets, which conveys a more accurate indication of the level of banking business being undertaken by the bank groups.[17] Hungary is the only PCPE where foreign banks account for more than 10 per cent of total banking assets.[18] By way of comparison, in the United States foreign banks account for roughly 21 per cent of the total.[19] In terms of lending activities, foreign banks

*Table 7.2* Overview of foreign bank experience in PCPEs, 1992 to 1994

| *Country* | *Regulatory restrictions on foreign banks* | *Number of foreign Banks in 1994* (% of total banks) | *Foreign bank assets* (*% of total banking assets*) | *Foreign bank lending* | | *Foreign bank profitability* |
|---|---|---|---|---|---|---|
| | | | | *Lending growth* (*% absolute change*) | *Market share* (*% of total market*) | |
| *Czech Republic* | None | 21<br>(36) | 9.47<br>(as of 30/11/94) | 107.5<br>(first nine months of 1994) | 1/1/94: 2.34<br>11/1/94: 3.71 | Foreign banks *marginally* more than domestic banks[a] |
| *Hungary* | None | 20<br>(47) | 19.26<br>(end-1994) | – | 1993: 14.77<br>1994: 14.44 | Foreign banks *considerably* more than domestic banks[b] |
| *Poland* | None | 12<br>(13) | 3.15<br>(as of 30/9/94) | 917 between 1992–1994<br>• 417 in '92<br>• 500 in '93 | 1992: 0.65<br>1993: 2.00<br>1994: 4.00 | Foreign banks *considerably* more than domestic banks[c] |
| *Russia* | Many | 18<br>(0.007) | 7.0<br>(estimate) | – | – | – |

*Notes:*

[a] In the Czech Republic, as of November 1994, foreign banks accounted for 7.9 per cent of total gross banking profits, and 14.5 per cent of total net profits.

[b] In Hungary, at the end of 1994, foreign banks accounted for 68 per cent of total net profits.

[c] In Poland, as of September 1994, foreign banks accounted for 23 per cent of total gross banking profits.

– = not available

*Source:* National Bank of Poland (1995); State Banking Supervision of Hungary (1994, 1995); Czech National Bank internal data; Analytical Centre Under the President of the Russian Federation (1994); own calculations.

account for insignificant levels in PCPEs, with the exception of Hungary where they still lend less than one-sixth of the total. These low lending levels, moreover, exist despite the rapid (absolute) growth shown by foreign bank lending levels between 1992 and 1994. This is true in Poland in particular.

On the other hand, the profitability figures suggest that foreign banks have been profitable in these markets, particularly compared with domestic banks. Reasons include the high costs of maintaining the branch networks for local banks and, more importantly, the fact that many local banks are provisioning for their NPLs. The absence of any such differential in the Czech Republic reflects to a large extent the Czech financial restructuring whereby NPLs were placed in a separate consolidation bank.[20] In Hungary and Poland, an additional reason is that there continue to exist state-owned banks which may not be profit-oriented.[21]

There are clearly numerous reasons for the relatively low levels of foreign bank involvement in these PCPEs, including concerns of macroeconomic and political instability and the changing legal requirements. Here we draw attention to some that arise even in the East German case. First of all, for outside banks it is difficult to develop a local deposit base owing to the lack of a branch network and portfolio of enterprises for which the banks manage deposit business (i.e. cash management). While this may have been an obstacle to the expansion of West German bank lending in the East, it is a particular obstacle for foreign banks which would have to 'import' funds to on-lend, thus taking on cross-border risk. Furthermore, the experience of West German banks in the East underscores the vast expense necessary to build a branch network. Even with the high levels of investment, West German banks were unable to take away deposits to any significant degree from the local Savings Banks. In other PCPEs, the legacy of the monopoly of the Savings Banks over deposits is likely to be at least as hard to penetrate. In Russia, the Savings Banks held 83 per cent of deposits on 1 January 1993, and still had 61 per cent by March 1995.[22] In addition, inter-bank markets in these countries are often not highly developed making funds both more costly and perhaps not available.[23]

From the East German experience we learn that building a branch network involves costs to the parent bank beyond the financial investment, as it places strains on the bank to fill the local staffing requirements. This is particularly evident in terms of qualified lending officers. To put this problem into perspective, according to a McKinsey &

Company survey, lending skills are in short supply even in mature banking systems:

> In the United States ... many banks have concluded that it is no longer feasible to maintain the skills of hundreds of loan officers throughout their branch systems.[24]

In addition to this constraint on lending activity, a further one is capital committed by the parent bank, which limits the amount of overall lending the bank can extend.[25] Foreign banks have limited amounts of capital, and thus are constrained in the amounts they can allocate to each particular country.

Even where foreign banks enter the market, they have to undergo a learning process to develop their local information and customer base. In addition, unlike the West German banks in the East, foreign banks in PCPEs are not the source of such heightened expectations to develop the local economy.[26] As a result of these factors and the constraints outlined, foreign banks tend to develop their lending activities gradually, with high levels of loans to other banks in the early period of development.[27] At the same time, foreign banks' initial lending business tends to focus on multinationals (MNCs), often existing overseas customers of the parent bank. In Russia, a report by the Analytical Centre Under the President found that while foreign bank activities were insignificant in terms of their volumes, these banks tended to operate in what they called 'ecological niches', including serving MNCs and joint-ventures.[28] A report in the Czech Republic similarly noted:

> It is well known that most foreign banks that have obtained a licence in the Czech Republic are not in a hurry at all with crediting Czech companies unless these are either giants with more or less monopoly status in the market or firms with foreign participation.[29]

In the same report, a banker from *Commerzbank* noted:

> As far as small and medium-sized firms are concerned, we believe that these firms will remain under the Czech banks' domain.

This emphasis on business with foreign companies also occurs in East Germany, but the level of foreign ownership in PCPEs is much lower than West German levels in the East, thus making this market segment much smaller. Against this tendency, there are suggestions that some foreign banks in PCPEs are beginning to widen their loan portfolios to include local firms, smaller enterprises as well as the largest ones.[30]

The foregoing analysis focuses primarily on deposit and lending activities. The East German experience reinforces the point that it would be unrealistic to expect foreign banks to take on the major lending risks of the transition. Nevertheless, there are important areas in which foreign banks can contribute to the process. Foreign banks introduce new products and services to customers in the market.[31] They can accelerate the growth of financial markets, especially the inter-bank market (which they rely upon for financing, particularly in the initial phase following their entry), but also foreign exchange and derivative markets.[32] They engage in training local bankers through seminars and, moreover, staffing these banks over time as locals who work in the foreign banks eventually return to domestic institutions. The primary reason for training local bankers, apart from the simple desire to help develop the country's financial system, is that for most foreign banks their most important customer segment in the early years of operation in particular consists of *other banks*.

Recent events in Central and Eastern Europe suggest that foreign banks may be given a greater opportunity to acquire market share by purchasing domestic institutions on favourable terms. Stemming from European Union directives on opening domestic financial sectors, the continued sorry state of most domestic banks and the more general international forces touched upon in the outset of the book, we may well find closer examples to the West German ideal case of virtually complete foreign ownership of banks. This led The *Economist* in 1998 to observe that, 'A year from now, a domestically owned East European bank may well be a rarity'.[33] Before speculating upon what this might mean for the region – and this book certainly suggests some possible consequences – we should not overlook the obstacles to foreign banks actually entering on such a grand scale. As the same *Economist* article goes on to say:

> So is it bonanza time for international banks seeking East European bargains? Up to a point. But empire-building in Eastern Europe is not necessarily cheap or easy.

## A closing word

This book has sought, first, to broaden the conventional framework on banking reform in PCPEs by emphasising the learning process and framing the discussion in the context of institutional change. Second, it has provided an extensive discussion of the East German limiting case, including case studies of two West German banks, drawing on interviews as well as internal data gathered in the course of the fieldwork. Third, it has examined the German *Hausbank* system and underlined its important role in managing risk while, at the same time, analysing why it has encountered difficulties in the East. The analysis of the *Hausbank* system has also drawn on sociology and psychology to add perspective to financial and economic data. Fourth, it has used the East German case to suggest implications for banking in other PCPEs, and in particular for the role of foreign banks. Given that foreign banks are unlikely to play the lead role in financing the transition, it is perhaps justified that the emphasis in the literature on the financial system has been focused on domestic banks.

The last point notwithstanding, the current international financial system is demonstrating increasingly that capital will flow more freely and rapidly, and an effect of this trend is that domestic financial institutions will become prone to inflows which may destabilise their countries' financial systems and create banking crises in their wake. The growth of global capital markets will only lead to further disintermediation of banks, and pressure on local banks to withstand the growth of foreign institutions across borders. Witness the events today in Europe, as Economic and Monetary Union (EMU) is widely expected to bring with it massive consolidation in the European financial services industry, across financial institutions, exchanges and related providers. While it is unfortunately outside the scope of this work to begin to analyse such issues, it is hoped that the study can provide a helpful conceptual framework and methodology for further research.

# Appendix 1: Timetable of Events

*All specific banking events are emboldened.

## Before GEMSU

**1989**

| | |
|---|---|
| 9 October | Large demonstration (100 000+) protesters in Leipzig chanting:'*Wir sind das Volk*' ('We are the people'). |
| 18 October | Resignation of SED General Secretary Erich Honnecker, who is replaced with Egon Krenz. |
| 4 November | 1 million East Germans demonstrate in East Berlin. |
| 9 November | The Berlin Wall is opened following months of protests and thousands of East Germans fleeing to the West via Hungary and Czechoslovakia. |
| 28 November | Chancellor Helmut Kohl announces a ten-point programme which addresses the creation of common policy institutions in East and West Germany leading to an eventual unification. |

**1990**

| | |
|---|---|
| 1 February | East German Prime Minster Hans Modrow proposes a plan for unity after discussions in Moscow. |
| 13 February | Prime Minister Modrow visits Bonn and Chancellor Helmut Kohl suggests negotiations on economic and monetary union. |
| 1 March | The *Treuhandanstalt* established. |
| **Early March** | ***Deutsche Bank* enters into negotiations with the *Treuhandanstalt* with regard to the bank's role in the East.** |
| **6 March** | **Decision to introduce a new banking system: the GDR Parliament passes a law (*Gesetz über die Anderung des Gesetzes über die Staatsbank der DDR*) which introduces a two-tier banking system, but with the Staatsbank remaining as the central bank.** |
| 18 March | First free elections in the history of East Germany. The 'Alliance for Germany' (a coalition of the Christian Democratic Union (CDU), Democratic Awakening, and the German Social Union) favouring rapid monetary and economic union followed by full unification, wins with overwhelming support. |
| **19 March** | **The creation of the *Deutsche Kreditbank (DKB)* as the commercial operations are hived off the Staatsbank.** |
| **17 April** | ***Deutsche Bank* signs a letter of intent with *Deutsche Kreditbank* to form a joint venture.** |
| 18 May | The GEMSU Treaty is signed by the governments of the FRG and GDR. |

1990

17 June — The East German Parliament approves '*Treuhandgesetz*,' which later becomes an integral part of the unification treaty.

21/22 June — The GEMSU Treaty is ratified by the parliaments of the FRG and GDR.

* * * *

**1 July — GEMSU: The Deutschmark becomes the sole legal tender in the whole of Germany, and the *Bundesbank* its sole central bank. In addition, *Deutsche Bank* and *Dresdner Bank* acquire the former *Deutsche Kredit Bank (DKB)*, forming separate joint ventures.**

**23 July 1990 — *Deutsche Bank* announces that it will invest an additional DM 700 mn into its joint venture, raising its total capital investment to DM 1 bn and its stake to 84.7 per cent.**

23 August — The East German Parliament votes to seek accession to the FRG through Article 23 of the German Constitution.

31 August — The 'Unification Treaty' is signed by the FRG and GDR governments.

3 October: — Formal (political) Unification: the GDR ceases to exist, and the (West) German Constitution is extended to include the five *neue Bundesländer*.

* * * *

2 December — First general elections. The CDU wins by a large margin, and fosters expectations with promises, such as 'no new tax increase will be needed to finance German unification,' and 'nobody will be worse off but a lot of people will feel better after unification.'

**27 December — *Deutsche Bank* gains 100 per cent control over the joint venture by purchasing the remaining 15.3 per cent from the *THA* for an undisclosed amount.**

31 December — The end of the transferable rouble trade system among East European countries, and also of guarantees for East German exports to the USSR. East German exports to Eastern Europe experience a massive decrease.

1991

**1 February — East German Savings Banks and Credit Cooperatives restricted to up to two-thirds of refinancing through presenting their own promissory notes.**

**31 December — The completion of the transfer of the West German payment system to the *neue Bundesländer*.**

**1992**

**2 January** **Refinancing quotas for East German Savings Banks and Credit Cooperatives are reduced from DM 25 bn (the level they were set at on 1 July 1990) to DM 10 bn.**

**October** **The Bundesbank winds up its administrative office in the East.**

**November** **East German bank refinancing quotas lowered to 'normal' West German levels.**

1995

January The *Treuhandanstalt* closes.

# Appendix 2: State Support Programmes through the Specialised Banks[a]

## Loan programmes

| *Programme* | *Eligibility* | *Conditions* | *Application* |
|---|---|---|---|
| **Equity Capital Assistance Programme** | • Natural persons not older then 55 in: industry and commerce, and the liberal professions | **Uses**:<br>Raise equity capital base for:<br>Business start-ups<br>Acquisition of SMEs (including privatisation)<br>Investment to consolidate private sector company<br>**Maximum loan**: DM 700 000 (for privatisations up to DM 2 mn; for equity increase up to 40% of investment, with 15% more from investor; to strengthen the company, up to 100%)<br>**Term**: up to 20 years<br>**Interest rate**: 1–3 years free; year 4: 2%; year 5: 3%; year 6: 5%; from year 7: market rate<br>**Processing fee**: 2% **Guarantee charge**: 0.5%<br>**Disbursement**: 100% | ***Deutsche Ausgleichsbank* via *Hausbank*** |
| **Equity Capital Assistance Partnership Components** | • Independent SMEs with an investing partner willing to supply DM 100 000 or more and management support | Provides 'equity loans' to support the capital of the partner<br>**Maximum amount**: DM 5 mn in absolute terms; 2.5 times the liable funding of the partners in relative terms<br>**Term**: 20 years; after 10 grace years repayment in 20 equal half-yearly instalments<br>**Interest rate**: same as above | ***Deutsche Ausgleichsbank* via *Hausbank*** |
| **ERP Business Start-Up Programme** | • New businesspeople in industry and commerce and the liberal professions | **Projects to**:<br>• acquire companies including follow-up investment within 3 years of the start of the company.<br>• take over shares in a management capacity<br>• finance the first inventory of goods<br>**Maximum amount**: DM 1 mn (for up to 50% of eligible costs)<br>**Term**: up to 15 years (20 for construction projects)<br>**Interest rate**: currently 5.5% p.a.[b]<br>**Grace period**: up to 5 years<br>**Disbursement**: 100% | ***Deutsche Ausgleichsbank* via *Hausbank*** |

| *Programme* | *Eligibility* | *Conditions* | *Application* |
|---|---|---|---|
| ***Deutsche Ausgleichsbank* Business Start-Up Programme** | • Natural persons<br>• Companies in industry and commerce<br>• Liberal professions | **Projects to**:<br>• set up independently in business<br>• secure the business in the long term within 8 years of the start<br>**Maximum loan**: DM 1.5mn (for up to 50% of the eligible costs; as supplementary support, up to 75%)<br>**Term**: up to 10 years<br>**Interest rate**: currently 5.65% p.a.[b)]<br>**Grace period**: up to 2 years<br>**Disbursement**: 98% | ***Deutsche Ausgleichsbank* via *Hausbank*** |
| **ERP Company Reinforcement Programme** | • Companies in trade and industry with annual turnover of up to DM 50 mn<br>• Liberal professions (excluding healing professions) | **Investment to**:<br>• start or take over<br>• expand or convert<br>• fundamentally rationalise companies<br>**Maximum loan**: DM 1 mn (up to 50% of eligible costs)<br>**Term**: up to 15 years (20 for construction projects)<br>**Interest rate**: currently 5.5% p.a.[b)]<br>**Grace period**: up to 2 years<br>**Disbursement**: 100% | ***Kreditanstalt für Wiederaufbau* via *Hausbank*** |
| ***KfW* Programme for SMEs** | • Companies in industry and commerce with annual turnover of up to DM 1 bn<br>• Liberal professions | Investment to set up, secure, and expand companies<br>Maximum loan: DM 10 mn<br>As financing for investment projects:<br>• up to two-thirds – where turnover over DM 100 mn<br>• up to three-quarters – where turnover below DM 100 mn<br>of the eligible costs<br>**Term**: up to 10 years<br>**Interest rate**: currently 5.25%[b)]<br>**Grace period**: up to two years<br>**Disbursement**: 96% | ***Kreditanstalt für Wiederaufbau* via *Hausbank*** |
| ***KfW/Treuhand* Industry Programme** | Manufacturing companies and industrial service companies owned by the THA | **Investment to**:<br>• adjust to the market<br>• remove obstacles to privatisation<br>Amount of loan: up to 50% of investment costs (can be combined with other support funding)<br>**Term**: up to 10 years<br>**Interest rate**: below capital market rate<br>**Grace period**: 2 years<br>**Disbursement**: 100% | ***Kreditanstalt für Wiederaufbau* via *Hausbank*** |

## Guarantee programmes

| *Programme* | *Eligibility* | *Conditions* | *Application* |
|---|---|---|---|
| **Federal Guarantee Programme for Investors in the New *Länder*** | Existing and new companies | 80% indemnity guarantee for:<br>• loans to fund investment projects<br>• loans to fund operating resources related to the realisation of investment<br>**Guarantee sum**: DM 20 mn minimum<br>**Length of guarantee**: flexible<br>**Costs**:<br>• application fee: 0.5% of sum guaranteed (up to DM 25 000) 50% returned in event of rejection/withdrawal; for approvals, fee deducted from subsequent charges<br>• commission: 0.25% of sum guaranteed; thereafter each 1 April and 1 October 0.25% of the residual sum guaranteed | ***C & L Treuarbeit* via *Hausbank*** |
| ***Deutsche Ausgleichsbank* guarantee programme** | Companies in industry and commerce | 80% indemnity guarantee<br>**Guarantee sum**: between DM 1 mn and DM 20 mn<br>**Length of guarantee**:<br>• for loans for investment projects maximum 15 years (23 for construction)<br>**Costs**:<br>• processing fee of 0.5% of the sum guaranteed, up to DM 30 000 (only on approval)<br>• charge of 0.9% p.a. on the residual sum guaranteed | ***Deutsche Ausgleichsbank* via *Hausbank*** |
| **Guarantees from the *Bürgschaftsbanken*[c]** | • Persons setting up in business<br>• SMEs<br>• Liberal professions | 80% indemnity guarantee<br>**Guarantee sum**: up to DM 1 mn<br>**Length**: maximum 15 years (23 for construction)<br>**Costs**:<br>• processing fee between 0.75% and 1% of the sum guaranteed<br>• commission: between 0.8% and 1% of the residual sum guaranteed | **The relevant *Bürgschaftsbank* via *Hausbank*** |

*Notes*:

[a] The table does not include a number of environmental programmes which are handled via the *Hausbank*. It does not some include other loan programmes that may be handled by the *Hausbank*, such as European Investment Bank (EIB) loans. *THA* guarantee programmes are not included.

[b] Rates as of January 1994.

[c] Including the following *Bürgschaftsbanken*: *Berlin-Brandenburg GMbH; Brandenburg GMbH; Mecklenburg-Vorpommern GMbH; Sachsen GMbH; Sachsen-Anhalt GMbH; Thüringen GMbH.*

*Source*: Federal Ministry of Economics (1994).

# Appendix 3: Bank Activity in the East

*Table* A3.1 Total deposits of non-banks in the East, 1990–4[a]

| *Type of deposit (DM mn)* | *1990* | | *1991* | *1992* | | | | *1993* | | | | *1994* | | | |
|---|---|---|---|---|---|---|---|---|---|---|---|---|---|---|---|
| | *GEMSU* | *Dec.* | *Dec.* | *Mar.* | *Jun.* | *Sep.* | *Dec.* | *Mar.* | *Jun.* | *Sep.* | *Dec.* | *Mar.* | *Jun.* | *Sep.* | *Dec.* |
| Demand deposits | 50 393 | 72 702 | 63 206 | 55 022 | 56 046 | 57 609 | 64 338 | 57 235 | 59 231 | 62 193 | 71 911 | 63 903 | 66 066 | 67 995 | 76 659 |
| Time deposits | 1 277 | 15 909 | 28 689 | 34 811 | 37 234 | 43 674 | 44 546 | 50 756 | 51 648 | 52 084 | 54 603 | 57 581 | 55 196 | 52 778 | 51 610 |
| Savings deposits/ certificates | 120 366 | 64 735 | 63 068 | 65 689 | 66 418 | 67 919 | 73 157 | 75 692 | 76 793 | 78 643 | 84 726 | 86 776 | 88 315 | 90 403 | 96 667 |
| Total deposits | 172 036 | 153 346 | 154 963 | 155 522 | 159 698 | 169 202 | 182 041 | 183 683 | 187 672 | 192 920 | 211 240 | 208 260 | 209 577 | 211 176 | 224 936 |

*Note*: [a] Not including East Berlin.
*Source*: *Deutsche Bundesbank, Regionalergebnisse der monatlichen Bilanzstatistik für Kreditinstitute in Ostdeutschland; Landeszentralbanken* data.

*Table* A3.2 Breakdown of total deposits in the East by bank group, 1990–4*a*

| *Total deposits (DM mn)* | *1990* | | *1991* | *1992* | | | | *1993* | | | | *1994* | | | |
|---|---|---|---|---|---|---|---|---|---|---|---|---|---|---|---|
| | *GEMSU* | *Dec.* | *Dec.* | *Mar.* | *Jun.* | *Sep.* | *Dec.* | *Mar.* | *Jun.* | *Sep.* | *Dec.* | *Mar.* | *Jun.* | *Sep.* | *Dec.* |
| West German commercial banks | 39 971 | 40 889 | 36 070 | 33 479 | 34 713 | 38 603 | 41 311 | 40 428 | 41 059 | 41 296 | 47 904 | 44 889 | 45 673 | 43 981 | 48 617 |
| East German savings banks | 101 496 | 87 670 | 93 521 | 95 649 | 97 758 | 101 749 | 109 500 | 111 413 | 114 056 | 117 158 | 126 632 | 125 454 | 126 812 | 128 470 | 135 665 |
| East German credit cooperatives | 20 058 | 23 650 | 24 592 | 25 563 | 26 313 | 27 821 | 30 195 | 30 916 | 31 506 | 32 597 | 35 141 | 34 288 | 34 595 | 35 640 | 37 751 |
| Other financial institutions | 11 016 | 1 137 | 0 780 | 0 835 | 0 921 | 1 072 | 1 142 | 1 211 | 1 367 | 2 260 | 2 021 | 4 187 | 3 326 | 3 945 | 4 109 |
| All banks | 172 541 | 153 346 | 154 963 | 155 526 | 159 705 | 169 245 | 182 148 | 183 968 | 187 988 | 193 311 | 211 698 | 208 818 | 210 406 | 212 036 | 226 132 |

*Note*: [a] Not including East Berlin.
*Source*: *Deutsche Bundesbank, Regionalergebnisse der Monatlichen Bilanzstatistik für Kreditinstitute in Ostdeutschland; Landeszentralbanken* data.

*Table* A3.3 Breakdown of time deposits in the East, by bank group, 1990–4[a]

| *Time deposits (DM mn)* | *1990* | | *1991* | *1992* | | | | *1993* | | | | *1994* | | | |
|---|---|---|---|---|---|---|---|---|---|---|---|---|---|---|---|
| | *GEMSU* | *Dec.* | *Dec.* | *Mar.* | *Jun.* | *Sep.* | *Dec.* | *Mar.* | *Jun.* | *Sep.* | *Dec.* | *Mar.* | *Jun.* | *Sep.* | *Dec.* |
| East German savings banks | 0 144 | 3 157 | 10 570 | 14 477 | 15 726 | 17 840 | 19 627 | 22 992 | 23 558 | 23 752 | 23 923 | 25 389 | 24 278 | 22 940 | 21 559 |
| West German commercial banks | 1 260 | 8 668 | 11 355 | 11 733 | 12 356 | 15 370 | 13 800 | 15 076 | 15 201 | 15 084 | 16 749 | 17 733 | 16 983 | 15 623 | 16 388 |
| East German credit cooperatives | 0 161 | 3 259 | 6 477 | 8 246 | 8 746 | 9 926 | 10 688 | 12 137 | 12 256 | 12 368 | 12 656 | 12 836 | 12 020 | 11 678 | 11 471 |

*Note*: [a] Not including East Berlin.
*Source*: *Deutsche Bundesbank, Regionalergebnisse der Monatlichen Bilanzstatistik für Kreditinstitute in Ostdeutschland; Landeszentralbanken* data.

*Table* A3.4 Total bank lending in the East, 1991–4

| *Loan type (DM mn)* | *1991* | *1992* | | | | *1993* | | | | *1994* | | | |
|---|---|---|---|---|---|---|---|---|---|---|---|---|---|
| | *Dec.* | *Mar.*[a] | *Jun.* | *Sep.* | *Dec.* | *Mar.* | *Jun.* | *Sep.* | *Dec.* | *Mar.* | *Jun.* | *Sep.* | *Dec.* |
| Enterprise loans[b] | 116 841 | 33 341 | 36 293 | 37 803 | 37 930 | 38 876 | 39 696 | 43 433 | 42 683 | 43 727 | 47 738 | 50 721 | 52 879 |
| Loans to self-employed persons | 12 852 | 13 580 | 15 685 | 17 704 | 19 423 | 20 834 | 22 805 | 24 945 | 27 197 | 28 632 | 30 246 | 31 882 | 34 071 |
| Personal loans | 20 603 | 22 085 | 24 447 | 26 586 | 29 028 | 30 107 | 32 190 | 34 323 | 36 882 | 38 258 | 41 270 | 44 803 | 48 872 |
| Public housing loans | 1 409 | 1 476 | 1 979 | 2 748 | 4 588 | 4 845 | 5 722 | 6 279 | 9 362 | 8 148 | 8 577 | 9 332 | 14 187 |
| Total loans | 151 705 | 70 482 | 78 040 | 84 075 | 90 969 | 94 662 | 100 413 | 108 980 | 116 124 | 118 765 | 127 831 | 136 738 | 150 009 |

*Notes*:
[a] After March 1992, the lending statistics do not include *Staatsbank Berlin* and *DKB* accounts.
[b] Does not include *KfW/DtA* loans.
*Source*: *Landeszentralbanken* data.

*Table* A3.5 Term structure[a] of bank lending in the East, 1991–3

| *Loan maturity (DM mn)* | *1991* | *1992* | | | | *1993* | | | |
|---|---|---|---|---|---|---|---|---|---|
| | *Dec.* | *Mar.*[b] | *Jun.* | *Sep.* | *Dec.* | *Mar.* | *Jun.* | *Sep.* | *Dec.* |
| Short-term[c] | 63 410 | 29 257 | 30 555 | 29 991 | 28 841 | 28 229 | 26 829 | 28 047 | 24 368 |
| Medium-term[c] | 2 672 | 2 905 | 3 216 | 3 571 | 3 940 | 3 786 | 4 097 | 4 044 | 4 395 |
| Long-term[c] | 63 621 | 14 735 | 17 813 | 21 179 | 24 572 | 27 695 | 31 600 | 36 287 | 41 117 |
| Total | 129 703 | 46 897 | 51 584 | 54 741 | 57 353 | 59 710 | 62 526 | 68 378 | 69 880 |

*Notes*:
[a] Term structure data not available for 1994.
[b] After March 1992, the data does not include *Staatsbank* and *DKB* accounts.
[c] 'Short-term' is up to and including 1 year; 'medium-term' is more than 1 year but less than 4; 'long-term' is 4 years or more.
*Source*: *Landeszentralbanken* data (East German banks and West German commercial banks, excluding Mortgage banks).

*Table* A3.6 Bank lending in the East, by bank group, 1991–4

| *Lending group (Dm mn)* | *1991* | *1992* | | | | *1993* | | | | *1994* | | | |
|---|---|---|---|---|---|---|---|---|---|---|---|---|---|
| | *Dec.* | *Mar.*[a] | *Jun.* | *Sep.* | *Dec.* | *Mar.* | *Jun.* | *Sep.* | *Dec.* | *Mar.* | *Jun.* | *Sep.* | *Dec.* |
| West German commercial banks | 116 562 | 32 790 | 36 293 | 37 803 | 39 137 | 39 038 | 40 349 | 42 539 | 42 850 | 42 811 | 46 329 | 48 357 | 51 763 |
| East German savings banks | 23 747 | 25 190 | 23 308 | 31 503 | 34 898 | 36 819 | 39 663 | 42 802 | 46 665 | 48 003 | 50 438 | 53 630 | 57 849 |
| East German credit cooperatives | 9 977 | 10 858 | 11 819 | 12 535 | 13 299 | 14 048 | 14 762 | 14 488 | 15 991 | 16 399 | 17 021 | 17 897 | 18 643 |
| Total | 150 286 | 68 838 | 71 420 | 81 841 | 87 334 | 89 905 | 94 774 | 99 829 | 105 506 | 107 213 | 113 788 | 119 884 | 128 255 |

*Note:* [a] After March 1992, the data does not include *Staatsbank* and *DKB* accounts.

*Source:* *Landeszentralbanken* data.

# Notes and References

## Introduction

1. Gelman (1987, p.237).
2. Lansman, Ergin and Griepp (1989, p.3).
3. Cited in Lansman, Ergin and Griepp (1989, p.6).
4. Calne (1965, p.29).
5. Calne (1965, p.28).
6. Offe (1992b, p.5).
7. Rostowski (1993a).

## 2 The banking system in the transition: a conceptual framework

1. Kornai (1992) presents a comprehensive analysis. Ericson (1991) offers a short but focused overview of the main characteristics of the CPE. Åslund (1989), Hewett (1988) and Nove (1986) examine the historical and institutional development of the Soviet economic system, the prototype for the East European systems.
2. Kornai (1992, pp.91–110).
3. Kornai (1980) introduced the term, and then developed it further (Kornai, 1986). A brief discussion can be found in Kornai (1992, pp.140–5).
4. Ibid. See Kornai (1992, pp.229–34) for a brief overview.
5. Kornai (1992, p.234).
6. Ericson (1991, p.22).
7. Kornai (1992, p.487).
8. Olson (1992, p.63).
9. Ericson (1991, p.11).
10. The literature on the financial system of the CPE is rather limited. Garvy (1966) is the most widely referred-to source. In addition, Peebles (1991), Zwass (1979), Podolski (1973), Grossman (1968) offer similar comprehensive treatments. Catte and Mastropasqua (1993) examine banking reforms in CPEs in the 1980s.
11. Ericson (1991, pp.19–20).
12. Kornai (1992, p.141) presents a more detailed schematic diagram (than Figure 2.1), demonstrating the constrained money flows in the CPE.
13. Kornai, 1992, p.132.
14. Grossman (1968, p.4) categorised the household sector as possessing a higher degree of 'moneyness' than the enterprise sector.
15. Lenin (1964, p.106). The work cited was republished with the original having being written approximately 50 years earlier.
16. Garvy (1966, p.53).
17. Nove (1969, pp.215–6; decrees appear in n.30, p.412.
18. Kornai (1992, p.545).
19. Martin (1992).

20. All of the systems were subject to 'reform', some to a greater and others to a lesser extent. In the USSR, there were the Kosygin reforms (1965) which were intended to increase enterprise autonomy and, of course, there were the *perestroika* reforms (1986–91), which modified the principle of state ownership to a certain extent (Robins, 1991b). In Hungary, the New Economic Mechanism (1968) attempted to increase enterprise autonomy and to decrease the extent of planning. In Yugoslavia, workers' self-management (1960s) was tried to overcome some of the problems with state ownership.
21. Kornai (1993).
22. Lipton and Sachs (1990a, p.99).
23. Dornbusch (1991), for example, argued that the transition should be carried out as quickly as possible, and proposed a '7-day' plan for the process, leaving financial sector reform for the seventh day. McKinnon (1993), on the other hand, put forward the case for gradualism. Pickel (1992a) examines the issues confronting both approaches.
24. Summers (1992); Dornbusch (1991); Fischer and Gelb (1991); Kornai (1990).
25. Countries such as Poland, for example, with extreme macro-imbalances were forced to address these at an early stage (1990) while others such as Czechoslovakia with more stability could concentrate initially more on structural issues. In addition, the level of decentralisation which existed was also important, since it gave an indication of the extent to which the formal institutional structure had already been modified (and thus the degree to which alternative 'formal' institutional arrangements were put in place). Czechoslovakia, for instance, was fortunate with respect to its macro-situation but needed to begin virtually from scratch in overhauling its institutional structure and implementing structural reform. Hungary, Poland and Yugoslavia had made some progress on the institutional front, but were burdened with severe macroeconomic problems. The USSR and Bulgaria manifested the worst of both worlds.
26. While Aghion and Burgess (1993, pp.304–6) reviewed the issues and argued that 'capital *will and will have to come in large part from domestic sources*' (emphasis in original), capital could come from domestic or foreign sources or, most likely, from some combination of the two.
27. Calvo and Kumar (1993, p.3).
28. Listfield and Montes-Negret (1994); Blommestein and Lange (1993, Part 2); and Folkerts-Landau, Garber, and Lane (1993) discuss the development of payment systems in PCPEs.
29. Rostowski (1993a).
30. Calvo and Coricelli (1993) argued that the large fall in output in many PCPEs during the transition was due to the underdeveloped state of credit markets.
31. As throughout the chapter, our analysis remains highly stylised, focusing on problems which were common to the PCPEs, albeit to differing degrees. Some examples from specific countries are mentioned for illustrative purposes, and further studies are suggested. Dittus (1994a, 1994b) and Thorne (1993) present comprehensive, empirical overviews on a country-by-country basis of banking developments and problems in the PCPEs.

32. Dittus (1994a) finds evidence of credit rationing by banks in PCPEs.
33. Stiglitz and Weiss (1981). See Chapter 6 for a discussion.
34. Gomulka (1993); Perotti (1993).
35. See McKinnon (1993) and also Bönker (1993, p.11) concerning tax evasion.
36. Hexter (in Fries, 1994, p.40).
37. Prill (1995, p.185).
38. Lane (1995, p.191). Karailiev and Petkova (1993, pp.210–11) also examine problems in Hungary. Dedek (1995) and Johnson (1994) discuss similar problems in the Czech Republic.
39. Dedek (1995, p.110).
40. Ibid., p.123.
41. For a survey of the venture capital industry in PCPEs, see 'Hopes and Fears', *Business Central Europe*, (February 1995, pp.7–11).
42. Dedek (1995, p.120).
43. See Fries (1994, p.40).
44. Buch (1994); Dittus (1994a, pp.14–25); Calvo and Kumar (1993, pp.13–15).
45. Blommestein and Lange (1993, p.14).
46. Ligeti (1993) makes this point based on the Hungarian experience.
47. See Rostowski (1993b).
48. Bofinger (1992) observed in Poland that the ratio of inter-enterprise credit to bank credit was 70 per cent in 1988 and increased to 150 per cent in 1990.
49. Calvo and Coricelli (1992, p.83) found in Poland that 'the expansion of bank credit in the third quarter [1990] was matched by a contraction of interenterprise credit, leaving total credit for enterprises roughly unchanged'.
50. Winiecki (1993).
51. Aghion and Carlin (1994) and Long (1993) discuss problems, incentives and possible roles for banks.
52. Begg and Portes (1992, p.10).
53. Hardy and Lahiri (1992); McKinnon (1991).
54. McKinnon (1993, p.251).
55. McKinnon (1991, p.147).
56. Caprio and Levine (1994, pp.7–9); Pleskovic (1994, pp.15–16); Schmieding and Buch (1992, p.5); Hinds (1990, pp.130–2).
57. Prill (1995, pp.37–40) estimates that 75 per cent of the Russian banks were pocket banks based on a typology of Russian banks he creates based on their incentive structures. Also see Robins (1991a, pp.45–6).
58. Caprio and Levine (1994, pp.7–9); Dittus (1994a, pp.53–9); Pleskovic (1994, pp.13–5); Calvo and Kumar (1993, p.16); Szöke (1991); Hinds (1990).
59. Calvo and Kumar (1993, pp.13–15) observe that in Poland, at the end of 1991, 20–30 per cent of bank assets were estimated to be non-performing, with more recent estimates (1993) showing between 25–60 per cent in SOBs.
60. Hinds (1990, pp.147–8).
61. Aghion and Carlin (1994, p.26).
62. Ábel jjand Gatsios (1993); Aghion and Burgess (1993, pp.316–17); Miszei (1993).

63. Saunders and Sommariva (1993, pp.936–7).
64. Begg and Portes (1992, pp.7–8).
65. Dittus (1994a, p.60).
66. Johnson (1994, p.983). A similar observation was made by Schiffman (1993, p.1066): 'To assess the technical and commercial feasibility of restructured enterprises in diverse fields requires skills of analysis which most banks in Former Soviet Union countries probably do not have at the present time'.
67. Schmieding and Buch (1992, p.5).
68. Thorne (1993, p.961).
69. See Winiecki (1992).
70. Douglass North, whose work provides the foundation for this section, received the Nobel Prize for Economics in 1993.
71. Akerloff's (1970) classic article on the market for 'lemons' demonstrated the problems caused by asymmetric information for economic agents who, in the case of the used car business, are unable to distinguish on the basis of price and thus employ other forms of judging quality.
72. Coase's (1960) work on transaction costs and the importance of property rights in developing efficient contracts provided the underpinning for much of the recent work.
73. North (1990, p.3).
74. Sjöstrand (1993, p.7).
75. North (1990, p.53).
76. Ibid. (1990, p.42).
77. Ibid. (1990, p.36).
78. Ibid., p.91.
79. Neuber (1993, p.12).
80. Rose (1993).
81. Etzioni (1993). 'Friction (psychological, sociological, political)', he writes (p.59), 'is a major social science variable'.
82. Ibid., p.51.
83. Bönker (1993, pp.10–14). Also see Johnson (1994) and Neuber (1993).
84. Johnson, Kroll and Horton (1992).
85. Kirichenko (1993, p.8).
86. Winiecki (1992, p.14).
87. Saunders and Walter (1992, p.118) (emphasis in original).
88. Brainard (1990) recognised that capital markets in market economies were many years away for PCPEs, with shorter-term prospects depending on banks. Volcker (1990) and Corrigan (1990) presented similar arguments.
89. Gibb (1993, p.474); Dedek (1995).
90. See Calvo and Kumar (1993).
91. Griffith-Jones and FitzGerald (1995); Buch (1994, pp.16–32); Dhar and Selowsky (1994); Pleskovic (1994, pp.17–20); Calvo and Kumar (1993, pp.14–15).
92. Regarding the former USSR, Peck (Nordhaus, *et al.*, 1991, p.364) argued that the outstanding debts would represent a tremendous burden on the budget if they were to be taken on board. Tanzi (1992) drew upon the Chilean experience, arguing that the absorption of bad loans by the government made a negative impact on its fiscal position.

93. See van Wijnbergen (1992).
94. Claassen (1993).
95. Nuti (1992b, p.212).
96. Fries (1994, p.33) and Begg and Portes (1992).
97. Institute for East-West Studies (1994), Rostowski (1994, pp.8–12), and Mortimer (1993) summarise the approaches and problems that have developed.
98. Prill and Robins (1994).
99. Andreas Prindl (1992), however, a banker by trade (Chairman of Nomura Bank International in London), even in a short article devoted considerable attention to the need for a bankers' training institute and a bankers' association along with the need – with the help of foreigners – to develop technical skills.
100. Rostowski (1993c).
101. Ibid., p.3.
102. Arrow (1962) introduced experience into an economic growth model, on the assumption that learning is linear and hence (positive) experience is accumulated over time.
103. Parker and Lewis (1981, p.17).
104. See Lall (1987) and also (1993).
105. Levinthal and March (1993), for instance, outline 'myopias' which inhibit the learning process.
106. Arrow (1962, p.172).
107. Deutsch (1966).
108. Ibid., p.164.
109. Deutsch (1966, p.96) offers an example: 'the greater learning capacity or adaptability of one army relative to another can be predicted if, other things being equal, it has greater facilities of communication and transport and a greater "operational reserve" of uncommitted man power and equipment'.
110. Ibid., p.169.
111. Ibid., p.248.
112. See North (1990, p.104).
113. See Deutsch (1966, pp.247ff.)
114. Wagener (1994, pp.25–6).
115. Szego (1993); Talley (1993); Lacoue-Labarthe (1992).
116. Stiglitz (1992, p.165) discusses the need to protect consumers of banks.
117. Diaz-Alejandro (1985, p.13).
118. Prill and Robins (1994, pp.9–10) model this behaviour graphically, showing that shocks to the learning curve of banks could be minimised through bank supervision.
119. McKinnon produced several works on the design of the financial system in the transition to a market economy. This discussion draws largely from McKinnon (1993); a similar argument is found in McKinnon (1991, Chapter 11).
120. McKinnon (1993, p.251).
121. Rostowski (1993a, pp.447–8).
122. Rostowski (1993c, p.3).
123. Rostowski draws largely on the work of Simons (1936), calling for warehousing and payment companies to carry out payment functions (for

which they could either charge fees or receive interest on their reserves) alongside non-bank financial institutions (NBF Is) which would be responsible for intermediation functions (similar to mutual funds). Friedman (1959) has also suggested a 100 per cent reserve banking system.

124. Rostowksi (1993c, p.16).
125. Other proposals separate the long-term from the shorter-term development of the banking system, arguing that banks' freedom to operate could be increased over time, thus allowing banks to *evolve* into a larger role. Phelps *et al.* (1993, p.31) recommend a transformation whereby mutual and investment funds could become universal banks over time, during which they could develop the necessary infrastructure to provide traditional commercial banking services. Scott (1992) outlines a useful framework which separates transitional objectives from fundamental objectives, also envisioning an evolution over time in the scope of bank activities but in the opposite direction: commercial banks could *gradually become universal* once skills were developed and supervision vastly improved.
126. Begg and Portes (1993, p.18).
127. Ibid.
128. Lipton and Sachs (1990a, p.131). Also see Long and Sagari (1991, pp.436–7).
129. Thorne (1992).
130. Pohl and Claessens (1994).
131. Gray and Hanson (1993); Steinherr (1993); Saunders and Walter (1992), though they recommend a Japanese model in the short- to medium-term, and a German model in the long-term; Schmieding and Buch (1992); Corbett and Mayer (1991).
132. Corbett and Mayer (1991).
133. Saunders and Walter (1992, p.118).
134. Corbett and Mayer (1991, p.62).
135. Phelps *et al.* (1993, p.24).
136. Grosfeld (1994) cautions against excessive concentration of control in banks – through lending *and* shareholding – arguing that it may not lead to dynamic enterprise restructuring. Phelps *et al.* (1993) voice similar concerns.
137. Brainard (1990, p.19).
138. Yip (1995) examines the twinning programme experience in Poland.
139. Steinherr (1993, p.1048).
140. Zecchini (1995); Brada, Schönfeld and Slay (1995); and Aghion and Burgess (1993) provide overviews of the issues, while Wallich (1995) reviews the World Bank experience in PCPEs and Rodlauer (1995) that of the IMF.
141. Terrell (1986), where he also presents objections to these arguments.
142. See Walter (1988, pp.113–22) for more detail.
143. Ibid.
144. Stiglitz (1989a, p.63).
145. Corbett and Mayer (1991, pp.58–9).
146. See, Caprio and Levine (1994, pp.9–10); Pleskovic (1994, p.15); Blommestein (1993); Steinherr (1993, p.1048); Thorne (1993); Chambers and Hyland (1992).
147. Aghion and Carlin (1994).

148. See 'Poland: Bank Privatisation May Take Longer Than Planned', *Rzeczpospolita*, 6 (May 1995) (English abstracts), and also 'Too many banks', *The Banker*, (November 1994, pp.55–60).
149. Rostowski (1993a); Saunders and Walter (1992); Schmieding and Buch (1992).
150. Saunders and Walter (1992, p.120). They break the notion of efficiency into two components: (1) *static efficiency*, which is 'modelled as the all-in weighted average spread [differential] between rates of return provided to ultimate savers and the costs of funds to users'; and (2) *dynamic efficiency*, which is 'characterized by high rates of financial product and process innovation through time'.
151. Rostowski (1993a, p.459).
152. Pigott (1986) makes this point. One such study, Odle (1981), presents a highly critical appraisal of foreign bank activities in the developing world, advocating a Marxist-type perspective of no foreign participation in the real or financial sectors of the economy.
153. See Cho (1985).

## 3 Context and approach of the investigation

1. Rostowski (1993a).
2. For a detailed overview see Kindleberger (1984, Chapter VII). See also Hu (1975, pp.7ff.).
3. Weber (1995, p.38). Dyson (1986, pp.120ff.) illustrates the important role these banks played in assisting German industry in the latter part of the nineteenth century.
4. Weber (1995, p.39).
5. Hu (1975, p.9). *Commerzbank* was at that time called '*Commerz and Discontobank.*'
6. Ibid., p.12. Its deposits grew from 4.8 mn marks in 1871 to 71.8 mn in 1894, and to 779.5mn in 1908.
7. Kindleberger (1984, p.128).
8. Ibid., p.127.
9. *Dresdner Bank Annual Report* (1989, p.7).
10. Axel Osenberg, 'Deutsche Bank moves east,' *Banking World* (June 1991, p.24). Osenberg was a board member of the joint-venture formed in 1990 between *Deutsche Bank* and *Deutsche Kreditbank* (see Chapter 4).
11. 'Reclaiming the East,' *Bank Systems and Technology* (June 1992, p.58), quoting *Commerzbank* director Peter Kraemer.
12. For a brief account, see Andrew Fisher, 'Banks' Big Adventure,' *Financial Times* (11 August 1995, p.12).
13. See Kindleberger (1984, pp.419–20).
14. Hultman (1990, p.6) describes a foreign branch as 'an office of an institution located outside the country under the laws of the country in which the institution is organized.'
15. The only banks not privatised were the local Savings Banks and Credit Cooperatives which are discussed below.
16. This meant that the banks were not given incentives to support (poorly performing) SOEs owing to their significance in the banks' portfolios.

17. As Schrettl (1992, p.147) observed, 'the State Treaty [GEMSU] contains practically all the elements usually considered indispensable in programmes of transition.' Winiecki (1992) argued that the GDR was aided far more by its imported institutional structure from West Germany than by the large capital injections it received from West Germany.
18. Phelps *et al.* (1993).
19. Giersch, Paqué–and Schmieding (1992, pp.262–6) provide an exposition of these conditions.
20. Offe (1992b, pp.1–2).
21. Carlin and Richthofen (1995, p.2).
22. Schulmann (1992, p.132).
23. Dornbusch and Wolf (1992, p.245).
24. Rostowski (1993c, p.5).
25. Edwards and Lawrence (1994, pp.4–5).
26. Carlin and Richthofen (1995); Deeg (1994); Griffin (1994).
27. See Wagner (1993), for example.
28. Carlin and Richthofen (1995); Deeg (1994); Griffin (1994).
29. Deeg (1994, p.37) for instance, found that, 'state loans and guarantees were critical to the process of building a credit market in the East.'
30. Deeg (1994) argues that that the East is undergoing a process of 'normalisation,' under which 'banks are assuming an Eastern role in industrial development and governance that is largely consistent with the role that has evolved in western Germany.' One of the proponents of the contemporary school (see Chapter 4), Deeg holds that 'the market behaviour of banks in the East is consistent with their increasingly risk-averse behaviour in the West.' (1994, p.5).
31. Carlin and Richthofen (1995): Griffin (1994).
32. Carlin and Richthofen (1995, p.14).
33. Schama (1989, p.xiii).
34. Edwards and Lawrence (1994, pp.5–6).
35. The closure of the privatisation agency (*Treuhandanstalt*), for instance, occurred after the author had gathered valuable internal data on liquidity loans (Chapter 5) and interviewed its staff.
36. A *Deutsche Bundesbank* report (1994f) noted that these banks could be considered 'representative' of all East German banks since they accounted for about four-fifths of the business volume of East German banks and more than 90 per cent of all interest volume.
37. 'Other Organisations' include research institutes, government institutions, bank and industry associations, chambers of commerce and academics. The *Bundesbank* category includes its regional offices (*Landeszentralbanken*). In addition to the Specialised Banks, other banks include *Dresdner, IKB* and *Sal. Oppenheim*, among others.
38. Author's interviews.
39. The data for these are collected primarily from nine banks, including: *Bayerische Hypotheken- und Wechsel-Bank AG; Bayerische Vereinsbank AG* (not including *Vereins- und Westbank AG); Berliner Bank AG; Berliner Handels- und Frankfurter Bank; Commerzbank AG; Deutsche Bank AG; Dresdner Bank AG; SchmidtBank KGaA;* and *Vereins- und Westbank AG*.

40. Moreover, the data presented were gathered through a mailing to the credit departments of the participating banks, rather than based on any published figures. (Author's interview with a manager from the *Bundesverband deutscher Banken*, 27 July 1994).
41. Weber (1995, p.68).

## 4 Economic, institutional and banking development after GEMSU

1. Akerloff *et al.* (1991, p.1).
2. Sinn and Sinn (1992, pp.29–30).
3. Bofinger and Cernohorsky (1992) present comparative data. Also see Giersch, Paqué and Schmieding (1992, pp.266–7) and Siebert, Schmieding and Nunnenkamp (1992).
4. Dornbusch and Wolf (1994, p.161). The OECD (1990–1, p.14) placed the fall in *real* GDP at 31.4 per cent in 1991. The higher early drop was due to significant inflation in the East after GEMSU, particularly for consumer goods. Inflation levels in the East were: 14.2 per cent in 1991; 11.2 per cent in 1992; 8.8 per cent in 1993; and 3.4 per cent in 1994 (*German Brief*, 13 January 1995, p.7).
5. Dornbusch and Wolf (1994, p.161).
6. OECD (1990–1, p.42). See Siebert, Schmieding and Nunnenkamp (1992, p.93) for a detailed, sectoral breakdown.
7. Sinn and Sinn (1992, p.29). Also see Akerloff, *et al.* (1991, pp.6–7).
8. Akerloff, *et al.* (1991, p.8).
9. Sinn and Sinn (1992, p.29). Their calculation does not include, however, the roughly 700 000 people who had taken early retirement up to the end of 1991, or the roughly 540 000 commuters who worked in West Germany. The OECD (1990–1, p.50) presents similar calculations.
10. Dornbusch and Wolf (1994, p.161).
11. *Deutsche Bundesbank* (1990b, p.15).
12. The following allowances were made. The rate of M 1 = DM 1 was offered: (a) to balances not exceeding M 2000 for persons born after 1 July 1976; (b) to balances not exceeding M 4000 for persons born between 2 July 1931 and 1 July 1976; and (c) to balances not exceeding M 6 000 for persons born before 2 July 1931. For details, see *Deutsche Bundesbank* (1990c).
13. *Deutsche Bundesbank* (1990b, p.16).
14. An in-depth look at events leading up to GEMSU from the *Bundesbank* perspective which focuses on the divisions between then *Bundesbank* President Karl Otto Pöhl and German Chancellor Helmut Kohl can be found in Marsh (1992, pp.196–27), and a more concise account in Görtemaker (1994, pp.235–8).
15. Not all were agreed on this point, even though the black market exchange rate had been more than 4 M = 1 DM prior to GEMSU. Sinn and Sinn (1992) argued that based on purchasing power of the Mark in the East, the conversion rates did not adequately compensate East Germans. This view was controversial, however, and many estimates of purchasing power were offered. A useful summary table of these is in Sinn and Sinn (1992, p.54).

16. Görtemaker (1994, p.145). As an aside, an opinion poll conducted a day before the announcement predicted that the SPD would win a clear majority of the vote, with expected support at more than twice the level projected for the CDU.
17. Dornbusch and Wolf. (1994, p.158).
18. Sinn and Sinn. (1992, p.70).
19. Autarky was evident on an aggregate level in the *closed* nature of the GDR economy. Exports in the GDR represented 20 per cent of GDP while in West Germany exports were 35 per cent. (OECD, 1990–1, pp.26–7) It was also evident on a *Kombinat* level, with the *Kombinate* each remaining relatively self-sufficient, what von Thadden (1994a, p.4) described as 'an economy within an economy.'
20. The OECD (1990–1, pp.86–91) outlines the reasons for restructuring.
21. According to the OECD (1990–1, p.16), the *Kombinate* increased their share of net product in East Germany from 55.3 per cent in 1950 to 95.7 per cent in 1988. During this period, in 1972, the Honecker government had nationalised virtually all of the existing SMEs. Distribution in the labour market showed a similar monopolisation by the *Kombinate.*
22. In 1989, services in the East accounted for 5.5 per cent of the total value added in the economy, whereas in West Germany they accounted for 29 per cent. Mining and manufacturing accounted for 53.4 per cent in the East against 35.9 per cent in West Germany (OECD 1990–1, p.24) This, of course, explains why the service sector was able to grow after GEMSU.
23. Siebert *et al.* (1992, p.71).
24. Extensive survey research (Akerloff *et al.*, 1991) suggested that this reasoning was misguided. That is, East Germans were more concerned with the prospect of unemployment than with lower wages – in other words, raising wages was not what East German workers would have preferred (given the unemployment levels it was to bring).
25. In economic terms, Akerloff *et al.* (1991, p.16) stated the problem simply: 'at prevailing Eastern wages and world market prices most Eastern firms that produce tradable goods are unable to cover even their short-run costs of production.' Hallet, Ma and Mélitz (1994) used simulations – based on the IMF's MULTIMOD – to demonstrate that the unrealistically high wages would take decades to correct.
26. OECD (1990–1, p.51, 1992–3, p.61).
27. This phenomenon suggests that wage inflation might have occurred *no matter the exchange rate that was applied.*
28. Akerloff *et al.* (1991, pp.56–64) list reasons for the wage increases, including: (1) that economic union created a single labour market where only one wage could prevail (and where West German wages did not fall); (2) that East German workers had a strong sense that for equity concerns they should be paid the same as West Germans; (3) that East German unions put strong pressure on Eastern wages; (4) that West German unions placed similar pressure on wages to protect West German jobs – i.e. slow migration, and enhance union solidarity East and West; and (5) that management offered no effective resistance to demands for higher wages. Schrettl (1992, p.153) extends the latter view, arguing that the high wages served as a bargaining point: 'In resisting wage demands, employers would

have deprived themselves of the twin advantages of (i) being able to buy the Treuhandanstalt's assets relatively cheaply, and (ii) maintaining public pressure on the government to continue existing or even provide further subsidies for investors and employers in eastern Germany.'

29. Ardagh (1991, pp.462–5) offers a vivid account of the poor state of the environment in East Germany, and the issues involved in its improvement. Also see Merkl (1993, pp.249–52).
30. OECD (1990–1, p.89).
31. Akerloff *et al.* (1990, pp.26–30) offer a thorough analysis of the low productivity levels in East Germany after GEMSU.
32. The study measured productivity (as a percentage of West German productivity) on a sectoral basis as follows: Fuel and energy (45 per cent); Chemicals (55 per cent); Construction materials (40 per cent); Steel industry, non-ferrous metals (45 per cent); Mechanical engineering and construction of motor vehicles (55 per cent); Electronics, data processing, precision engineering and optical goods (50 per cent); Textiles (55 per cent); Food Industry (40 percent) (*Deutsche Bank*, 1989, pp.8–11).
33. OECD (1990–1, p.25).
34. Ibid., p.43.
35. Beintema and van Ark (1993). They found, however, that performance was relatively good in certain sectors, including food products, beverages and leather products, with productivity levels above 50 per cent of those in West Germany, while machinery and transport equipment sectors performed poorly, with levels of just over 20 per cent of those in West Germany.
36. Dornbusch and Wolf (1992, p.239).
37. Akerloff *et al.* (1991) argued that the loss of product markets represented the second crucial negative effect – in addition to the 'price–cost squeeze' – on the East German economy.
38. OECD (1990–1, p.29). Also see Siebert, *Schmieding* and Nunnenkamp (1992, p.71).
39. See Sinn and Sinn (1992, pp.37–9) for a discussion of this issue. This dilemma was common to all ex-CMEA members.
40. Sinn and Sinn (1992, p.38).
41. *Deutsches Institut für Wirtschaftsforschung, 'Wochenbericht,'* 12 (21 March 1991, p.127).
42. OECD (1992–3, pp.13–24).
43. Akerloff *et al.* (1991, p.13).
44. Ibid., p.28.
45. The *THA* was created in March 1990 but was given little scope for privatisation at that time. It was given this scope at GEMSU with the passage of the 'Trusteeship Act' (*Treuhandgesetz*) on 17 June 1990, after which time it began rapidly to dispose of its portfolio. The *THA* became the focus of both extreme praise and criticism, and the literature on it voluminous. Fischer, *Hax* and Schneider (1993) offer the most comprehensive treatment. For English sources, Balz (1992) offers a critical appraisal of the *THA*, while Carlin and Mayer (1992) offer a more favourable account. *Deutsche Bundesbank* (1994e) looks specifically at the financial aspects of the *THA*.

46. Bös and Kayser (1995, p.84). The unification treaty, which took effect on 3 October 1990, repeated these functions virtually word-for-word (Article 25).
47. Carlin and Mayer (1992, pp.327–8), and (1994, pp.191–2) examine the creation of these boards, which we discuss further in Chapter 6.
48. Enterprises were broken down into six categories: (1) profitable; (2) expected to be profitable in 1992; (3) could be successfully privatised; (4) appear capable of being profitable but have inadequate plans; (5) unlikely to become profitable; (6) unable to be made profitable (Carlin and Mayer, 1992, p.329).
49. Ibid., p.329. 'Potentially viable' meant that the enterprise would fall into the first four categories outlined above.
50. von Thadden (1994a, p.6) citing the 'Treuhand Act' (*Gesetzblatt der DDR I*, p.300).
51. Merkl (1994, pp.214–15) outlines the criticisms which were levied against the *THA*.
52. See Watson (1992, p.187).
53. von Thadden (1994a, p.10). Also see Esser (1994b, p.119).
54. OECD (1995, p.161).
55. Although the *THA* itself ceased its operations at the end of 1994, several agencies were created, including the Federal Institute for Unification-Caused Special Tasks, in order to monitor the agreements that had been secured on employment and investment levels (*Economist Intelligence Unit*, on *Reuters-News-Service*, 24 October 1994) For details, see OECD (1995, p.73).
56. *Treuhandanstalt* (1994a, 31 May, p.2).
57. *The Economist* (24 December–6 January 1994, pp.93–4).
58. '*Die Treuhand hat Geschichte geschrieben,' Trierer Volksfreund* (3 December 1994).
59. The precise figure was DM 204 619 bn (*Deutsche Bundesbank Monthly Report*, February 1995, p.58).
60. Sinn and Sinn (1992, pp.81ff.) present a comprehensive account of the history behind restitution, the legal and institutional issues involved and the implications for the privatisation process, including a good overview of the different categories of persons along with their entitlements under the law.
61. For an overview of the development of East German property law, see Jeffress (1991, pp.529–32).
62. Sinn and Sinn (1992, p.88) offer a detailed account of the specific cases of restitution that emerged.
63. This decision was meant to appease the Soviet Union and lead it to acquiesce in unification. The decision was challenged in the German Federal Constitutional Court by more than 10 000 expropriated parties, but it was ruled that legal agreements between the Soviet Union and West Germany took precedence over legal claims to compensation based on constitutional principles (Merkl, 1994, p.201).
64. Siebert (1991, p.296). The reason that ownership remained uncertain was that there had been more than one expropriation in the East – i.e. multiple claimants for the same property.

65. The cost of financially compensating former owners was clearly a factor in choosing restitution as opposed to compensation, as was the lobbying and potential votes of West Germans who, after all, were the primary beneficiaries of it (see Chapter 6). In extreme cases, or cases where the investment was important for the public good, compensation could be offered. But these cases were the exception, not the rule.
66. According to Sinn and Sinn (1992, p.83), natural restitution carried out through the municipal authorities has proved to be a complete failure. By October 1991 only about 3.3 per cent of the claims had been settled; 90 per cent of the decisions regarding the restitution of firms were being contested and were thus not yet legally valid. In an interview with the author, one attorney confirmed on the basis of his experience that in the early days municipal cases often took more than a year to sort out.
67. Some facets of the former East German property law were maintained, notably the East German law forbidding property transfer, originally devised to prevent speculation. After GEMSU, this law was used to prevent property transfer until claims could be processed. In other words, an old East German law was kept in place only with a new purpose (author's interview).
68. 'Investing in East Germany: Restitution Nightmares,' *German Brief* (10 June 1994, p.4) citing data from the *Institut der deutschen Wirtschaft.*
69. *Gesetz zur Beseitigung von Hemmnissen bei der Privatisierung von Unternehmen und zur Förderung von Investitionen,* (22 March 1991) (*Bundesgesetzblatt,* Part I, No.20, 28 March 1991, pp.766–89).
70. Sinn and Sinn (1992, pp.94–6).
71. The modification process continues. In September 1994, the *Financial Times* reported, The upper house of Germany's parliament has passed a law to compensate former property owners in East Germany. The law, which will speed up investment decisions in the five eastern states, follows three years of wrangling over terms and funding. (Judy Dempsey, 'Germany Passes Property Law,' *Financial Times,* 26 September 1994, p.2)
72. Author's interview.
73. *Zeitschrift für offene Vermögensfragen (ZOV)* and *Zeitschrift für Vermögens- und Investitionsrecht (VIZ).*
74. We explore risk management by banks in Chapter 6.
75. Sheng and Cho (1993).
76. Ibid., p.8.
77. Schrettl (1992).
78. Giersch, Paqué and Schmieding (1992, p.262).
79. Schrettl (1992, p.149).
80. Esser (1994a, pp.28–9). The West German 'social market economy' has been the source of a large literature. The father of the term, Alfred Müller-Armack (1965), presents a brief but vague account of its principles.
81. Randlesome (1994, p.187). The decision to subsidise capital rather than wages attracted some criticism. (Sinn and Sinn, 1992, pp.174–9) Akerloff *et al.* (1991) argued for a wage subsidy, as did Begg and Portes (1993).
82. *Deutsche Bundesbank* (1995a, pp.48–9).
83. *Deutsche Bundesbank* (1992c, p.21).

84. Ibid., p.22.
85. Ibid., p.22.
86. Vitols (1994, p.5). About 60 per cent of all bank loans to small enterprises in West Germany have maturities of more than one year, and most of these have maturities of four years or more (Vitols, 1994, p.6).
87. *Deutsche Bundesbank* (1992c, p.28).
88. The 'German Unity Fund' was created on 16 May 1990, under which the federal government and the West German *Länder* would raise DM 115 bn to finance unification. (F. Protzman, 'Germans in Accord on Financing Unity,' *The New York Times*, May 17 1990, as cited in Jarausch and Granson, 1994, p.153.)
89. *Deutsche Bundesbank Monthly Report* (1993, p.59).
90. OECD (1992–3, p.70). In a study of the *Institut der deutschen Wirtschaft*, fourth-fifths of responding enterprises cited high capital costs as a major deterrent to investment (Smyser, 1993, p.179).
91. Harm (1992a, p.7). We use the term '*Mittelstand*' rather than 'SME' when referring to Germany.
92. Simon (1992).
93. William J. Holstein, 'Think Small: The Export Lessons to be Learned from Germany's Midsize Companies,' *Business Week* (November 4 1991, pp.58–65).
94. The senator was Elmar Pieroth (Merkl, 1993, pp.272–3).
95. *Treuhandanstalt* (1992, 1993).
96. Hummel, Ludwig *et al.* (1994, p.92).
97. Harm (1992a, p.32) observes that

    > a lot was achieved by the government providing liquidity, while the banks of the private sector bear the risk and are compensated for it. This way, a market inefficiency is overcome while avoiding the mistakes of centralised administration.

98. *Kreditanstalt für Wiederaufbau* (1993, p.1).
99. The *KfW* approves about 99 per cent of the applications it receives in the East. The large demand for loans after GEMSU placed the *KfW* under pressure to review (quickly) all the applications it had received. The decision to approve a loan application was based on a quick check of whether the borrower met the required criteria (see Appendix 2, p. 000) and whether the purpose of the loan was within *KfW* guidelines. (author's interview).
100. The margin is generally 1 per cent when the *Hausbank* takes the full liability for the loan, but decreases as risk-sharing between the KfW and the *Hausbank* is introduced (see below).
101. *Kreditanstalt für Wiederanfbau* Annual Report (1990, p.40).
102. *Kreditanstalt für Wiederanfbau* Annual Report (1992, p.29). The maximum is 50 per cent in West Germany.
103. One estimate (Harm, 1992a, p.11) placed the general KfW share at roughly 41 per cent of the borrower's financing package, though it did not specify the year.
104. As a result, the loan approval rate for the *DtA* has been slightly lower in the East than for the *KfW* (about 96 per cent of all applications) and the lending process somewhat longer (about two months). (author's interview). These

results may also be caused by the more difficult screening involved in start-ups as opposed to existing enterprises.

105. *Deutsche Bundesbank* (1992c, pp.22–3).
106. *Deutsche Bundesbank* (1990b, p.19).
107. What the *Deutsche Bundesbank* (1995a, p.46) called 'aid towards self-help', these funds were transitional in order to enable the East to develop its infrastructure while maintaining satisfactory living standards for the people.
108. Public transfers between West and East German governments, on regional and local levels do not generally get intermediated by the banking system (in the first instance). On the other hand, West German banks provide significant levels to the German government. (*Deutsche Bundesbank*, 1997). The transfer process would warrant a complete discussion in its own right. These transfers have been significant in the East, and regional and local governments have played a significant role in their allocation. The East German *Länder* each developed industrial policies with elaborate schemes for privatisation and various financing and support packages. To compete for investment, the *Länder* publicised these programmes, took on financial advisors, and introduced high-profile advertising. The *Investment Atlas for Saxony*, for example, outlines the regional advantages, industrial and sectoral structure, opportunities for support and corresponding contacts for the *Land* Saxony. The *Atlas* was prepared by the Saxony Economic Development Corporation with the support of Deutsche Bank.
109. The OECD (1991–2, p.37) estimates that in 1992, of the total DM 218 bn in transfers to East Germany, only 25 per cent was used for investment purposes, whereas 55 per cent was used for consumption, subsidies and interest payments. (The other 20 per cent was marked 'other'.) Moreover, the OECD measure of public transfers includes ERP funds (i.e. Specialised Bank loans) which, equalling 11 per cent of the total, are virtually *all* used for investment purposes. This makes the low level of investment overstated somewhat in any event. The use of public transfers primarily for consumption reasons is another reason why they have not featured more prominently in the analysis.
110. According to the OECD (1990–1, p.102), following an agreement in March 1991, between the Treuhandanstalt, the Federal government and the new Länder on the principles for cooperation, the Treuhandanstalt appears to have become more firmly committed to financing investment and other restructuring expenditures on the part of firms for which purchasers are not readily apparent.
111. *Deutsche Bundesbank* (1990b, p.16).
112. The *Bundesbank* uses the measure of 'business volume' rather than balance sheet size to compare banks. Business volume is the 'balance sheet total plus endorsement liabilities on rediscounted bills, own drawings in circulation discounted and credited to borrowers, and bills from the banks' portfolios dispatched for collection prior to maturity' (Edwards and Fischer, 1994, p.100).
113. Weber (1995, p.38).
114. Edwards and Fischer (1994, pp.107–8).
115. See Weber (1995, pp.54–6).

116. Ibid., p.38.
117. Ibid.
118. Harm (1992a); Vitols (1994).
119. Edwards and Fischer (1994, pp.75–83) provide a detailed description of the different legal forms.
120. Ibid., p.75.
121. Ibid.
122. Ibid. The decrease in turnover reflects the changeover in legal status in many of these businesses to *GMbH* or *AG* status.
123. Some *GMbHs* are quite large, bigger than *AGs*.
124. In Chapter 6 we examine more closely the governance role of German banks *vis-à-vis* the *Mittelstand.*
125. Schneider-Lenné (1992) provides a clear and concise overview of the control levers. A more comprehensive analysis is Baums (1992), with a detailed, legal review provided by Roggenbuch (1992).
126. Prill (1995) provides a detailed discussion on the importance of proxy holdings in the governance of non-financial enterprises.
127. All *AGs* must have a supervisory board, as well as all *GMbHs* with more than 500 employees, though in the latter case the board has less extensive rights. It cannot, for instance, dismiss the management of an enterprise, a right which is accorded to supervisory boards in *AGs*. The main functions of the supervisory board are outlined in the Stock Corporation Act (*Aktiengesetz*) and are not explored here in detail.
128. There are periodic accusations against the banks for exercising monopolistic practices by virtue of their control levers. The Gessler Commission, however, appointed by the Minister of Finance, prepared a study during the period 1974–9 and found little support for the accusations being made against banks. For a summary of the findings, see Krümmel (1980).
129. Edwards and Fischer (1994, pp.1–11) offer a concise overview of this literature.
130. Gerschenkron (1968, p.137). Hu (1975, pp.7–17) presents a brief historical overview of the large role the German banks have played in the country's economic development.
131. See Esser (1990). Harm (1992b) also investigates 'the myth in the Anglo-Saxon literature: that German banks own or control German industry', and argues that 'banks have been vindicated by all major studies examining the banking system'. Dyson (1986) argues that German banks have become less disposed to assist firms in distress.
132. Edwards and Fischer (1994) find no evidence that banks provide plentiful and lower-cost finance to industry as a result of their universal status and institutional levers of control.
133. Sabel, Griffin and Deeg (1993, p.13) note that

    > management [in large firms] could not bring the level of internal finance high enough to make bank debt superfluous until the early 1970s, when pension reform gave them an opening to act.

    This is not to say that the Big Banks did not maintain a significant share of business – primarily non-lending services – with these enterprises.

134. See Deeg (1993, pp.168–70).
135. Deeg (1992, p.184). See also Sabel, Griffin and Deeg (1993) for a thoughtful presentation of the major strands of the contemporary view.
136. Quack and Hildebrandt (1995b, p.11); Vitols (1994); and Harm (1992a), especially the table on p.24.
137. Sabel, Griffin and Deeg (1993, pp.17–24) and also Mullineux (1994, p.25).
138. From 1978 to 1982, Big Bank *Mittelstand* loans as a per centage of total corporate lending rose from 28.3 per cent to 37.2 per cent. The rise, however, took place as the Big Banks' share of the overall corporate loan market fell from 15.4 per cent to 11.9 per cent. That is to say, Big Banks saw a *relative* increase in *Mittelstand* lending as lending to large enterprises fell.
139. Buck (1987, pp.190–3) and Garvy (1966, pp.145–50) provide more detailed discussions on the development of the Staatsbank.
140. Garvy (1966, p.146).
141. Buck (1987, p.197).
142. Ashauer (1990, p.9). He offers a detailed description of savings bank activity in East Germany, including a geographic breakdown of the branch network.
143. Garvy (1966, p.145).
144. Buck (1987, pp.193–7) examines these banks' functions and development.
145. To enhance their business standing in the West, these banks were registered as *AG*s. (Buck, 1987, p.196)
146. *Gesetz über die Anderung des Gesetzes über die Staatsbank der DDR.*
147. The *DKB*, created on 19 March 1990, initially had a balance sheet volume of M 286 bn, with a portfolio of more than 7000 enterprises (*'Privatisierung bis Jahresende'*, *Neue Zeit*, 24 February 1994, p.10).
148. Shinasi, Lipschitz and McDonald (1990, p.151).
149. Author's interview. Buck (1987, p.198) notes that the actual per centage of women working in banks was 80 per cent, though another account puts the figure at 95 per cent ('The Problems of Unity', *Euromoney*, September 1990, p.11).
150. Daniel Ben Ami, 'Bankers in the Front Line', *Banking World* (February 1991, p.17).
151. Based on the prevailing market exchange rate of M 7 = DM 1 (Shinasi, Lipschitz and McDonald, 1990, p.144, n. 2), and on the average 1989 exchange rate of DM 3.081 = £1 (*Deutsche Bundesbank, Monthly Report, Statistical Section*, March 1995, p.76).
152. For a technical, legal account of the institutional changes in the banking system following GEMSU, see Robertz (1990).
153. See Deeg (1994, pp.8–15) for a detailed discussion on the integration processes of both bank sectors, with particular emphasis on the internal political dimension.
154. Meinecke (1993, p.90).
155. FIBOR is the Frankfurt Interbank Offer Rate. The claims were in essence interest-bearing government bonds. Redemption beginning in July 1995 involved 2.5 per cent of the claims' nominal value being paid back annually (Schütte, 1993, p.183, n. 2).
156. The *RIKO* (*Rückstellungen für Richtungskoeffizienten*) fund was established at the *Staatsbank* to reconcile the official exchange rate with the one used for

trade with non-CMEA countries. Trade with these countries was conducted using the 'valuta mark' (VM) rather than the Mane. While the official conversion rate was VM 1 = DM 1, an unofficial, depreciated rate was used in practice. In 1989, for example, this rate was VM 1 = M 4.4. Thus if an importer brought in goods worth DM 100, he would pay M 100 to the Foreign Trade Company handling the transaction and an additional M 340 to the fund. Similarly, the export of goods worth DM 100 would involve M 100 being paid to the exporter via the Foreign Trade Company with an additional M 340 coming from the fund. The liability at GEMSU for the *Staatsbank* derived from the export surpluses the GDR had experienced (i.e. an export subsidy). For details, see Mayer and Thumann (1990, p.53).

157. This was written into the State (GEMSU) Treaty (Annex I, Article 8, paragraph 4 (2)) (*Deutsche Bundesbank*, 1990*b*, p.24).
158. We discuss this point in more detail in Chapter 6. We should note, however, that the East German banks were requested to prepare balance sheets which had to be audited and then submitted to the Federal Banking Supervisory Office by not later than 15 March 1991, but were unable to meet this deadline, largely due to valuation problems of the old loans (*Deutsche Bundesbank,* Annual Report, 1991, p.113).
159. Shinasi, Lipschitz and McDonald (1990, p.152).
160. *Deutsche Bundesbank, Annual Report* (1991, p.114). Due to these problems, claims were often allocated in the early stages as book entries with no funds being transferred until a later date.
161. *Deutsche Bundesbank* (1992a, p.23).
162. *Deutsche Bundesbank* (1994c, p.38).
163. *Deutsche Bundesbank* (1993b, pp.49–50) presents a breakdown of the funds allocated.
164. The precise figure was DM 75.263 bn (*Deutsche Bundesbank Monthly Report,* May 1995, p.57).
165. For a discussion of these instruments of monetary policy, see *Deutsche Bundesbank* (1989b, pp.44–80).
166. According to the *Bundesbank*, the minimum conditions for trade bills are that they must be 'backed by three parties known to be solvent, they must fall due within three months of purchase and they should be good trade bills', (*Deutsche Bundesbank*, 1989b, p.46).
167. The *Bundesbank* accepts various forms of collateral, including: (1) Bills (including trade bills); (2) Treasury Bills with a maturity under one year; (3) Bonds and debt register claims of the Federal Government, a *Land* government or a Federal Special Fund; (4) Other Bonds and Debt Register Claims; (5) Equalisation claims *Deutsche Bundesbank,* (1989b, p.50).
168. Based on a *Bundesbank* decision of 17 May 1990. The promissory notes were also backed by provisional claims made on the equalisation fund (Deutsche Bundesbank, *Annual Report*, 1990, p.123).
169. Shinasi, Lipschitz and McDonald (1990, p.151).
170. The combined average business volume in 1991 was approximately DM 140 bn for East German Savings Banks and Credit Cooperatives as against the total West German level of DM 5,243 bn (*Deutsche Bundesbank Monthly Report, Statistical Section,* March 1995, p.16). The East German figure was computed as follows: these banks held 24.1 per cent of their total business

volume as loans to non-banks (*Deutsche Bundesbank*, 1994*f*, p.46), these loans totalling DM 33.724 bn (Landeszentralbanken data).

171. *Deutsche Bundesbank* (1990b, p.18).
172. *Reuters-News-Service* (5 December 1991).
173. Announcement made on 2 October 1991 (*Reuters-News-Service*). For a complete breakdown of the decrease in rediscount quotas over time, see *Deutsche Bundesbank* (1992a, p.11).
174. *Deutsche Bundesbank, Annual Report* (1990, p.123).
175. David Goodhart, 'Management: Teaching Potential Capitalists – The *Deutschebank* at the Leipzig Fair', *Financial Times* (19 March 1990, p.14).
176. Plessing (1993, pp.137–8). The old debt of the *BSB* amounted to DM 7 bn and was refinanced by the *Staatsbank* in the early stages. In addition, the *BSB* was given the option to access the Equalisation Fund for compensation for NPLs, making them – in effect – guaranteed (*Treuhandanstalt, Pressemitteilung*, 7 September 1991).
177. In sheer physical terms, the conversion represented a massive undertaking. The *Bundesbank* noted that it had supplied its main branches in the East with 'several hundred tonnes of currency worth a total of some DM 28 million' (*Deutsche Bundesbank*, 1990a, p.25).
178. Plessing (1993, p.136).
179. Darrell Delamaide, 'The Provincial Powerhouse', *Euromoney* (October 1991, pp.67–8).
180. *German Brief* (13 January 1995, p.10).
181. Plessing (1993, p.138). The Credit Cooperatives remained East German-owned.
182. *Deutsche Bundesbank* (1990b, p.16).
183. *Deutsche Bundesbank* (1994f). We present a full discussion of these banks' activities in Chapter 5.
184. Katharine Cambell, 'International Capital Markets: Staatsbank Refinancing Total Stands at DM 24 bn', *Financial Times* (7 September 1990, n. 36). For a report on the refinancing activities of the Staatsbank Berlin, see Garry Evans, 'Staatsbank Can Sit Back', *Euromoney Supplement* (September 1992, p.51).
185. By October 1991, roughly DM 85 bn had been raised. ('Germany: Staatsbank Berlin Needs to Raise a Further DM 30 bn on the Capital Markets', *Frankfurter Allgemeine Zeitung* and *Boersen Zeitung* (English abstracts)).
186. *Staatsbank Berlin, Geschäftsbericht* 1993.
187. *KfW* Advertisement, 'German Banking and Finance Survey', *Financial Times* (17 May 1995, p. II'. 'In the unification treaty, it was envisaged that all or part of the Staatsbank would be transferred to a public-law institution after completing its tasks'. ('Germany: Merger of Staatsbank with *KfW* is complete', *Boerson Zeitung* (English abstract), 29 July 1994, which also provides an overview of the *Staatsbank* performance after GEMSU).
188. Schütte (1993, pp.176–7) based on his interviews in the *Staatsbank*. This figure roughly corresponds to the total outstanding credit at GEMSU (see Table 4.2). Schütte provides a breakdown of the old loans by bank and further divides them into nominal and real values.
189. Plessing (1993, p.137).
190. For details, see 'Germany: Privatisation of Deutsche Kreditbank Begins', *Boersen Zeitung* (English abstracts) (31 August 1994). For an overview of the

activities of the *DKB* since GEMSU, see Peter Stebner, *'Privatisierung bis Jahresende', Neue Zeit* (24 February 1994, p.10).

191. Schütte (1993, pp.175–6).
192. Schütte (1993, p.177). According to the *THA*, 'Under the terms of the so-called Debt Remission Regulations [*Entschuldungsverordnung*] of September 30 1990, a remission of the company from existing or inherited debts can be effected wholly or partly for the purpose of restructuring the company or enhancing its effectiveness' (*Treuhandanstalt*, (n. o.)).
193. Of the total of DM 101 bn at GEMSU, the *THA* absorbed between DM 77–78 bn of the old loans, DM 15.6 bn were recovered through liquidations, and DM 7 bn were covered in sale agreements by the purchasers. The *THA* also paid an additional DM 28 bn in interest on these loans (Hornef, 1994a, pp.21, 32). Schmieding and Buch (1992) were quite critical of this approach, arguing that the case-by-case approach led to a virtual global write-off in the end, but with far more expenses, delays and administrative burdens.
194. In a strong critique of the gains made by the banks without bearing risks, *Der Spiegel* claimed that the West German banks – especially *Deutsche Bank* and *Dresdner Bank* – earned more than DM 5 bn per year for managing the collection of these loans in the first three years after GEMSU. (*'Das Zinsenwunder im Osten', Der Spiegel,* October 1994, p.55). While the precise 'fee' paid to the West German banks is not clear, it is important to distinguish between this management fee and the actual interest payments on the loans. While the majority of the interest payments for the old loans went to the DKB, the institution taking responsibility for them, some (West German) banks took responsibility for the old loans and were entitled to the interest payments due. *DG Bank*, for example, took on more than DM 16 bn in old debt from the *BLN*'s books when it acquired it. The overall interest payments for the bad debts were significant. An OECD (*Economic Survey,* 1990–1, p.101) estimate for 1990 placed the level of interest payments at roughly DM 7 bn for the first quarter of 1991 alone.
195. *'Treuhand: Noch keine Entscheidung über Privatisierung der Deutschen Kreditbank', Handelsblatt* (23 February 1994, p.13). Of this decrease, the bulk was due to the debt reduction in *THA* enterprises, falling from DM 85.7 bn in 1990 to DM 8.6 bn by the end of 1993.
196. 'Germany: Deutsche Kreditbank would retain autonomy under Bayerische Landesbank', *Frankfurter Allgemeine Zeitung* (English abstracts) (6 January 1995). The agreement was that DKB would keep its name but be integrated into the Bayerische Landesbank East German network.
197. *Reuters-News-Service* (23 October 1992).
198. 'Thirty-five years after it came into force, the *Deutsche Bundesbank* Act of July 26, 1957 (Federal Law Gazette I, p.745) has for the first time been amended (by the Fourth Act Amending to the *Deutsche Bundesbank* Act) with respect to major provisions governing the way the *Bundesbank* is organised'. (*Deutsche Bundesbank,* 1992b, p.48). In the lead-up to its re-organisation, there were sharp disagreements among the *Länder* themselves, and also between the *Länder* and the Federal government, over what the final structure should be. Each of the five new *Länder* wanted to be represented on the *Bundesbank* governing council, and a political battle ensued

between the *Länder* and the Federal government. In the end, the Federal government's view that the bank should be streamlined was adopted, and an organisational consolidation occurred, whereby some of the *Länder* in the East shared a *Bundesbank* main branch (*Landeszentralbank*). Nine main branches remained as a result of the reorganisation, including: (1) the *Land* of Baden-Württemberg; (2) the Free State of Bavaria; (3) the *Länder* of *Berlin and Brandenburg;* (4) the Free Hanseatic City of Bremen and the *Länder* of Lower Saxony and *Saxony Anhalt*; (5) the Free and Hanseatic City of Hamburg and the *Länder* of *Mecklenburg-Western Pomerania* and Schleswig-Holstein; (6) the *Land* of Hesse; (7) the *Land* of North Rhine-Westphalia; (8) the *Länder* of Rhineland-Palatinate and Saarland; and (9) the *Free State of Saxony* and the *Land* of *Thuringia* (The East German *Länder* are shown in italic). For details, see *Deutsche Bundesbank* (1992b, pp.48–53).

199. A discussion of the functions of the Federal Banking Supervisory Office and its relationship with the *Bundesbank* can be found in Böhnel (1995).
200. Shinasi, Lipschitz and McDonald (1990, p.154). The Banking Supervisory Office in the FRG could, under certain circumstances, grant exemptions to the banking law to East German banks.
201. Only basic financial data were required from East German banks until the end of 1990. For details on the specific requirements and concessions, see *Deutsche Bundesbank, Annual Report* (1990, p.117).
202. *Deutsches Institut für Wirtschaftsforschung, 'Wochenbericht',* (51/52, 19 December 1991, p.727).
203. David Waller, 'Service with a Smile', *Financial Times* (4 May 1994, p.II). Another reason overlooked by the reporter is that East Germans would perhaps not be able to handle the immediate introduction of sixty new products, thus leading the bank to opt for a gradual increase.
204. *Industrie- und Handelskammer zu Leipzig, Jahresbericht*, 93/94, p.9.
205. *Deutsche Bundesbank* (1990a, p.30).
206. The old system was the *Einheitliches System der Elektronischen Rechentechnik*, which means 'standard system of electronic data processing' (*Deutsche Bundesbank*, 1990*a*, p.26).
207. The details of the transfer process can be found in *Deutsche Bundesbank* (1990*a*, pp.30–1).
208. The increasing adoption by banks and their customers of west German accounting and payment methods, the reduction of transport times and the further expansion of processing capacities in the computer centres of the banking industry and the *Bundesbank* in 1991 helped to ensure that, in both paperless and paper-based payments, the banking industry largely managed to achieve the processing periods customary elsewhere in west–east and east–west payments as well as within the new Länder. Hardly any complaints [reach the *Bundesbank*] about unduly long processing periods for credit transfers. Temporary backlogs which occurred in individual payments computer centres in the processing of requests for the investigation of the whereabouts of credit transfers and cheque or direct debit collections not carried out at all, or in time, have meanwhile been eliminated by means of elaborate staff and organisational measures. (*Deutsche Bundesbank, Annual Report*, 1991, p.117)
209. Author's interview.

210. Marsh (1992, p.217).
211. Author's interview.
212. Author's interview. The internal system was called a '*Buro Kommunikation System*' (BKB). *Deutsche Bank*, like the *Bundesbank*, also negotiated a few unofficial lines, it sharing the same building in Berlin with the *Bundesbank*.
213. West German Savings Banks were not allowed to buy their East German counterparts yet needed to improve the latter's operations in order to serve their West German customers in the East – i.e. the East was an extension of the competition between Savings Banks and Big Banks in West Germany ('The Problems of Unity', *Euromoney*, September 1990, p.11).
214. *Bundesverband deutscher Banken* (1994, p.5).
215. Friedmann (1995, p.968).
216. *Bankenverband mittel- und ostdeutscher Länder* (1995, p.4).
217. These figures represent the total branches of *all* private banks in East Germany, rather than the nine reporting banks from which the previous investment figures were taken (see Chapter three). Since the nine reporting banks possess the vast majority of the branches, however, the two sets of figures should roughly correspond.
218. Friedmann (1995, p.968).
219. *Deutsche Sparkassen- und Giroverband e.V.* (1994, p.3).
220. Deeg (1994, p.8).
221. *Bundesverband deutscher Banken* (1994, p.6).
222. According to the *BDB* report (1994, p.6), 'training intensity is defined as the ratio of the number of staff who received training to the total number of workers'.
223. Deeg (1994, p.8). More than 7500 East German staff have received training at the German *Sparkassen* Academy in Bonn. In addition, the *Ostdeutsche Sparkassen* Academy Berlin-Rahnsdorf was in the process of being built in 1994 (*Deutsche Sparkassen- und Giroverband e.V.*, 1994, p.5).
224. *Deutsche Sparkassen- und Giroverband e.V.* (1994, p.4).
225. Of the 33 000 West German (Private) Bank employees in the East, 4600 had been trainees (Friedmann, 1995, p.968).
226. *Deutsche Sparkassen- und Giroverband e.V.* (1994, p.4).
227. Wagner (1993, p.1010).
228. Carlin and Richthofen (1995, p.17).
229. Deeg (1994, p.22).
230. *Bundesverband deutscher Banken* (1994, p.6).
231. A senior *Deutsche Bank* manager argued that if other industries had taken the banks' approach of not only supplying high financial investment, but also management transfers on a large scale, they might have developed faster and better. He argued that the banks had no choice but to pursue this strategy – as opposed to manufacturers who could produce in the West and sell in the East – because for banks 'all business is local'. (Author's interview).

## 5 Overall financial flows and bank activities

1. West German Commercial Banks do not include West German Savings Banks and Credit Cooperatives. Some data presented (*Landeszentralbanken*

data) include West German (private) Mortgage Bank loans. Where this is the case, it will be noted. Our focus is not on mortgage lending, as such, and in any event the Mortgage Banks are to a large extent owned by the Big West German Banks (see Edwards and Fischer, 1994, p.106), and thus are grouped under the heading 'West German Commercial Banks'. This is noted as a guide to the reader since in Figure 4.2 Mortgage Banks are grouped under 'Specialist Banks'.

2. The *Bundesbank* (1995a, p.47) reports that of the total Specialised Bank loans approved between 1990 and 1994, approximately 86 per cent were paid out. Of West German Commercial Bank corporate loans between 1990 and 1993, 79 per cent of the loans approved were paid out (see Table 5.7). It is not always clear whether Berlin is included in the various flows, though this is noted in the cases where it is known.
3. *Handelsblatt* (15 December 1994, on *Reuters-News-Service*).
4. Ibid.
5. The decline seems to have continued since. Loans through the *DtA* were reported to have declined by 17 per cent in the first half of 1995 compared with the first half of 1994, and the number of enterprises supported by 22 per cent (*Handelsblatt*, 31 July 1995, on *Reuters-News-Service*).
6. There is some evidence of regional variations. The *Bürgschaftsbanken* data represent an average of two regions: in Berlin-Brandenburg we find a much larger role for the West Commercial Banks (79 per cent in 1992, 68 per cent in 1993) and a much smaller role for the East German Savings Banks (6 per cent in 1992, only 2 per cent in 1993). For loans guaranteed by the *Bürgschaftsbank Sachsen* between 1990 and 1994, West German Commercial Banks handled roughly 60 per cent of the number of applications and also of the total loan volume (letter to the author from the *Bürgschaftsbank Sachsen*, 1 June 1995).
7. *Bundesverband der deutscher Banken* (1994, pp.10–11).
8. Of ERP-Start-Up funds in the East in 1992, West German Commercial Banks handled 40 per cent, whereas in West Germany they handled only 18.5 per cent. For the Capital Assistance Programme the corresponding figures for 1992 were 40.8 per cent and 22.1 per cent, respectively. In 1993, West German Commercial Banks handled 33.7 per cent of ERP Start-Up funds versus only 10.9 per cent in West Germany.
9. The *KfW* does not analyse the differences in distribution between East and West Germany. In addition, the data on the distribution of *KfW* loans 'refer to the entire lending volume of the *KfW*, and lending to the *Mittelstand* accounts for only 40 per cent,' (Harm. 1992a, p.11) Nonetheless, *KfW* staff reported in a letter to the author (13 June 1995) that it is unlikely that there are significant differences between East and West Germany.
10. Housing modernisation loans totalled DM 36.3 bn between 1990 and 31 March 1995.
11. Carlin and Richthofen (1995, p.20).
12. Carlin (1993, p.11). Also see Merkl (1994, p.216).
13. Aghion and Carlin (1994, p.28).
14. Seidel (1994). Of the enterprises financed by the *KfW*, 69 per cent of East German ones were start-ups. West German-owned enterprises tended to originate less as start-ups (44 per cent of all West German-owned) and more as

purchases of enterprises or investments into existing ones. See also Carlin and Mayer (1995).

15. *Treuhandanstalt* (1993, p.23).
16. Balz (1992, p.18). *THA* figures confirm that the majority of MBOs had less than 200 employees. In September 1993, 2537 MBOs, 2227 (88 per cent) had 100 employees or less (*Treuhandanstalt*, 1993, p.15).
17. *Deutsche Bundesbank* (1994a, p.24). The figures refer to all enterprises domiciled in Germany, excluding financial institutions and housing, regardless of the owners' origins.
18. *Institut für Wirtschaftsforschung Halle* (1993, p.39). In 1992, West German-owned enterprises invested DM 27.1 bn out of a total of DM 43.1 bn, in 1993, DM 35.8 bn out of a total of 55.5 bn and in 1994, DM 35 bn out of a total of DM 60.6 bn.
19. Interviews with the author.
20. Carlin and Richthofen (1995, p.20).
21. There are various off-setting considerations here. West German-owned enterprises possess more own funds and thus are more likely to have funded a larger proportion of their investment through intra-enterprise transfers with own funds; equally, however, West German-owned enterprises are more creditworthy than East German enterprises and hence may have been able to borrow more, a conclusion strongly supported in this book. Again, East German firms tend to be small firms which are – in general terms – more dependent on external finance, bank loans especially. Against this, large firms tend to be West German-owned, and these borrow in larger amounts.
22. Deeg (1994, p.36), based on a *Handelsblatt* article.
23. See Vitols (1994, pp.14–15).
24. *IKB Deutsche Industriebank, Annual Report*, 1991, 1992, p.33.
25. Ibid., p.36.
26. In 1991, under the *KfW*'s Investment Loan Programme, 65 per cent of total loans went to enterprises with some degree of foreign participation. Of these, 33 per cent went to wholly West German-owned enterprises, and another 28 per cent to firms with West German participation (*Kreditanstalt für Wiederaufbau, Annual Report*, 1991, p.32).
27. OECD (1995, p.62). During these years the transfers were roughly equal to 4 per cent of West German GDP.
28. Bofinger and Cernohorsky (1992, pp.8–9).
29. *Deutsche Bundesbank* (1997, p.18).
30. Ibid., p.28.
31. *Deutsche Bundesbank* (1994e, p.28) reports that *THA* borrowing from capital markets rose from DM 4.9 bn in 1991, to DM 19.4 bn in 1992 and to DM 77.5 bn in 1993.
32. *Deutsche Bundesbank* (1994e, p.29).
33. The *Bundesbank* argues that it would make more sense to include *THA* flows as part of the overall budget, a change which would increase transparency of fund transfers to the East which will ultimately be paid for by the German state budget (*Deutsche Bundesbank*, 1994e, p.19).
34. Quoted by Carlin and Richthofen (1995, p.25). The data is from the *Bundesverband deutscher Kapitalbeteiligungsgesellschaft (BVK)* based on the

*'BVK-Statistik 1993'* report. The data were derived from a survey of members and non-members of the association. It may understate the total amount of equity investment in the East since some non-members did not participate.

35. *BVK* data as presented in Hummel, Ludwig, *et al.* (1994, p.65).
36. *Deutsche Sparkassen- und Giroverband e. V.* (1994, p.18).
37. *Deutsche Bank AG, Annual Report,* 1993, p.14.
38. *Süddeutsche Zeitung* (English Abstracts) (26 October 1994).
39. The East German Investment Trust plc, *Annual Report and Accounts,* 31 March 1994, p.10, and 31 March 1995, p.2.
40. See especially Deeg (1994).
41. *Deutsche Bundesbank* (1994f, p.33).
42. Sinn and Sinn (1992, p.78).
43. Sinn and Sinn (1992, p.77) cite examples of this displacement in food products, where shares of some West German goods (of the total consumed in the East) in 1990 were: 96 per cent for coffee; 94 per cent for canned soups, and 90 per cent for fruit-flavoured cottage cheese. The authors argue that the sharp displacement was due to the much higher quality of West German goods in addition to the heavy advertising campaign undertaken by West German exporters. There was also a psychological desire for East Germans to purchase goods which they had for so long only heard about or seen on television but could not obtain.
44. Higher consumption by households does not necessarily decrease the level of total deposits since the funds may flow from the enterprises selling the goods back to the banks. In the East, however, a high percentage of sales were West German imports.
45. The *net migration* from East to West Germany (i.e. subtracting migration from West to East) was: 359 126 in 1990; 169 476 in 1991; 87 825 in 1992; and 53 286 in 1993 (*Statistisches Bundesamt,* cited in Sahm, 1995, Chapter II).
46. These levels were identical to those of a year earlier (Calculated from *Bundesbank* and *Landeszentralbanken* data).
47. *Deutsche Bundesbank* (1995a, p.44).
48. *Deutsche Bundesbank* (1994f, p.39).
49. There are no figures available on the number of new accounts by bank group. It is probable that the Savings Banks would have a higher market share of customers (as a percentage of the total) than deposits since they target a wider (i.e. lower net-worth) market than the Big Banks. This is supported by Hanspeter Gondring of the *Sparkassen- und Giroverband Hessen-Thüringen* who in a letter to the author (23 August 1995) reported that Savings Banks in the East have a market share of 70 per cent of retail customers (as against about 50 per cent in West Germany). Another report similarly noted that 'in a typical East German community, three quarters of the residents are Savings Bank customer' ('Savings Banks Profit From Close Community Ties', *International Herald Tribune,* June 2 1995, p.18).
50. *Deutsche Bundesbank, Regionalergebnisse der monatlichen Bilanzstatistik für Kreditinstitute in Ostdeutschland; Landeszentralbanken* data; own calculations. This figure does not include East Berlin.
51. *Deutsche Bundesbank, Bankenstatistik* (March 1995, pp.62, 70).

52. Calculated from *Landeszentralbanken* data. Disaggregated data not available for 1990 or 1994. Does not include East Berlin.
53. One survey of retail customers in the Berlin area found that more than a third of both private and self-employed persons cited location/availability (*Erreichbarkeitsmotiv*) as the main motivation for choosing a bank (Kapelle, Schreiber and Meyer, 1994, p.9).
54. *Deutsche Sparkassen- und Giroverband e. V.* (1992)
55. Author's interview.
56. Kapelle, Schreiber and Meyer (1994, p.5) found that the East German Savings Banks and Credit Cooperatives were by far the best-known (*Gute Bekanntheit*) in the Berlin area.
57. While the switch was based on certain tangible factors, such as the lower cost of the East German goods and their improved quality since the time of GEMSU, there is evidence that East German consumers simply preferred East German goods. In a (1995) survey by *Der Spiegel*, while 53 per cent of respondents noted that their purchasing decision were driven by quality and price, 45 per cent claimed that they would buy East German goods if possible; the remaining (only) 2 per cent expressed a preference for West German products (*'Stolz Aufs Eigene Leben'*, *Der Spiegel*, 27, 1995, p.43). The irony, of course, is that many of these goods were being produced by West German-owned enterprises under an East German product name. Accounts of this consumer behaviour are found in Woldt (1992); Sinn and Sinn (1992, p.78); and 'Is eastern Germany really bouncing back?' *The Economist* (6 August 1994, p.55).
58. Those that fled would probably have been the most natural customers for the West German commercial banks since they were not reluctant to move, and likely were higher net-worth individuals – either by virtue of the funds they possessed at GEMSU or their earning potential which enabled them to live in West Germany. Indeed, of those that left in 1989, nearly 60 per cent were between the ages of 18 and 40. That is to say, they were in the prime earning and saving period of their lives and, further, were likely to have been more open-minded than the older generation about moving their accounts to a West German bank (*Statistisches Bundesamt*, cited in Sahm, 1995, Chapter II).
59. *Reuters-News-Service* (27 June 1990).
60. *Deutsche Bundesbank* (1994f, p.39).
61. Calculated from *Landeszentralbanken* data. Disaggregated data not available for 1990 or 1994. Does not include East Berlin.
62. Sinn and Sinn (1992, p.38).
63. High net-worth individuals may have preferred the West German banks' more sophisticated services. In a letter to the author, a member of the Savings Bank Association of Hessen-Thüringen writes, 'some of the (West German) commercial banks are already being successful in their attempts to draw highly profitable customer segments away from the (East German) savings banks'.
64. Calculated from *Landeszentralbanken* data. Disaggregated data not available for 1990. Does not include East Berlin.
65. See Judy Dempsey, 'Old Family Houses Return', German Banking and Finance Survey, IV, *Financial Times* (31 May 1994, p.IV).

66. As noted in Chapter 3, the banking associations are political organisations designed to represent the interests of their member banks.
67. *Landeszentralbanken* data.
68. *Landeszentralbanken* data, as presented in Hummel, Ludwig-*et al.* (1994, p.45).
69. As prescribed by the *Deutsche Bundesbank* (1990c, p.40),

    > The Deutsche Mark shall be introduced via the financial institutions of the GDR. The conversion of GDR Mark into Deutsche Mark shall be *exclusively through accounts with these institutions*. There shall be no direct exchange of cash (emphasis added).

    The Savings Banks held the majority of personal accounts and thus shouldered the biggest administrative burden in the exchange. Hans Giese, a director of the West German Savings Bank Association, remarked,

    > There are 16 million people in East Germany, and 15 million of them go to the savings banks to change their Ostmarks to Deutschmarks. People had to queue for hours and hours ('The Problems of Unity', *Euromoney*, September 1990, p.11).

70. Carlin and Richthofen (1995, p.18) make this point. Also see Deeg (1994, p.8).
71. 'Financial cowboys' DM 400 m round-up', *Financial Times* (18 August 1993, p.2).
72. *Deutsche Bundesbank* (1992a, p.23).
73. In June 1992, East German Savings banks had 33.7 per cent of their liabilities in (low-cost) demand deposits, as opposed to only 15.1 per cent for West German Savings Banks. East German Credit Cooperatives had 35.4 per cent in demand deposits against 15.2 per cent for their West German counterparts (*Deutsche Bundesbank*, 1992a, p.21).
74. See *Deutsche Bundesbank* (1994f).
75. Apart from having to pay more for deposits, East German banks' refinancing privileges with the Bundesbank had been terminated and they were having to refinance at the higher securities repurchase rate rather than the discount rate. In 1993, for example, security repurchases carried a refinancing rate of approximately 0.5 per cent (50 bp) above the discount rate (*Deutsche Bundesbank Monthly Report*, August 1994, p.59).
76. See *Deutsche Bundesbank* (1994f).
77. Not including loans by West German Mortgage banks.
78. *Financial Times* (4 May 1994, Section 11).
79. Kurt Kasch, Senior Vice President of Deutsche Bank, quoted in 'On your own', *The Banker* (March 1995, p.29).
80. As we noted in Chapter 3, since the West German banks established branch networks in the East, the only available balance sheet and profitability figures are those which the banks choose to release. These figures often conflict and aggregate data must be pieced together from various sources. Since more interviews were conducted with *Deutsche Bank*, and since there was in general more information available on it – particularly from published sources – it is the subject of the more detailed analysis.

81. *'Deutsche Bank* Moves East', *Banking World,* (June 1991, p.24).
82. 'The Battle Plans of Hilmar Kopper', *Euromoney* (January 1994, p.42).
83. The *Financial Times* reported that, 'the deal, after weeks of speculation about *Deutsche Bank's* intentions, immediately raised questions from the Federal Cartel Office in West Berlin' ('Deutsche Bank Unveils Venture with East Germans', *Financial Times,* 18 April, 1990, p.1). The *International Herald Tribune* also printed an article entitled, 'In East, *Deutsche Bank* Inroad Heightens Monopoly Fears' (*International Herald Tribune,* April 18,1990, p.1).
84. Krupp (1990). Many reports claimed that *Deutsche Bank* took over 118 branches, and one even claimed that the DKB did not know how many branches it had ('Rebuilding a Sector: West German Banks are Rushing into East Germany', Survey Section, *Financial Times,* 19 June 1990, p.4).
85. *DKB* took a 47 per cent stake, with the remaining 4 per cent divided between three East German enterprises: Interhotel; Konsum (the consumers' society); and the synthesis works at Schwarzheide (*Banking World,* June 1991, p.24).
86. Bank director Axel Osenberg quoted in 'Deutsche Bank Moves East', *Banking World* (June 1991, p.24).
87. Interviews with *Deutsche Bank* managers.
88. On 23 July 1990, *Deutsche Bank* announced that it would invest an additional DM 700 mn into the joint-venture, raising its total capital investment to DM 1 bn and its stake to 84.7 per cent. (*Financial Times,* 24 July 1990, p.21). On 27 December 1990, *Deutsche Bank* gained 100 per cent control of the venture by purchasing the remaining 15.3 per cent from the *THA* for an undisclosed amount (*Financial Times,* 3 January 1991, p.19).
89. Author's interview.
90. 'An Air of Vulnerability', *Euromoney* (July 1991, p.76).
91. Author's interview.
92. The importance of the appearance of the branches, in aesthetic terms, should not be underestimated. It is a point that was bought up in nearly all of the author's interviews with bankers.
93. 'The Battle Plans of Hilmar Kopper', *Euromoney* (January 1994, p.42).
94. 'Deutsche Bank Moves East', *Banking World* (June 1991, p.24).
95. *Reuters-News-Service* (26 April 1992). It is likely that part of the *Deutsche Bank* agreement was to continue to employ a significant proportion – if not all – of the former *Kreditbank* employees. Even if it was not part of the agreement, *Deutsche Bank* would have severely tarnished its image if it had initiated large-scale staff cutbacks.
96. Griffin (1994, p.405).
97. 'Kopper Steers Deutsche East', *Financial Times* (16 January 1991, p.21).
98. *Commerzbank* (1990).
99. 'Strained Relations Among West Germany's Big Banks', *The Economist* (1 September 1990, p.77).
100. 'The cake was so-to-say distributed, and there was nothing left for Commerzbank.' Author's interview with *Deutsche Bank* managers.
101. Author's interview with *Commerzbank* manager.
102. 'Reclaiming the East', *Bank Systems and Technology* (June 1992, p.58). *Commerzbank* Chairman Walter Seipp was reportedly furious that *Commerzbank* did not get (many) existing branches ('An Air of Vulnerability', *Euromoney,* July 1991, p.75).

103. Photographs taken by the author (June 1994).
104. 'An Air of Vulnerability', *Euromoney* (July 1991, p.76).
105. Ibid. The article does not specify whether customers are depositors, or both depositors *and* borrowers.
106. *Commerzbank* Chairman Walter Seipp commented, 'We come as a complete newcomer. There have been cases where companies have been threatened with having their credits terminated if they go to another bank' (*Financial Times*, 29 October 1990, p.23).
107. Confirmed in author's interviews with banks and the *THA*.
108. From *Deutsche Bank's* perspective, the good fortune of 'inheriting' such a large volume of liquidity loans was the reward for early 'commitment' to the East (author's interview with *Deutsche Bank* manager).
109. The figure is computed as follows. For total loans paid out, *Deutsche Bank* shows the following figures: 1990: DM 6 347 000; 1991: DM 6 710 000; 1992: DM 6 735 800; 1993: DM 3 097 086. The total for the four years is DM 20 406 255. On the basis that margins for 1990 and 1991 were 3 per cent, and for 1992 and 1993 were 1.5 per cent, the total interest income is computed.
110. It is likely that *Commerzbank's* share was even higher since *Deutsche Bank's* figures seem to include Berlin which is not the case for *Commerzbank*.
111. 'An Air of Vulnerability', *Euromoney* (July 1991, p.75). Figures on the profitability of individual branches are not publicly available.
112. *Dresdner Bank* (1991).
113. *Deutsche Bank* Chairman Hilmar Kopper disclosed the profits in the *Financial Times* (16 January 1991, p.21) and on *Reuters-News-Service* (24 June 1991).
114. Krupp (1994a, p.2). Another report noted that *Deutsche Bank* would not realise any profits until 1996 ('Germany: Transfers to East Germany Remain Essential', *Frankfurter Allgemeine Zeitung* (English Abstracts on *Reuters-News-Service*, 29 September 1995).
115. Based on author's interviews with *Deutsche Bank* employees.
116. Author's interview with *Deutsche Bank* managers. The estimate refers to the first two years after GEMSU.
117. The following account by the OECD (1990–1, p.102) supports this view

> 'liquidity credits have been granted increasingly on the basis of "corporate plans" ... In the event, plans have often been liberally interpreted by enterprises, and investment funds have been claimed based on rudimentary market strategies. Not only has the Treuhandanstalt often found plans to be highly unrealistic but it appears that relatively few enterprises have in fact produced corporate plans at all: by May 1991 only 66 out of 333 enterprises in east Berlin had provided reconstruction plans'.

118. According to Kurt Kasch, Senior Vice President, *Deutsche Bank*, Berlin (*Reuters-News-Service*, 9 November 1993) and from Table 5.10).
119. Estimations based on *Deutsche Bank* internal data. The decline in enterprise customers was not seen in self-employed persons and private customers. Nevertheless, the rate of growth in those customer areas did slow down.
120. *Handelsblatt* (21 June 1993, p.12).

121. 'Kopper Steers Deutsche East', *Financial Times* (16 January 1991, p.21).
122. *Tagesspiegel* (18 May 1993, p.26).
123. *Neue Zeit* (10 November 1993, p.10).
124. *Deutsche Bank* and *Commerzbank* have different overall strategies regarding their organisational approaches to offering a broad range of financial services. While *Deutsche Bank* pursues a 'foundation' approach, using subsidiaries and its own name to sell these services, *Commerzbank* employs a 'cooperative' approach, involving cooperative agreements with *other* financial institutions (see Gaebe, 1993, p.108).
125. *Handelsblatt* (18 May 1993, p.13).
126. 'Banks Used Up Credit Scope for East Germany', *Reuters-News-Service* (19 January 1995).
127. *Financial Times* (9 October 1990, p.27).
128. 'Rise in Bad Loans in East Germany Seen – *Commerzbank*', *Reuters-News-Service* (27 May 1993).
129. It is difficult to generalise and these lessons are extended to West German banks more generally based on selected interviews with other banks as well as other published accounts which are referred to. As we noted (Chapter 3), these banks account for the largest and third largest presence in the East by West German banks.
130. In terms of general staff, both banks faced burdens. *Deutsche Bank* had to shoulder the high cost of the large workforce, while *Commerzbank* had to search for employees and, in the process, strain its capacity in West Germany.
131. The estimate level for 1994 was 132.2 per cent (*German Brief*, 13 January 1995, p.6).
132. *Deutsche Bundesbank* (1994e, p.26).
133. Carlin and Mayer (1994, p.204). This is not to suggest that finance was the only significant input in short supply in the East. According to George Krupp (1994b, p.1) of *Deutsche Bank*, most enterprises also lacked 'convincing strategies, marketable products, competitive sales levels and an equity (own-funds) base that supports these' (*Den meisten Unternehmen fehlen heute ... überzeugende Konzepte, marktgängige Produkte, ein leistungsfähiger Vertrieb und vor allem Eigenkapital*')(own translation).
134. *Bundesverband der deutschen Industrie* (1994). This analysis of the results of the survey is supplemented by the author's interview with the person responsible for the survey.
135. Hummel, Ludwig *et al.* (1994). The research involved telephone interviews with personnel from 14 enterprises, a telephone survey of a further 113 enterprises, and a mail survey of roughly 1000 enterprises. In addition, interviews were conducted with Commercial Banks, *Bürgschaftsbanken* and venture capital funds.
136. See Carlin (1993).
137. *Deutsche Bundesbank* (1994c, p.28). The study found that trends in the construction and distribution sectors were much more favourable.
138. See *Deutsche Bundesbank* (1993a).
139. *Landeszentralbanken* data (Hummel, Ludwig *et al.*, 1994, p.47).
140. The data given are for 1992 and 1993 because the 1991 figures include the loans from the *Staatsbank Berlin* and the *DKB*. Even with these loans

included, there is still a marked decrease in loans to manufacturing, but to show this in absolute terms would overstate the drop – i.e. lending to manufacturing enterprises at the end of 1991 was DM 58 787 mn.

141. Hummel, Ludwig *et al.* (1994, p.47).
142. Author's interview with *BDI* manager.
143. *Deutsches Institut für Wirtschaftsforschung, 'Gesamtwirtschaftliche und unternehmenische Anpassungsfortschritte in Ostdeutschland'*, Zehnter Bericht, 15/94 (14 April 1994), Berlin.
144. This is certainly the case in West Germany and in other economies.
145. *'Trotz des umfangreichen Förderinstrumentariums klagen kleine und mittlere Unternehmen über Finanzierungsprobleme'* (Hummel, Ludwig *et al.*, 1994, p.2).
146. Hummel, Ludwig *et al.* (1994, p.26). Enterprises with under 50 employees went from 11 per cent experiencing problems to 26 per cent in the period, whereas those with 50–200 went from 32 to 19 per cent, those with 200–500 went from 39 to 13 per cent and those with 500 or more from 41 to 16 per cent.
147. *DIW Wochenbericht*, 11/92 (18 March 1993, p.107).
148. For manufacturing enterprises, those with under 200 employees experienced far more problems owing to a lack of collateral (21 per cent of those with under 20 employees and 29 per cent of those with 20–200 employees, as against only 6 per cent of those with more than 200 employees). With respect to long-term bank loans, not a single enterprise with more than 200 employees complained of financing problems, whereas for enterprises with under 20 employees the figure was 12 per cent and for 20–200 it was 21 per cent (Hummel, Ludwig *et al.*, 1994, p.79).
149. Hummel, Ludwig *et al.* (1994, p.30).
150. Based on the author's interview with the *BDB* manager who was responsible for the study (27 July 1994). Also see *BDB* (1994, p.10). Harm (1992a, p.22) observes the same problem with data on *Mittelstand* loans in West Germany.
151. *KfW* 1993, *Annual Report*, p.23. In the period, industrial *Mittelstand* made up only 17 per cent of the total number of *Mittelstand* borrowers sponsored by the *KfW*; in other words, roughly one-sixth of borrowers received half of the funds – i.e. the East German *Mittelstand* received on average three times more than West German *Mittelstand* borrowers.
152. Seidel (1994, p.15).
153. Seidel analysed balance sheets of *KfW*-sponsored enterprises for the period 1990–3. He found that a total of DM 32.8 bn of *KfW* funds were made available to industrial *Mittelstand* in the East, of which DM 24.2 bn (74 per cent) went to East German-owned enterprises (Seidel, 1994, p.18). We should note that of the East German enterprises financed, a significant proportion were start-ups (69 per cent). West German-owned enterprises tended to be more concentrated on purchases of enterprises or investments into existing ones.
154. Wieczorek (1994, p.4).
155. Ibid., pp.1–3. This figure includes those formed through *THA* sales. The number may be overstated somewhat, moreover, since it includes registered enterprises which are not in operation (see Randlesome, 1994, pp.189–90)
156. *Reuters-News-Service* (15 April 1994).

157. Author's interview.
158. 'Je *größer ein Unternehmen,* um so unkomplizierter *gestaltet sich die Antragstellung'* (*Bundesverband der deutschen Industrie,* 1994, p.4). (own translation). According to a separate account,

> In many sectors, such as chemicals, a loan is made only in cases in which a Western company is a major shareholder or the firm continues under a Treuhand guarantee'. (Kasch, Lowenthal and Cassuto. 'Financing German Reunification', *The Bankers Magazine,* September/October 1994, p.61)

159. Hummel, Ludwig *et al.* (1994, p.88).
160. *Deutsches Institut für Wirtschaftsforschung, 'Gesamtwirtschaftliche und unternehmenische Anpassungsfortschritte in Ostdeutschland'*, Sechster Bericht, 39/92 (24 September 1992), Berlin.
161. *Kreditanstalt für Wiederaufbau* (Seidel, 1994).
162. Carlin and Richthofen (1995, p.22).
163. The implication is that these enterprises are less dependent on innovating in terms of their products, these being simple inputs to West German businesses. This is not to suggest, however, that firms which are suppliers do not innovate. The West German *Mittelstand* are a case in point.
164. The *BDI* survey was administered by sending questionnaires to smaller, member federations of the *BDI* which were asked to distribute it to their members, so it is difficult to know whether certain industries are overrepresented. One *BDI* manager notes that the survey is 'not the most academic' but offers a wide sample of enterprises and is in agreement with some of the larger surveys undertaken by the German research institutes, some of which we have referred to (author's interview).
165. The *BDI* agreed with this observation and noted that it had been raised by various banks as a criticism of the survey's 'uniqueness' to East Germany (author's interview).
166. Quack and Hildebrandt (1995b); Mullineux (1994); Vitols (1994); Harm (1992a).
167. Edwards and Fischer (1994, pp.88–93) present empirical evidence based on *Bundesbank* data for the period 1965–71. Quack and Hildebrandt (1995b, p.10) similarly point out that 'the majority of [West] German SMEs rely mostly on internal mobilisation of financial resources'.
168. The *BDB* (1994, p.8) makes this observation.
169. The *BMWi* study noted a shortage of own funds as an obstacle to *Mittelstand* in the East (Hummel, Ludwig *et al.,* 1994, p.4). The German Economics Ministry reported that loans through the *DtA* in the East were roughly twice as large as those in West Germany owing to the low levels of own funds possessed by East German enterprises (*Handelsblatt,* 31 July 1995, on *Reuters-News-Service*). The *Handelsblatt* also reported a survey of East German *Mittelstand* which found that some 40 per cent of them had own funds levels below 10 per cent (*'Noch kein Rückgang bei Pleiten in Sicht'*, *Handelsblatt,* 6 June 1995, p.1).
170. Elsser (1994); *Deutsche Bundesbank* (1995b), (1994c); (1993a).
171. The West German figure is based on a large sample – more than 17 000 – of enterprise balance sheets (*Deutsche Bundesbank,* 1994a, p.29). The figure has declined slowly from 18.3 per cent in 1989.

172. Elsser attributes the difference in the own-funds levels to a larger proportion of *THA*-owned enterprises in the *Bundesbank* sample. *Deutsche Bundesbank* (1995b, p.56) also notes that the *KfW* sample contained more service enterprises which on the whole have performed better than manufacturing enterprises since GEMSU. In the *Bundesbank* study, it was noted that enterprises in construction and distribution sectors had higher levels of own funds.
173. *Deutsche Bundesbank* (1995b, p.63).
174. See Edwards and Fischer (1994, Chapter 3); also Harm (1992b, p.25).
175. Further evidence of the own-funds problem in addition to the studies we have mentioned is found in the *DIW Wochenbericht*, 13/93 (1 April 1993, pp. 150ff), and *DIW Wochenbericht*, 20/94 (19 May 1994, p.323).
176. *'Kalte Schulter'*, *Wirschatfs-Woche* (25 February 1994, pp.22–5).
177. In West Germany, firms younger than eight years old account for 75 per cent of all insolvencies (Harm, 1992a, p.19).
178. Harm (1992a, p.19).

## 6 The *Hausbank* System in the East after GEMSU

1. Author's interview.
2. Ibid.
3. Yates and Stone (1992, p.1).
4. Steil (1990, p.10).
5. Knight (1973, p.233). The work was first published in 1922, and has been recognised as the founding work in the study of risk and uncertainty.
6. The seminal work is Luce and Raiffa (1957). See also Yates and Stone (1992, p.14). The terms 'objectivity' and 'ignorance' correspond to Knight's 'risk' and 'uncertainty'.
7. Ellsberg (1961).
8. Camerer and Weber (1992).
9. March and Shapira (1987, p.1407). Managers are shown to be less interested in quantifying risk than they are in 'feeling' it, whatever that may mean.
10. Shapira (1993) discusses several of these studies. See also Viscusi and Magat (1992).
11. Kunreuther, Hogarth, and Meszaros (1993), and Hogarth and Kunreuther (1989).
12. Shapira (1986, p.1410) (emphasis is in original). The finding was based on interviews with 50 American and Israeli executives. The results match those in the survey by MacCrimmon and Wehrung (1986) which involved questionnaire responses from 509 high-level executives in Canadian and American firms (including 128 interviews with Canadians in the sample).
13. Yates and Stone (1992, p.15).
14. March and Shapira (1987). If managers simply accepted a fair bet they would not be seen as adding particular value through their knowledge and experience.
15. Wood (1992, p.599). Donaldson (1989) presents a detailed examination of the many facets of credit risk.
16. We are leaving out of account a number of other factors which may figure in the pricing of the loan – for example, the banks' overall market penetration strategy.

17. Diaz-Alejandro (1985) compares banks with butcher shops and makes the point that butcher shops require no information on their customers, provided they pay cash and, moreover, that the butcher will sell as much meat as he can at a given price. Banks, on the other hand, require extensive information on their borrowing customers, and often may not give as much credit as a customer would like at a given interest rate.
18. A senior credit officer of a major European bank remarked,

    Of course, financial ratios and local information are important. But one of my most reliable sources of judgement on credit risk is having my assistant observe the behaviour of a client waiting for a credit negotiation meeting to begin. (Wuffli and Hunt, 1993, p.93)

19. Donaldson (1989, p.13).
20. Stiglitz and Weiss (1981) is the seminal article.
21. Yates and Stone (1992, p.323).
22. Champernowne (1969, p.2).
23. Diamond (1984) points out that banks have a key advantage over depositors in being able to diversify portfolios and hence handle higher individual risks.
24. See Markowitz (1991).
25. Schumpeter (1939, p.116). The bank–borrower relationship suggests a dynamic interaction, over time, between banker and borrower – what Schumpeter points out as 'the necessity of looking after customers and constantly feeling their pulse' (p.117).
26. Wuffli and Hunt (1993, p.96).
27. Diamond (1984), also Diamond (1991).
28. Diamond (1991, p.690).
29. Fama (1985, p.36): 'Inside debt is defined as a contract where the debtholder gets access to information from an organization's decision process not otherwise publicly available'.
30. Sharpe (1990) argues that over time the relationship may favour the bank because the firm becomes 'informationally captured', meaning that it is costly for the firm to switch banks because other banks do not possess the same relationship-specific information and would, therefore, not be prepared to offer the same lending conditions. Moreover, adverse selection may occur whereby the termination of a bank–borrower relationship signals to other banks that the borrower has become less creditworthy.
31. von Thadden (1994b, p.15).
32. Although the benefits of bank–borrower relationships are widely recognised in the literature, there have been theoretical arguments that these relationships – based on the benefits to the bank – do not adequately explain the special status of the long-term borrower, particularly regarding why the borrower gets favourable rates (Blackwell and Santomero, 1982).
33. Binks, Ennew and Reed (1992, p.39).
34. Fama (1985, p.37) argues that having a bank as a delegated monitor provides value to the borrower:

    The value of the signals from a bank about the creditworthiness of an organization's fixed payoff contracts is attested by the fact that many organizations pay periodic monitoring fees for lines of credit from banks even though they do not take the resources offered.

35. The *Allfinanz* strategy involves bank diversification into new markets so that the bank offers a wide portfolio of products, including insurance, leasing and mortgage lending. This diversification not only benefits the bank in terms of portfolio diversification of risk across products, but also allows the bank to sell higher-earning products to a single customer in addition to lower-earning products. In addition, it provides the bank with further information on the borrower, thus reducing the level of ambiguity in lending decisions. In the process, as the customer commits to a wider product range with the bank, the bank–borrower relationship is further strengthened (Sabel, Griffin and Deeg, 1993; also Walter and von Rosen, 1995). This is not to suggest that cross-selling is a purely German approach. Most banks try to market a package of products to a single customer. As banking markets become more competitive, lending spreads usually decline and give banks incentives to sell additional higher value-added products. One bank uses the metaphor of 'McDonalds', with the loan seen as the hamburger or 'centre of the plate', and the french fries, drinks, and so on, as additional products. Lending is often considered the key component in building the bank–borrower relationship and allowing the bank to sell these additional products.
36. Berger and Udell (1995, p.3). They also present a literature survey of empirical and theoretical work on the topic.
37. Peterson and Rajan (1994, p.35).
38. Corbett (1987).
39. Fukada and Hirota (1993).
40. Hoshi, Kashyap and Scharfstein (1990). Aoki (1990) draws similar conclusions.
41. See Edwards and Fischer (1994, pp.1–11).
42. As we noted in Chapter 4, in the official literature on state support programmes, the term '*Hausbank*' is always used for the bank which *handles* the flows for the enterprise.
43. Edwards and Fischer (1994) and Sabel, Griffin and Deeg (1993) also recognise this point. In addition, Quack and Hildebrandt (1995b, p.12) observe the growing existence of a 'double *Hausbank*' arrangement with SMEs.
44. Quack and Hildebrandt (1995b, p.1).
45. Cable (1985) found evidence of a relationship between bank involvement and corporate profitability in a sample of 48 *AG*s. Elston and Albach (1994) and Elston (1993) present evidence that close bank ties lead to less liquidity constraints.
46. Mullineux (1994).
47. Mullineux (1994, p.10).
48. Gröschel (1993). His argument is based on trust in relationships and corresponding lower transaction costs due to less significant informational asymmetries.
49. Mullineux (1994, p.25).
50. Kopper (1992, p.4).

51. In Mullineux's interviews (1994, p.10) with West German bankers, the view was expressed (although not unanimously) that subsidised loans have become less significant over time as bank–borrower relationships develop.
52. *'Kredit in Ostdeutschland nur gegen überhöhte Sicherheiten', Frankfurter Allgemeine Zeitung* (18 March 1994, p.15).
53. Sabine Richter, *'Das Kreditrisiko im Osten ist siebenmal höher', Welt am Sonntag* (31 January 1993, p.23). The article does not identify the bank, but says it is one of the Big Banks and not *Commerzbank* (i.e. *Deutsche Bank* or *Dresdner Bank*).
54. Author's interviews with bankers.
55. *'Die Risikobereitschaft der privaten Banken in den neuen Bundesländern ist durchweg größer als in Westdeutschland. Sie gehen bis an die Grenze des Vertretbaren. Zu berücksichtigen ist aber, daß eine realistische Risikobeurteilung außerordentlich schwierig ist. Die Abschätzung der tatsächlichen Risiken und Schwierigkeiten ist viel problematischer als anfangs geglaubt'*. (own translation) *(Bankenverband mittel- und ostdeutscher Länder e.V., Argumente: Zur Risikobereitschaft der Banken*, mimeo). The report was not an official one, but rather a statement of the views of bankers for discussion purposes.
56. Colin Jones, 'Meeting of the Ways', *The Banker* (May 1990, p.62).
57. *Reuters-News-Service* (27 May 1993).
58. One of the *THA*'s initial tasks was to establish the value of its portfolio. Enterprises were instructed to provide opening balance sheets in DM for 30th October 1990. Although initially viewed as a straightforward accounting exercise that would be completed within months, this task was transformed into a major project of enterprise evaluation and financial restructuring which lasted two years. (Carlin, 1993, p.16).
59. *Gesetz über die Eröffnungsbilanz in Deutscher mark und die Kapitalneufestsetzung (Bundesgesetzblatt II*, 889, 1169, 1245). According to the *Deutsche Bundesbank* (1993a, p.31), Section 36 of the act allowed adjustments to be made to the opening balance sheet on assets, special reserves and debts, until the end of the financial year 1994.
60. A view expressed by a number of West German bankers in interviews with the author. Edwards and Fischer (1994, p.147) encountered the same response in similar interviews.
61. The Chief Executive of *Commerzbank*, Martin Kohlhaussen, stated, 'we simply don't have the credit information and the company history which normally form the basis of a lending decision' (David Waller, 'Service with a Smile', *Financial Times*, 4 May 1994, p.II).
62. Griffin (1994, p.401).
63. This view was illustrated in case studies compiled by Bischof, von Bismark and Carlin (1992).
64. Griffin (1994, p.402).
65. Ibid., p.405.
66. Kasch, Lowenthal and Cassuto (1994, p.61). See also 'Common Goals, Divided Loyalties', *Euromoney* (February 1992, p.41). Conventional bank lending differs from project finance in that loans are made not against projections of what the loan will be used for – although this is considered – but primarily on the record of the borrower. As Donaldson (1989, p.4) explains:

A traditional bank lender normally makes the strength of the borrower the main basis for a decision as to whether to lend. Naturally he takes account of the nature of the loan, the reason for which the borrower needs it, the sources of repayment and so on; but these are mainly ways of assessing the borrower's strength. As long as the borrower remains sound it will meet its obligations.

67. Hummel, Ludwig *et al.* (1994, p.90); and also *BDI* (1994, pp.4–5).
68. *Euromoney* reported that in February 1992 there were only 'the beginnings of a property market in cities such as Dresden, Leipzig, and Berlin' ('Common Goals, Divided Loyalties', *Euromoney*, February 1992, p.41).
69. Griffin (1994, p.410). In an interview with the central credit control department of *Deutsche Bank* in Frankfurt, ambiguity surrounding restitution was viewed as by far the most significant obstacle to credit business in the East (author's interview with Reinhard Bracker, Dieter Müsse and Eva Zipplies, 28 July 1994).
70. *Bundesverband deutscher Banken,* 1992, 1993, 1994.
71. Mullineux (1994, p.7).
72. Some have disputed whether it is really a 'system' at all. Esser (1994a, p.29) argues that it consists of 'single programmes and measures, not parts of an integrated, fully harmonised conception'. Dahrendorf (1990) argues

    there is no 'system' which could be called 'social market economy'; there is only a reality which has come about under special, though not necessarily unique circumstances.

    Our point, however, is simply that the institutions *collectively* enable lending flows to occur.
73. Harm (1992a, p.18).
74. Vitols (1994, p.14).
75. See Gibb (1993, p.467).
76. Kocka (1994) provides a comprehensive treatment of the problems experienced in transplanting West German institutions onto the East, examining the transplant of political institutions, religious institutions and the West German educational system.
77. Kocka (1994, pp.177–8) explains the process under which this decision was made. The key instruments were the State Treaties, which can be found in English translation in Hancock and Welsch (1994, pp.339–70).
78. Portes (1993, p.2).
79. Smyser (1993, p.156) discusses EC legal and institutional issues with respect to GEMSU.
80. For further of this concept see Henzler (1992, p.24); Offe (1993, p.12); Kocka (1994, p.188); Esser (1994a, p.21).
81. Dornbusch and Wolf (1994, p.155). Dornbusch, of course, also proposed a '7 day plan' for PCPEs to complete the transition to a market economy (Chapter 2).
82. *Bundesbank* President Hans Tietmeyer (1993) claimed that West Germany shares a common history, culture, and language with East Germany, but the significance of these factors is the subject of dispute. See Offe (1993,

p.14), and also Judy Dempsey, 'The Wall is Gone but the Burden remains', *Financial Times*, (5–6 November 1994, Section II, pp.I, XIV).

83. Offe (1993, p.1) disputes the often-used analogy, 'After we Germans have coped and managed so impressively after 1945, the new post-1989 reconstruction should be but little more than child's play'.
84. Ibid., p.15.
85. Ibid., p.35.
86. See Offe (1993, p.28), who calls the relative comparisons 'lasting deprivations', based on the idea that East Germany had been politically and legally but not economically unified.
87. Offe (1993, p.10) argues:

    > Compared to the post-1945 short-lived and half-hearted denazification experience, the post-1989 purges of political, judicial, administrative, intellectual, managerial and professional elites was much more protracted and comprehensive.

    Von Lazar (1991, p.34) outlines the difficult process of identifying persons who belonged to the *Stasi* and functioned as 'informants, spies, or torturers'.
88. Offe (1993, p.31).
89. Lehmbruch (1994).
90. *Bundesverband deutscher Banken* (1994, p.6). Of the total 20 979 workers in the branch networks, 4488 came from West Germany, with the other 16 491 being from East Germany. It should be noted, however, that the vast majority of the West Germans filled management positions. At the management level, then, the balance would be much more even if not biased in favour of West Germans.
91. von Thadden (1994a). He observed (p.9), for example, that between GEMSU and July 1991, the percentage of West German higher-level managers in the *THA* increased from 0 to 91 per cent.
92. 'Justice in East Germany: On the Verge of Collapse', *German Brief* (8 March 1991, pp.2–3).
93. Merkl (1994, p.203).
94. The (incremental) changes made to the laws on restitution in response to the delays and obstacles to investment were outlined in Chapter 4. Administrative changes were also made to allow the *THA* to decide ownership in some cases of privatisation in order to avoid the long municipal channels. But within the *THA* there were internal regulations and a separate legal department, and all but the most pressing privatisation cases were delayed in any case (author's interview)
95. Author's interviews. One lawyer explained that the laws surrounding restitution were complicated and untried, and that they posed an extreme challenge for lawyers – even 'educated lawyers' – East and West, since the new laws contained aspects of East and West German law. 'In some cases', he noted, 'an unqualified staff has to apply an unprecedented and highly complicated law'.
96. The reason for the delay was that judges in East Germany, many of whom had come over from the West, were without their support staff (*Rechtspfleger*) who do most of the actual work, and East German staff needed to learn to work within the new institutional framework (author's

interview). This point was confirmed at a subsequent interview with the *KfW*.

97. Confirmed in author's interviews with the *KfW* and *DtA*.
98. Griffin (1994, p.403).
99. Carlin and Richthofen (1995, p.21).
100. *'Geldhäuser knüpfen das Netz noch dichter'*, *Die Wirtschaft* (November 1993, p.20).
101. Author's interview.
102. This point was explained at length in interviews with bankers and also with another chamber of commerce. Similar sentiments were expressed in a telephone interview with a Deputy Director of the Rostok Chamber of Commerce (15 September 1994), and also with several bankers. A *Commerzbank* manager commented that the chamber personnel knew 'absolutely nothing' about (West German-style) banking (author's interview).
103. Kasch, Lowenthal and Cassuto (1994, p.61).
104. Peter Lee, 'Common Goals, Divided Loyalties', *Euromoney* (February 1992, p.41).
105. Randlesome (1992). Karin Wagner (1993) found training to be lacking in the East and a constraint on enabling East German managers to perform close to West German standards.
106. The sample consisted of 159 West German firms in industry and service sectors (OECD 1990–1, p.89).
107. Cited in Randlesome (1992, p.78).
108. Hummel, Ludwig *et al.* (1994, p.53). On a scale of 1 (very high), 2 (high) and 3 (low), banks rated the general qualifications of East German entrepreneurs as an obstacle to making long-term loans at 1.3, of which financial management was rated at 1, and marketing at 1.6. The same survey conducted on *Bürgschaftsbanken* revealed a slightly more favourable assessment of East German entrepreneurs, rating them overall at 1.5, with a 1.8 in financial management and 1.3 in marketing (p.62).
109. 'Joining the Extended Family – The Varying Fortunes of the German Mittelstand', *Financial Times* (29 June 1993, p.9).
110. *'Das Vertrauen seitens der Kreditwirtschaft in die geschäftsführische und kaufmännische Qualifikation ostdeutscher Unternehmer ist nicht sehr ausgeprägt'*. (own translation) (*BDI*, 1994, p.6).
111. Interviews with Sal. Oppenheim Bank and *Deutsche Industrie Holding*. According to the latter, while all *DIH*-owned companies have West German managers, 'Western managers are not a guarantee of success. Some were "dropouts" in the West. In most cases, they were not the best people that you could reach'.
112. One young West German offered three reasons which were being discussed 'on the street' for why West Germans had come over to East Germany. First, to seek promotion that does not exist for them in West Germany. Second, due to failure in their job in West Germany, or to escape or avoid a coming failure. Third, to escape problems, often personal, in West Germany and to start over. He added that the last group was often the most capable but, unfortunately, the smallest of the three (author's interview). It was also suggested by a *Deutsche Bank* manager that

many West Germans came over to use East Germans to front for them in opening a business (author's interview).

113. While the (two) companies remain anonymous, they are both undergoing change. One from meeting plan targets to becoming sales driven; the other, from distributing goods under scarcity (a shortage economy) to selling them in a market under conditions of abundance.
114. Antal and Merkens (1993, p.82).
115. Author's interview.
116. Deeg (1994, p.42).
117. Mullineux (1994, p.23). This view was expressed by a number of bankers in interviews with the author.
118. Research in West Germany suggests that increasing numbers of Mittelstand borrowers expect assistance from banks in addressing non-bank related matters (Schamp, Linge and Rogerson, 1993, p.112).
119. Brandkamp (1993). Of the 87 start-ups in the sample, the responses were: No advice (28.7 per cent); Professional consultants (28.7 per cent); local chambers of commerce (26.4 per cent); friends from West Germany (24.1 per cent); and banks (18.4 per cent).
120. According to the *KfW*, the decision to open this office was taken at a meeting between then Minister of the Economy, Hausemann, and *KfW* Chairman, Gert Vogt, to discuss the problems involved in informing enterprises about public programmes (author's interview).
121. *Bundesverband der deutschen Industrie* (1994, p.10). Enterprises in the survey assessed both West and East German banks, and their criticisms cannot be taken to have been exclusively aimed at West German banks. For the sake of the analysis, however, we maintain that since West German banks were the primary *Hausbanken* to most enterprises, particularly in the first two years after GEMSU while the East German banks were developing their capabilities, we can apply the comments to West German banks.
122. Emphasised by enterprises in the *BDI* survey (1994, p.7).
123. Carlin and Richthofen (1995, p.13).
124. 'Scandalous', *The Economist* (7 August 1993, p.75). Also see, 'Eastern Shortages: Stock Offerings', *The International Herald Tribune* (April 20 1994, p.21). The latter piece suggests that a possible reason for the lack of IPOs is that East German enterprises are not yet able to meet the reporting requirements of the West German stock regulations. According to Jörg Walter, president of the Berlin Stock Exchange, 'Not a single one of the stocks on the Polish or Czech exchanges could have met the standards of the German market'.
125. Deeg (1994, p.24). Carlin (1993, p.22) emphasises West German doubts about East German managerial capacity. This view was expressed by *DIH* in an interview with the author.
126. 'The view from *Deutsche Bank*', *Barron's* (18 November 1991, p.24). In an exceptional instance, *Deutsche Bank*'s increase in its equity stake in Daimler-Benz in 1975, was designed to prevent the Shah of Iran from purchasing the company ('The Battle Plans of Hilmar Kopper', *Euromoney*, January 1994, p.30).
127. Deeg (1994, p.29).

128. In terms of overall venture capital provided – of which banks have accounted for more than half – as of 1993 Germany's total venture capital raised was less than one-quarter of that in the United Kingdom, and less than half of that in France (EVCA, 1994, p.56).
129. Letter to the author from a consultant who worked with the *THA* before joining Roland Berger & Partner *GMbH*. This view is supported by data gathered by Carlin and Mayer (1995) who found that of *THA* privatised enterprises 72.5 per cent became majority-owned (i.e. a single owner with greater than 50 per cent). The average was particularly high for large enterprises (i.e. more than 500 employees), of which 89.4 per cent were majority-owned. In many cases, the *THA* did not sell complete enterprises, but combinations of physical and human resources to which were attached financial incentives to turn these successful enterprise with *the addition of sound marketing and management principles*, most often from outside the East (Bischof, von Bismark and Carlin, 1993) (emphasis original).
130. Balz (1992, p.9). Balz presents his own view at a conference rather than the official view of the *THA*.
131. This view was argued by Roesler (1994) and Carlin (1993). Once it recognised the need for MBOs, the *THA* found ways to enable East Germans to purchase businesses. First, in most cases the *THA* freed the enterprise of its prior debt burden: this was the case for approximately 90 per cent of MBOs (*Die Wirtschaft*, 1994, p.36). Second, all enterprise assets not essential to the business were stripped (by the *THA*) to reduce the purchase price, operating costs and financing needs. On the latter point, the buyer was given an option to lease the requisite property and buy it at a later date. Third, the *THA* commonly accepted less than the purchase price up front with the balance paid in instalments. Fourth, in some cases, *THA* liquidity guarantees were extended beyond the sale. By February 1994, there were 2622 MBOs in the East, the majority being in the service and construction sectors rather than in manufacturing (Treuhandanstalt, 1992, p.15). There is no indication that this trend changed between 1992 and 1994. For more on MBOs in the East, see Balz (1992) and also 'The Chance of the 90's: Investing in Eastern Germany' (Treuhandanstalt 1992, p.17).
132. Roesler (1994, p.510).
133. See Sinn and Sinn (1992, pp.86, 117).
134. 'Germany', in EVCA (1994, p.110). At the end of 1992, the total amount of venture capital investment in West Germany was DM 1687 mn, which then dropped significantly to DM 402 mn in 1993. The OECD (1993–4, p.104) observed: 'In Germany, as in most of continental Europe, the institution of venture capital is poorly developed'.
135. Banks provided 51.6 per cent of total venture capital in Germany in 1992, and 52.2 per cent in 1993 (EVCA, 1994, p. 110).
136. von Thadden (1994a, pp.20–1) quotes *Deutsche Bank* Chairman Hilmar Kopper: 'It is not the primary task of banks to develop entrepreneurial activity. This would go against the classical division of roles in a market economy and, in the end, would be beyond the banks' capabilities'.
137. Ardagh (1991, pp.119–20) outlines banks' risk aversion and suggests possible explanations for it.

138. The insurance industry, for example, is restricted from investing in unlisted companies and pension funds do not exist.
139. Sabel, Griffin and Deeg (1993, p.10). The authors note that one reason for this is the 1952 Capital Market law imposed high corporate and personal taxes on dividend income relative to interest from debt. The OECD (1995, pp.16–17, n. 139) observes that (only) 5.5 per cent of German households own shares, the lowest level in the OECD. Also see *Deutsche Bundesbank* (1991a) and *Deutsche Beteiligungsgesellschaft*, 'Challenges for German Industry are Opportunities for the Development Capital Market', in EVCA (1994, p.17). This fixed-income bias is changing somewhat, albeit slowly. See, Conner Middelmann, 'New-found Enthusiasm for Equities', German Banking and Finance Survey, *Financial Times* (17 May 1995, p.VI).
140. 'Mittelstand Need Persuading', Survey on Venture Capital Development, *Financial Times* (September 23 1994, p.VII).
141. 'Challenges for German Industry are Opportunities for the Development Capital Market', *Deutsche Beteiligungsgesellschaft*, in EVCA (1994, p.17).
142. Quack and Hildebrandt (1995*b*, p.9). The postwar generation of owners is growing near retirement age, however. The next generation may be more open to the idea of diluting their ownership share either to play a smaller role in the business on the one hand, or perhaps to expand it in absolute terms on the other. They may also simply decide to sell it.
143. Saxony accounted for 37 and 36 per cent of all lending in the East in the years 1992 and 1993, respectively (Landeszentralbanken data).
144. '*Schommer kritisiert Scheu der banken vor dem Risiko*', *Handelsblatt*, (22 February 1994, p.4).
145. Carlin and Mayer (1992, p.339). The data was supplied by the *THA*.
146. It is, of course, possible that those interviewed did not wish to admit that information was obtained.
147. Mayhew and Seabright (1992, p.117).
148. Given all these points, there seems little basis for the view put forward by Carlin and Mayer in a more recent work (1994, p.204):

    > The reason why interest is now being shown by West German banks in lending to East German firms is that viable companies are beginning to emerge. The monitoring and control functions of supervisory boards have been central to this development. Through their position on supervisory boards, banks accumulate valuable information on the quality of prospective borrowers. Banks are therefore just at the point of being confident that they can identify sound investments.

149. Harm (1992a, p.5). Sabel, Griffin and Deeg argue (1993, p.23), however, that 'advisory board positions do not normally provide the banks with a chance to influence management'.
150. One *Commerzbank* manager confirmed in an interview that he sits on two advisory boards, but claims that he has 'no communication' with the loan officer who is responsible for the enterprises in question.
151. Author's interview with a *Landeszentralbank* manager (Leipzig), who noted that: 'In the West, the *Hausbank* relationship is formally between institutions, but really goes through a single person on a single level'.

152. This according to Reiner Rusch, General Manager of *Deutsche Bank* Leipzig (*Asian Finance*, 'Big Three Line up Branches and Loans', 15 September 1990, p. 15).
153. Peter Lee, 'Common Goals, Divided Loyalties', *Euromoney* (February 1992, p.42).
154. Ibid.
155. Author's interview with a *Commerzbank* manager.
156. The *Bundesbank* (*Annual Report*, 1991, p.114) reported that 'there still remains a heavy burden for staff with banking experience. This is particularly true for the loan business'. Training, after all, is only half of the learning process, and doesn't make up for a lack of experience (as we discussed in Chapter 2).
157. Edwards and Fischer (1994, p.147). The authors note further that, 'new officers spend a significant amount of time in junior positions within the loan department, developing the necessary skills for loan assessment by observing the practices of their superior'.
158. Author's interview with a *Deutsche Bank* manager
159. Quack and Hildebrandt (1995b, p.18).
160. The view expressed in the author's interviews with other banks.
161. Griffin (1994, p.411).
162. The process is more complicated for *DtA* loans than for *KfW* loans because the *DtA* bears default risk in a larger percentage of the loans. According to one *DtA* manager, the total application for a new borrower contains some 73 pages, and to be approved must be accompanied by an approval from the local chamber of commerce. Once the complete application is submitted, there are frequently further information requests made of the *Hausbank*.
163. While *KfW* loans carry no interest rate risk, they allow the *Hausbank* a maximum margin of 1 per cent (when the *Hausbank* bears the full default risk for the loan) and a lower margin in the (limited) cases where the default risk is shared between the *Hausbank* and the *KfW*.
164. According to one report, in 1991 there were more than 670 official programmes on offer ('Rebuilding Europe', *The Wall Street Journal Europe*, January 26 1995, p.1). Later reports claimed more than 800 ('Nahezu Null', *Wirtschafts Woche*, 18, 27 April 1995, 25). Many of those interviewed referred to a 'war of paper' and described the process of sorting out the programmes as 'horrifying'. One *Deutsche Bank* manager stated that there was sufficient information about the programmes, but that this information – contained in stacks of pamphlets – still needed to be communicated to potential borrowers (author's interview).
165. Author's interview with a member of the German Bankers' Association.
166. In addition to bankers, this view was noted in interviews with a *KfW* manager, who observed that there are few defaults on these loans.
167. Jarausch (1994, p.204). Dennis (1993, p.171) cited a 1993 survey in *Der Spiegel* which found that 64 per cent of West Germans and 74 per cent of East Germans agreed with the statement, 'The Wall has gone but the wall in people's heads grows'.
168. Trommsdorff (1994) contains a collections of papers on psychologica aspects of GEMSU, the central message being that while the transpla

worked well on certain (formal) levels, underlying psychological 'condition-factors and processes' (*Bedingungsfaktoren und Prozesse*) are relevant and must be taken into account.

169. Dennis (1993, pp.170–1).
170. Our reference to the term 'colonialism' is not meant to be a value judgement on West Germans but rather to characterise how the transplant and the *system* that was put in place may have been perceived by East and West Germans. That is to say, 'colonialism' is used as a functional description of this system, rather than to imply that it was based on reasons of exploitation as the term is often understood. East Germans did, after all, vote to become part of West Germany and, in a material sense, see their living standards improves markedly after GEMSU largely as a result of West German transfers paid for by West German taxpayers.
171. 'Ex-Chancellor Schmidt Criticizes Reforms In East Germany as Too Drastic, Too Fast', *The Wall Street Journal Europe* (Friday–Saturday, July 1–2 1994, p.8). The *Guardian* also reported that, 'Big Brother also looks like a colonial master race of *Wessis* who profess to educate the boorish *Ossis* but do so in their own economic interest'. ('Capitalism's Disgruntled New Arrivals', The *Guardian*, 27 November 1991, p.21).
172. Radice (1995, p.23).
173. Schrettl (1992, p.148).
174. Sinn and Sinn (1992, p.86, n. 12); also Schrettl (1992, p.151).
175. Merkl (1994, p.203).
176. Fieldhouse (1981, pp.6–7).
177. Glaessner (1994, p.159). Pickel (1992a, p.180) also points out that GEMSU led to 'the socio-psychological and political disempowerment of large sectors of the East German population ("colonization" creation of a *de facto* group of second-class citizens)'.
178. A leading East German playwright wrote,

    > Along a wide (Western) media front, East German culture is being convinced that it never really existed. Attacks on East German authors ... represent only a symptom. Whether film, art or theater, everything which could be seen as a necessary, unique cultural development in GDR intellectual history is being retrospectively eliminated. (Wolfgang Kil on the Intellectual Colonization of East Germany, 29 June 1990, cited in Jarausch and Granson, 1994, pp.171–2)

179. Görtemaker (1994, p.142) writes:

    > The results virtually amounted to a complete Federal Republic takeover of the GDR. Bonn offered to accept responsibility for the GDR economy, monetary stability, unemployment, pensions, welfare, and the infrastructure, but requested that the entire West German economic order be introduced in East Germany as well. The adaptation of the GDR to the Federal system was to be sealed in a state treaty on the 'establishment of a united economic and social area' in which the West German law and West German government would prevail. Thereafter, even budget decisions of the GDR parliament would be dependent upon West German consent.

    See also Radice (1995, p.31).

180. Author's interview. Similar problems were mentioned by a manager of Sal. Oppenheim Bank.
181. Harris (1967). Harris' work is derived from earlier studies by Berne (1961).
182. The use of transactional analysis in the book is thus based on criteria of helpfulness rather than academic standing in the field of psychoanalysis, a field in which the author claims no particular expertise. Moreover, we are extending transactional analysis somewhat to *characterise* East and West Germans' dominant psychological states. Transaction analysis applies to transactions which, unfortunately, we do not have since the author did not engage in participant observation of (for example) loan negotiations between West German bankers and East German borrowers. Nevertheless, the analysis helps us to understand the likely interaction between these groups based on the experiences conveyed in interviews and other accounts.
183. So as not to confuse the discussion we do not use the terms 'Child' and 'Parent', which have a different meaning within the framework of transactional analysis.
184. Harris (1967, p.20). The author's interview with a member of the *Bundesbank*'s Supervision Department was particularly revealing. He insisted that standards for bank licences needed to be equalised across East and West Germany because (unqualified) East German bankers might receive licences and then work in the West. The standards included the number of years in a management position, the educational background, and the total experience carrying out banking business on West German standards. He admitted that – by definition – these standards would exclude most East Germans. Further, he argued that West German bankers were better able to operate in the East because they were 'more skilled in the business', and pointed out that the East German Savings Banks had experienced significant losses due to their inexperience (see Chapter 5). When asked why West German banks had also suffered high levels of loan losses, he was unable to respond, seeing no connection between the two., evidencing a dominant Parent which adheres to a position based on a taught, normative basis rather than based on experience and an evaluation of the evidence (author's interview).
185. Herbert Henzler (1992, p.24), Chairman of the German office of McKinsey & Company.
186. Author's interview.
187. Maaz (1990, p.53). Maaz's book, *Behind the Wall*, has been the source of criticism for 'putting the whole of Germany onto the couch and analysing it'. Maaz admits (p.210) that, 'I don't see it as a scientific work, but rather as an account of personal experiences', adding that the book was written in twelve weeks. Nevertheless, it is based on more than a decade of psychiatric work at the Protestant Psychiatric Clinic in Halle, in which Maaz had more than 5000 patients.
188. Author's interview.
189. Harris (1967, p.51). Thus, many of the perceived problems by borrowers may have simply been due to a lack of understanding of how the lending process works, particularly through the Specialised Banks.
190. Approximately one-third of the enterprises felt the loan process took too long (*BDI*, 1994, p.3). According to a Director of the Leipzig Chamber of

Commerce, delays in processing loans represented the biggest problem to East German borrowers (author's interview).

191. *Bundesverband der deutschen Industrie* (1994, p.6); Hummel, Ludwig *et al.* (1994, p.90). The experience of one East German entrepreneur, highlights a basic adjustment problem, whereby East German entrepreneurs were unable to comply with an institutional state support structure which functions efficiently in West Germany. He set up a business after GEMSU. In 1992, he was advised by his *Hausbank* that he could obtain a loan package consisting of *KfW* loans and a state subsidy – what he called 'a gift'. The problem was that in order to receive the gift he needed to produce a balance sheet – a standard request in West Germany. For him, producing a balance sheet took almost two years, given that his business involved making small plastic containers and parts and was not computerised. During this time, he was forced to substitute bridging loans for the state subsidy at the market rate from his *Hausbank* (author's interview).
192. A manager of Deutsche Leasing observed this problem in his four years of experience with East German borrowers (author's interview, 1 August 1994).
193. *BDI* (1994, p.5).
194. Another important difference with the postwar period is that BIS capital adequacy guidelines did not exist then. These guidelines – that total capital must equal at least 8 per cent of risk-weighted assets – constrain banks' ability to take on risky debt. Hilmar Kopper (1992, p.9) discusses how these guidelines have made German banks more conservative in their lending practices. For a full discussion of the issue of capital requirements in the German banks, see Rudolph (1993).
195. *BDI* (1994, p.5).
196. Ashauer (1990, p.21); also Jeffries and Melzer (1987, pp.188–9).
197. Mentioned in interviews with the author, particularly in the *THA*.
198. '*Unsere Unternehmen müssen einfach lernen, auch mal einer Bank den Stuhl vor die Tür zu setzen, wenn sie nicht bessere Konditionen anbietet*'. (own translation) ('*Auf den Trimmpfad*', *Wirtschafts-Woche*, 14 February 1992, p.18). Wolfram Krause was the board member responsible for finance (*Treuhand-Finanzvorstand*).
199. Harris (1967, p.77) defines the second rule of communication in Transactional Analysis: 'When stimulus and response cross on the P-A-C transactional diagram, communication stops'.
200. A similar Parent characterisation was evident in the following interview with an East German professor:

    > Here in East Germany, everything had to be refurbished in order to conform to the bureaucratic prescription of the west. I think part of this process represented the inferiority of the west Germans. The first thing they did was to implant western conditions here. You felt they were uneasy if things did not look like what they were accustomed to. The furniture. The towels. Everything western had to be transplanted on the east. ('The Wall is Gone but the Burden Remains', *Financial Times*, 5–6 November, Section II, p.I).

201. Expectations were crucial in keeping East German people content and *contained* while the inevitable pain of the transition would take hold.

The unified labour market drove – and accelerated – the process towards GEMSU and the policies it would bring. The unified labour market and corresponding migratory pressures appeared long before GEMSU, beginning with the fall of the Berlin wall on 9 November 1989 (Schrettl, 1992).

202. Roesler (1994, p.512). Also see Jarausch and Granson (1994, pp. 122–4) for a review of Chancellor Kohl's campaign promises in March 1990.
203. Schrettl (1992, p.146) refers to this boosting of expectations as the 'Paretian Promise', that 'nobody will be worse off and many will be better off'. Marsh (1992, p.212) presents a discussion of the way in which Chancellor Helmut Kohl raised expectations regarding the reconstruction process in East Germany.
204. The scrutiny continues: In October 1995, the German Finance Ministry announced that it would investigate allegation against West German banks which had 'profited from cheap takeovers' in the East (*Reuters-News-Service*, 28 October 1995).
205. Author's interview. The *BDI* (1994, p.11) pointed out that there were no significant differences in East and West interest rates.
206. 'East German Savings Banks Predict More Than 7500 Bankruptcies by end 1995, Roughly a Third of all in Germany'. (*Süddeutsche Zeitung*, English abstracts, 11 August 1995).
207. In the author's interviews, there were many references to the struggle going on between the *THA* and the banks, most evident in the changing policies over the level of liquidity loans. In addition, the media was littered with position statements by Chancellor Helmut Kohl that the banks were not doing enough in the East (such as 'Kohl says German banks doing too little in the East', *Reuters-News-Service*, 11 February 1994), with responses from the German Bankers Association, among others, in defence of the banks' position.
208. Schrettl (1992, p.149).
209. 'Treuhandanstalt: Are the Banks Being Blackmailed?', *German Brief* (5 March 1993, p.21).
210. A short history of the proposal can be found in Hornef (1994b).
211. It was widely noted in interviews that the *Bankenmilliarde* was created in a defensive manner to improve the banks' image, not under the banks' initiative to seek out and invest in viable opportunities. A Director of *DIH* also observed that *DIH* was created by *Deutsche Bank* for primarily political reasons (author's interview).
212. The critique most widely cited in the media came from Heinrich Hornef (1994b) of the *THA*, who argued that, '*Die Geschichte der Bankenmilliarde ist alles andere als eine Erfolgsstory*' ('The Bankenmilliarde is anything but a success story'.) Hornef observed that many companies were purchased by outside investors, thus demonstrating that the enterprises were potentially viable but that the banks were not interested in taking the risk of purchasing them.
213. Author's interview.
214. 'Treuhandanstalt: Are the Banks Being Blackmailed?', *German Brief* (5 March 1993, p.21).

215. It is highly likely, in fact, that East German banks' borrowers faced greater difficulties since these banks did not have more creditworthy West German enterprises in their portfolios.
216. Deeg (1994, p.35).
217. *Deutsche Bundesbank* (1994f, p.39). A member of the Savings Bank Association reported that about 80 per cent of the Savings Banks' loan portfolio in the East consisted of business start-up loans (letter to the author, 23 August 1995).
218. Deeg (1994, p.35) makes this point. In the UK economy, a survey by the British Chambers of Commerce found that of small firms surveyed, less than half feel that the bank understands their business when they deal with it at a regional level, whereas 70 per cent feel it does so when dealing at a local level (see *Business Briefing*, 2 June 1995, p.5).
219. 'Savings Banks Profit From Close Community Ties', *International Herald Tribune* (June 2 1995, p.18) We should not overlook the fact that as the President of the Association it is Köhler's purpose to present the member banks in the best possible light. A member of the Savings Bank Association also noted that the Savings Banks have a 'more thorough knowledge of local conditions', in addition to 'excellent personal contact' with their customers (letter to the author, 23 August 1995).
220. Vitols (1995).
221. Quack and Hildebrandt (1995b, p.13) report that West German Savings Banks operate a database that includes more than 100 000 firms, which they call 'unique in the German banking sector'.
222. Vitols (1995, p.6).
223. Sabel, Griffin and Deeg (1993) argue that the Big Banks underwent large-scale decentralisation in the 1970s and 1980s to expand their *Mittelstand* portfolio, yet still experienced screening and monitoring problems, often resulting in loan losses.
224. Systematic risk was high in the East because bank portfolios had *more risky companies* than in the West due to the large number of start-ups. Many bankers had lending logs showing the majority of East German enterprises as higher lending risks. The rating system would attach a letter 'grade' to rate the risk level of a company. The lower the letter (such as '*C*' or '*D*' as opposed to '*A*' or '*B*') the riskier the enterprise (*source*: author's interviews with bankers). In any event, bankers in the East consistently expressed the view that portfolio diversification was not undertaken in line with the theory of negative covariance (though they did not explicitly use the term in the interviews). In other words, they do not seek to diversify their portfolio as widely as possible, but rather choose sectors which they believe will be successful.
225. The Big Banks' international business accounts for between one-third and just less than one-half of their balance sheets, and in some cases an even higher share of their earnings (Weber, 1995, pp.41–3).
226. Harm (1992b, p.4).
227. With respect to *THA* liquidity loans, *Deutsche Bank* was clearly the most overstretched, but *Commerzbank* still handled not insignificant levels and – like *Deutsche Bank* – served its West German customers.
228. See Deeg (1994, p.35).

229. Edwards and Fischer (1994, pp.103–4).
230. Vitols (1995, p.9). Edwards and Fischer (1994, p.99) note that

> the traditional functions of the lower tier – the savings banks – are implicitly defined by the special savings bank laws passed under Land [state] legislation, with which these banks must comply in addition to the banking act.

231. 'Savings Banks Profit From Close Community Ties', *International Herald Tribune* (June 2 1995, p.18).
232. The *Bundesbank* (1994f) reports that for 1991 and 1992 profit levels were similar for East and West German Savings Banks and Credit Cooperatives. A more recent report (*Deutsche Bundesbank*, 1994b) finds that this continued in 1993, where profit levels were virtually identical for both bank groups, equal to that of the Big Banks (overall result), and moreover, higher than the average of all categories of banks in Germany. The data are consistent with the view expressed in a letter (21 August 1995) to the author from the Secretary of the Managing Board of the *Stadt- und Kreissparkasse Leipzig*:

> we can confirm that the Sparkassen in Germany are not able to assume higher risks simply because they are publicly owned. Sparkassen have to work as responsible as other institutes do. And there hasn't been pressure on the Sparkassen to do so.

233. Quack and Hildebrandt (1995a) argue that French banks are not successful in building long-term relationships with SMEs owing to the banks' 'concentration on financial information in credit decisions' and also their frequent changes of customer advisors.
234. In interviews with employees of *Deutsche Bank* there was a noticeable tension amongst employees in the East who had the impression that they were misunderstood. Griffin (1994, p.399) came to a similar conclusion based on his interviews, as the following episode illustrates:

> The same branch manager, for example, related how top Frankfurt managers' unfamiliarity with East German ways created bitter controversy between Frankfurt and Berlin and also between Frankfurt and Potsdam over the banks' marketing strategies in the East.

235. Griffin (1994, pp.411–12).
236. This is argued by Deeg (1994, pp.33,40), and Griffin (1994, p.406).
237. This point was mentioned frequently in the interviews with the author.
238. This is a problem found in mature banking systems as well. Wuffli and Hunt (1993, p.100) note,

> Because the life of a loan is often longer than the job tenure of the loan officer responsible for it, and because credit committees tend to dilute responsibility, true accountability for loans and losses is rare.

This was certainly one of the causes of the high volumes of NPLs made in Latin America in the 1970s and early 1980s.

## 7 The East German experience in perspective

1. *Bankenverband mittel- und ostdeutscher Länder* (1997/8).
2. *Deutsche Bundesbank* (1995a).
3. Pickel (1992a, p.179).
4. See Maaz (1990).
5. Griffin (1994) makes this argument.
6. Quack and Hildebrandt (1995b, p.11). Unfortunately, the authors do not mention what type of companies made up the sample.
7. Pohl and Claessens (1994, pp.12–13).
8. Prill (1995).
9. See, 'Going West?', *Business Central Europe* (October 1995, pp.48–50).
10. Kopper (1992, p.7).
11. Horst Köhler, 'A savers' solution', *The Banker* (14 February 1995, p.14).
12. Gibb (1993, p.474).
13. '*Deutsche Bank*: Klient über alles', *Segodnya* (11 July 1995).
14. This section draws on the findings of Robins (1995b). The study consisted of one week each in the Czech Republic, Hungary, Poland and Russia. In addition to collecting data, interviews were conducted with domestic and foreign bankers, regulators and bank customers.
15. In each of the countries, however, informal restrictions have played a role in recent years. Licensing moratoria and arrangements whereby foreign banks are expected to 'contribute' to the system (e.g. purchase a local bank with problems) have inhibited somewhat the number entering. These restrictions, however, came after the initial wave of foreign banks entered the markets and thus are unlikely to have kept out many other foreign banks. One exception which received attention is in Poland where some German banks – most notably *Deutsche Bank* – had been unable to obtain a banking licence (see '*Deutsche Bank* Wants to Extend Operation in Poland', *Reuters-News-Service*, 27 January 1994), although Deutsche and Dresdner had received licences by 1995.
16. Russia is the only country in which domestic banks successfully lobbied to keep out foreign banks. Restrictions were imposed on foreign banks through decrees issued in November 1993 and June 1994, including: an aggregate limit of 12 per cent on foreign capital in the system; borrowers restricted to only one local currency account (which is already with a local bank); restrictions on operations with residents for banks which began these later than 15 November 1993; a minimum deposit level of 55 000 ecu (roughly US $72 000) thereby restricting foreign banks to high net-worth customers; a limit of one branch office in addition to the foreign bank's main branch in Russia; and higher minimum capital requirements on foreign banks (US $5 mn) than on local banks (roughly US $610 000) (Robins, 1995b, p.23).
17. Asset levels may not capture off-balance sheet activities, however, an area where foreign banks are likely to be particularly active due to their smaller balance sheet size, higher skill levels and broader experience in such activities. Given that much attention has been devoted to the intermediation function of banks, the asset levels are a reasonably good measure of bank activity.

18. The relatively higher levels of foreign bank involvement in Hungary are largely due to the data which include all joint-venture banks with more than 50 per cent foreign ownership as foreign banks. In addition, the figures include the large off-shore consortium Central European International Bank (CIB) (see Zdeborsky and Gellert, 1992). In 1993, the CIB accounted for more than 11 per cent of the total assets of all foreign and joint-venture banks (calculated from CIB, *Annual Report*, 1993).
19. This represents the level as of 30 June 1994. See United States Department of the Treasury (1994, p.4).
20. The higher profitability of Czech domestic banks compared with domestic banks in Hungary and Poland also reflects the strong concentration of the Czech banking sector and the lack of advantages such as tax holidays, given to foreign banks when entering the market.
21. In Hungary, for example, small private banks accounted for the remaining 32 per cent of total net banking profits, whereas large Hungarian banks – most state-owned – accumulated net losses equal to 45 per cent of total net profits for the banking sector (State Banking Supervision of Hungary, 1995).
22. Prill (1995, p.121).
23. In Hungary, foreign banks had enjoyed a 'swap window' whereby the central bank allowed them to exchange foreign currency for Hungarian forints to meet their liquidity requirements. In December 1994, this window was closed by the central bank (officially for monetary policy concerns) which provoked protests by foreign banks, underlining the importance they attached to this facility. As a result, the window was reopened though the levels allowed were lowered somewhat.
24. Wuffli and Hunt (1993, p.99).
25. This is true in the case of subsidiaries which are treated as local banks and expected to maintain the same capital adequacy requirements. For branches, such as those of the West German banks in the East, the capital of the parent bank is used thus giving more freedom to the local branch to extend higher lending volumes. Even in the case of branches, however, there is some degree of monitoring by the central banks of branch lending volumes to ensure the soundness of the banks (e.g. in Poland branches now must commit local capital in any event), and these banks also have internal limits on cross-border exposure which further limits the lending levels of branches. In any event, the issue of branches versus subsidiaries has been a contentious one in PCPEs, the Czech Republic being the most notable case in which several foreign branches were established and accused by local banks of lending exceedingly large amounts by virtue of their branch status. In Hungary, foreign banks may only enter via subsidiaries, and in Poland it appears that branch licences – though legally permitted – are no longer given.
26. One of the findings of interviews conducted (Robins, 1995b) was a clear lack of consensus among policy-makers, regulators and local bankers on the expectations of the role of foreign banks in PCPEs.
27. In Poland, in 1992 43.9 per cent of foreign bank assets were loans to other banks, a figure which fell gradually from 41.5 per cent in 1993 and 35.9 per cent in 1994 (National Bank of Poland, 1995).

28. Analytical Centre Under the President of the Russian Federation (1994).
29. '*Commerzbank hodlá v Ceské republice postupovat i nadále velmi aktivne*', *Hospodársué Noviny* (10 January 1995, p.10.)
30. See, 'Going West?', *Business Central Europe* (October 1995, pp.48–50).
31. In Poland, for example, foreign banks developed the commercial paper market and also improved cash management services for business by initially sending daily faxes with account information and later moving to a fully electronic system.
32. In the PCPEs, foreign banks worked with regulators to develop the necessary infrastructure for these markets and, at the same time, built networks between financial institutions to enable the infrastructure to be utilised as it was developed. (Robins, 1995b)
33. 'Bracing for a Buying Binge', *The Economist* (August 15 1998, p.66).

# Bibliography

## Books and articles (including statistical sources)

Ábel, István and Konstantine Gatsios (1993). 'The Economics of Bankruptcy and the Transition to a Market Economy,' *CEPR Discussion Paper*, 878 (December).

Adam, Jan (1989). *Economic Reforms in the Soviet Union and Eastern Europe since the 1960s*, London: Macmillan.

Aghion, Philippe and Robin Burgess (1993). 'Financing and Development in Eastern Europe and the Former Soviet Union: Issues and Institutional Support,' in Alberto Giovannini (ed.), *Finance and Development: Issues and Experience*, Cambridge: Cambridge University Press.

Aghion, Philippe and Wendy Carlin (1994). 'The Economics of Enterprise Restructuring in Central and Eastern Europe,' mimeo.

Akerloff, George A. (1970). 'The Market for "Lemons:" Quality Uncertainty and the Market Mechanism,' *Quarterly Journal of Economics*, 84(3), 488–500.

Akerloff, George A., A.K. Rose, J. Yellen and H. Hessenius (1991). 'East Germany in from the Cold: The Economic Aftermath After Currency Union,' *Brookings Papers on Economic Activity*: 1, 1–105.

Allison, Graham T. (1971). *Essence of Decision*, Boston: Little, Brown & Co.

Amberger, Hartmut (1992). '*Dresdner Bank*'s Strategy in the Former German Democratic Republic,' in Alfred Steinherr (ed.), *The New European Financial Market Place*, London: Longman.

Analytical Centre Under the President of the Russian Federation (1994). 'Report on Foreign Bank Participation in the Russian Economy,' mimeo (an English summary of the main findings appears in *Commersant Daily*, 189, 6 October 1994).

Antal, Ariane Berthoin and Hans Merkens (1993) 'Cultures and Fictions in Transition: Challenges Facing Managers and Employers in East German Companies,' *Journal of General Management*, 19(1) (Autumn), 76–86.

Aoki, Masahiko (1990). 'Toward an Economic Model of the Japanese Firm,' *Journal of Economic Literature*, 28 (March), 1–27.

Ardagh, John (1991). *Germany and the Germans*, London: Penguin.

Arrow, Kenneth (1962). 'The Economic Implications of Learning by Doing,' *Review of Economic Studies*, 29(1), 155–73.

Ashauer, Gunter (1990). *'Das Bankwesen in der Deutschen Demokratischen Republik,' Sparkasse*, 1, (107 *Jahrgang*), 8–25.

Aslund, Anders (1989). *Gorbachev's Struggle for Economic Reform*, London: Pinter.

Balz, Manfred (1992). 'Commercial Privatisation in Germany 1992,' paper prepared for the CEEPN Conference (Ljubljana) (November 1992), mimeo.

*Bankenverband mittel- und ostdeutscher Länder* (various years), *Annual Reports*, other reports and summary statistics.

——— (1994). *'Geschäftsentwicklung in den neuen Bundesländern per 31.12.1993'*.

——— (1995). *'Geschäftsentwicklung der privaten Banken in den neuen Bundesländern,'* Berlin.

——— (1997/8). *'Die privaten Banken und ihr Verband in den neuen Bundesländern,'* Berlin.

Baums, Theodor (1992). 'Corporate Governance in Germany: The Role of Banks,' *The American Journal of Comparative Law*, 40, 503–26.

Begg, David and Richard Portes (1992). 'Enterprise Debt and Economic Transformation: Financial Restructuring of the State Sector in Central and Eastern Europe,' *CEPR Discussion Paper*, 695 (June).

——— (1993). 'Eastern Germany Since Unification: Wage Subsidies Remain a Better Way,' *Economics of Transition*, 1(4), 383–400.

Beintema, Nienke and Bart van Ark (1993). 'Comparative Productivity in East and West German Manufacturing Before Unification,' *CEPR Discussion Paper*, 895 (February).

Benston, George J. (1990). *The Separation of Commercial and Investment Banking*, London: Macmillan.

——— (1994). 'Universal Banking,' *Journal of Economic Perspectives*, 8(8) (Summer), 121–43.

Berger, Allen N. and Gregory F. Udell (1995). 'Relationship Lending and Lines of Credit in Small Firm Finance,' *New York University Salomon Center Working Paper Series*, S-95-5.

Berle, Adolf A. and Gardiner C. Means (1932). *The Modern Corporation and Private Property*, New York: Harcourt, Brace & World.

Berne, E. (1961). *Transactional Analysis in Psychotherapy*, New York: Grove Press.

Binks, M.R., C.T. Ennew, and G.V. Reed. (1992). 'Information Asymmetries and the Provision of Finance to Small Firms,' *International Small Business Journal*, 11(1) (October–December), 35–46.

Bischof, Robert, Gottfried von Bismark and Wendy Carlin (1993). 'From Kombinat to Private Enterprise: Two Case Studies in East German Privatisation,' in John Heath (ed), *Revitalizing Socialist Enterprise: A Race Against Time*, London: Routledge.

Blackwell, Norman R. and Anthony M. Santomero (1982). 'Bank Credit Rationing and the Customer Relation,' *Journal of Monetary Economics*, 9, 121–9.

Blejer, Mario I. and Sylvia B. Sagari (1992). 'Hungary: The Initial Stages in the Financial Sector Reform of a Socialist Economy in Transition,' *Applied Financial Economics*, 2, 33–42.

Blommestein, Hans J. (1992). 'Sound Banking for a Strong Market,' *The OECD Observer*, 117 (August–September), 19–22.

——— (1993). 'Financial Sector Reform and Monetary Policy in Central and Eastern Europe,' in Donald E. Fair and Robert J. Raymond (eds), *The New Europe: Evolving Economic and Financial Systems in East and West*, Dordrecht: Kluwer.

Blommestein, Hans J. and Jean R. Lange (1993). *Transformation of the Banking System: Portfolio Restructuring, Privatisation and the Payments System*, Paris: OECD.

Bofinger, Peter (1992). 'The Experience with Monetary Policy in an Environment with Strong Microeconomic Distortions.' paper presented at the conference, *Economic Consequences of the East*, mimeo.

Bofinger, Peter and Ivan Cernohorsky (1992). 'Some Lessons from Economic Transformation in East Germany,' *CEPR Discussion Paper*, 686 (June).

Böhnel, Johannes (1995). 'Supervision of Financial Markets,' in Norbert Walter and Rüdiger von Rosen (eds), *German Financial Markets*, Cambridge: Gresham Books, Woodhead Publishing, 15–35.

Bönker, Frank (1993). 'Building Capitalism in Eastern Europe: State and Determinants of Institutional Reform in Bulgaria, Hungary, the Czech Republic, and Slovakia,' paper prepared for the Conference, 'Constitutional Politics and Economic Transformation in Post-Communist Societies,' Collegium Budapest (17–19 December), mimeo.

Borish, Michael S., Millard F. Long and Michel Noël (1995). 'Restructuring Banks and Enterprises: Recent Lessons from Transition Countries,' *World Bank Discussion Paper*, 279.

Bös, Dieter and Gunter Kayser (1995). 'The Last Days of the Treuhandanstalt,' in Paul Cook and Colin Kirkpatrick (eds), *Privatisation Policy and Performance: International Perspectives*, London: Prentice-Hall Harvester Wheatsheaf, 84–100.

Brada, Josef C., Roland Schönfeld and Ben Slay (1995). 'The Role of International Financial Institutions in Central and Eastern Europe,' *Journal of Comparative Economics*, 20, 49–56.

Brainard, L.J. (1990). 'Reform in Eastern Europe: Creating the Capital Market,' *AMEX Bank Review Special Papers*, 18.

Brandkamp, M. (1993). *'Erfolgsaussichten von Unternehmensgründungen in den fünf neuen Bundesländern,' Zeitschrift für Betriebswirtschaft-Ergänzungsheft*, 1, 109–44.

Brus, Wlodzimierz and Kazimierz Laski (1989). *Marx to the Market*, Oxford: Clarendon Press.

Bryman, Alan (1989). *Research Methods and Organization Studies*, London: Routledge.

Bryson, Phillip J. (1992). 'The Economics of German Reunification: A Review of the Literature,' *Journal of Comparative Economics*, 16, 118–49.

Buch, Claudia M. (1994). 'Dealing with Bad Debt – Lessons from Eastern Europe,' *Kiel Working Papers*, 642 (July).

——— (1995). 'Monetary Policy and the Transformation of the Banking System in Eastern Europe,' *Kiel Working Papers*, 676 (February).

Buck, Hannsjörg F. (1987). 'The GDR Financial System,' in Ian Jeffries and Manfred Melzer (eds), *The East German Economy*, London: Croom Helm, 149–201.

*Bundesverband deutscher Banken (BDB)* (1992). *'Die Aktivitäten der Privaten Banken in den neuen Bundesländern,'* Köln: *Informationen des Bundesverbandes deutscher Banken.*

——— (1993). *'Die privaten Banken in den neuen Bundesländern: Entwicklung und Perspektiven,'* Köln: *Eine Informationen des Bundesverbandes deutscher Banken.*

——— (1994). *'Die privaten Banken in den neuen Bundesländern: Aufgabe, Engagement und Perspektiven.'* Köln: *Bundesverband deutscher Banken Informations-Dienst.*

*Bundesverband der deutschen Industrie (BDI)* (1994). *'Kreditvergabepraxis der Banken und Sparkassen in den neuen Bundesländern: Ergebnisse einer BDI-Umfrage und erste Schlußfolgerungen,'* Köln: *BDI* (7 April), mimeo.

*Bundesverband Kapitalbeteiligungsgesellschaften (1993). Annual Report.*

*Bürgschaftsbank Berlin-Brandenburg* (various years). Internal data.

*Bürgschaftsbank Mecklenburg-Vorpommern GmbH (1993). Geschäftsbericht.*
Cable, J.R. (1985). 'Capital Market Information and Industrial Performance: the Role of West German Banks,' *Economic Journal*, 95, 118–32.
Caldwell, Bruce (1982). *Beyond Positivism: Economic Methodology in the 20th Century*, London: Unwin Hyman.
Calne, R.Y. (ed.) (1984). *Transplantation Immunology Clinical and Experimental*, Oxford: Oxford University Press.
Calne, R.Y. (1965). 'Organ Transplantation,' *Discovery Journal of Science*, 26(3) (March), 28–32.
Calvo, Guillermo A. and Fabrizio Coricelli (1992). 'Stagflationary Effects of Stabilization Programs in Reforming Socialist Countries: Enterprise-side and Household-side Factors,' *The World Bank Economic Review*, 6(1), 71–90.
——— (1993). 'Output Collapse in Eastern Europe,' *IMF Staff Papers*, 40(1) (March), 32–52.
Calvo, Guillermo A. and Jacob A. Frenkel (1991a). 'The Role of Capital Markets,' in Paul Marer and Salvatore Zecchini (eds), *The Transition to a Market Economy*, Paris: OECD.
——— (1991b). 'Credit Markets, Credibility, and Economic Transformation,' *Journal of Economic Perspectives*, 5(4) (Fall), 139–48.
——— (1991c). 'From Centrally Planned to Market Economy,' *IMF Staff Papers*, 38(2), (June), 268–99.
Calvo, Guillermo A. and Manmohan S. Kumar (1993). 'Financial Sector Reforms and Exchange Arrangements in Eastern Europe,' *IMF Occasional Paper*, 102, Part 1 (February).
Camerer, Colin and Martin Weber (1992). 'Recent Developments in Modelling Preferences: Uncertainty and Ambiguity,' *Journal of Risk and Uncertainty*, 5, 325–70.
Cameron, Ronald (ed.) (1972). *Banking and Development: Some Lessons of History*, Oxford: Oxford University Press.
Caprio, Gerard Jr and Ross Levine (1994). 'Reforming Finance in Transitional Socialist Economies,' *The World Bank Research Observer*, 9(1), 1–24.
Carlin, Wendy (1993). 'Privatisation and Deindustrialization in East Germany,' *CEPR Discussion Paper*, 892 (December).
Carlin, Wendy and Colin Mayer (1992). 'Restructuring Enterprises in Eastern Europe,' *Economic Policy*, 7(7), 311–52.
——— (1994). 'The Treuhandanstalt: Privatisation by State and Market,' in O. Blanchard, K. Froot and J. Sachs (eds), *The Transition in Eastern Europe*, vol. 2, Chicago: University of Chicago Press, 189–207.
——— (1995). 'Structure and Ownership of East German Enterprises,' paper prepared for the Economics of Transition, CEPR–NBER–TCER Conference (Tokyo) (6–7 January 1995) (as cited in OECD, 1995).
Carlin, Wendy and Peter Richthofen (1995). 'Finance, Economic Development and the Transition: The East German Case,' *Wissenschaftszentrum Berlin für Sozialforschung Discussion Paper*, FS I 95–301.
Cato Institute (1992). Papers presented at the Cato Institute Tenth Annual Monetary Conference, 'Money in Transition: From Plan to Market,' (5–6 March).
Catte, Pietro and Cristina Mastropasqua (1993). 'Financial Structure and Reforms in Central and Eastern Europe in the 1980s,' *Journal of Banking and Finance*, 17, 785–817.

Central European International Bank (CIB) (1993). *Annual Report.*

Chambers, Fred and David Hyland (1992). 'Building a Banking System from Scratch – Advice for the Emerging Market Economies,' *Banking World* (March), 22–4.

Champernowne, D.G. (1969). *Uncertainty and Estimation in Economics,* vol. 1), Edinburgh: Oliver & Boyd.

Checchi, Daniele (1993). 'Creation of Financial Markets in (Previously) Centrally Planned Economies,' *Journal of Banking and Finance,* 17, 819–47.

Cho, Kang Rae (1985). *Multinational Banks: Their Identities and Determinants,* Ann Arbor: UMI Research Press.

Cho, Yoon Je (1986). 'Inefficiencies from Financial Liberalization in the Absence of Well-Functioning Equity Markets,' *Journal of Money, Credit, and Banking,* 18, (2) (May), 191–9.

Claassen, Emil-Maria (1993). 'Cleaning the Balance Sheets of Commercial Banks in Eastern Europe and Their Role in Corporate Governance,' *Weltwirtschaftliches Archiv,* 129, 600–9.

Clifton, Eric V. and Mohsin S. Kahn (1993). 'Interenterprise Arrears in Transforming Economies,' *IMF Staff Papers,* 40(3) (September), 680–96.

Coase, Ronald (1960). 'The Problem of Social Cost,' *Journal of Law and Economics,* 3, 1–44.

Collins, Susan M. and Dani Rodrick (1991). *Eastern Europe and the Soviet Union in the World Economy,* Washington, DC: IIE.

*Commerzbank* (1990–3). *Annual Reports.*

*Commerzbank* (1990). '*Commerzbank* in East Germany: Quickly Expanding its Own Network' (August).

Copeland, Thomas E. and J. Fred Weston (1988). *Financial Theory and Corporate Policy,* 3rd edn, New York: Addison-Wesley.

Corbett, Jenny (1987). 'International Perspectives on Financing: Evidence from Japan,' *Oxford Review of Economic Policy,* 3(4) (Winter), 30–55.

Corbett, Jenny and Colin Mayer (1990). 'Banks and Corporate Investment: Institutional Reform in Socialist Economies,' St. Antony's College, Oxford and City University Business School, London, mimeo.

——— (1991). 'Financial Reform in Eastern Europe: Progress with the Wrong Model,' *Oxford Review of Economic Policy,* 7(4), 57–75.

Corrigan, E. Gerald (1990). 'The Role of Central Banks and the Financial System in Emerging Market Economies,' *Federal Reserve Bank of New York Quarterly Review* (Summer), 1–7.

Czech National Bank (n.d.). Internal data.

Dahrendorf, Ralf (1990). *Reflections on the Revolution in Europe,* London: Chatto & Windus.

van Damme, Eric (1994). 'Banking: A Survey of Recent Microeconomic Thought,' *Oxford Review of Economic Policy,* 10(2) (Winter), 14–33.

Dedek, Oldrisch (1995). 'Problems of Financing Small and Medium-sized Enterprises in the Czech Republic,' in Stephany Griffith-Jones and Zdenek Drábek (eds), *Financial Reform in Central and Eastern Europe,* New York: St Martin's Press, 105–25.

Deeg, Richard E. (1992). *Banks and the State in Germany: The Critical Role of Subnational Institutions in Economic Governance,* unpublished PhD thesis, MIT (June).

——— (1993). 'The State, Banks, and Economic Governance in Germany,' *German Politics*, 2(2) (August), 149–76.

——— (1994). 'Banking on the East: The Political Economy of Investment Finance in Eastern Germany,' *Wissenschaftszentrum Berlin für Sozialforschung Discussion Paper*, FS I 94–303.

Dennis, Mike (1993). *Social and Economic Modernization in Eastern Germany from Honnecker to Kohl*, London: Pinter Publishers.

Denzin, Norman K. (1989). *The Research Act*, Englewood Cliffs: Prentice-Hall.

Deutsch, Karl W. (1966). *The Nerves of Government*, New York: The Free Press.

*Deutsche Ausgleichsbank* (1990–3). *Annual Reports.*

*Deutsche Bank* (1989) *Deutsche Bank Research Report*, Frankfurt: *Deutsche Bank.*

——— (1990). *Special: East Germany*, Frankfurt: *Deutsche Bank.*

——— (1990–3). *Annual Reports.*

*Deutsche Bank* Press Information (various years). Various reports.

*Deutsche Bank* Research (1992). 'Two Years of Successful Treuhandanstalt Privatisation,' *Focus: Germany*, 89 (4 August).

*Deutsche Beteiligungs* AG (1992/3). *Geschäftsbericht.*

*Deutsche Bundesbank* (1990). 'The monetary union with the German Democratic Replubic', *Deutsche Bundesbank Monthly Report*(July), 13–28.

——— (1990–2). *Regionalergebnisse der monatlichen Bilanzstatistik für Kreditinstitute in Ostdeutschland*, from 1 July 1990 to 1992.

——— (1990–3). *Annual Reports.*

——— (Various issues). *Bankenstatistik.*

——— (Various issues). *Deutsche Bundesbank Monthly Report, Statistical Section.*

——— (1989). 'The *Deutsche Bundesbank*: Its Monetary Policy Instruments and Functions,' *Deutsche Bundesbank Special Series*, 7, 3rd edn (July).

——— (1990a). 'Technical and Organisational Aspects of the Monetary Union with the German Democratic Republic,' *Deutsche Bundesbank Monthly Report* (October), 25–31.

——— (1990b). 'The Monetary Union with the German Democratic Republic,' *Deutsche Bundesbank Monthly Report* (July), 13–28.

——— (1990c). 'Terms of the Currency Conversion in the German Democratic Republic on July 1, 1990,' *Deutsche Bundesbank Monthly Report* (June), 40–8.

——— (1991a). 'The Significance of Shares as Financing Instruments,' *Deutsche Bundesbank Monthly Report* (October), 21–8.

——— (1991b). 'Promoting economic activity in the new Länder,' *Deutsche Bundesbank Monthly Report* (March), 15–26.

———. (1992a). *Abschlußbericht* (October).

——— (1992b). 'Restructuring the Bundesbank,' *Deutsche Bundesbank Monthly Report* (August), 48–53.

——— (1992c). 'Interest Subsidies and Other Financial Assistance in United Germany,' *Deutsche Bundesbank Monthly Report* (August), 21–8.

——— (1993a). 'Balance Sheet Ratios and Earnings of East German Enterprises in 1991,' *Deutsche Bundesbank Monthly Report* (July), 27–38.

——— (1993b). 'The Significance of Subsidiary Budgets in the Context of German Unification,' *Deutsche Bundesbank Monthly Report* (May), 43–57.

——— (1993c). 'Overall Financial Flows in Germany in 1992,' *Deutsche Bundesbank Monthly Report* (May), 19–41.

——— (1994a). 'West German Enterprises' Profitability and Financing in 1993,' *Deutsche Bundesbank Monthly Report* (November), 19–39.

——— (1994b). 'The Profitability of German Credit Institutions in 1993,' *Deutsche Bundesbank Monthly Report* (October), 19–47.

——— (1994c). 'East German Enterprises' Profitability and Financing in 1992,' *Deutsche Bundesbank Monthly Report* (July), 19–32.

——— (1994d). 'Overall Financial Flows in Germany in 1993,' *Deutsche Bundesbank Monthly Report* (May), 19–43.

——— (1994e). 'The Finances of the Treuhand Agency,' *Deutsche Bundesbank Monthly Report* (April), 17–31.

——— (1994f). 'The Profitability of East German Savings Banks and Credit Cooperatives in 1991 and 1992,' *Deutsche Bundesbank Monthly Report* (April), 33–47.

——— (1995a). 'Progress in the Adjustment Process in Eastern Germany and the Contribution of Economic Promotion Measures,' *Deutsche Bundesbank Monthly Report* (July), 37–54.

——— (1995b). 'East German Enterprises' Profitability and Financing,' *Deutsche Bundesbank Monthly Report* (July), 55–64.

——— (1997). 'Trends in Public Sector Debt since German Unification,' *Deutsche Bundesbank Monthly Report* (March), 17–31.

*Deutsche Industrie-Holding (1993) Prospectus.*

*Deutsches Institut für Wirtschaftsforschung, Berlin,* and *Institut für Weltwirtschaft Kiel.*(various issues). *'Gesamtwirtschaftliche und unternehmerische Anpassungsfortschritte in Ostdeutschland,' Kiel Discussion Papers.*

*Deutsches Institut für Wirtschaftsforschung,* Berlin (various issues). *Institut für Weltwirtschaft Kiel* (various issues). *'Wochenbericht'* .

*Deutsche Sparkassen- und Giroverband e.V.* (1992). *Ostdeutsche Wirtschaft im Wandel: Bestandsaufname und Perspektiven eines Aufholprozesses,* Stuttgart: Deutscher Sparkassenverlag.

——— (1994). *Leistungen der Sparkassenorganisation in den neuen Bundesländern. Eine Gesamtbilanz,* Meckenheim: Druck Centre.

Dhar, Sanjay and Marcelo Selowsky (1994). 'Dealing with the Bad Debt Problem in Transition Economies,' *Finance and Development* (June), 44–47.

Diamond, Douglas W. (1984). 'Financial Information and Delegated Monitoring,' *Review of Economic Studies,* 51 (3) (July).

——— (1991). 'Monitoring and Reputation: The Choice Between Bank Loans and Directly Placed Debt,' *Journal of Political Economy,* 99 (4) (August), 689–721.

Diamond, Douglas W. and Philip H. Dybvig (1983). 'Bank Runs, Deposit Insurance and Liquidity,' *Journal of Political Economy,* 91 (31), 401–19.

Diaz-Alejandro, Carlos (1985). 'Good-bye Financial Repression, Hello Financial Crash,' *Journal of Development Economics,* 19, 1–24.

Diesing, Paul (1972). *Patterns of Discovery in the Social Sciences,* London: Routledge & Kegan Paul.

*Die Wirtschaft* (1994). *Privatisierte* Berlin: *Die Wirtschaft.*

Dittus, Peter (1994a). 'Corporate Governance in Central Europe: The Role of Banks,' *BIS Economic Papers,* 42 (August).

——— (1994b). 'Bank Reform and Behaviour in Central Europe,' *Journal of Comparative Economics,* 19(3) (December), 335–61.

Donaldson, T.H. (1989). *Credit Risk and Exposure in Securitization and Transactions*, London: Macmillan.

Dornbusch, Rudiger (1991). 'Strategies and Priorities for Reform,' in Paul Marer and Salvatore Zecchini (eds), *The Transition to a Market Economy*, Paris: OECD.

Dornbusch, Rudiger and Alejandro Reynoso (1989). 'Financial Factors in Economic Development,' *American Economic Review*, 79, 204–9.

Dornbusch, Rudiger and Holger Wolf (1992). 'Economic Transition in Eastern Germany,' *Brookings Papers on Economic Activity*, 1, 235–72.

——— (1994). 'East German Economic Reconstruction,' in O. Blanchard, K. Froot and J. Sachs (eds), *The Transition in Eastern Europe*, vol. 1, Chicago: University of Chicago Press, 155–90.

Downes, Patrick and Reza Vaez-Zadeh (eds) (1991). *The Evolving Role of Central Banks*. Washington, DC: IMF.

*Dresdner Bank* (1989–93). *Annual Reports*.

——— (1991). *'Die Dresdner Bank in den fünf neuen Bundesländern'* (July), mimeo.

Dyba, K. and J. Svenjar (1992). 'Stabilization and Transition in Czechoslovakia,' paper presented at NBER Conference on 'Transition in Eastern Europe,' (Cambridge, Massachusetts) (February), mimeo.

Dyson, K. (1986). 'The State, Banks, and Industry: The West German Case,' in A. Cox, (ed.), *State, Finance and Industry: A Comparative Analysis of Post-War trends in Six Advanced Industrial Economies*, Brighton: Wheatsheaf, 118–41.

The East German Investment Trust plc (1994, 1995). *Annual Report and Accounts*.

Eckstein, Harry (1975). 'Case Study and Theory in Political Science,' in Fred I. Greenstein and Nelson W. Polsby (eds), *Handbook of Political Science* vol. 7, Reading, Mass.: Addison-Wesley.

Edwards, Jeremy (1987). 'Recent Developments in the Theory of Corporate Finance,' *Oxford Review of Economic Policy*, 3(4), 1–12.

Edwards, Jeremy and Klaus Fischer (1994). *Banks, Finance and Investment in Germany*, Cambridge: Cambridge University Press.

Edwards, Vincent and Peter Lawrence (1994). *Management Change in East Germany*, London: Routledge.

Eisenhardt, Kathleen M. (1989). 'Building Theories from Case Study Research,' *Academy of Management Review*, 14(4), 532–50.

Ellman, Michael (1989). *Socialist Planning*, (2nd edn), Cambridge: Cambridge University Press.

Ellsberg, Daniel (1961). 'Risk, Ambiguity, and the Savage Axioms,' *Quarterly Journal of Economics*, Volume 78(4) (November), 643–69.

Elsser, Stefan (1994). *'Auswertung der Bilanzdaten ostdeutscher Unternehmen,' KfW: Aktuelle volkswirtschaftliche Themen*, 8.

Elston, Julie A. (1993). 'Firm Ownership Structure and Investment: Theory and Evidence from German Panel Data,' *Wissenschaftszentrum Berlin für Sozialforschung Discussion Paper*, FS IV 93–28.

Elston, Julie A. and Horst Albach (1994). 'Bank Affiliations and Firm Capital Investment in Germany,' *Wissenschaftszentrum Berlin für Sozialforschung Discussion Paper*, FS IV 94–10.

Ericson, Richard E. (1991). 'The Classical Soviet-type Economy: Nature of the System and Implications for Reform,' *Journal of Economic Perspectives*, 5(4) (Fall), 11–27.

Esser, Josef (1990). 'Bank Power in West Germany Revised,' *West European Politics*, 13(4), 17–32.
——— (1994a). 'Model Germany in the 1990s?', paper presented at the conference, 'The State and Economic Crisis in 20th Century Germany,' (University of Nottingham) (14–16 April), mimeo.
——— (1994b). 'Germany: Symbolic Privatizations in a Social Market Economy,' in Vincent Wright, ed., *Privatization in Western Europe: Pressures, Problems and Paradoxes*. London: Printer Publishers.
Etzioni, Amitai (1988). *The Moral Dimension*, New York: Free Press.
——— (1993). 'A Socio-economic Perspective on Friction,' in Sven-Erik Sjöstrand (ed.), *Institutional Change: Theory and Empirical Findings*, Armonk: M.E. Sharpe, 47–60.
European Investment Bank (1990–3). *Annual Reports.*
EVCA (1994). *EVCA Yearbook*, KPMG/EVCA.
Falke, Andreas (1994). 'An Unwelcome Enlargement? The European Community and German Unification,' in M. Donald Hancock and Helga A. Welsh, (eds), *German Unification: Process & Outcomes*, Boulder: Westview Press.
Fama, Eugene F. (1985). 'What's Different About Banks?,' *Journal of Monetary Economics*, 15, 29–39.
Federal Ministry of Economics (1994). *Economic Incentives in Germany's New Federal States: An Overview*, Bonn: Federal Ministry of Economics, Task Force New *Länder*.
Fieldhouse, D. K. (1981). *Colonialism 1870–1945: An Introduction*, London: Weidenfeld & Nicolson.
Fischer, Stanley and Alan Gelb (1991). 'The Process of Socialist Economic Transformation,' *Journal of Economic Perspectives*, 5(4) (Fall), 91–105.
Fischer, Wolfram, Herbert Hax and Hans Karl Schneider (eds) (1993). *Treuhandanstalt: Das Unmögliche Wagen*, Berlin: Akademie Verlag.
Flemming, John and J.M.C. Rollo (eds) (1992). *Trade Payments and Adjustment in Central and Eastern Europe*, London: EBRD/RIIA.
Folkerts-Landau, David, Peter Garber and Timothy Lane (1993). 'Payment System Reform in Formerly Centrally Planned Economies,' *Journal of Banking and Finance*, 17, 849–68.
Forsyth, W. (1992). 'The Socialist Financial System: The Case of the DDR,' in D.H. Gowland (ed.), *Finance in Eastern Europe*, Aldershot: Dartmouth.
Franks, Julian and Colin Mayer, (1990). 'Capital Markets and Corporate Control: A Study of France, Germany, and the UK,' *Economic Policy* (April), 189–231.
Frenkel, Allen B. and John D. Montgomery (1991). 'Financial Structure: An International Perspective,' *Brookings Papers on Economic Activity*, 1, 257–310.
Friedman, Milton (1953). *Essays in Positive Economics*, Chicago: University of Chicago Press.
——— (1959). *A Program for Monetary Stability*, New York: Fordham University Press.
Friedmann, Günter (1995). 'Private Banken: Pioniere des "Aufbau Ost"', *Kreditwesen*, 967–9.
Fries, Steven (ed.). (1994). 'Transition: Private Sector Development and the Role of Financial Institutions,' *EBRD Working Paper*, 13.
Fry, Maxwell J. (1988). *Money, Interest, and Banking in Economic Development*, Baltimore: Johns Hopkins University Press.

Fukada, Atsuo and Shin'ichi Hirota (1993). '"Main Bank" Relationships and Capital Structure in Japan,' Kyoto Sangyo University, mimeo.

Gaebe, W. (1993). 'Changing Strategies of Financial Corporations in the Federal Republic of Germany,' in Eike W. Schamp, Godfrey J.R. Linge and Chris M. Rogerson (eds), *Finance, Institutions and Industrial Change: Spatial Perspectives*, Berlin: Walter de Gruyter, 103–17

Garvy, George (1966). *Money, Banking and Credit in Eastern Europe*, New York: Federal Reserve Bank of New York.

Gelman, Simon (ed.) (1987). *Anesthesia and Organ Transplantation*, Philadelphia: W.B. Saunders Co.

George, Alexander L. (1979). 'Case Studies and Theory Development: The Method of Structured, Focused Comparison,' in Paul Gordon Lauren (ed.), *Diplomacy: New Approaches in History, Theory and Policy*, London: Free Press.

Gerschenkron, Alexander (1962). *Economic Backwardness in Historical Perspective*, Cambridge, Mass.: Belknap Press.

——— (1968). *Continuity in History and Other Essays*, Cambridge: Harvard University Press.

Gibb, Allan A. (1993). 'Small Business Development in Central and Eastern Europe – Opportunity for a Rethink?,' *Journal of Business Venturing*, 8, 461–86.

Giersch, Herbert, Karl-Heinz Paqué and Holger Schmieding (1992). *The Fading Miracle*, Cambridge: Cambridge University Press.

Gill, John and Phil Johnson (1991). *Research Methods for Managers*, London: Paul Chapman Publishing.

Glaessner, Gert-Joachim (1994). 'Parties and the Problems of Governance During Unification,' in M. Donald Hancock and Helga A. Welsh (eds), *German Unification: Process & Outcomes*, Boulder: Westview Press, 139–61.

Glaser, Barney G. and Anselm L. Strauss (1967). *The Discovery of Grounded Theory*, Chicago: Aldine Publishing Company.

Goldsmith, Raymond W. (1969). *Financial Structure and Development*, New Haven: Yale University Press.

Gomulka, Stanislaw (1993). 'The Financial Situation of Polish Enterprises 1992–1993 and its Impact on Monetary and Fiscal Policies,' London School of Economics, Department of Economics and Centre for Economic Performance (December).

Görtemaker, Manfred (1994). *Unifying Germany*, London: Macmillan.

Gould, Stephen Jay (1983). *Hen's Teeth and Horse's Toes*, Harmondsworth: Penguin Books.

Gray, Cheryl W. and Rebecca J. Hanson (1993). 'Corporate Governance in Central and Eastern Europe,' *World Bank Working Paper*, 1182 (September).

Greenwald, B. and J.E. Stiglitz (1990). 'Macroeconomic models with Equity and Credit Rationing,' in R.G. Hubbard (ed), *Information, Capital Markets and Investments*, Chicago: University of Chicago Press.

Griffin, John R. (1994). 'Investment and Ownership in a Volatile Economy: Big Banks and the Case of the East German Economic Transition,' *Politics & Society*, Volume 22(3), 389–420.

Griffith-Jones, Stephany and E.V.K. FitzGerald (1995). 'Financial Sector Development in Central and Eastern Europe,' in Stephany Griffith-Jones and Zdenek Drábek (eds), *Financial Reform in Central and Eastern Europe*, New York: St Martin's Press, 223–46.

Gröschel, Ulrich (1993). *'Hausbankprinzip, Struktur des Bankensystems und Marktstabilität,' Sparkasse* (November), 510–13.

Grosfeld, Irena (1994). 'Financial Systems in Transition: Is there a Case for a Bank Based System?', *CEPR Discussion Paper,* 1062 (November).

Grossman, Gregory (ed.) (1968). *Money and Plan: Financial Aspects of East European Economic Reforms,* Berkeley: University of California Press.

Guitián, Manuel (1993). 'From the Plan to the Market: Banking and Financial Reform Aspects,' in Donald E. Fair and Robert J. Raymond (eds), *The New Europe: Evolving Economic and Financial Systems in East and West.* Dordrecht: Kluwer.

Gummesson, Evert (1988). *Qualitative Methods in Management Research,* Lund: Studentlitteratur.

Habermeier, Karl (1995). 'Prospects for Self-sustaining Growth in Eastern Germany,' in Robert Corker *et al.*, 'Uniting Germany: The First Five Years. Performance and Policy Issues', *IMF Occasional Paper,* 125, Washington DC: IMF (May), 62–72.

Hancock, M. Donald and Helga A. Welsh (eds) (1994). *German Unification: Process & Outcomes,* Boulder: Westview Press.

Hardy, Daniel C. and Ashok Kumar Lahiri (1992). 'Bank Insolvency and Stabilisation in Eastern Europe,' *IMF Staff Papers,* 39(4) (December), 778–800.

Harm C. (1992a). 'The Financing of Small Firms in Germany,' *World Bank Policy Research,* WPS 899.

——— (1992b). 'The Relationship between German banks and the Large German Firms,' *World Bank Policy Research,* WPS 900.

Harris, Thomas A. (1967). *I'm OK – You're OK,* London: Pan Books.

Hassard, John (1988). 'Overcoming Hermeticism in Organization Theory: An Alternative to Paradigm Incommensurability,' *Human Relations,* 41(3), 247–59.

von Hayek, F.A. (1978). *Denationalising Money: The Argument Refined,* London: Institute for Economic Affairs.

Hellwig, Martin (1991). 'Banking, Financial Intermediation and Corporate Finance,' in Alberto Giovannini and Colin Mayer (eds), *European Financial Integration,* Cambridge: Cambridge University Press.

Henzler, Herbert (1992). 'Managing the Merger: A Strategy for the New Germany,' *Harvard Business Review* (January-February), 24–29.

*Hermes Kreditversicherungs-AG* (1993). *Annual Report.*

Hewett, Ed A. (1988): *Reforming the Soviet Economy: Equality Versus Efficiency,* Washington DC: The Brookings Institution.

Hinds, Manuel (1990). 'Issues in the Introduction of Market Forces in Eastern European Socialist Economies,' in Report IDP – 0057, Office of the Vice President, Europe, Middle East, and Africa Region, The World Bank.

Hirschman, Albert O. (1970). *Exit, Voice, and Loyalty,* Cambridge, Man.: Harvard University Press.

——— (1990). 'Good News is Not Bad News,' *The New York Review of Books,* 37(15) (11 October), 20.

Hofstede, Geert (1984). *Culture's Consequences: International Differences in Work-Related Values,* abridged edn, London: Sage.

Hogarth, Robin M. and Howard Kunreuther (1989). 'Risk, Ambiguity, and Insurance,' *Journal of Risk and Uncertainty,* 2, 5–35.

Hornef, Heinrich. (1994a). 'Pressekonferenz der Treuhandanstalt' (25 July).

——— (1994b). *'Was ist aus der Bankenmilliarde geworden?,'* Press Conference (14 February), mimeo.

Hoshi, T., A. Kashyap, and D. Scharfstein (1990). 'The Role of Banks in Reducing the Costs of Financial Distress in Japan,' *Journal of Financial Economics*, 27(1), 67–88.

Hu, Yao-Su (1975). *National Attitudes and the Financing of Industry*, London: PEP, 41, Broadsheet (December).

Hughes Hallet, Andrew, Yue Ma and Jacques Mélitz (1994). 'Unification and the Policy Predicament in Germany,' *CEPR Discussion Paper*, 956 (May).

Hultman, Charles W. (1990). *The Environment of International Banking*, Englewood-Cliffs: Prentice-Hall.

Hummel, Marlies, Udo Ludwig *et al.* (1994). *'Finanzierungsprobleme kleiner und mittlerer Unternehmen der gewerblichen Wirtschaft in den neuen Bundesländern,' Kurzexpertise im Auftrag des Bundesministeriums für Wirtschaft, ifo Institut für Wirtschatfsforschung* and *Institut für Wirtschaftsforschung Hall* (July), mimeo.

Husain, Aasim M. (1994). 'Private Sector Development in Economies in Transition,' *Journal of Comparative Economics*, 19, 260–71.

*IKB Deutsche Industriebank* (1991/1992, 1992/1993). *Annual Report.*

*Industrie- und Handelskammer Leipzig* (1993/1994). *Jahresbericht 1993/1994.*

*Institut für Wirtschaftsforschung Halle* (1993). *'Ostdeutschland 1993 & 1994: Aufbau Trotz Rezession im Western,' Frühjahrsgutachten.*

Institute for East-West Studies (1994). 'Accelerating Bank Privatization in Central and Eastern Europe,' Conference Report (Sophia, Bulgaria), mimeo.

Jacobsson, Staffan (1993). 'The Length of the Infant Industry Period: Evidence from the Engineering Industry in South Korea,' *World Development*, 21(3), 407–19.

Jarausch, Konrad H. (1994). *The Rush to German Unity*. Oxford, Oxford University Press.

Jarausch, Konrad H. and Volker Granson (eds) (1994). *Uniting Germany: Documents and Debates 1944–1993*, Oxford: Berghahn Books.

Jeffress, Dorothy Ames (1991). 'Resolving Rival Claims on East German Property Upon German Unification,' *Yale Law Review*, 101(1), 527–49.

Jeffries, Ian and Manfred Melzer (eds) (1987). *The East German Economy*, London: Croom Helm.

Jick, Todd D. (1983). 'Mixing Qualitative and Quantitative Methods: Triangulation in Action,' in John van Maanen (ed), *Qualitative Methodology*, London: Sage, 135–48.

Johnson, Juliet Ellen (1994). 'The Russian Banking System: Institutional Responses to the Market Transition,' *Europe Asia Studies*, 46(6), 971–95.

Johnson, Simon (1994). 'Private Business in Eastern Europe,' in O. Blanchard, K. Froot and J. Sachs (eds), *The Transition in Eastern Europe*, vol. 2, Chicago: University of Chicago Press, 245–91.

Johnson, Simon, Heidi Kroll and Mark Horton (1992). 'New Banks in the Former Soviet Union: How Do They Operate?', in Anders Aslund and Richard Layard (eds), *Reforming the Russian Economy*. London: Pinter, 183–209.

Kapelle, Günter, Dagmar Schreiber and Dagmar Meyer (1994). *'Köpenick 94: Umfrage zur Nutzung von Banken im Stadtbezirk Berlin-Köpenick,'* SIGMA-Institut Berlin (24 June).

Karailiev, Emil N. and Ivanka D. Petkova (1993). 'Reforming the Financial System in Central and Eastern Europe,' in Donald E. Fair and Robert J. Raymond (eds), *The New Europe: Evolving Economic and Financial Systems in East and West*, Dordrecht: Kluwer.

Kasch, Kurt, Franklin Lowenthal and Alexander E. Cassuto (1994). 'Financing German Reunification,' *The Bankers Magazine* (September–October), 60–2.

Kindleberger, Charles Poor (1984). *A Financial History of Western Europe*, London: Allen & Unwin.

Kirichenko, Nikita (1993). 'Banks' Credits Policy: Trust One Client Out of Seven,' *Commersant*, 40(191) (13 October), 8–10.

Knight, Frank H. (1973). *Risk, Uncertainty and Profit*, Chicago: University of Chicago Press.

Kocka, Jürgen (1994). 'Crisis of Unification: How Germany Changes,' *Daedalus*, (123) (1) (Winter), 172–92.

Koehler, Fritz K. (1992). 'Investment in the New German Federal States,' *Case Western Reserve Journal of International Law*, 24(3) (Summer), 495–88.

Kohlhaussen, Martin (1994). *'Pressegespräch anläßlich der Eröffnung der Commerzbank- Filiale am Thomaskirchhof,'* (6 September).

Kopper, Hilmar (1992). 'German Banks – What Role Do They Really Play?', *The Gilbart Lecture 1992*, The Chartered Institute of Bankers (27 October).

Kornai, Janos (1980). *Economics of Shortage*, Amsterdam: North-Holland.

——— (1986). 'The Soft Budget Constraint,' *Kyklos*, 39 (1), 3–30.

——— (1990). *The Road to a Free Economy*, New York: W.W. Norton.

——— (1992). *The Socialist System: The Political Economy of Communism*, Oxford: Clarendon Press.

——— (1993). 'The Evolution of Financial Discipline under the Postsocialist System,' *Kyklos*, 46, 315–36.

Koslowski, Rey (1992). 'Market Institutions, East European Reform and Economic Theory,' *Journal of Economic Issues*, 26(3) (September) 673–705.

*Kreditanstalt für Wiederaufbau* (1990–3) *Annual Reports*.

——— (1993) 'Kreditanstalt für Wiederaufbau: Financing Partner for Investments in the New Federal Länder and Berlin (East),' Frankfurt: *KfW*.

——— (1994a). 'Functions and Activities,' Frankfurt: *KfW*.

——— (1994b). '*KfW*: Your International Financing Partner in Germany,' Frankfurt: *KfW*.

Krümmel, H.J. (1980) 'German Universal Banking Scrutinised,' *Journal of Banking and Finance*, 4, 33–55.

Krupp, Georg (1990). *'Die Deutsche Bank geht in der DDR optimistisch an den Start,' Presse-Information*, Berlin (27 June).

——— (1994a). *'Zukunft Deutschland – zwischen ökonomischer Verpflichtung und gesellschaftlicher Verantwortung,'* Bonn (13 April).

——— (1994b). *'Für die Deutsche Bank geht das Engagement in Ostdeutscheland weit über die Perspektive des eigenen Instituts hinaus,' Presse-Information, Deutsche Bank*, Bonn/Frankfurt am Main (13 April).

Kuhn, Thomas S. (1970). *The Structure of Scientific Revolutions* 2nd edn, Chicago: University of Chicago Press.

Kunreuther, Howard, Robin Hogarth and Jacqueline Meszaros (1993). 'Insurer Ambiguity and Market Failure,' *Journal of Risk and Uncertainty*, 7, 71–87.

Lacoue-Labarthe, Dominique (1992). 'Setting Up a Safe and Sound Banking System in Central and East European Countries,' The University of Birmingham, International Finance Group, WP 92–07.
Lall, Sanjaya (1987). *Learning to Industrialize*, London: Macmillan.
——— (1993). 'Understanding Technology Development,' *Development and Change*, 24, 719–53.
Landeszentralbanken (1990–4). Selected data.
Lane, Sarah. J. (1995). 'Business Starts During the Transition in Hungary,' *Journal of Business Venturing*, 10, 181–94.
Lansman, Steven L., M. Arisan Ergin and Randall B. Griepp (1989). 'History of Cardiac Transplantation,' in John Wallwork (ed), *Heart and Heart-Lung Transplantation*, London: W.B. Saunders Co., 3–19.
von Lazar, Arpad (1991). 'Work and Unity: Germany The Morning After,' *Harvard Business Review* (March–April), 32–43.
Lee, Raymond M. (1993). *Doing Research on Sensitive Topics*, London: Sage.
Lehmbruch, Gerhard (1994). '*Institutionen, Interessen und sektorale Variationen in der Transformationsdynamik der politischen Ökonomie Ostdeutschlands*,' *Journal für Sozialforschung*, 34. *Jg. Heft* 1.
Lenin, Vlaoimir I. (1964). *Collected Works*, vol. 26, London: Lawrence & Wishart.
Levinthal, Daniel A. and James G. March (1993). 'The Myopia of Learning,' *Strategic Management Journal*, 14, Special Issue (Winter), 95–112.
Ligeti, Sàndor (1993). 'Problem Loans,' *University College of North Wales Research Papers in Banking and Finance*, 13.
Lincoln, Yvonna S. and Egon G. Guba (1985). *Naturalistic Inquiry*, Newbury Park: Sage.
Lipschitz, Leslie and Donough McDonald (eds). (1990). 'German Unification: Economic Issues,' *IMF Occasional Paper*, 75 (December).
Lipton, David and Jeffrey Sachs (1990a). 'Creating a Market Economy in Eastern Europe: The Case of Poland,' *Brookings Papers on Economic Activity*, 1, 75–147.
——— (1990b). 'Privatisation in Eastern Europe: The Case of Poland,' *Brookings Papers on Economic Activity*, 2, 293–341.
Listfield, Robert and Fernando Montes-Negret (1994). 'Modernizing Payment Systems in Emerging Economies,' *World Bank Policy Research Working Paper*, 1336 (August).
Long, Millard F. (1993). 'Financial Aspects of Enterprise Restructuring,' in Donald E. Fair and Robert J. Raymond (eds), *The New Europe: Evolving Economic and Financial Systems in East and West*. Dordrecht: Kluwer.
Long, Millard and Sylvia B. Sagari (1991). 'Financial Reform in the European Economies in Transition,' in Paul Marer and Salvatore Zecchini (eds), *The Transition to a Market Economy*, Paris: OECD.
Luce, R.D. and H. Raiffa (1957). *Games and Decisions*, New York: Wiley.
van Maanen, J. and D. Kolb (1985). 'The Professional Apprentice: Observations on Fieldwork Roles in Two Organizational Settings,' in S.B. Bacharach and S. M. Mitchell (eds), *Research in the Sociology of Organisations*, vol. 4, Greenwich, Conn.: JAI Press, 1–33, 154, 161–165 (as cited in Bryman 1989).
Maaz, Hans-Joachim (1990). *Behind the Wall: The Inner Life of Communist Germany*, New York: W.W. Norton.
MacCrimmon, Kenneth R. and Donald A. Wehrung (1986). *Taking Risks: The Management of Uncertainty*, New York: Free Press.

March, James G. and Zur Shapira (1987). 'Managerial Perspectives on Risk and Risk Taking,' *Management Science*, 33(11) (November), 1404–18.

Markóczy, Lívia (1994). 'Modes of Organizational Learning,' *International Studies of Management and Organisations*, 24(4), 5–30.

Markowitz, Harry M. (1991). 'Foundations of Portfolio Theory,' *The Journal of Finance*, 46(2) (June), 469–77.

Marsh, David (1992). *The Bundesbank: The Bank that Rules Europe*, London: Heinemann.

Martin, Peter (1992). 'Banking Reform in Czechoslovakia,' *RFE/RL Research Report*, 1(15) (10 April), 29–33.

Mayer, Colin (1989). 'Myths of the West: Lessons from Developed Countries for Development Finance,' background submission to the 1989 World Bank Development Report on Financial Systems and Development, mimeo.

——— (1993). 'In the Image of the West: Creating Financial Systems in Eastern Europe,' in Donald E. Fair and Robert J. Raymond (eds), *The New Europe: Evolving Economic and Financial Systems in East and West*, Dordrecht: Kluwer.

——— (1994). 'The Assessment: Money and Banking: Theory and Evidence,' *Oxford Review of Economic Policy*, 10(4) (Winter), 1–10.

Mayer, Thomas and Gunther Thumann (1990). 'German Democratic Republic: Background and Plans for Reform,' in Leslie Lipschitz and Donogh McDonald (eds), 'German Unification: Economic Issues,' *IMF Occasional Paper*, 75 (December).

Mayhew, Ken and Paul Seabright (1992). 'Incentives and the Management of Enterprises in Economic Transition: Capital Markets Are Not Enough?,' *Oxford Review of Economic Policy*, 8(1), 105–29.

McKinnon, Ronald (1973). *Money and Capital in Economic Development*, Washington, DC: The Brookings Institution.

——— (1991). *The Order of Economic Liberalization: Financial Control in the Transition to a Market Economy*, Baltimore: Johns Hopkins University Press.

——— (1993) 'Macroeconomic Control in Liberalizing Socialist Economies: Asian and European Parallels,' in Alberto Giovannini (ed), *Finance and Development: Issues and Experience*, Cambridge: Cambridge University Press.

Medawar, P.B. (1965). 'Transplantation: The Scientific Background,' *Discovery Journal of Science*, 26(3) (March), 22–6.

Meinecke, Hans Dieter (1993). 'The Restructuring of the Banking System in the Former German Democratic Republic,' in Hans J. Blommestein and Jean R. Lange (eds), *Transformation of the Banking System: Portfolio Restructuring, Privatisation and the Payments System*, Paris: OECD.

Mendelson, Morris and Junius W. Peake (1993). 'Equity Markets in Economies in Transition,' *Journal of Banking and Finance*, 17, 913–29.

Merkl, Peter H (1993). *German Unification in the European Context*, University Park, Pennsylvania: The Penn State University Press.

——— (1994). 'An Impossible Dream? Privatising Collective Property in Eastern Germany,' in M. Donald Hancock and Helga A. Welsh (eds), *German Unification: Process & Outcomes*, Boulder: Westview Press, 199–221.

Merton, Robert K. (1967). *On Theoretical Sociology*, New York: Free Press.

Miles, Mathew B. and A. Michael Huberman (1984). *Qualitative Data Analysis*, London: Sage.

Mills, C. Wright. (1957). *The Sociological Imagination*, Oxford: Oxford University Press.

Mintzberg, Henry (1983). 'An Emerging Strategy of "Direct" Research,' in John van Maanen (ed.), *Qualitative Methodology*, London: Sage, 105–16.

Miszei, K. (1993). *Bankruptcy in the Post-Communist Economies of East Central Europe*, New York: Institute for East-West Studies.

Mole, John (1990). *Mind Your Manners*, London: The Industrial Society.

Moretti, Marina (1992). 'Stabilization-cum-structural Adjustment Policies and the Financial System: Lessons from Bolivia,' *Development Studies Working Papers*, Queen Elizabeth House and *Centro Studi Luca d'Agliano*, 47 (June).

Morgan, Gareth and Linda Smircich (1980). 'The Case for Qualitative Research,' *Academy of Management Review*, 5(4), 491–500.

Mortimer, Kate (1993). 'Banking Privatisation Policy in Poland and Czechoslovakia,' mimeo.

MTA (1994). '*"Az átalakuló magyar bankrendszer" kutatási program: Bankok számok és adatok tükrében*,' MTA/PTI, Budapest (August), mimeo.

Müller-Armack, Alfred (1965). 'The Principles of the Social Market Economy,' *The German Economic Review*, 3(2), 89–104.

Mullineux, Andy (1992). 'Banks, Privatisation and Restructuring in Poland,' *International Financial Group Working Paper*, IFGWP-02, The University of Birmingham.

——— (1994). 'Small and Medium-sized Enterprise (SME) Financing in the UK: Lessons from Germany,' *Anglo-German Foundation for the Study of Industrial Society*, London: The Chameleon Press Ltd.

Murrel, Peter (1991). 'Can Neoclassical Economics Underpin the Reform of Centrally Planned Economies?', *Journal of Economic Perspectives*, 5(4), 59–76.

——— (1992). 'Evolution in Economics and in the Economic Reform of the Centrally Planned Economies,' in Christopher Clague and Gordon C. Rausser (eds), *The Emergence of Market Economies in Eastern Europe*, Oxford: Basil Blackwell.

National Bank of Poland (1995). 'Information on Bank Operations with Foreign Capital as well as Foreign Capital Participation in the Polish Banking System,' General Inspectorate of Bank Supervision, Warsaw (January).

Nelson, Richard R. and Sidney G. Winter (1982). *An Evolutionary Theory of Economic Change*, Cambridge, Mass.: The Belknap Press of Harvard University.

Neuber, Alexander (1993). 'Adapting the Economies of Eastern Europe: Behavioural and Institutional Aspects of Flexibility,' Cambridge, Mass., mimeo.

Nordhaus, William D. *et al.* (1991). 'Do Borders Matter? Soviet Economic Reform After the Coup,' *Brookings Papers on Economic Activity*, 2, 321–40.

North, Douglass C. (1990). *Institutions, Institutional Change and Economic Performance*, Cambridge: Cambridge University Press.

Nove, Alec (1969). *An Economic History of the USSR*, Harmondsworth: Penguin.

——— (1986). *The Soviet Economic System*, 3rd edn, Boston: Allen & Unwin.

Nuti, Domenico Mario (1986). 'Hidden and Repressed Inflation in Soviet-type Economies: Definitions, Measurements and Stabilization,' *Contributions to Political Economy* (5 March), 37–82.

——— (1989). 'Feasible Financial Innovation Under Market Socialism,' in Christie Kessides, Timothy King, Mario Nuti and Catherine Sokil (eds),

*Financial Reform In Socialist Economies. EDI Seminar Series*, Washington, DC: World Bank.

——— (1992a). 'The Role of the Banking Sector in the Process of Privatisation,' *EEC Economic Papers*, 98 (November).

——— (1992b). 'Privatisation of Financial Institutions,' in Peter Newman, Murray Milgate and John Eatwell (eds), *The New Palgrave Dictionary of Money and Finance*, London: Macmillan, 212–14.

Odle, Maurice A. (1981). Multinational Banks and Underdevelopment, New York: Pergamon Press.

OECD (1990–1, 1992–3, 1993–4, 1995). *Economic Survey: Germany*, Paris: OECD.

Offe, Claus (1992a). 'Designing Institutions for East European Transitions,' mimeo.

——— (1992b). 'German Reunification as a "Natural Experiment"', *German Politics*, 1(1) (April), 1–12.

——— (1993). 'Economic "Hardware" and Institutional "Software" in the Two German Transitions to Democracy: Comparing post-1945 West Germany and post-1989 East Germany,' mimeo.

Olson, Mancur (1992). 'The Hidden Path To a Successful Economy,' in Christopher Clague and Gordon C. Rausser (eds), *The Emergence of Market Economies in Eastern Europe*, Oxford: Basil Blackwell.

Patton, Michael Quinn (1990). *Qualitative Evaluation and Research Methods*, 2nd edn, London: Sage.

Parker, Chris and Ralph Lewis (1981). 'Beyond the Peter Principle – Managing Successful Transitions,' *Journal of European Industrial Training*, 5(6), 17–21.

Parker, John (1993). 'Survey of Eastern Europe,' *The Economist* (13 March), 1–22.

——— (1994). 'A Survey of Germany,' *The Economist* (21 May).

Parsons, John E. (1986). 'Credit Contracts in the GDR: Decentralized Investment Decisions in a Planned Economy,' *Economics of Planning*, 20(1), 28–51.

Peebles, Gavin (1991). *A Short History of Socialist Money*, London: Allen & Unwin.

Perotti, Enrico C. (1993). 'Bank Lending in Transition Economies,' *Journal of Banking and Finance*, 17, 1021–32.

Perry, F.E. (1984). *The Elements of Banking*, 4th edn, London: Methuen, in association with The Institute of Bankers.

Peterson, Mitchell A. and Raghuram G. Rajan (1994). 'The Benefits of Lending Relationships: Evidence from Small Business Data,' *The Journal of Finance*, 49(1) (March), 3–37.

Pettigrew, Andrew M. (1987). 'Context and Action in the Transformation of the Firm,' *Journal of Management Studies*, 24(6) (November), 649–70.

Pfeffer, Jeffrey (1982). *Organizations and Organization Theory*, London: Pitman.

Phelps, Edmund S., Roman Frydman, Andrzej Rapaczynski and Andrei Shleifer (1993). 'Needed Mechanisms of Corporate Governance and Finance in Eastern Europe,' *EBRD Working Paper*, 1 (March).

Pickel, Andreas (1992a). 'Jump-starting a Market Economy: A Critique of the Radical Strategy for Economic Reform in Light of the East German Experience,' *Studies in Comparative Communism*, 25, 177–91.

——— (1992b). 'Towards the New Germany: The Logic of Rapid Unification and Social Experiment of Radical Marketization in the GDR,' in William D. Graf (ed.), *The Internationalization of the German Political Economy*, New York: St. Martin's Press.

Pigott, Charles A. (1986). 'Financial Reforms and the Role of Foreign Banks in Pacific Basin Nations,' in Cheng Hang-Sheng (ed), *Financial Policy and Reform in Pacific Basin Countries*, San Francisco: Federal Reserve Bank of San Francisco.

Pleskovic, Boris (1994). 'Financial Policies in Socialist Countries in Transition,' *World Bank Policy Research Paper*, 1242 (January).

Plessing, W.D. (1993). 'The Privatisation of Banks in the Former German Democratic Republic,' in Hans J. Blommestein and Jean R. Lange (eds), *Transformation of the Banking System: Portfolio Restructuring, Privatisation and the Payments System*, Paris: OECD.

Podolski, T.M. (1973). *Socialist Banking and Monetary Control: The Experience of Poland*, Cambridge: Cambridge University Press.

Pohl, Gerhard and Stijn Claessens (1994). 'Banks, Capital Markets and Corporate Governance: Lessons from Russia for Eastern Europe,' *World Bank Policy Research Working Papers*, 1326 (July).

Popper, Karl R. (1977). *The Logic of Scientific Discovery*, 9th impression, London: Hutchinson.

Portes, Richard (ed.) (1993). *Economic Transformation in Central Europe: A Progress Report*, London: CEPR and Luxembourg: EC.

Powell, Walter W. and Paul J. Dimaggio (eds) (1991). *The New Institutionalism in Organisational Analysis*, Chicago: University of Chicago Press.

Prill, Oliver (1995). *Financial Sector Reform in the Soviet Union/Russia since 1987: Options and Consequences*, unpublished D.Phil thesis, Oxford University.

Prill, Oliver and Gregg Robins (1994). 'Incentives and the Learning Process: Implications for Banking in the Transition to a Market Economy,' contribution to the Eighth Annual AMEX International Economics and Finance Essay Competition, mimeo.

Prindl, Andreas (1992). 'Building a Banking System from Scratch – Advice for the Emerging Market Economies,' *Banking World* (March), 18–20.

Prowse, Stephen (1994). 'Corporate Governance in International Perspective,' *BIS Economic Papers*, 41 (July).

Quack, Sigrid and Swen Hildebrandt (1995a). *'Das Geheimnis der Banken: Zum Einfluß von Organisationsstrukturen und Personalpolitiken deutscher und französicher Kreditinstitute im mittelständischen Unternehmensgeschäft,' Wissenschaftszentrum Berlin für Sozialforschung Discussion Paper*, FS I 95–103.

——— (1995b). 'Hausbank or Fournisseur? Bank Services for Small and Medium Sized Enterprises in Germany and France,' *Wissenschaftszentrum Berlin für Sozialforschung Discussion Paper*, FS I 95–102.

Radice, Giles (1995). *The New Germans*, London: Michael Joseph.

Randlesome, Colin (1992). 'East German Managers: From Karl Marx to Adam Smith,' *European Management Journal*, 10(1) (March), 74–9.

——— (1994). *The Business Culture in Germany*, Oxford: Butterworth/ Heinemenn.

Robertz, Margie (1990). *'Die Entwicklung des Bankensystems in der ehemaligen DDR,' Recht in Ost und West* (November), 321–7.

Robins, Gregg S. (1991a). *The Soviet Banking System Within the Context of Change: Problems, Progress and Prospects*, Unpublished M.Phil thesis, Oxford University.

——— (1991b). 'Entrepreneurialism and Gorbachev's USSR: Their Present Incompatibility,' *The Oxford International Review*, 1(1), 24–8.

——— (1992). 'The Soviet Economy and the *Perestroyka* Years,' *Problems of Communism* (May–June), 139–44.

——— (1995a). *Banking in a Transition Economy: East Germany after Unification*, Unpublished D.Phil thesis, Templeton College, Oxford University.

——— (1995b). 'Expectations and Realities Surrounding Foreign Bank Participation in the Czech Republic, Hungary, and Poland,' mimeo.

Rodlauer, Markus (1995). 'The Experience with IMF-supported Reform Programs in Central and Eastern Europe,' *Journal of Comparative Economics*, 20, 95–115.

Roe, Alan (1992). 'Financial Sector Reform in Transitional Socialist Economies,' *An EDI Policy Seminar Report*, 29.

Roesler, Jörg (1994). 'Privatisation in Eastern Germany – Experience with the Treuhand,' *Europa-Asia Studies*, 46(3), 505–17.

Roggenbuch, Harald E. (1992). *Begrenzung des Anteilbesitzes von Kreditinstituten an Nichtbanken – Gesetzliche Regelungen, Empirische Befund, sowie Anlage- und Gesellschaftspolitische Bedeutung*, Frankfurt: Peter Lange.

Rose, Richard (1992). 'East Europe's Need for a Civil Economy,' in Richard O'Brien (ed.), *Finance and the International Economy*, Oxford: Oxford University Press, AMEX Bank Review Prize Essays, 6.

——— (1993). 'Contradictions Between Micro- and Macro-Economic Goals in Post-Communist Societies,' *Europe-Asia Studies*, 45(3), 419–44.

Rostowski, Jacek (1993a). 'Problems of Creating Stable Monetary Systems in Post-Communist Economies,' *Europe-Asia Studies*, 45(3), 445–61.

——— (1993b). 'The Inter-enterprise Debt Explosion in the Former Soviet Union: Causes, Consequences, Cures,' *CEPR Discussion Paper*, 142 (April).

——— (1993c). 'The Banking System, Credit and the Real Economy in Economies in Transition,' mimeo.

——— (1994). 'Banking Sector Reform in Post-Communist Economies – A Gradualist Agenda,' mimeo.

Rudolph, Bernd (1993). 'Capital Requirements of German Banks and the European Community Proposals on Banking Supervision,' in Jean Dermine (ed), *European Banking in the 1990s*, 2nd edn, Oxford: Blackwell, 373–85.

Sabel, Charles F., John R. Griffin and Richard E. Deeg (1993). 'Making Money Talk: Towards a New Debtor–Creditor Relation in German Banking,' Conference on Relational Investing, Columbia University School of Law (6–7 May), mimeo.

Sahm, Christoff (1995). *Transformation and Integration in East Germany: Objective and Subjective Changes*, Unpublished D. Phil thesis, Oxford University.

Saunders, Anthony and Andrea Sommariva (1993). 'Banking Sector and Restructuring in Eastern Europe,' *Journal of Banking and Finance*, 17, 931–57.

Saunders, Anthony and Ingo Walter (1992). 'The Reconfiguration of Banking and Capital Markets in Eastern Europe,' in Horst Siebert (ed), *The Transformation of Socialist Economies*, Symposium 1991, Institut für Weltwirtschaft an der Universität Kiel, Tübingen: J.C.B. Mohr, 101–30.

Schama, Simon (1989). *Citizens*, London: Penguin Group.

Schamp, Eike W., Godfrey J.R. Linge and Chris M. Rogerson (eds) (1993). *Finance, Institutions and Industrial Change: Spatial Perspectives*, Berlin: Walter de Gruyter.

Schiffman, Henry N. (1993). 'The Role of Banks in Financial Restructuring in Countries of the Former Soviet Union,' *Journal of Banking and Finance*, 17, 1059–72.

Schmieding, Holger and Claudia Buch (1992). 'Better Banks for Eastern Europe,' *Kiel Discussion Papers*, 197 (December).

Schneider-Lenne, Ellen R. (1992). 'Corporate Control in Germany,' *Oxford Review of Economic Policy*, 8(3), 11–23.

Schnelldienst (1991). *'Infrastrukturenpässe in den neuen Bundesländern,' Jahrgang* 44 (February), 3–4.

Schonfeld, A. (1965). *Modern Capitalism*, London: Oxford University Press.

Schrettl, Wolfram (1992). 'Transition with Insurance: German Reunification Reconsidered,' *Oxford Review of Economic Policy*, 8(1), 144–55.

Schulmann, Horst (1992). 'Comment on the paper presented by Anthony Saunders and Ingo Walter', in Horst Siebert (ed), *The Transformation of Socialist Economies*, Symposium 1991, Institut für Weltwirtschaft an der Universität Kiel, Tübingen: J.C.B. Mohr, 131–4.

Schumpeter, Joseph A. (1939). *Business Cycles*, vol. I, New York: McGraw Hill.

——— (1949). *The Theory of Economic Development*, Cambridge, Man.: Harvard University Press.

Schütte, Tjark (1993). 'Bad Debt Problems and Enterprise Restructuring in Eastern Germany,' *Communist Economies and Economic Transformation*, 5(2), 161–85.

Scott, David H. (1992). 'Revising Financial Sector Policy in Transitional Socialist Economies: Will Universal Banks Prove Viable?', *World Bank Working Paper*, 1034 (November).

Seidel, Petra (1994). *'Der industrielle Mittelstand in den neuen Bundesländern 1990 bis 1993,'* Kreditanstalt für Wideraufbau.

Shapira, Zur (1986). 'Risk in Managerial Decision Making,' unpublished ms, Hebrew University. (as cited in March and Shapira, 1987).

——— (1993). 'Ambiguity and Risk-taking in Organizations,' *Journal of Risk and Uncertainty*, 7, 89–94.

Sharpe, Steven A. (1990). 'Asymmetric Information, Bank Lending, and Implicit Contracts: A Stylized Model of Customer Relationships,' *The Journal of Finance*, 45(4) (September), 1069–87.

Shaw, Edward S. (1973). *Financial Deepening in Economic Developmen*, New York: Oxford University Press.

Sheng, Andrew and Yoon Je Cho (1993). 'Risk Management and Stable Financial Structures,' *World Bank Policy Research*, WPS 1109 (March).

Shinasi, Garry J, Leslie Lipschitz and Donough McDonald (1990). 'Monetary and Financial Issues in German Unification,' in Leslie Lipschitz and Donough McDonald (eds), 'German Unification: Economic Issues,' *IMF Occasional Paper*, 75 (December), 144–54.

Siebert, Horst (1991). 'German Unification: The Economics of Transition,' *Economic Policy*, 6 (October), 289–340.

Siebert, Horst, Holger Schmieding, and Peter Nunnenkamp (1992). 'The Transformation of a Socialist Economy: Lessons of German Unification,' in Georg Winckler (Moderator), *Central and Eastern Europe in Transition*, Washington, DC: IMF/Austrian National Bank.

Simon, Hermann (1992). 'Lessons from Germany's Midsize Giants,' *Harvard Business Review* (March–April), 115–23.

Simons, Henry C. (1936). 'Rules Versus Authority in Monetary Policy,' *Journal of Political Economy*, 44(1), 1–30.

Singh, Ajit (1994). 'How do Large Corporations in Developing Countries Finance their Growth?', in Richard O'Brien (ed), *Finance and the International Economy*, 8, Oxford: Oxford University Press.

Sinn, Gerlinde and Hans-Werner Sinn (1992). *Jumpstart: The Economic Unification of German*, Cambridge, Man.: MIT Press.

Sjöstrand, Sven-Erik (ed.) (1993). *Institutional Change: Theory and Empirical Findings*, Armonk: M.E. Sharpe.

Smith, Roy and Ingo Walter (1993). 'Bank–Industry Linkages: Models for Eastern European Economic Restructuring,' in Donald E. Fair and Robert J. Raymond (eds), *The New Europe: Evolving Economic and Financial Systems in East and West*, Dordrecht: Kluwer.

Smyser, W.R. (1993). *The German Economy: Colossus at the Crossroads*, 2nd edn, Harlow: Longman.

*Staatsbank Berlin* (1990–3). *Geschäftsbericht*.

State Banking Supervision of Hungary (1994). *Annual Report.*

——— (1995). Internal data.

Stark, David (1990). 'Privatisation in Hungary: From Plan to Market or From Plan to Clan?', *East European Politics and Societies*, 4(3) (Fall), 351–92.

Steil, Benn Lawrence (1990). *The Use of Currency Options in Hedging Foreign Exchange Exposure Risk*, unpublished D.Phil thesis, Nuffield College, Oxford University.

Steinherr, A. (1993). 'An Innovatory Package for Financial Sector Reforms in Eastern European Countries,' *Journal of Banking and Finance*, 17, 1033–57.

Stewart, Rosemary *et al.* (1994). *Managing in Britain and Germany*, New York: St Martin's Press.

Stiglitz, Joseph E. (1989a). 'Financial Markets and Development,' *Oxford Review of Economic Policy*, 5(4), 55–68.

——— (1989b). 'Markets, Market Failures, and Development,' *American Economic Review*, 79, 197–203.

——— (1992). 'The Design of Financial Systems for the Newly Emerging Democracies of Eastern Europe,' in Christopher Clague and Gordon C. Rausser (eds), *The Emergence of Market Economies in Eastern Europe*, Oxford: Basil Blackwell.

Stiglitz, Joseph E. and Andrew Weiss (1981). 'Credit Rationing in Markets with Imperfect Information,' *American Economic Review*, 71, 393–410.

Summers, Lawrence (1992). 'The Next Decade in Central and Eastern Europe,' in Christopher Clague and Gordon C. Rausser (eds), *The Emergence of Market Economies in Eastern Europe*, Oxford: Basil Blackwell.

Sundararajan, V. (1991). 'Financial Sector Reform and Central Banking in Centrally Planned Economies,' in Patrick Downes and Reza Vaez-Zadeh (eds), *The Evolving Role of Central Banks*, Washington, DC: IMF.

Szegö, Giorgio (1993). 'Introduction,' *Journal of Banking and Finance*, 17, 773–83.

Szöke, Magdolna (1991). 'Some Aspects of Building Up New Financial Structures: Reflections About the Hungarian Way,' in Richard O'Brien and Sarah Hewin (eds), *Finance and the International Economy*, Oxford: Oxford University Press. The AMEX Bank Review Prize Essays, 4.

Talley, Samuel H. (1993). 'Fail-proof Banking Systems: Would they be Feasible and Desirable?', *World Bank Working Papers*, 1095 (February).

Tanzi, Vito (ed) (1992). *Fiscal Policies in Economies in Transition*, Washington, DC: IMF.

——— (1993). *Transition to Market: Studies in Fiscal Reform*, Washington, DC:IMF.

Terrell, Henry S. (1986). 'The Role of Foreign Banks in Domestic Banking Markets,' in Cheng Hang-Sheng (ed), *Financial Policy and Reform in Pacific Basin Countries*, San Francisco: Federal Reserve Bank of San Francisco.

von Thadden, Ernst-Ludwig (1994a). 'Centralized Decentralization: Corporate Governance in the East German Economic Transition,' mimeo.

——— (1994b). 'Long-term Investment and Monitoring in Financial Relationships,' (June) mimeo.

Thorne, Alfredo. (1992). 'Issues in Reforming Financial Systems in Eastern Europe: The Case of Bulgaria,' *World Bank Working Paper*, 882 (April).

———(1993). 'Eastern Europe's Experience with Banking Reform: Is there a Role for Banks in the Transition?', *Journal of Banking and Finance*, 17, 959–1000.

Tietmeyer, Hans (1993). 'The New Europe: Evolving Economic and Financial Systems in East and West,' in Donald E. Fair and Robert Raymond (eds), *The New Europe: Evolving Economic and Financial Systems in East and West*, Dordrecht: Kluwer.

Treuhandanstalt (1990–4). Internal data.

——— (1992). *Treuhand-Initiative Mittelstand* (September).

——— (1993). *Treuhand-Initiative Mittelstand* (September).

——— (1994a). *'Monats-informationen der THA.'* Treuhandanstalt, Zentrales Controlling, various issues.

——— (1994b). 'Overview,' Central Controlling Office, various issues.

——— (n.o.). 'The Chance of the 90s: Investing in Eastern Germany,' Pamphlet.

Trommsdorff, Gisela (ed) (1994). *Psychologische Aspekte des sozio-politischen Wandels in Ostdeutschland*, Berlin: Walter de Gruyter.

United States Department of the Treasury (1994). *National Treatment Study*.

*Verband der Bürgschaftsbanken* (1992) *Jahresbericht* .

——— (1993/1994) *Verbandsbericht der deutscher Bürgschaftsbanken*.

Viscusi, W. Kip and Wesley A. Magat (1992). 'Bayesian Decisions with Ambiguous Belief-aversion,' *Journal of Risk and Uncertainty*, 5, 371–87.

Vitols, Sigurt I. (1995). 'German Banks and the Modernization of the Small Firm Sector: Long-term Finance in Comparative Perspective,' *Wissenschaftszentrum Berlin für Sozialforschung Discussion Paper, FS I 95–309*

Vittas, Hari (1995). 'Introduction,' in Robert Corker *et al.* (eds), 'Uniting Germany: The First Five Years. Performance and Policy Issues,' IMF Occasional Paper, 125, Washington DC: IMF (May), 1–8.

Volcker, Paul (1990). 'The Role of Central Banks,' in *Central Banking Issues in Emerging Market-Oriented Economies: A Symposium*, Kansas City: Federal Reserve Bank of Kansas City (May).

Volcker, Paul A., Miguel Mancera and Jean Godeaux (1991). *Perspectives on the Role of a Central Bank*, Washington, DC: IMF.

Wagener, Hans-Jürgen (1994). 'What Type of Capitalism is Produced by Privatisation?,' Europa-Universität Viadrina, Frankfurt Oder, mimeo.

Wagner, Helmut (1993). 'Reconstruction of the Financial System in East Germany: Description and Comparison with Eastern Europe,' *Journal of Banking and Finance*, 17, 1001–19.

Wagner, Karin (1993). *'Qualifizierungsbedarf in ostdeutschen Betrieben,' Wissenschaftszentrum Berlin für Sozialforschung Discussion Paper*, FS I 93–307.

Wallich, Christine I. (1995). 'What's Right and Wrong with World Bank Involvement in Eastern Europe,' *Journal of Comparative Economics*, 20, 57–94.
Walter, Ingo (1988). *Global Competition in Financial Services*, Cambridge: Ballinger.
Walter, Norbert and Rüdiger von Rosen (eds) (1995). *German Financial Markets*, Cambridge: Gresham Books, Woodhead Publishing.
Watson, Alan (1992). *The Germans: Who Are They Now?*, London: Mandarin.
Weber, Manfred (1995). 'Universal Banks,' in Norbert Walter and Rüdiger von Rosen (eds), *German Financial Markets*, Cambridge: Woodhead Publishing, 36–72.
Wegner, Manfred (1993). *Die Neuen Bundesländer in der EG. Baden-Baden: Nomos Verlagsgesellschaft.*
Wertheimer, Max (1945). *Productive Thinking*, New York: Harper & Bros.
Whyte, William Foote (1984). *Learning from the Field*, Beverly Hills: Sage.
Wieczorek, Freidrich (1994). *'Aufbau mittelständischer Strukturen in den neuen Bundesländern,' Bundesministerium für Wirtschaft*, Berlin office (March), mimeo.
van Wijnbergen, Sweder J.G. (1992). 'Economic Aspects of Enterprise Reform in Eastern Europe,' in Richard O'Brien (ed), *Finance and the International Economy*, Oxford: Oxford University Press.
Williamson, Oliver (1979). 'Transaction-cost Economies: The Governance of Contractual Relations,' *Journal of Law and Economics*, 22, 233–61.
——— (1985). *The Economic Institutions of Capitalism*, New York: Free Press.
Winiecki, Jan (1992). 'Shaping the Institutional Infrastructure,' in Horst Siebert (ed), *The Transformation of Socialist Economies*. Symposium 1991, Tübingen: J.C.B. Mohr.
——— (1993). *Post-Soviet-Type Economies in Transition*, Aldershot: Avebury.
Woldt, Fritz (1992). 'Retailing in East Germany,' *International Journal of Retail & Distribution Management*, 20(6), 11–15.
Wolf, Thomas A. (1991). 'The Lessons of Limited Market-oriented Reform,' *Journal of Economic Perspectives*, 5(4) (Fall), 45–58.
Wood, Doug (1992). 'Default Risk,' in Peter Newman, Murray Milgate and John Eatwell (eds), *The New Palgrave Dictionary of Money and Finance*, London: Macmillan.
The World Bank (1986). 'Report on International Workshop on Commercial Bank Lending for Small Enterprises and Operation of Credit Guarantee Schemes,' *London Business School*, 35 (as cited in Gibb, 1993).
——— (1989). *The World Development Report*, Oxford: Oxford University Press.
Wuffli, Peter A. and David A. Hunt (1993). 'Fixing the Credit Problem,' *The McKinsey Quarterly*, 2, 93–106.
Yates, J. Frank and Eric R. Stone (1992). 'The Risk Construct,' in J. Frank Yates (ed), *Risk Taking Behaviour*, New York: John Wiley, 1–25.
Yelle, Louis E. (1979). 'The Learning Curve: Historical Review and Comprehensive Survey,' *Decision Sciences*, 10(2), 302–28.
Yin, Robert K. (1989). *Case Study Research*, London: Sage.
Yip, Anna (1995). 'Foreign Banks and the Banking Reforms of Poland: A Study of the Twinning Programme,' unpublished M.Phil. thesis, Oxford University.
Zdeborsky, G. and A. Gellert (1992). 'Central European International Bank in the New Banking System of Hungary,' in Andreas Prindl (ed), *Banking and Finance in Eastern Europe*, New York: Woodhead-Faulkner, 136–44.

Zecchini, Salvatore (1995). 'The Role of International Financial Institutions in the Transition Process,' *Journal of Comparative Economics*, 20, 116–38.
Zwass, Adam (1979). *Money, Banking and Credit in the Soviet Union and Eastern Europe*, Armonk: M.E. Sharpe.

## Newspapers and periodicals

*Asian Finance*
*Bank Systems and Technology*
*The Banker*
*The Bankers Magazine*
*Banking World*
*Barron's*
*Boersen Zeitung*
*Business Briefing*
*Business Central Europe*
*Business Week*
*Die Bank*
*Die Wirtschaft*
*Der Spiegel*
*The Economist*
*Economist Intelligence Unit*
*Euromoney*
*Financial Times*
*Frankfurter Allgemeine Zeitung*
*German Brief*
*The Guardian*
*Handelsblatt*
*Hospodársué Noviny*
*International Herald Tribune*
*Neue Zeit*
*The New York Times*
*Reuters-News-Service*
*Rzecpospolita*
*Segodnya*
*Sparkasse*
*Süddeutsche Zeitung*
*Tagesspeigel*
*The Wall Street Journal Europe*
*Trierer Volksfreund*
*Welt am Sonntag*
*Wirtschafts-Woche*

# Index

Lightning Source UK Ltd.
Milton Keynes UK
UKHW010219191119
353757UK00001B/90/P

9 781349 412440

Essentials of Bi